ADVANCE PRAISE

GW00580218

"David Benatar has provided his university and the rest of us with rare and profoundly disturbing insights. His detailed account of the fall of the University of Cape Town, the most prestigious institution of higher education in Africa, is a warning to all of us. He chronicles what happens when an institution gets fixated on the colour of people's skin and other forms of tribalism, and starts caving in to intimidation, threats and violence; when fundamentals like equality before the law, the rule of law and the right to free inquiry are abandoned. I am sure that future generations will discover in this important and brilliant book, patterns and dynamics that led to the university's present academic, moral, and social decline."

Flemming Rose, author of *The Tyranny of Silence*, Editor-in-Chief of Friheden, and former Culture Editor of *Jyllands-Posten*.

THE FALL OF
THE UNIVERSITY OF CAPE TOWN

Africa's leading university in decline

DAVID BENATAR

Politicsweb Publishing

Typesetting: Obsidian Worlds Publishing

ISBN 978-3-9822364-1-4 (eBook)

ISBN 978-3-9822364-2-1 (Paperback)

ISBN 978-3-9822364-3-8 (Paperback)

To Elisa Galgut and Greg Fried,
two colleagues of great intellect and integrity,
for whose friendship I am grateful.

CONTENTS

LIST OF ABBREVIATIONS

ANC   African National Congress (the governing party in South Africa).

AU   Academics' Union.

COI   Committee of Inquiry (the second stage of a staff disciplinary process).

BAC   Black Academic Caucus, UCT.

DAC   Dean's Advisory Committee.

DP   Duly Performed (a certification that a student has met the coursework requirements and may sit the final examination).

DPR   Duly Performed Refused.

DVC   Deputy Vice-Chancellor.

EE   Employment Equity.

EFF   Economic Freedom Fighters (the third largest political party in South Africa).

FEC   Faculty Examinations Committee.

FHS   Faculty of Health Sciences, UCT.

FMF   Fees Must Fall.

IOL   Independent Online (the online platform of the Independent Newspapers).

IRTC   Institutional Reconciliation and Transformation Commission.

PAIA   Protection of Access to Information Act.

PASMA   Pan Africanist Student Movement of Azania.

PASS   Professional, Administrative, and Support Staff.

PIC   Preliminary Investigating Committee (the initial stage of a staff disciplinary process).

RMF   Rhodes Must Fall.

SAJS   *South African Journal of Science.*

SRC   Students' Representative Council.

UCT   University of Cape Town.

UKZN   University of KwaZulu Natal.

VC   Vice-Chancellor (equivalent of a university president in the United States).

PREFACE

Universities, like almost everything else of (positive) value, are much easier to destroy than they are to build. That applies to the physical infrastructure, such as the buildings, but even more to the intangible features of a university. The latter include the scholars and scholarship, the teachers and teaching, the students and the learning.

Destructive forces have been eroding the University of Cape Town (UCT), Africa's leading university. The damage will not easily be undone. It might even be irreversible. Time will tell. In the interim, this book tells the sad, true tale of what has been transpiring at UCT. It is a saga of lunacy, criminality, pandering, and identity politics. The mad and the bad – the deranged, deluded, the depraved – have been granted endless latitude in bullying and persecuting others. The abandonment of reason, and its associated virtues, is patent.

The decline began in 2015 with the Rhodes Must Fall (RMF) protest that resulted in the offending statue's removal within a month (and which spawned similar protests abroad). Emboldened by their success, the protestors issued new and ever-increasing demands later that year and then again in 2016 and 2017. Their methods also became criminal – including intimidation, assault, and arson. The university leadership capitulated to this behaviour, and this fostered a broader and now pervasive toxic environment within the institution.

I introduce the book further in Chapter 1 – and provide a guide for those who wish to read only parts of the book. In what remains of this Preface, I offer some preliminary terminological comments, as well as my thanks to various people who have contributed in some way to this book.

Throughout the book I put all racial classifications – such as "black", "coloured", "Indian" and "white" – in scare quotes. (The exceptions are where I am quoting others who have not done so.) I do so in order to signal just how problematic these categories are. One would have hoped that no such signalling would be necessary, especially in post-Apartheid South Africa. Unfortunately, the lessons have not been learned. Here is a reminder of what those opposed to Apartheid were saying *during* Apartheid:

> South African law divides people into racial categories – 'Black', 'White', 'Coloured' and 'Asiatic'. While it is sometimes difficult to bypass such terms we need to avoid thinking in these categories and to stop using them in our day-to-day lives. We need to think post-apartheid, act post-apartheid and live post-apartheid.[1]

Given the linguistic practices that predominate in South Africa nearly three decades after the end of apartheid, it would seem that thinking, acting and living "post-apartheid" did not, after all, involve the abandonment of these categories. It should have been otherwise. I cannot avoid these terms given that they pervade UCT and South Africa more generally. However, I can offer a constant reminder that it should be different. Readers who are bothered about the scare quotes, should be more bothered about the categories themselves.

Readers who are not from South Africa may require some explanation of how the word "liberal" is used in this country. Whereas in the United States it is often used as a term of opprobrium by those on the right to refer to everybody on the (or their!) left, in South Africa it is regularly used as a pejorative term by those on the far left in a way that connotes "right-winger". Real liberals are neither on the far right nor the far left of the political spectrum. They are liberals because they support (individual) liberty. This goes hand in hand with non-racialism, and tolerance of views that one dislikes. Liberalism also requires toleration of practices that are either harmless or which harm only those who consent to them. These liberal ideals tend to be antithetical to those on the ends of the political spectrum. Indeed, both the right and the left have more in common with one another than either would like to admit. It is sometimes difficult to distinguish them. (If, for example, German, Polish, and Hungarian nationalists are right-wingers, why are African nationalists not?[2])

Although I am familiar with the convention of using only surnames to refer to people, it is a convention I eschew for reasons of courtesy.[3] I thus use either first name and surname, or title and surname.

I have made every effort to ensure the accuracy of what I have written, and to check facts. If, despite this, any readers believe that there are factual errors, they should please draw these, along with supporting evidence, to my attention. I shall endeavour to do what I can to rectify the error in a public forum.

A retired UCT colleague who, given the climate at UCT and despite his retired status, wishes to remain anonymous, first suggested that I publish (some version of) this book. He had proposed that the various articles I had written about UCT should be gathered together into a single volume. While grateful for his suggestion, I initially rejected it. However, as UCT continued its descent, I became more persuaded that it was a good idea. As I began to think about it seriously, I realised that there were many gaps that needed to be filled with new chapters. These new chapters constitute over seventy percent of the book's word count.

I am also grateful to many others for their contributions. I interviewed dozens of people – mainly academic and administrative staff, but also some students – around campus. Almost all of them are unnamed in this book, in order to protect them. They provided information and documents that were invaluable in depicting trends in various parts of the university as well as details in specific cases that I discuss. Only a fraction of what I was told has been recounted in the pages that follow.

UCT's Institutional Planning Department provided me with demographic information that I had requested. (They did not know why I was asking for the information, but they helpfully provided it, which is as it should be.)

A former student, who also wishes to remain anonymous, provided some helpful research assistance on a few questions. William Daniels, a former librarian at UCT, was a reliable source of elusive information. He also commented expertly on what I had written about the suppression of art at UCT. Other colleagues, who will remain unnamed here, provided helpful comments on parts of the book. I am happy to thank, by name, Dr Elisa Galgut for having read much of the manuscript and for having provided not only helpful comments but also encouragement. My thanks also go to Jess du Toit for serving as a sounding board, and for her comments on some of the chapters.

Professor Anton Fagan kindly gave me permission to republish our co-authored paper that appears as Chapter 13 in this book. Dr James Myburgh gave me permission to republish that paper and all others I had initially published in Politicsweb,[4] which he edits. Given these origins, it is apt that this book is published under the imprint of Politicsweb Publishing.

My parents read the entire manuscript, and offered valuable comments. They and my brothers, Michael and Brian, provided moral support. I am grateful to Michael for discussions, and to Brian for the special skills he brought to the project and for his enthusiastic assistance.

Finally, this book is dedicated to two friends, Dr Elisa Galgut and Dr Greg Fried. They have been islands of good sense, courage, and decency in an institution increasingly characterised by the opposite traits.

Chapter 1
INTRODUCTION

The University of Cape Town (UCT) is, by several measures,[1] the leading university not only in South Africa but also in Africa as a whole. To put this in context, there is some competition within South Africa[2] but not much within the rest of the continent. Non-comparatively, the quality of UCT has been uneven. At various points in its history, including the present, there have certainly been pockets of excellence (including a few Nobel Laureates). It has many proud alumni, both in South Africa and abroad, who value the excellent education they received. There have also been swathes of respectability, and zones of mediocrity or worse. However, UCT had promise – opportunities to expand the excellence and respectability. That promise was broken in 2015, although the seeds of this were planted earlier.

The precipitous downward trajectory began, but did not end, with the criminal protests from 2015 to 2017. The capitulation to these forces helped foster a broader toxic environment within the university. The protests may have ended, at least for now, leading to an impression beyond the university that normality has returned. However, the new toxic environment has become entrenched and the institution has been captured. While it is impossible to prognosticate, there are good reasons for thinking that UCT may have passed a tipping point and will not recover. That does not mean that the decline will be readily visible from the outside (or on the inside to those without insight) in the short term.

The underlying cause of these problems is a virulent strain of pathological racial politics. To readers unfamiliar with the South African situation this may sound like the identity politics common on campuses in the United States, the United Kingdom, and Canada, for example. However, there is reason to think that the problem at UCT is far worse, not least because those claiming victimhood are the politically dominant majority rather than minorities.

Is the situation at UCT (and at South African universities more generally) *actually* worse? There are clearly many disturbing stories emanating from universities in other countries. It is very difficult to make a comparison without intimate knowledge of these particular universities. The situation may appear less bad there than it actually is, only because I do not have the insider's view of them that I have of UCT. Thus, part of the value of writing this book is to provide a fairly detailed insight into the situation at UCT. Those with experience of other universities can then make comparisons. Those with experience of universities in such countries as the United States, Canada, and United Kingdom, may be especially interested in comparing their experience with what has been happening at UCT. In particular they may be interested to see what difference it makes when those they call "minorities" are the politically dominant majority.

There are, of course, connections between what has been happening at UCT (and at South African universities more generally) and what has been happening at universities in the United States, for example. Judging by the timing of developments there seem to have been influences in both directions.

In their book, *The Coddling of the American Mind*, Greg Lukianoff and Jonathan Haidt wrote of a shift, in 2013, toward a growing intolerance among university students, who began "asking for 'triggering' material to be removed from courses".[3] There was also a growing trend towards disinvitation of speakers whose ideas students found offensive, and the disruption of talks when disinvitation failed. Moreover, Mr Lukianoff and Professor Haidt noted a new rationale for such censorship – a medicalized one. Students were claiming that some ideas were impeding their ability (or the ability of other students) to function.[4] The authors of *The Coddling* call this the "culture of safetyism",[5] but it might also be called, perhaps more provocatively but also more comprehensively, a "culture of weaponised fragility". Those in the thralls of this culture may be delicate but they are not shrinking violets. If you do not defer to their sensibilities, they will mob you. Safety for them, but not for you.

In South African universities too, students have begun to weaponize their own purported psychological frailty in order to silence or punish others. Consider one trivial but bizarre (and somewhat amusing) example. On 31 October 2018, five staff members at UCT dressed up in Halloween costumes, which they wore as they invigilated an examination. Well-adjusted people would have seen this as a light-hearted antic intended to ease stress at an examination. Unfortunately, contrary to all weather forecasts (and weather history), "snowflakes" can be found in a Cape Town spring. A number of students complained, including one who tweeted: "I'm struggling to understand how UCT allowed such things to happen. An exam is already traumatizing and yet invigilators came like this. UCT better stop preaching 'your mental health is important during these stressing times'".[6]

UCT responded quickly, stating that "this should not have been allowed" and that the "matter has been addressed urgently with the invigilators concerned to ensure that it does not occur again in the future".[7] This led one regular critic of UCT to tweet: "I cannot believe #UCT apologized to students and censured staff for wearing ghost costumes. They [that is, UCT] literally did nothing to people trying to actually burn the place down ... Arson – Terrifying. Costumes? Not so much".[8]

In other words, it has not been only the *American* mind that has demanded coddling. As in the United States, the intolerance was not new. However, just as something changed in the United States, something changed in South Africa too. The medicalization of the intolerance was one new feature, but probably not the predominant one. In South African universities and more specifically at UCT, there was a sudden intensification and more vigorous expression of already robust racial grievances, by not only students but also by academic and other staff. This occurred within a couple of years of the campus changes beginning to emerge in the United States.

PATHOLOGICAL RACIAL POLITICS

Given South Africa's notorious history of legalized racial discrimination, which persisted into the early 1990s, racial grievance may seem entirely reasonable. In some ways it is. There are certainly enduring effects of historical racial discrimination, most especially economic ones, which, in turn, impact on educational opportunities, personal safety, health and well-being. It is no accident that the great bulk of impoverished South Africans are "black". They suffer in myriad ways as a result. This is well known and is so obvious that no further argument is required here to demonstrate this.

However, the intensity, scope, and expression of racial grievance in South African universities significantly exceeds the bounds of reason. Perhaps this is why it is out of kilter with the attitudes of ordinary South Africans of all races. Despite recent racially incendiary language from African National Congress (ANC) and Economic Freedom Fighters (EFF) politicians, the South African Institute of Race Relations found high levels of racial harmony among South Africans.[9]

For example, when interviewees were asked which (of a provided list of) issues should be the priorities for the government, the top ones were "creating more jobs",[10] "fighting corruption",[11] "improving education",[12] and "fighting crime".[13] Only 2% of all respondents saw racism as a top priority. This included only 2% of "Blacks", 0% of "Coloureds", 6% of "Indians" and 5% of "Whites".[14]

Fifty-seven percent of South Africans – 64% of "Blacks", 26% of "Coloureds", 37% of "Indians" and 39% of "Whites" – thought that race relations had improved since 1994. Fourteen percent saw no change, and 26% of all South Africans – 20% of "Blacks", 51% of "Coloureds", 44% of "Indians, and 47% of "Whites" – thought that they had become worse.[15]

The majority (58%) of South Africans thought that job appointments should be made on merit, with special training for the disadvantaged. Fifty-five percent of "Blacks" and 68% of "Whites" assented to this. Only 10% of South Africans (13% of "Blacks" and 1% of "Whites") thought that only "blacks" should be appointed to jobs "for a long time ahead".[16]

Most South Africans (64%) thought that "talk of racism / colonialism" arises "from politicians seeking excuses for their own failures". Sixty percent of "Blacks", 66% of "Coloureds", 75% of "Indians" and 89% of "Whites" thought this.[17] When asked whether "different races need each other for progress" and whether "there should be full opportunities for all", 88% of respondents agreed: 86% of "Blacks", 96% of "Coloureds", 100% of "Indians" and 98% of "Whites".[18]

If these figures are to be believed, then the dominant (even if not the majority) attitudes on South African campuses, and especially at UCT, are far removed from the views of ordinary South Africans. The climate of racial grievance on campus more closely resembles the race-baiting found among South African politicians – and more specifically among politicians on the left of the political spectrum. This is ironic, given that politicians and those in the university community are among the most privileged members of South African society. (We should not underestimate the capacity of those elites to whip up racial hatred – and even violence – among the broader population in conducive circumstances.)

Curiously, those fostering and exploiting unreasonable racial grievance, at least at UCT, include some of those who have come to South Africa from elsewhere in Africa. For example, a number of key players in UCT's Black Academic Caucus (BAC), fall into this category. I hasten to add that many others who have come from elsewhere in Africa do *not* participate in such divisive politics. Some, however, have come to pastures that are (thus far) greener, and now they are playing with a fire that, with the wrong winds, can be expected to turn South Africa into the kind of place they left. The ironies are greatest when they come from places like Zimbabwe – which was transformed from a bread basket into a basket case, in part because of the toxic racial politics of those seeking to divert attention from their own misrule. Such people have learned nothing from the experiences of their own country. They now champion attitudes and practices that may destroy ours.

There are a number of reasons why the racial grievance that saturates life at UCT is unreasonable. First, while the Apartheid regime and those who supported it bear an immense responsibility for the current legacies of discrimination, South Africa has had a democratically elected government for more than a quarter of a century. During that time, it has chalked up some impressive achievements but also some crucial failures. Corruption, (new and extensive) systems of patronage, looting of the public purse, squandering of resources, and other ills have resulted in many people being no better off now than they were in 1994. For example, and of special relevance to universities, most primary and secondary schooling is, by some metrics, even worse than it was previously.[19] South Africa has educational outcomes that are worse than other middle-income countries, and even worse than many low-income African countries.[20] The vast majority of schools in South Africa are dysfunctional.[21] It is unreasonable not to recognize the important role that post-1994 failings play in explaining current inequities. If primary and secondary schooling are in an abysmal state, with poor "blacks" disproportionately affected by this, it is unreasonable to think that universities – especially elite ones – can proportionately reflect the demography of the country.

Second, it is either pathological or cynical to level reflex accusations of "racism". Given the current environment, doing precisely this is an effective means of getting one's own way or silencing opponents. Nevertheless, it is dishonest, and it trivialises real racism. By "real racism", I have in mind here not only racial enslavement, terror, oppression, and segregation, but also more subtle – but nevertheless real – forms of discrimination and prejudice. However, there is a difference between something's being a subtle but real instance of racism and it's not being an instance of racism. *A fortiori*, there is a difference between *explicit* racism and the absence of racism. Yet, this does not stop some people from alleging explicit racism when there is no racism at all.

False accusations of racism are also damaging, both to the

individuals accused and to the long-term interests of society. The societal damage results from the chilling effect of spurious accusations of racism. There are surely *some* ("white") racists, but they are much rarer at UCT than we would be led to believe by opportunists and those who are paranoid. Given how regularly such accusations are made, one would think that UCT is no different from a racially exclusive, conservative, Afrikaans-medium university in 1960. Even in 1960 UCT was very unlike such a university. The implication of equivalence is even more ludicrous now.

Of course, it is easy to *say* that UCT is not a hotbed of (anti-"black") racism – just as it is easy to say that it *is*. This is why I am not merely going to say it. I am going to *demonstrate* it in this book by discussing a number of accusations of racism. In *every* instance that I have probed, the accusation is clearly without merit or is unsubstantiated. It is not possible to investigate every case: there are simply too many. However, if every case that is examined proves to be groundless, one begins to discern a pattern. Moreover, if one shows that a person's cry of "racism" in one case is groundless, one should be distrustful of that same person's allegations in other cases. (A story about a little boy and a wolf comes to mind.)

I cannot discount the possibility that some of those crying racism may be justified in doing so. Indeed, I would be surprised if there were *no* anti-"black" racism at UCT. However, given the innumerable false cries of "racism" and the strong social taboos against anti-"black" racism, we need compelling evidence to believe allegations of anti-"black" racism. As this book will make clear, much of what passes for evidence for such claims does not actually support them.

None of the foregoing is intended to deny the difficulties experienced by, for example, poor or educationally disadvantaged students arriving at an unfamiliar institution and trying to navigate it, especially for those who are not fluent in English, the dominant language of instruction. This is exactly why UCT has, for a very long time, sought to soften that landing by providing many forms of support, including orientation and academic support. In many cases this only mitigates rather than eliminates the difficulties. However, it is a mistake, sometimes a narcissistic one, to think that just because one is facing some difficulty, it must be on account of racism, or to think that some people who seem privileged are not facing profound difficulties of their own. Life is hard for everyone, albeit to varying degrees.[22] Some of the hardship is attributable to racism, but there are many other reasons why life is hard. Moreover, many of those at the vanguard of complaints are not poor, educationally disadvantaged students. They are fluent English speakers and come from privileged backgrounds or have been educated at elite primary and secondary schools.

Third, the irony is that the less "black" students and staff have had to complain about, the more strident and aggressive the cries of "racism" have become. It does not matter that there are more "black" students than "white" students,[23] that there are many more "black" staff than "white" staff[24] (although not quite yet more "black" *academic* staff[25]), that most of the senior administrative positions – university executive and deans – are occupied by "blacks", that there are explicit and extreme racial preferences *in favour of* "blacks" in admissions, appointments, mentoring, and funding, for example, or that an increasing number of building names have been "decolonized".[26] Nor does it matter that most "whites" are either pandering to the narrative of anti-"black" racism or cowering in silence while the narrative is peddled. None of this is a bar to a paranoid sense of victimization.

IDENTITY POLITICS

The result is that thoroughly decent people who abhor racism are tainted with a label that, in the current context, is comparable in its social effect to a racist slur in a genuinely racist society. Racist slurs, like false accusations of racism: (a) are levelled on the basis of the recipient's purported "race", and (b) have the effect of silencing or at least diminishing or dominating the recipient. Just as there is no socially effective response to a racist slur in contexts in which racist slurs work, so there is no such response to a false accusation of racism in contexts in which such accusations work. It does not matter that all evidence is to the contrary. Those with the social power to level the accusation can make it stick. It is both puerile and vicious.

Any "white" who attempts to ward off a false accusation of racism is accused of "white fragility".[27] The social power dynamics thus create a catch-22 situation. If you are a "white" falsely accused of racism, you can either accept it, in which case you are "acknowledging" your racism, or you can deny it, which is then taken as evidence of your alleged racism. There is no point citing evidence that one is not racist, or that the accusation is false, because that too is taken as a sign of "white fragility". Indeed, it is viewed as worse to deny it because then one is not even acknowledging the purported problem. In this way, allegations of racism become "unfalsifiable". There are no conceivable facts that would be accepted as counting against the allegation.

The intellectual bankruptcy of this should be apparent, but those who can only understand these matters when the victims are "black", should consider the racist allegation, all too common in the past, levelled against "blacks" for being "uppity" or "cheeky". Where such a charge has had social force, the victim had two choices – either remain silent, which could then be interpreted as assent by acting chastened, or "prove" the allegations by objecting. Or imagine a scenario in which complaints by "blacks" of (real) racism could routinely and effectively be dismissed, with social effectiveness, as "black fragility". "Blacks" would then face the choice between accepting racism and being accused of "black fragility".

The point is that facts do (or should) matter.[28] If somebody makes an allegation of racism, it is an allegation that must be evaluated. It may be true, or it may not be, or it may be partly true. There may also be instances where it is very difficult or impossible to determine which of these it is, but none of this means that the allegation should not be evaluated on the basis of evidence rather than on the basis of the identity of either the person levelling the accusation or the person against whom it is levelled.

Some people think that their so-called "lived experience" must be accepted rather than subjected to evaluation. Some even go so far as think that questioning some people's "lived experience" itself amounts to racism. This is a serious mistake, even though there is a kernel of truth in the concept of "lived experience". The kernel of truth is that experiencing something oneself *can* sometimes give one an insight that is lacking in others who know of something only through the reports of those experiencing them. The problem is that experiences can also be mistaken. There is a conceptual difference between perception and reality. Some perceptions are mistaken. Sometimes the mistaken perceptions are those of people claiming that something is racist – false positives – and sometimes the mistaken perceptions are of those denying that something is racist – false negatives. The only way to evaluate perceptions is by subjecting them to scrutiny and determining whether they are supported by the facts. That may often not be easy, but the correct solution to difficult determinations is not automatic deferral to one conclusion.

One way in which those levelling false accusations of racism respond to counter evidence is to accuse those offering that evidence of "gaslighting"[29] them. This term is a favourite in the *vade mecum* of the "woke". "Gaslighting" refers to psychological manipulation of people in which one gets them to doubt their memories, perceptions, judgements and – in the most extreme cases – their sanity. The problem with this response is that there is a world of difference between psychological *manipulation* and rational *argument*. If you provide somebody with an argument – evidence and logical inferences – you may be showing them that they are mistaken, but that does not mean that you are psychologically manipulating them. There *is* something wrong with those who cannot understand that distinction.

False accusations of racism actually encourage a kind of racism among the unprincipled. The unprincipled are often so keen to avoid the charge of racism that they will even act in one kind of racist way to evade it – namely by holding darker people to lower standards than they would hold paler people. Of course, *this* form of racism is entirely congenial to those race-baiters who wield false charges of racism. What they really want is to get their own way. They do not see – or do not care – that they are not being treated as fellow adults. It is those who refuse to patronise them in this way who are accused of racism.[30]

The foregoing argument should be sufficient. However, those who view everything through the lens of identity are likely to reply that I simply do not understand what it is like to be part of a group that has been stereotyped, discriminated against and oppressed. I should not have to offer the following response, and I would have preferred not to, but if it is the only response that my critics will understand, then let me offer it: I *do* understand. I have not experienced being "black", but for all the differences, there are also many similarities with being Jewish.

I shall start with a Jewish joke. Two Jewish friends bump into one another in the street. The first says to the second: "Tell me, Abe, did you get that job as a newsreader for which you applied?" Abe replies: "N-n-n-n-n-n-n-n-no; d-d-d-d-d-damn antisemites!"[31]

We can well imagine – although I have never heard – a parallel joke involving two "black" friends. Many Jews, like many "blacks", have a tendency to see prejudice and discrimination even when it does not exist. This hypersensitivity is likely a by-product of a hypervigilant scanning of the environment for (sometimes subtle but) real threats. This does not mean that their perceptions are always veridical. They are not. Jews and "blacks" (and others) need to subject their intuitive reactions to the corrective of rational scrutiny. For example, there are helpful principles – which I shall not discuss here – for determining when criticism of Jewish cultural practices is antisemitic and when it is not. The same is true for determining whether criticism of a practice of some or other "black" culture is racist.

It may come as a surprise to some of those calling for the decolonization of the curriculum at UCT that the so-called "colonized" curriculum is not the cultural heritage of all those they label as "whites". For example, it is not part of the cultural heritage of Jews, even when Jews are "white". While Jews have, for millennia, had their own institutions of higher learning, these were yeshivot rather than universities. Jews were excluded from the latter until relatively recently.

It is not uncommon for ultra-orthodox Jews to disparage what they (too) call "Western" thought or philosophy, which they see as alien to Jewish thought. Plenty of self-professed "progressives", including Jewish ones, will recognise this sentiment as conservative closed-mindedness. Where these progressives are themselves Jewish, they do not typically cleave to Jewish thought. Yet the same people are falling over themselves to pay obeisance to "black" versions of the same characterization of "Western" thought as alien. That difference speaks to a lack of principle. Moreover, the idea that one has to eschew "foreign" intellectual contributions, or at least combine them with those of one's own cultural group is a self-crippling mentality about which I say a little more in Chapter 2.

Consider statuary and building names next. There are certainly difficult ethical questions to ask about who should be memorialized in these ways. As I note in Chapter 3, I recommend a healthy cynicism about such memorializations, given that unsavoury characters are disproportionately represented among those honoured in these ways. *Everybody* else who is memorialized is a flawed human being, because everybody is flawed. If memorials were to be established only for the perfect, there would be no memorials. Once we recognise that being flawless is not a necessary condition for being honoured through memorials, we have to acknowledge that there has to be some weighing of the good and the bad of the person, along with some other considerations.

How we do that weighing is not my question here. Instead, I want to ask how reasonable is it to be *traumatised* by the presence of statues of colonizers, racists, and antisemites? Similarly, how reasonable is it to be debilitated by buildings named after people who "are not like you"? How important is it to fell those statues and change those building names? My answer is "not very".

I think that this is true of Cecil John Rhodes's statue. I also think it true of the Arch of Titus (who besieged, captured, and sacked Jerusalem in 70 CE, sending many Jews into a diasporic exile, where they have suffered nearly two thousand years of discrimination, oppression and periodic ethnic cleansing, including genocide). Yet, I do not think that TitusMustFall. Similarly, I do not think that the busts of Abbott Lawrence Lowell, former President of Harvard University, should be removed from display at that university, even though he supported quotas limiting the number of Jews admitted to Harvard.

Some "black" students and staff have complained that too many buildings are still named after "whites", or that still too few are named after "blacks". They think that this makes UCT inhospitable to "blacks" and congenial to (all) "whites". What are we to make of these claims?

The vast majority of the buildings at UCT are named after gentiles – RW James, PD Hahn, Leslie, Centlivres, Beattie, Fuller Hall,[32] Baxter Hall, John Day, Immelman, Snape, Neville Alexander, and AC Jordan, for example.[33] There are, of course, some buildings and rooms named after Jews[34] but there are also some buildings named after "blacks".[35] I realise of course, that Jews are a very small minority at UCT, but they were once a much larger minority. In any event, the question I am asking is not how strong a claim different groups have for name changes. Majorities arguably have stronger claims than minorities. I am thus *not* arguing against UCT's diversifying of the demographics after whom buildings are named.

Instead, the questions are whether the erstwhile building nomenclature is really so affirming of all those people of whom it is said to be affirming, and whether being part of a university where the buildings are not named after enough people from one's own racial, ethnic or cultural group is so psychologically damaging that the climate is hostile to one. My answers to *those* questions are negative. Thus, if Jewish students at UCT were complaining (now or at the peak of their numbers) that UCT was providing an inhospitable environment because most of the buildings are named after gentiles, I would think that they needed to grow up.

THE FAECAL FULCRUM

At UCT, and in South Africa more generally, the turning point was 9 March 2015. On that date, a superannuated undergraduate,[36] Chumani Maxwele, threw human faeces on the statue of Cecil John Rhodes that occupied a central position on the UCT campus, thus triggering the Rhodes Must Fall and associated "decolonization" protests.[37] These protests soon spread to other South African universities, with ripple effects at Oxford, Harvard and other universities abroad. Later that year, the Fees Must Fall (FMF) protests began at the University of the Witwatersrand in Johannesburg and rapidly spread to UCT and other South African universities. The target of these protests was not only fees. "Decolonization", although never defined, was another demand. There were dozens of other demands too – including for increased worker wages, compulsory lecture recordings, even more extreme racial preferences than were already in place, renaming more buildings, and the provision of free tampons and sanitary pads in all residences.[38] Later the demands included that no "black" student should be excluded on either academic or economic grounds.[39] (It is an implication of this demand that even if a "black" student were repeatedly failing *all* of his or her courses, that student should not be excluded from UCT.)

South Africa's higher education sector was crippled by the so-called "Fallist" protests in 2015, 2016, and 2017. Hundreds of millions of rands' damage was done,[40] a monetary cost that the country could not afford and which made it even more difficult to fulfil demands like free tertiary education. However, the monetary costs were not the only ones, or even the most enduring ones. The human costs were immense.

Not all universities responded alike. At the University of the Witwatersrand, then Vice-Chancellor, Adam Habib, took a firm stand against unacceptable behaviour.[41] The same was not true at UCT, where Vice-Chancellor Max Price's administration was ever pliant. There was widespread support at UCT for the removal of Cecil John Rhodes's statue, but as the protests transformed into disruptions and became more extreme, the radicals lost the support of large sectors of the university.

However, UCT's leadership seemed uninterested in what became the vast majority of law-abiding students and staff.[42] Instead, they pandered to the criminal element, abandoning many staff and students to appalling treatment. The upshot was an unusually high rate of resignations, traumatization, withdrawal, and even suicide. Some of this is recounted in various chapters in this book.

It should go without saying that those causing the trouble and actively supporting it are in their element. They will no doubt want to dismiss my characterization of events – and will likely do so on racial grounds. If past experience is any indication, they will want to argue that "racist whites" resistant to "transformation" are disgruntled because they are "no longer in control". There are many problems with this narrative, but perhaps the one most accessible to those who view everything through the prism of race is that the misery has been felt across the racial spectrum. Did Bongani Mayosi, the Dean of the Faculty of Health Sciences, take his own life because he was a racist "white" who was resistant to transformation? Or was it instead because UCT became a deeply toxic place, hostile to those not (sufficiently) compliant with the agenda of those polluting the institutional environment?[43]

PRELUDES

Although 2015 was a turning point – the point at which the pathology intensified markedly – there were many dramatic preludes, which gave a taste of things to come.

For example, as far back as 1986, students at UCT disrupted lectures by visiting Irish politician, public intellectual, and academic, Conor Cruise O'Brien. Dr O'Brien had been a strong supporter of the Anti-Apartheid movement but rejected an academic boycott which, during his visit to UCT, he dismissed as "Mickey Mouse stuff". This outraged certain students and staff at UCT. The student disruptions resulted in then Vice-Chancellor, Dr Stuart Saunders, advising Dr O'Brien that he, Dr Saunders, "couldn't guarantee" Dr O'Brien's "protection on campus" and said that if Dr O'Brien tried to speak again, "violence was likely to result".[44] As a result, Dr O'Brien's visit was terminated prematurely.

Among the arguments advanced by those disrupting Dr O'Brien's visit, and those justifying that disruption, was that there is "no free speech in an unfree society".[45] While the naïve might have accepted that as a justification, some of us knew, at the time, that it was a rationalization of intolerance. The subsequent history has borne out the more cynical view. It should now be apparent that for the intolerant left (as opposed to the liberal left) there is "no free speech even in a free society", at least if the speech is not congenial to the intolerant left. Even in post-Apartheid South Africa, those on the intolerant left often feel entitled to silence those with whom they disagree. Indeed, they are doing so *more* now that they did before – perhaps because they now *can* do so more than they could in the Apartheid era.

Even more disturbing is a campus killing and the reaction to it. At approximately 11h10 on Friday 28 January 2005, Associate Professor Brian Hahn was assaulted outside the administrative suite of the Mathematics Department by Dr Maleafisha Stephen ("Steve") Tladi.[46] Dr Tladi had just left the administrative office where he had been looking for an item of stationery.[47] He hit Professor Hahn, hard and repeatedly over the head with a sturdy umbrella. The blows were hard enough that the *umbrella* was "completely wrecked" in the process. Professor Hahn fell backwards to the floor, his head hitting the vinyl-tiled concrete floor. Dr Tladi, a thick-set, vigorous young man, clad in heavy footwear stomped repeatedly on Professor Hahn's face. One eyewitness said that Dr Tladi drove "the sole and heel of his foot, very forcefully and deliberately, vertically down" onto Professor Hahn's head.

This witness interposed himself between Dr Tladi and Professor Hahn, pushed Dr Tladi away and restrained him. Dr Tladi would not leave the scene until he had recovered his glasses. One witness found two pairs of glasses on the ground. She brought both of them to Dr Tladi and he took one of them. Professor Hahn was taken to hospital but died of his injuries some days later.

Before arriving at UCT, Steve Tladi had left, without completing, the PhD programme at Brown University in the United States. In 1999 he began a PhD at UCT, where he also started a contract lectureship. By 2003 a decision had to be taken whether to convert his contract post into a permanent position. Professor Hahn, who was then the Head of Department, was asked to make an assessment of Mr Tladi's performance. While Professor Hahn felt unable to recommend Mr Tladi for a permanent position, he did suggest that Mr Tladi be afforded the opportunity to make his case to a departmental committee.

Mr Tladi was afforded that opportunity in early September 2003. Instead of addressing his performance in teaching, research, administration, he flew into a rage about personal matters and claimed that people were acting against him. He used abusive language towards members of the committee. When he sought to leave the meeting, one member of the committee, Associate Professor Sizwe Mabizela calmed him down. Mr Tladi became contrite and apologised. After he left the room, the committee unanimously concluded that Mr Tladi was not a suitable candidate for a permanent appointment. He was advised in writing that his contract appointment would cease at the end of 2003.

Mr Tladi submitted his thesis in January 2004 and was awarded the degree in December that year. He requested to stay at UCT until January 2005 in order to "finalise matters". Associate Professor Chris Gilmour, who had succeeded Brian

Hahn as Head of Department, granted him permission to retain his office until the end of January 2005. Within days of that deadline, Dr Tladi fatally assaulted Professor Hahn.

Decent people would be appalled at the brutal murder of an academic, especially by one of the former students in his department. Their public statements would be ones of shock, outrage, sorrow, and commiserations with Professor Hahn's family. The actual response from far too many groups and individuals was indecent. It exploited Professor Hahn's murder in a most unseemly fashion.

For example, the executive committees of the Academics' Association,[48] Employees' Union, National Education Health and Allied Workers' Union, Black Staff Association, the Students' Representative Council, and the interim steering committee members of the Black Caucus wrote an open letter to then Vice-Chancellor Njabulo Ndebele.[49] In one short sentence they extended condolences to the Hahn family. In another sentence they rejected "all acts of violence as a means to address or resolve disputes or disagreements within the university". However, the vast bulk of the letter was devoted to their "transformation" agenda.

First, they objected that "official UCT communication portrays Dr Tladi as an outsider" (even though he was neither a student nor a staff member in January 2005). Second, they objected that the University did not "refer to him as Dr Tladi, but as an ex-student" which they said "contrasts sharply with the reporting on other recent and unfortunate incidents involving former staff members of the university, where past association and due regard for academic pedigree are referred to without reservation". It is not clear what they had in mind here, but I am not aware of other incidents in which the *assailant*, rather than a victim, had an academic title, which was then not mentioned. Third, they said that "the university should take far more seriously the concerns about the prevailing race relations at the institution" where many staff were "being made to feel marginalised, alienated, angry, and unworthy". The authors of the letter called, inter alia, for "an open public debate around the slow pace of transformation and institutional culture at the university".

In summary, the first two points about transformation were that the killer was given insufficient respect. The implication of the third point, if it has anything to do with the killing of Professor Hahn, is that the killing may not have occurred if the authors' transformation agenda had been more vigorously pursued.[50] In other words, two lines were devoted to the real tragedy and then the rest of the letter was devoted to grinding the authors' prized axe. This sounds like a case of "condolences to the mourners, and now back to us".

This is not to say that tragedies never occasion a broader discussion. If, for example, there is yet another mass shooting or yet another killing of an African American man by the police in the United States, it is entirely appropriate to speak about the need for better gun control or for less violent policing. This is partly because doing so does not take the attention away from the actual victims. More importantly, the broader issue is germane. The tragedy really does result (in large part) from poor gun control or from police brutality.

Neither of these was true in Steve Tladi's killing of Brian Hahn. First, talking about transformation shifts the focus from the actual outrage – a homicide. Second, transformation is simply irrelevant in Dr Tladi's case. That is, unless you assume, as the Open Letter's signatories seem to have done, that Dr Tladi should have been offered an appointment. It is only if he was rightfully aggrieved that the question of transformation arises, even if one condemns the action that he took. However, the decision not to offer Dr Tladi a permanent appointment was an entirely reasonable one. He had been afforded the opportunity of a contract lectureship – an opportunity not afforded many PhD students. He had performed poorly and had demonstrated serious personality problems. The entire committee, irrespective of their "race" had agreed upon this.

Subsequent events testified to the wisdom of the departmental committee's decision. Dr Tladi was released on R500 bail into the custody of his wife, a lawyer. While out on bail he was charged with assaulting her.[51] According to her statement, he removed the shade off a lamp and then hit her on the forehead with the lamp's wooden stand. She had to seek medical care for the resultant wound. After a psychiatric assessment the court ruled that Dr Tladi was "not guilty [of murdering Professor Hahn] because of mental illness" and was detained as a State patient.

Curiously, he was released less than two years later as a State outpatient, and was subsequently employed as a Senior Lecturer in the School of Mathematical Sciences and Computer Sciences at the University of Limpopo. In a widely circulated email in 2019, he wrote as follows:

> In January 1989, after ten years of operative work as Legasa, I became undercover intelligence officer of Mphatho wa Magasa and, under orders from Mphatho wa Magasa, carried out abroad secret assignment of the combat nature. In 1990, I succeeded in infiltrating the leadership of the BSU, CASA, LASO, ASA, SOCA and had meetings with its leaders in Worcester, Boston, and Providence. Mphatho wa Magasa and the government appreciated my work by giving me my first Order of the BOPTREE Banner in May 1992, 1993, & 1996. I received a new assignment of Mphatho wa Magasa which involved the founder and the leader of the MAM 400W Pr.Dr. Hahn. I arranged a secret, eye-to-eye meeting with Pr.Dr. Hahn in Cape Town and destroyed him in January 2005; I returned home safely in September 2009. In 2005, under Mphatho wa Magasa orders, I organized

a combat operation in the Cape Peninsula, and carried it out successfully. While giving awards for this mission to me, the leadership repeated the promise I had heard already at Mphatho wa Magasa headquarters: "Wa Mphatho will never forget what you have done, and will help and support not only you but your families as well." I shall omit the details of my work in other areas. I appeal to you with the request to rehabilitate myself, to restore our party membership and to return to us our military ranks and decorations. CERTIFICATION OF REHABILITATION: Issued to the former Prof.Dr. Maliafisha Maleafisha, born in 1969, convicted on 7 December 2004 by the Military Collegium of the Supreme Court for committing the crime in accordance with article 07-2004-12 of the Criminal Code of the Republic of South Africa to years of imprisonment. He is rehabilitated in accordance with paragraph A, article 3 of the law of the Republic on the rehabilitation of political repressions of 24 May 1994.

In other words, mental illness and not the pace of transformation was what led to Dr Tladi killing Professor Hahn. The real problem with the "institutional culture" of UCT was that a homicide by a mentally disturbed person could be turned into an opportunity for a wide array of campus organizations to complain *not* about the killing of a gentle and decent man, but instead about UCT's not being sufficiently welcoming to his killer. That is either deeply pathological or morally heinous.

The only redeeming feature of this saga is that the departmental committee had decided not to offer Dr Tladi a permanent position. It would have been a massive error of judgement to have appointed him, but despite all the pressure to "transform", the committee kept its head. The same cannot be said elsewhere at UCT. The most glaring example is UCT's appointment, in 2007,[52] of a Deputy Registrar in charge of legal affairs.

It had been decided that the Registrar's office was in need of transformation. UCT created new posts in this office and "explicitly sought a Black candidate for the new post of Deputy Registrar: Legal Services".[53] The incumbent of this position "would be responsible for providing special legal services, providing leadership and support on legal matters, providing advice on draft legislation, and legal compliance" among other tasks. The post was also created "with a view to succession issues" because "the university believed that it had to change to meet the equity policy in respect of its staff". It thus "explicitly advertised for a Black person to fill the post".[54]

When one becomes fixated on satisfying a racial or other demographic requirement, one can lose sight of other much more important considerations. That happens *often*, but not always as obviously as on this occasion. UCT appointed, as its inhouse legal adviser, somebody who had been disbarred from legal practice in the United States[55] and who had been arrested on charges of failure to pay child support and was facing charges of forgery, larceny and the unauthorized practice of law.[56] In appointing Paul Ngobeni, UCT was unaware of this, although a simple internet search would have revealed Mr Ngobeni's[57] evolving legal troubles. The point is that UCT never bothered to do that search, probably because it was far too focused on the race of the person they were seeking to appoint. That is how UCT came to hire, as its legal advisor, somebody who later became a "fugitive from justice".[58]

Having been the beneficiary of racial preference he was soon playing the race card at UCT and in South Africa more generally. For example, days after fourteen professors in UCT's Law Faculty entered a public discussion about John Hlophe, Judge President of the Cape High Court, and published a respectful and temperate letter to the *Cape Times*, in which they asked Judge Hlophe to "consider whether his continuation in high judicial office in our legal system will not further damage our constitutional democracy", Paul Ngobeni called their letter "a hi-tech lynching of the worst kind".[59] In the next paragraph he said that the "unprecedented attacks on Hlophe reflect demagoguery and irresponsible criticism by those who have long harboured a secret agenda to undermine blacks in higher judicial positions". Later in the piece he wrote that he did "not recall these same scholars and lawyers attacking fellow white judges with such venom during the apartheid years".[60]

He also played the race card in his professional work at UCT. For example, he called UCT's Registrar a racist[61], accused him of "an Apartheid-minded response",[62] and of "racist arrogance".[63] When a male member of staff laid a disciplinary complaint against a female student who was stalking and harassing him, Mr Ngobeni provided a contorted explanation for why the disciplinary tribunal would not prosecute the case. It included gratuitous, irrelevant and unsubstantiated claims based on the racial identities Mr Ngobeni imputed to the staff member and the student.

Mr Ngobeni did not remain long at UCT. The University initiated a disciplinary hearing against him. The findings were mixed – some in favour of the University and some in favour of Mr Ngobeni. However, an agreement was reached, under the terms of which the disciplinary case was annulled retroactively and Mr Ngobeni was given a golden handshake of R2.5 million.[64] These terms were not initially made public. At the time of Mr Ngobeni's departure it was said that he had "expressed his wish to leave UCT to pursue other interests".[65] It was only later that the details of the agreement were revealed.[66]

Mr Ngobeni's departure from UCT occasioned institutional self-flagellation – but not for having made the mistake of appointing him. Vice Chancellor Max Price wrote that he wished to "apologise for any inconvenience caused, particularly to Dr Ngobeni".[67] He then raised "wider transformation issues". He recognized that "this case is seen by some as reflective of issues relating to race, institutional climate and transformation at UCT".[68] He was not speaking here about the racial preferences that led to the appointment of a disbarred lawyer, or about the hostile environment created by that person levelling bogus accusations of racism. Instead, he was referring to the perceptions of anti-"black" bias at UCT. If UCT's parting ways with Mr Ngobeni is meant to illustrate this purported bias, then we have further evidence of just how detached this narrative is from the facts.

AFFIRMATIVE ACTION

The foregoing should not be construed – as my detractors are sure to do – as suggesting that Dr Tladi and Mr Ngobeni are *representative* of the consequences of affirmative action. They are *not* representative, but they are extreme examples of what happens when one fixates on people's race. There is a spectrum. The less likely somebody was to have been appointed in the absence of racial preference, the greater the costs of the appointment. Sometimes the costs are serious, sometimes they are mild and sometimes there are no costs. The last of these is where the racial preference is moot, not because it does not exist but rather because the person would have been appointed even in the absence of racial preference.

Affirmative action, and especially race-based affirmative action, is much more extreme in South Africa than it is elsewhere. Much of the racial preference that passes legal muster in South Africa is so explicit and extreme that it would be outright illegal in places such as the United States. Worse still, there are many instances of racial preference at UCT that *may* be illegal even in South Africa, but which pass under the judicial radar because they are covert. Details of such practices will be provided in Chapter 17.

Another way in which South African affirmative action is extreme is that those favoured are a (large) majority rather than a minority. Advocates of "transformation" want the demographics to resemble the demographics of the country. For reasons mentioned earlier and which will be discussed again later, it is delusional to think that this can happen (without serious cost) at elite universities, unless problems beyond the country's universities are fixed. Even then, there would be a time-lag, given the pipeline from primary to secondary to tertiary education, to advanced degrees, academic staff positions, and then the senior professoriate. (A further complication is that suitably qualified "blacks" are more likely to be recruited by other public organizations and by the more lucrative private market, where strong racial preferences are also operative.)

I shall discuss racial preferences later in the book, and especially in Chapter 17. What should be said now is that one cannot express unorthodox views such as these without paying a massive price, which is one way in which dissent is silenced and the orthodox view enforced. That too should become apparent in the course of this book.

DECISIONS

Writing this book presented me with a number of dilemmas. One of these was whether to name people or to obscure their identities. There are sometimes good reasons to use a name, just as there are sometimes good reasons not to. Thus, I have been employed a mixed practice – sometimes naming and sometimes not – and have employed the following principles in deciding which option to use in a given situation.

I generally leave victims unnamed (unless they prefer otherwise). I sometimes make exceptions when they are already publicly identifiable as the victims about whom I am writing. I am somewhat less concerned to protect perpetrators, but even they are often left unnamed. Office bearers are sometimes identifiable either from context or name, but they also have a lesser claim to anonymity.

Criticizing named individuals is not something I do lightly. I am aware that there is a human being behind the name – a fellow mortal with feelings and insecurities, who may be hurt by what I have to say. My default position is one of compassionate treatment. However, that presumption must be defeated when the vulnerable human becomes a perpetrator.[69] Compassion should not stand in the way of forthrightly challenging those who are doing wrongful damage to others. Of course, those people will disagree that that they are doing damage or at least that the damage is wrongful, but that too must be the subject of frank debate. There is no good reason to withhold arguments that are aimed at showing that they are mistaken in that regard too.

Some might claim that I am too confident in my arguments. They should know that I typically do not voice an opinion without first carefully investigating the relevant matter. However, I recognize that at least some of my arguments would benefit from sophisticated challenges. That might well result in their being refined and improved – or sometimes even discarded. It is a source of great dismay to me that I have yet to encounter any such challenges at UCT. The responses I receive to my arguments are typically either mischaracterizations of my own arguments or infantile objections to what I actually say. Moreover, they are advanced by people who are not actually willing to have a rational discussion. They much prefer to bully and ostracize. I wish it were different.

Another decision was when to stop writing. New outrages occur with great regularity. Some of the sagas I recount have not yet ended. Changes in policy and office-bearers occur with greater frequency than is healthy. However, this is already a long enough book, and its publication cannot be delayed until the fall of UCT is "complete". It has not even been possible to include reference to all manifestations of the pathology that have already occurred. This is because there are so many of them. Unless UCT changes course, the developments and changes will continue along the trajectory I describe in this book.

A related decision was whether to include any material about my own unpleasant experiences at UCT. Hitherto, the articles I have published have avoided instances in which I have been badly treated. I did that to convey the atmosphere at UCT without becoming autobiographical. However, I break that pattern here. I have been targeted more than most, probably because I have dared to express unpopular views and to criticize those who have behaved badly, irrespective of their purported racial identities. I see no reason why those case studies should not be included alongside others. What is important is that my experiences are not isolated, but part of a broader pattern.

Of course, UCT is not all bad. There are pockets of the University that still function really well and there are many, though a diminishing number, of people of goodwill. These are people who span the racial spectrum and who are willing to interact with one another as reasonable fellow-humans. Unfortunately, most of them are cowering at UCT – living in utter fear of the bullying race-baiters, afraid of being labelled as a racist or a coconut (depending on their hue). The University leadership has betrayed these people and consistently bowed to the worst elements. Perhaps this is partly because they – the University leadership – have exactly the same fears.[70] Perhaps it is partly because ideologues now hold a growing number of the more senior positions. Whatever the explanation, they bear a massive responsibility for what UCT has become and what it may still become. They must be held to account. This book is the beginning of such an accounting.

OUTLINE OF THE BOOK – AND A GUIDE FOR READERS

This book has a somewhat mixed format. About half of the chapters – but less than third of the word-count – are republications of articles published in response to then current events.[71] The other chapters were written later in order to tie these articles together, to fill in many gaps, and to provide further argument. Both types of chapter have a role to play. Instead of using the previously published material as it is, I could have drawn on it in writing something new. However, in doing so, something would have been lost. What the articles that were written contemporaneously with the events provide is a snapshot of UCT at particular times, and my response at those times. For example, instead of writing now what I feared UCT might descend into when Cecil John Rhodes's statue was expeditiously removed in response to student protests, I present my actual words at the time. Similarly, the chapters about academic freedom provide a contemporaneous account of its rapid erosion and the institutionalisation thereof.

A second way in which the chapters of this book differ is that some are very short, while others are much longer. This difference does not coincide with the distinction between previously published and not previously published chapters. However, the newer chapters are on average longer than the ones that were previously published.

A third way in which the chapters differ is that some focus on specific events or series of events, whereas others are more thematic or provide an overview. There is a good balance of each. This difference too does not coincide with any of the previous distinctions.

Those chapters that focus on specific events or sagas are often very detailed. These details are necessary. As I noted above, it is easy to *say* that UCT is or is not a hotbed of anti-"black" racism. It is common at UCT for such claims to be made and then endlessly repeated. However, that is mere assertion and hearsay. Such claims need to be substantiated if they are to be believed. To substantiate, evidence needs to be presented, and that requires detail.

Not everybody will want to read all the details. **Those who want to read only parts of the book can obtain guidance in two ways. First,** those chapters that cover specific events and sagas in detail are typically introduced with an initial few overview paragraphs, from which readers can gain a sense of what each of those chapters covers and what conclusions they reach. **Second,** I shall now provide an outline of the book and its constituent chapters – which readers who wish to read selectively can use to assist in their choice of selections. (Longer, more detailed chapters about specific events or sagas that some readers might want to skip are chapters 4, 12, 16, and 18.)

Following this introductory chapter, are Chapters 2 and 3 – both republications of articles written and published in the months following the beginning of the Rhodes Must Fall protests. Chapter 2 responds to the calls for "transformation" and "decolonization". In that chapter I note that these are slogans and that their meanings are not clear. I also caution against dangerous interpretations of these terms. Some people have suggested that I am "dismissive" of these ideas. I am most certainly dismissive of hackneyed slogans, and appropriately so. If these concepts can be interpreted more plausibly – and I make a few suggestions – then those interpretations are far from their sloganized usage.

Chapter 3 asks whether, in the wake of Cecil John Rhodes's statue falling, UCT must fall too. I indicate that I do not seek to defend Mr Rhodes or his statue, but I express concern about where UCT might be headed following the precipitous removal of that statue. I note that UCT was then at a crossroads and that there were some worrying indications about the direction it might take. Those concerns have subsequently proved to be very well founded.

Chapter 4, not previously published, documents an early instance of individuals being targeted. Four academics in the Humanities Faculty were subjected to a censure by their colleagues for objecting when the Dean, acting *ultra vires*, sought to block a proposal of theirs from being placed on the agenda of a Faculty Board meeting. One of those censured noted that if he and his fellow "accused" could be censured, others would soon suffer the same fate. That observation was prescient. It was not long before denunciations, ostracism, and bullying took firm root in UCT.

Chapter 5 is the first of a few chapters (5, 6, 11 and 14), most of which are previously published, focusing on the annual TB Davie Memorial academic freedom lecture and its descent into farce. The TB Davie Memorial Lecture was established in 1959 by students at the University of Cape Town. It is named after Thomas Benjamin Davie, Vice-Chancellor of UCT from 1948 until his death in 1955. Dr Davie[72] vigorously defended academic freedom against the apartheid regime's imposition of racial segregation on higher education in South Africa, a battle that was ultimately unsuccessful. Chapter 5 provides an account of, and argument against, the revocation of the invitation to Flemming Rose to deliver the TB Davie academic freedom lecture in 2016.

Chapter 6 continues the saga begun in Chapter 5. Until the middle of 2016, UCT's Academic Freedom Committee (AFC) did what it was meant to do – defend academic freedom. For example, when UCT's executive took the decision to rescind the AFC's invitation to Flemming Rose to deliver the annual academic freedom lecture in 2016, it did so over the protestations of the AFC. However, the AFC's term of office came to end around the middle of that year. Chapter 6 raises some concerns about the incoming committee and wonders whether they will defend academic freedom. Subsequent events make it clear that it would not.

Chapter 7 covers the ongoing lawlessness and criminal protests at UCT, as of September 2016, and UCT's capitulation to this behaviour. When that chapter was first published as an article, I warned about the dangers of further capitulation.

Chapter 8 reprints my response to the "concerned philosophers" who objected to my argument (in Chapter 7) that the rights of non-protesters ought to be protected against criminality even if this required the use of some force.

Chapter 9, which was first published in early 2017, was a response to Dr Price's Panglossian appraisal of UCT's condition at the end of 2016.

Chapter 10 chronicles the unfortunate change in the institutional climate at UCT by March 2017. Many examples are provided. It is a good "overview" chapter for readers who want a taste of how bad the situation had become by then.

Chapter 11 continues the story of the TB Davie Lecture. Mahmood Mamdani, who was invited to give this lecture in 2017, took the opportunity to defend the disinvitation of Mr Rose. Instead of defending academic freedom, Professor Mamdani criticized it. Chapter 11 evaluates his arguments and shows just how weak they were.

Chapter 12, written especially for this book, describes the saga of a student who engaged in a lengthy campaign of defamation against me. The same student had fraudulently signed an attendance register and also invaded the Philosophy Department where she harassed the administrative staff. This chapter shows how UCT pandered to her and failed to stand by me and those of my colleagues whom she had harassed. In doing so, it contributed to the climate of impunity for some, and the climate of hostility towards others. This chapter is one of a number of "case studies" in the book. Its detailed descriptions are among those that support the book's more general conclusions.

Chapter 13 was co-authored with Anton Fagan, UCT's WP

Schreiner Professor of Law. In it, we discuss the genocidal tweets of a UCT student Masixole Mlandu. We argue, on free speech grounds, that UCT was correct not to take disciplinary action against him for these words, but we note that freedom of expression could not have been UCT's actual motivation, given its poor recent record of protecting such expression. We also discuss UCT's failure to take appropriate action against Mr Mlandu for his criminal *actions*. He was among those protestors who had engaged in unlawful behaviour.

Chapter 14 returns to the academic freedom lecture. It discusses the invitation by the tamed AFC to Steven Salaita to deliver the 2019 TB Davie Memorial Lecture, which he entitled "The Inhumanity of Academic Freedom". While defending his right to speak, I comment on what this choice of invitation says about the tamed Academic Freedom Committee.

Chapter 15 is a response to a piece of pseudo-scholarship by one of the BAC's most vocal members, Adam Haupt. He begins his paper with the disinvitation of Flemming Rose (which he supported) and pivots to the criminal protests that shut UCT for weeks on end between 2015 and 2017 (which he also supported). His paper was an opportunity, as it so often is for him, to level charges of racism against those with whom he disagrees. In Chapter 15 I reveal the poverty of his arguments – and his double standards.

Chapter 16 is a detailed examination of a connected series of events in one of the MBChB classes in 2019. These came to a climax in a class meeting in which some students were berated and humiliated for allegedly being insufficiently compassionate. The irony was entirely lost on those doing the berating and humiliating. Moreover, careful attention to the facts shows that those they were criticizing were not guilty of the wrongs that were attributed to them. This case study is an indicator of the broader climate at UCT.

Chapter 17 focuses on racial preferences. It begins with an

argument against the use of such preferences and then describes the practice of quite extreme racial preference at UCT.

Chapter 18 discusses one very protracted hiring process – that of a Dean for the Faculty of Humanities. Racial preference loomed large in this process. One candidate was rejected by the Faculty on account of his race. There was then an ongoing battle between those wedded to the idea that person appointed must be "black" and those for whom the person appointed must be a "black African South African". The story is one of mismanagement, racism, xenophobia, not to mention electoral disruption in which one lecturer literally "bit the ballot".

Chapter 19 tells two connected stories – one about the so-called Institutional Reconciliation and Transformation Commission, and one about an inquiry into the suicide of Health Sciences Dean, Professor Bongani Mayosi.[73] Both arose from the viciousness of the 2015-2017 protests. Both were subject to the same methodological flaws, most important of which was to repeat narratives from an unrepresentative sample, instead of interrogating those narratives to determine their veracity. It is a case study in manufacturing and magnifying a narrative of UCT as hostile to "blacks".

Chapter 20 discusses the (attempted?) academic lynching of Professor Nicoli Nattrass, at the instigation of UCT's Black Academic Caucus and with the enthusiastic participation of UCT's leadership. This was in response to a commentary Professor Nattrass had published in the *South African Journal of Science*.

Chapter 21 chronicles Chumani Maxwele's parade of appalling behaviour. Mr Maxwele had initiated the Rhodes Must Fall protests and was deeply involved in the subsequent protests. He was among the students against whom interdicts were brought and he was among those who, for his protest-related criminality, was given amnesty. Although this chapter covers that saga too, its focus is on other, lesser-known but not less serious offences of his.

Chapter 22 responds to Dr Lwazi Lushaba's claim, in a lecture to his first year Political Studies students, that "Hitler committed no crime". Some attempted to defend Dr Lushaba by claiming that his statement was taken out of context. However, the broader context of the lecture does not provide an innocuous reading of his statement. It also shows an embarrassing level of ignorance and of ideologically saturated argument.

Chapter 23 is an update to Chapter 10. It demonstrates that the toxic climate described in March 2017 was ongoing in late 2020 and showed no sign of abating.

Chapter 24 is the conclusion. In this chapter, I first delve further into the Black Academic Caucus' role in UCT's decline. I then situate the developments at UCT in the national and international context, and demonstrate how those contexts have exacerbated the institutional problems. I present some vignettes of "useful idiots" who contributed to the problem. Finally, I consider UCT's future. I note that as bad as it is, it could be worse, and might still become so.

Chapter 2
WHAT ARE TRANSFORMATION AND DECOLONIZATION?

(Originally published: 29 June 2015)[1]

The decades-old call for "transformation" and "decolonization" of South African universities has recently been intensified. However, those demanding these changes almost never define their terms and when they do, they do so imprecisely. As a result, for all the talk of "transformation" and "decolonization", it is not clear what they refer to. This ambiguity may facilitate the halo effect that surrounds these terms. Whatever they are, they are regarded as something positive. Academics and students alike, piously intone them.

But slogans are no substitute for real argument. If one wants to establish some conclusion, one must use key terms as unambiguously and precisely as the underlying concepts permit. Consider first the term "transformation". A transformation is "a thorough or dramatic change". Not all such changes are positive and thus those who seek particular changes in the name of transformation need to make the case that the particular changes are desirable ones.

Among the changes being demanded is the transformation of the student and staff profiles to reflect the racial demographics of the country. (Sometimes the demand extends also to reflecting the sex demographics, but curiously only in those higher education domains in which females are under-represented.) However, a change is not merely an altered outcome; it is also the process whereby the alteration is made. For example, reducing inequality is a noble goal, but not every means of bringing about such a change is desirable. An appropriate means for reducing inequality is by making those who are poor better off than they were. An inappropriate means would be to reduce to poverty those who are not poor.

It is thus not enough to endorse the goal of having a student body that more closely matches the racial (and sex) demographics of the society. The means must also be appropriate. Thus, admitting, on the basis of their "race", vast numbers of students who are not at all prepared for university would be bad. It would set those students up for failure and would squander limited public resources.

To be clear, the university can, should, and does provide support to those students who have been disadvantaged by their inadequate schooling, but it can do so only for those students who are only moderately disadvantaged and could succeed with remedial help. Universities cannot compensate for twelve years of appalling primary and secondary education, which is the norm in South Africa's dysfunctional schools. If they could there would be no point in devoting more resources to improving basic schooling.

If the government is unable to deliver decent schooling, it

cannot expect the universities to make up all of the shortfall. The sad truth is that the pool of qualified university applicants is not all school leavers, but only a small proportion of them. Without improved schooling the student demographics at universities simply cannot resemble the demographics of the country. It is wishful, delusional thinking to imagine otherwise.

Similar points can be made about staff appointments. In hiring academic staff, universities can draw on only a very small subset of the entire population. The quarry for academic staff is not all adults or even all adults with PhDs. The aim is to appoint the best scholars and teachers from the pool of suitably qualified applicants. That pool bears very little resemblance to the national demographics.

In response to this, many advocates of "transforming" the staff profile argue that we have to alter our conception of "excellence" which, they say, is biased or "Eurocentric". It is very difficult to evaluate this claim in the abstract and thus those who offer it might make a more persuasive case if they could explicate the ways in which the current standards of "excellence" are questionable. Should we, for example, not be seeking staff who have a command of their field, have finely honed analytic skills, and can publish articles in good quality, international peer-reviewed journals, and books with fine academic presses?

Another feature of the university that is claimed to require "transformation" is the curriculum, which, it is said, needs to be "decolonialized" or "Africanized". It is very difficult to understand what exactly this is meant to imply. Universities are themselves colonial imports and thus if "Africanization" or "decolonization" meant ridding South Africa of all colonial influence then universities would have to go. That would be undesirable, of course, and nobody is seriously making that claim. European colonizers of Africa brought plenty of evil, but they also brought some good. It would be a great pity if, when the evil is finally being reversed, the good were also jettisoned.

So what does it mean to "decolonize" the curriculum? Sometimes the suggestion is that African ways of thinking should be affirmed and that "European" ways of thinking should not be privileged. One problem with this suggestion is that it oversimplifies "African" and "European" ways of thinking. For example, the ways of thinking that characterized European universities a few hundred years ago are not the ways of thinking that characterize them today. If European universities had insisted, as conservatives might have wanted, on preserving traditional European thinking, there would not have been the advances in knowledge that there have been.

Similarly, if advocates of "decolonization" insist on injecting traditional African ways of thinking, there would be a similar stultification. The success of modern universities is not based on self-consciously pursuing or affirming traditional or ethnic-specific ways of thinking. Instead, the goal is to pursue knowledge as a common human endeavour. Thus we should be interested in whatever methodologies and innovations work and adopt them irrespective of their origin. Europeans did not reject Indo-Arabic numerals on the grounds that they were not of European origin. (This is one illustration, by the way, that not everything brought to Africa by Europeans was European in origin.)

Just as Africa would be disadvantaged by getting rid of its universities, so it would be disadvantaged by ridding itself of the historical advances made in and adopted by those universities. The process is never complete, of course, which is why change should be welcomed – but only if change improves what universities do. Change for the sake of fitting an ethnic or nationalist agenda is unlikely to have that effect. Thus Africa should contribute to human knowledge but it needs to do so by demonstrating that it has something valuable to add rather than by arguing that it has something African to contribute. This is not to say that Africa has nothing valuable to contribute. Instead, it is to say that the selling point should be that it is valuable rather than that it is African.

Consider medicine, for example. It is possible that some traditional African medicines may have therapeutic value. Thus one possible African contribution is to investigate this scientifically (as is being done). The scientific methodology is crucial, however. It would be a mistake to reject this methodology as a "colonial epistemology" and to teach medical students to prescribe traditional remedies without scientific evidence that these remedies are safe and effective. It is only through advances made by the scientific methodology that European medicine shed itself – and not that long ago – of such errors as miasmatic theory, humorism, and phlebotomy as a standard "therapeutic" response. No doubt there are lingering (and new) errors in modern medicine that still need to be expunged by advancing knowledge.

Parts of the university curriculum, of course, are already Africanized in some sense. For example, the universities teach African languages and literature, African customary law, African religion and African dance. That is all entirely appropriate.

But not all disciplines lend themselves to Africanization. It is not clear, for example, what it would mean to "decolonize" physics or mathematics. Mathematics is mathematics. There is no such thing as European or African mathematics. There were certainly traditional African cosmologies, but like pre-modern Western cosmologies these are myth rather than science and thus are not suitable for inclusion in a science curriculum. They may reasonably be taught in religious studies or literature courses, but not in science.

What about my own discipline, Philosophy? The main source of confusion with demands to Africanize a philosophy curriculum is the ambiguity in the word "philosophy". Many people use the term to refer to any system of thought. However, that is not the way the word is used in the academic context. Indeed academic philosophy is not even the mere *study* of any systems of thought, for that would not differentiate philosophy from areas of anthropology and religious studies. Philosophy is characterized not only by being concerned with particular questions, but also by the particular methodologies it uses in responding to those questions. These methodologies, like those of mathematics and physics, are imports. Even if they can be applied to African thought, that would involve a kind of "colonization" – the African systems of thought are subjected to academic tools that are not indigenous.

But indigenousness is no more a marker of value than non-indigenousness is a marker of disvalue. Ideas, innovations, methodologies should be evaluated on their merits rather than on their provenance.

One psychological factor that impedes the recognition of this is the misplaced ("colonizing") pride of some people and the misplaced ("colonized") insecurity of others. A person's intellectual capacity and promise is not a function of what has been achieved by those who share his or her "race". "White" South Africans have no more reason to bask in the glow of intellectual achievements that were imported from Europe than "black" Africans have reason to be insecure about the impressiveness of those achievements. One has to have played some part in an achievement to be warranted in taking pride in it.

In any event not all "white" South Africans are descended from either colonialists or from the great centres of European learning. Some are descended from immigrants from non-colonial countries who learned English here and who failed to pass on their ancestral tongues to their children. They are first or second generation university graduates. Universities and their curricula were not part of their own "cultural heritage", but they embraced university learning – because it is valuable and despite its "cultural unfamiliarity".

Most "blacks" in South Africa are not immigrants to this country (although many are). Nevertheless, we should all be heartened by the words of the eminent Harvard philosopher, Robert Nozick, who asked whether it was absurd for him, "someone just one generation from the shtetl, a pisher from ... Brooklyn", even to touch on the work of monumental thinkers. He replied: "Of course it is. Yet it was ludicrous for them too. We are all just a few years past something or other, if only childhood. Even the monuments themselves, so serenely in command of culture and intellect, must have been children once and adolescents – so they too are immigrants to the realm of thought. It wouldn't hurt for an acknowledgement of this occasionally through their magisterial prose to peep."

POSTSCRIPT

Xolela Mangcu, then an Associate Professor of Sociology at UCT, responded to the above article, calling it a "racially offensive diatribe". If you had not read my article and read only his response, you would be excused for thinking that I had written something with the flavor of *Mein Kampf*. In fact, most readers of Professor Mangcu's reply were in exactly that position, because the so-called Independent Newspapers saw fit to publish his replies online, whereas my original article and my responses to his replies were restricted to the print edition of the *Cape Times*. For more on this outrageously partisan behaviour on the part of the Independent Newspapers, see Appendix 1. Below is my initial response to Professor Mangcu.

(Originally published: 3 July 2015)[2]

Xolela Mangcu's "Racially offensive diatribe has no place"[3] says much more about his own piece than it does about my article to which he which he was responding.

His response has the hallmarks of his (newspaper) writing in general – intemperate, unduly aggrieved, peppered with reference to books he has read, and thin on actual argument.

He begins, inauspiciously, with the sort of comment that if reversed would trigger the deep offence to which he is prone. He says that "white people are often given credit that is denied to black people of similar or better talent" and that if "David Benatar was black, he would not be enjoying the audience he does at UCT". Professor Mangcu should stop to ask himself how he would respond if somebody made a parallel claim about him.

Moreover, it is not clear that I have much of an audience at UCT, where my views on a wide arrange of subjects are typically outvoted. Insofar as there is an audience it is because the views I express are so rarely heard. Professor Mangcu would rather that they were not heard at all, which is why he "poisons the well" by labeling my sedate and carefully qualified argument as "racially offensive" – an "intellectually offensive" response.

A newspaper article does not afford one the space to address fully all the mistakes Professor Mangcu makes – which is why it is a pity that he has now refused to go through with a public debate with me to which he had previously agreed – but I'll summarize them here:

First, academics writing in newspapers do nothing for their readers when they attempt to dazzle them with references to an array of scholarly books. They need to present a self-contained argument, not references to one. Professor Mangcu would do us a service if instead of name-dropping and criticizing me for failing to do so, he actually explained what he means by "decolonization". This word has most definitely been sloganized in political discourse in South Africa. I explored some problems with the way the slogan is usually deployed. If he thinks that there is an interpretation of it that withstands these criticisms, he should say what it is.

Second, he claims that I "rehash" the "hackneyed argument that affirmative action sets up black students for failure", which "is the so-called 'mismatch theory'". He then proceeds to cite American arguments that purport to refute this. However, whether or not one supports Africanization, one must surely be aware that the circumstances in America (where "blacks" are a minority) and South Africa are very different, and that data from the former cannot simply "colonize" the local facts. Indeed, "mismatch theory", accurately interpreted, has limited application in South Africa, where our problem is the utter failure of the great majority of schools nationwide. Professor Mangcu should take up that important grievance more often.

Third, Professor Mangcu has misunderstood the principle of "no taxation without representation", which refers to representation in parliament not in universities. If the injustices of the past had been adequately addressed, our universities would be demographically more representative. However, the duty of universities is not to pretend that the past injustices have indeed been addressed by providing a façade of normalcy. Universities can do some remedial work but, as I said in my original article, we are heavily dependent on repair of the dysfunctional schooling system. Professor Mangcu seems to be in denial about this.

Fourth, there *is* a dearth of qualified "black" academics. This fact is not altered by calling it a "tired shibboleth". Nobody is trying, as Professor Mangcu claims, to keep "black academics out of the universities". It would be a massive relief if we had plenty of outstanding "black" academics in our staff applicant pools. The history of the country, however, has resulted in our not being so blessed. Again, if "black" students continue to be shortchanged in schools, failing either to matriculate or to attain a university pass, we cannot expect things to change dramatically for many decades to come. Given this, one again wonders why Professor Mangcu spends so little of his energy inveighing against our country's appalling schooling.

Despite his own claims, Professor Mangcu seems to recognize that there are too few qualified "black" academics, which is why he inquires about "incentives to keep black academics at UCT from leaving not only for government and the private sector, but for Wits University". Implicit here is a recognition both that we are hardly swimming in suitable "black" academics and that the few that there are have many more opportunities that entice them elsewhere.

Fifth, Professor Mangcu says that I have "chutzpa" to suggest that "Africa must prove that it has something to add to the [academic] world". If he had read what I actually said, he would have seen that I think that the academic requirement to prove that one has something of value to contribute applies to everybody and not only to Africa. I don't want the French, for example, strutting around telling us that they have something French to contribute. I want them to show that they have something valuable to contribute. (I am, by the way, very critical of much "French philosophy".) What would be a "chutzpa" would be to hold Africa to a lower standard than that to which we should hold everybody else.

Professor Mangcu also attributes to me the claim that "Africa equates tradition and Europe modernity". But only an inability or unwillingness to read carefully would lead one to think I had made that claim. What I did say, in the very words Professor Mangcu quotes, is that just as criticism of traditional "European" thinking was and is essential for academic progress, so criticism of traditional "African" thinking is also essential for such progress. Perfect symmetry. It is hard to see how this "is the most racially offensive piece" in my alleged "tirade".

Sixth, I never claimed, as Professor Mangcu alleges, that "while the humanities can be Africanized, this is not applicable to philosophy". What I did say is that there are some areas of inquiry – some in the humanities and others not – that lend themselves more to Africanization. Nor did I claim that philosophy is a science. I said that the methodologies of academic philosophy, like those of the sciences, are imports. Thus, in his subsequent fulminations, Professor Mangcu is posturing against a straw man rather than anything I actually said. He should read and write more carefully.

A final word about the caption underneath the photograph accompanying Professor Mangcu's article: "The idea that black students cannot do well at university is a self-fulfilling myth of professors who do not see it as their mission to nurture their potential, says the writer".

That idea does not appear in the published version of Professor Mangcu's article. However, let me make it absolutely clear that my colleagues and I are committed to nurturing all our students, irrespective of their "race" or any other irrelevant consideration. Indeed, my own department was a pioneer in introducing department-specific additional tutoring for struggling students (irrespective of their "race"), and we take a close personal interest in all of our many students.

Chapter 3
MUST UCT ALSO NOW FALL?

(Originally published: 30 June 2015)[1]

Cecil John Rhodes has fallen. Must UCT fall too? Vice-Chancellor Dr Max Price recently wrote to alumni to assure them that the University of Cape Town has been strengthened, not weakened by recent developments at sub-Saharan Africa's oldest and the continent's most prestigious university. He says that there is "no reason for concern that any of the events of the last three months compromise our commitment to academic excellence". I do not share his optimism. Although UCT currently retains its stature, worrying developments place this in jeopardy in the longer term.

I hold no brief for Mr Rhodes or for his statue. Indeed, I recommend a healthy cynicism not only concerning statuary, but also regarding eponymous buildings, structures, cities and countries. Rogues are disproportionately represented among those thus honoured and remembered.

My concern is thus not with a fallen Rhodes, but rather where this road leads. Those heading the charge have made it clear that this is only a symbolic beginning and they plan to rapidly "transform" the University of Cape Town. They want to have the university's staff and student profile reflect the demographics of the country and they want it forthwith. This, I have argued elsewhere constitutes a kind of denialism. The qualified pool of student and staff applicants does not reflect the demographics of the country, and there is thus no way that those chosen from that pool can do so – at least not without compromising quality.

Much of the blame for this unfortunate state of affairs must, of course, be placed at the door of South Africa's racist past. However, the great tragedy since the demise of Apartheid is that South Africa's government has done so little to fix the upstream problems – the quality of primary and secondary schooling – that stand in the way of normalizing the demographics of the tertiary education sector.

Indeed, the vast majority of schools in South Africa are dysfunctional. Government is failing at its job, and yet it and its cadres want to flagellate its premier universities for being demographically "untransformed" – or, more accurately, insufficiently "transformed". (That logical distinction is lost on ideologues.)

With regard to academic staff, the complaint is not merely that there are so few "blacks" among their number, but also that there are even fewer at the senior levels, most notably the professoriate. Dr Price wants to reassure alumni that "No one, black or white, is arguing that promotion criteria should be different for different members of faculty". That, as far as I know, is literally true, but it is also misleading.

The University has, in its latest Employment Equity Plan, quite explicitly stated that both the composition of all promotions committees and the criteria for promotion will need to be reviewed – purportedly "to ensure there are no inherent biases with respect to black and women candidates".

Avoiding bias is entirely appropriate but we need to be clear on what constitutes evidence of bias. It cannot be the outcome per se. If there are fewer "blacks" among the professoriate this need not be because of any inherent bias. It might instead be on account of upstream problems – including the dearth of quality job applicants from this demographic, the pressure to appoint disproportionately large numbers from this smaller pool, resulting in staff somewhat less likely on average – not in every case – to meet promotion criteria once they are appointed. At the very least, these possibilities cannot be excluded given the powerful "race"-based affirmative action pressures that are at play.

Of course, there are also many "white" males who do not ascend through all academic ranks – not every academic eventually becomes a professor – but in those instances, there is no institutional hand-wringing.

In practice, the mandate to alter both the constitution of promotion committees and the criteria for promotion has unleashed – and arguably even been pre-empted by – outrageous proposals that seriously threaten the integrity of UCT's promotion mechanisms. Thus far, the most extreme example is that of the Humanities Faculty.

Contrary to some prejudices about the humanities, the promotion criteria and processes in the Humanities Faculty at UCT have hitherto been appropriately rigorous – indeed more rigorous than a number of (but not all) other faculties at UCT. (This is not to say that no inappropriate promotions have slipped through.) Yet, in a revolutionary fit, drastic changes were devised in a very short space of time – all in the name of "transformation".

Higher university authorities have not (yet?) accepted all of the Humanities Faculty's suggestions, referring them back for reconsideration. However, one major change that has been approved is the inclusion of non-professors on the committee that decides on whom to promote to all ranks, including that of professor. Indeed, up to 49% of the committee may now consist of non-professors. Although there are some faculties at UCT where the inclusion of non-professors on the promotion committees is already the practice, there are excellent reasons for thinking it unwise and a threat to standards of excellence.

First, the idea that junior academics are able to adjudicate applications for promotion to more senior ranks is akin to thinking that (even postgraduate) students are equipped to examine doctoral theses. There are exceptions, but ordinarily those who have not attained the more senior rank are not qualified to decide whether somebody meets the criteria for promotion to such a rank.

Second, when non-professors sit on a promotion committee, they have a conflict of interest. They typically know that their own promotion applications will later come before the committee. Although they will not serve on the committee in the year in which they are applying for promotion, they know, when they are on the committee, that they are setting precedents for their own cases later. Moreover, there is scope for mutual back-scratching – whether conscious or subconscious: "You support my promotion application and I'll support yours!" The same is not true of professors who have nothing to gain from currying favour with those whose applications they are considering.

Various spurious justifications have been offered for changing the constitution of the promotions committee. One is that the new structure will be more representative. Because great care has long been taken to ensure that the committees included people of both sexes and different "races", it seems that this argument refers to representation of different academic ranks. While it is true that the new structure is more representative in this sense, it's also the case that this fact does not override the aforementioned problems with including non-professors on the committee.

Indeed, if greater representation were as powerful an argument as its proponents suggest, we should aim to include not only junior academic staff but also administrative staff and students. A committee thus constituted would be more representative of the university – but it would also be a much less qualified and thus a much worse committee.

Another argument for the new structure is that it will increase "transparency". It is true that those non-professors serving on the committee will gain a keener sense of its (now altered) workings, but if the confidentiality of the committee is preserved - which is essential for the effective and ethical functioning of promotions committees – there will be no greater transparency than there is now. (Promotions committees do already have external oversight – by representative deans from other faculties and by deputy vice-chancellors.)

Thus, the justifications offered for the changed structure are really excuses rather than (good) reasons. It is absolutely clear that the motivation for changing the structure is a "transformation" agenda. Indeed, in nominating members to serve on the new committee, nominees' "transformation" credentials were cited. There is good reason to suspect that some promotions will now be made on the basis of this agenda. (One sad by-product of this is that even those who do deserve to be promoted will have a doubt hanging over the merit of their promotion.)

The quality of the institution can survive some inappropriate promotions (as it has in the past), but if a critical mass is reached, the university may well begin a slow descent. By the time it becomes widely perceptible it will be too late.

In his letter to alumni, Dr Price also hailed the

"commitment to reasoned argument" within the university. This is most definitely not my experience. One reason why those without first-hand experience should be skeptical of Dr Price's claim is that politically loaded decisions made by groups of people are almost never made on the basis of reasoned argument. Uncritical thinking, logical fallacies, various irrationalities, dogmas, and perceived self-interest typically hold sway.

One might hope that matters would be different in a university, but (with very rare exceptions) they are not. For example, in one recent senior university forum, a careful argument I offered (against the promotion committee changes) was greeted with the response: "I cannot believe that somebody would say that." The statement was repeated as if its repetition would compensate for the absence of any actual argument to engage mine.

When the "transformation" card is played in university meetings, as it repeatedly is, almost everybody marches in lockstep. People fall over themselves in displays of political correctness, each paying obeisance to the mantras and slogans of contemporary South Africa – just as our conspecifics in other times and places have shamelessly attempted to demonstrate that they are true adherents of the orthodoxies of their respective contexts – true faithful of some or other religion, true revolutionaries, or true fascists, for example.

Dr Price is deftly handling a very difficult phase in the history of the University of Cape Town. He must balance the demands of disgruntled students and staff, the concerns of other staff, alumni and donors, and the constraints of conscience, among other considerations. This is an unenviable task, but it is his not mine.

My task is to speak plainly about how things are. In some ways UCT is much better than it has ever been. In other ways, it is worryingly worse. After Rhodes it is at a crossroads. Only the future will reveal whether the current political navigations will rescue UCT from the ire of revolutionaries without driving it onto the rocks of inadequacy. This peril would not exist if reasoned argument really did guide enough members of the university community.

Chapter 4
THE CENSURE

Consider the following scenario. Four members of UCT's Humanities Faculty, joined by fourteen others, seek to put a proposal on the agenda of the Faculty Board meeting. Their proposal is that a bust of Cecil John Rhodes be removed from the entrance of the Faculty Office. The Dean, acting beyond his authority, refuses to place the proposal on the agenda and repeatedly fails to explain why he believes he has the authority to do so.

The four core proposers thus decide to make use of a standing item on the agenda – questions for the Faculty Executive – to ask the Dean why he refuses to put their proposal on the agenda. At the meeting, the Dean responds by saying that the proposal is "based on a belief system" which should not be imposed on others and that because of "cultural diversity", we as a Faculty have an obligation to tolerate and protect diversity with regard to aesthetic tastes. Some people like the bust where it is. The Dean also says that the proposal does not concern an academic or resource allocation matter and thus does not constitute part of the Faculty Board's *core* business (even though the Faculty does sometimes consider proposals that are not part of its core business).

The core proposers push back, and the Dean says that he will "concede" to a Special Meeting of the Faculty Board to discuss the matter. However, he stipulates that non-academic staff and students in the Faculty will be allowed to vote at this meeting. In saying this, he is unilaterally altering the rules by prescribing that those who are not members of the Board will be entitled to vote at a Special Meeting of the Board. One of the core proposers reminds the Dean that, under the Statute, the Dean is the chairperson of the Board and may not rewrite its rules. He and the others are then silenced by the Dean and they walk out in protest.

If I told you that a motion of censure would follow these events, who would you think would be the object of that censure? You could be confident in answering that it would be the Dean. And you would probably be even more sure of your answer if I were to tell you that those bringing the motion of censure deemed themselves to be "progressives" at the vanguard of "transformation".

However, the scenario I have asked you consider differs in two ways from what actually happened. First, instead of the proposal being about the removal of a bust, it was actually about the Faculty taking a symbolic stand against the infliction of suffering and death on billions of victims. Perhaps your answer would remain unchanged with this correction – given how readily you might expect progressives to distance themselves from cruelty and how dim a view they would take of a dean breaking the rules in order to avoid such distancing.

If your answer would remain unchanged, consider a further specification not yet stated: The Dean is "black" and those seeking to make the proposal are perceived as "white". That specification should not make a difference, but this is UCT, where everything is viewed through the prism of "race" and people are held to different standards depending on their purported "race". The saga – a Carrollian-Orwellian-Kafkaesque hybrid - shows how naked racial politics and faux principles are employed to ostracise and silence some people in order to entrench the reigning orthodoxy.

THE ARTICLE

In October 2014, my colleague Dr Elisa Galgut and I published an opinion piece in UCT's then monthly newspaper.[1] We applauded UCT's condemnation of unfair discrimination, but we pointed to one serious injustice that UCT – like much of the world – routinely ignores. We noted that in doing so, UCT "both tacitly accepts and actively promotes the infliction of enormous suffering and death on almost unimaginable numbers of victims". We were speaking about the suffering and death inflicted by humans on non-human animals. In our piece, we called for the removal of animals and their products from the menu of university events.

Although justice for animals enjoys growing support, it is still a cause supported by only a minority of human beings. This is odd because desisting from eating animals and their products is actually a logical consequence of a basic moral principle that most people *do* accept – namely that it is wrong to cause *unnecessary* suffering to animals.

Over a billion animals are killed for food in South Africa every year. At least in the case of land animals, their deaths follow lives of misery and torment. Dr Galgut and I gave some examples of this suffering in our article:

> Most sows are still kept in gestation crates so small they cannot turn around. Egg-laying hens - 24 million of

them in South Africa at any given time - are de-beaked, and some de-clawed, without anaesthetic, before being crammed into cages so tightly that they are unable to spread their wings. They live their short, wretched lives in an area the size of an A4 piece of paper. A further 24 million chicks - the males, regarded as wasteful 'by-products' - are killed, usually by being ground up alive. Cows, impregnated in order to lactate, suffer great psychological distress at the loss of their calves, which are removed before they are weaned. Every year more than 200 000 male calves, useless to the dairy industry, are killed at birth or sold into impoverished settlements, where, deprived of their mothers' colostrum, most die in infancy.[2]

Fish "harvested" from the sea, unlike those in fish farms, are not reared in intensive conditions. However, they can suffer barotrauma when hauled from the ocean depths. Their deaths are horrific – as a result of asphyxia, decapitation or evisceration. Some people would like to believe that fish do not feel pain. The scientific evidence shows that they are mistaken.[3]

Is this suffering (and death) *necessary*? Does it produce a greater good (for humans) that cannot be produced in some other way? Not for most people – and certainly not for those eating at university events. They can fulfil all their nutritional requirements from other sources. Thus, those who really think that it is wrong to inflict unnecessary suffering on animals cannot consistently claim that what is done to fish and farmed animals is permissible. The corollary of this is that those who think that the way fish and farmed animals are treated is morally permissible must think that it is permissible to inflict *un*necessary suffering on animals.

Dr Galgut and I suggested that by "providing meat and other animal products at official functions, the University endorses and promotes these practices". We said that it is "hard to imagine that this barbarism will not, in time, be a source of institutional shame, and that future generations will not wonder how their predecessors - including our generation - could have exhibited such insensitivity". We asked why we should "wait to 'redress' what will then be a past injustice" instead of stopping the injustice now. To this end, we called on UCT "to put its principles of justice where its mouth is, and to pledge to take animal suffering off the menu at university functions".

Unsurprisingly, our proposal was ignored. This led Dr Galgut to pose a question to the University Executive at the March 2015 Humanities Faculty Board meeting.[4] Dr Galgut asked whether the Executive had given the proposal any consideration and, if so, what their response was.

Responding on behalf of the Executive, Professor Francis Petersen said that "the proposal had not been given consideration as no formal proposal had been received" and that those "who wished to make proposals for change were urged to do so through the appropriate governance structure". He said "that where food was served, the University catered for all dietary preferences including vegan".[5] He did not say whether cannibalistic preferences would also be catered for, but we can all be confident that they would not be. Professor Petersen seems to have missed the point that just as there would be ethical considerations against accommodating such preferences, there are similarly ethical considerations against accommodating other carnivorous preferences.

THE PROPOSAL

Given Professor Petersen's suggestion that a formal proposal be made, Dr Galgut and I, along with two other colleagues decided to put a formal proposal to the Humanities Faculty as a first step. On 13 August 2015, we submitted a proposal that animal products be removed from the menu of all official Faculty events.[6] We indicated that before the Faculty Board meeting, a longer list of co-proposers would be provided. This list of a further fourteen proposers was submitted on 2 September 2015.

In the interim, on 20 August 2015, the Faculty Manager advised me that the Dean[7] would "raise the proposal at the DAC [Dean's Advisory Committee] ahead of the next Board meeting". At the DAC meeting on 25 August there was time for only a perfunctory discussion of the matter. The Dean expressed his objection to the proposal, and I responded. He then said that he would "allow" the proposal to be placed on the agenda and suggested that the proposers would need to provide ballots, to which I replied that voting could be either via ballot or by a show of hands. He also expressed concern about how much Faculty Board time would be used and I assured him that the presentation would be no longer than six minutes, followed by discussion. In the days following the DAC, my co-proposers and I worked hard to produce a succinct presentation that would fit that time frame.

On the morning of 4 September, the Friday before the Faculty Board meeting, the Dean wrote to me to indicate that he would *not* include the proposal on the agenda. In support of his decision, he claimed that our proposal was "based on a belief system" which should not be imposed on others and that because of "cultural diversity, we as a Faculty have an obligation to tolerate and protect diversity with regard to dietary preferences".

I replied the same day, indicating my disappointment with his email. I cited three reasons. First, I did not believe that he was entitled to veto the proposal, and I copied the Registrar, asking him to clarify whether my interpretation was correct. Second, I indicated that the Dean had already agreed to have the matter included on the agenda and thus his latest email was a last-minute reversal. Third, I disagreed with the basis for his decision. Tolerance and cultural diversity cannot be invoked to justify racist and sexist *practices*. They should similarly not be invoked to justify speciesist practices. In other words, one cannot expect practices that wrongfully harm others to be tolerated.

The Dean did not reply. As the Registrar was indisposed, I was informed on 4 September that the Registrar-Designate, Royston Pillay, would be responding. By the evening of Monday 7 September I had received no response from the Registrar's office. I thus wrote again to Mr. Pillay, indicating the urgency of the matter, requesting his opinion and offering my explanation why I believed that, according to the UCT Statute, it was beyond the Dean's powers to veto the proposal. I noted that the Statute was not explicit but that a reasonable reading suggested the Dean was not entitled to act as he was acting.

At 07h06 on 8 September Mr. Pillay replied, with a copy to the Dean, indicating that a "member's right to have a motion included on the faculty board agenda is *implied,* given the provision that a special meeting must be called if 10 members so request". Mr. Pillay did also say "that the issue that is raised for the faculty board agenda should fall within the parameters of what the Statute records the board's responsibilities to be." I shall return to that matter later.

At 07h59 on 8 September, I wrote to Mr. Pillay, with a copy to the Dean, thanking him for confirming my interpretation. At 11h31 the Faculty Board agenda was distributed without the agenda item – and without any explanation from the Dean.

At 22h42 on 8 September, I wrote to the Dean, noting that in the light of the legal clarification from the Registrar-Designate, my colleagues and I presumed that the omission was an oversight and that a further agenda would be circulated with the proposal. However, I said that if that presumption were false, then we wished to pose a question to the Faculty Executive at the Faculty Board meeting. More specifically we wanted to know why our proposal was not included on the agenda. After all, the Dean had not deemed it necessary to explain his decision following input from the Registrar-Designate.

The next morning, the Dean responded by saying simply "My understanding of Royston's message is different from yours". Again, no explanation was provided, but he did agree to place our question on the agenda. I replied shortly thereafter, thanking the Dean, but also asking Mr. Pillay to state *explicitly* whether the Dean's interpretation or mine was the correct interpretation of his email.

Mr. Pillay replied saying that "A board member's right to have a motion included on the faculty board agenda is *implied* given the provision that a special meeting *must* be called if 10 members so request. In this narrow sense, there is prescription rather than discretion." He added "More generally though, I would have thought that role and functions of the faculty board – as captured in the Statute - would also be used as a yardstick to guide consideration as to what to include on an agenda, and whether there may be other options as to where else discussion of the item at hand may also be had."

I felt that this reply was too coy and that given the Dean's response a more explicit answer was needed. Thus, I wrote back to Mr. Pillay indicating that I had been hoping for a more explicit answer. In his reply, Mr Pillay said that the Statute's provision about a Special Faculty Board meeting "implies that the Dean does not have a right of veto". That seemed about as explicit as one could get from Mr Pillay.

THE FIRST MEETING

At the Faculty Board meeting on 10 September 2015, the Dean called on me to pose my question. He did not recuse himself from the chair for this item, and there was thus no independent chair to arbitrate on this procedural issue. I summarized the matter in a manner that the Dean seemed to find fair. He responded at length. Among the points he raised was his original comment about "imposing views" and "cultural practices". He also referred to the Statute's comments on the purview of the Faculty Board, a matter to which Mr. Pillay had referred in his initial two emails, but not in the last and most definitive one.

Before I responded to the Dean, I asked that he call on Mr. Pillay to comment on his answer. The Dean dismissed this idea. The Registrar did not volunteer a comment in the face of this. The Vice-Chancellor was also present, but he too remained silent. Thus, I began responding to the Dean's various points, but was cut short by him before I had finished. He said that he would concede to a Special Faculty Board meeting but that all administrative staff and students would also be invited to attend such a meeting and to vote at it.

I rose to respond, noting that we did not need the Dean to *concede* to a Special Faculty Board meeting because our right to that was *explicitly* stated in the Statute. (I also asked him why he would not allow the matter on a regular Faculty Board meeting if he were not opposed to its being placed on a Special Faculty Board meeting. He refused to answer that question.) In my response to his directive that all administrative staff and students would also be invited, I indicated that he did not understand the fact that administrative staff and students (except for their representatives) were not members of the Faculty Board, that they therefore had no right to attend or vote at such meetings, and that the Dean did not have a right to alter that state of affairs by fiat. In the process, I reminded the Dean that according to the UCT Statute the Dean is the *chairperson* of the Faculty Board and not its autocrat.

I had wanted to address other aspects of the Dean's response to my question, including the one about the purview of the Faculty Board. This was clearly an after-thought on the Dean's part, as it was not the originally cited reason for his decision. Nevertheless, while the Statute does describe the functions of the Faculty Board, which are primarily academic, it neither states nor implies that the functions of the Faculty Board are limited to the stated ones. Moreover, a number of motions have been placed on the Faculty Board agenda in the past that do not fall within the narrow scope of issues explicitly mentioned by the UCT Statute.

However, I was unable to make this point, because Associate Professor Xolela Mangcu interjected and was granted the floor by the Dean. Professor Mangcu began a tirade, accusing me of disrespecting the Dean, and again implicitly accusing me of racism. This then prompted Associate Professor Adam Haupt to express his anger, also changing the topic from the matter at hand to the topic of transformation.

While these two members of the Board were given freedom to complete their speeches, those who rose to speak in my support or against the Dean's answer, or to contribute any other point, were each cut short by the Dean and told to be silent and sit down.

A few of us then left the meeting, but not together. When Professor Skotnes, one of the core proposers, exited the room, the door banged behind her. She subsequently wrote to the Dean to indicate that while she was upset at what transpired in the meeting, she had *not* purposely banged the door in protest. Instead of taking this email in the calming spirit it was intended, the Dean responded by claiming that he was "not sure what this communication means or what you want me to do with it." Professor Skotnes replied that it simply meant that she did not want him to think that "the inadvertent slamming of the door was pointedly hostile". The Dean took this email to be a "direct insult" and forwarded it and the earlier correspondence (but not his subsequent reply to Professor Skotnes) to the entire Faculty

Board, the Vice-Chancellor, the Deputy Vice-Chancellors, Registrar, and others.

My view is that the Dean acted *ultra vires* in exercising a veto on the proposal for the Faculty Board Agenda. Whether or not that interpretation is correct, it was the interpretation implicitly provided in the Registrar Designate's final email (at 06h50 on 10 September 2015), when he stated categorically that "the provision therefore implies that the Dean does not have a right of veto".

The Dean and others may wish to create plausible doubt here by citing the fact that the UCT Statute is not explicit on this matter. However, even if one adopts that alternative interpretation, it remains true that the Dean acted in an unaccountable manner at various points. For example, he failed to explain why he disagreed with my interpretation of Mr. Pillay's initial email, so that we could have a reasoned exchange about that. He did not respond at all to the more explicit statement Mr. Pillay provided on 10 September. He also saw fit to direct that administrative staff and students would be allowed to attend and vote at the proposed Special Faculty Board meeting, which was *certainly* beyond his powers.

When a dean acts in this manner, members of the Faculty Board are entitled to call him to account. If he fails to account properly and makes up rules as he proceeds, the challenge must escalate. That does not cease to be true if the Dean is "black". It is thus astounding that those who believe that they are at the vanguard of "transformation" not only rush to the defence of a dean who has acted in a high-handed manner, but also seek to level accusations of racism at those holding the Dean to account.

The suggestion that the challenge to the Dean was "racially inflected" was scurrilous – but also part of a pattern of behaviour for both Xolela Mangcu and Adam Haupt[8]. It is curious that those who are so concerned about the Dean's being "at the receiving end of an attack on his integrity as a person" are so willing to attack the character of my colleagues and me by imputing racism to us. If they were the least bit attentive to the facts, they would have every reason to think that our actions were prompted by a Dean acting unaccountably, and no reason to think that the "race" of the protagonists had anything to do with it.

THE STATEMENTS

A few days after this meeting, the Black Academic Caucus (BAC) issued a statement condemning Professor Skotnes and me by name. Our accusers – the *members* of the BAC – hid behind the name of their collective. However, there is good evidence that the statement was drafted by the aforementioned Adam Haupt, and that the final revision was made by Dr Shose Kessi. The statement was copied to various people and groups, including RhodesMustFall, NEHAWU (National Education, Health and Allied Workers' Union), and the UCT Students' Representative Council.

The statement said that the events at the meeting "were a tragic disregard for inclusive transformation processes and a gross disrespect for the Dean of Humanities' call for such processes". It claimed that our proposal had "been taken seriously" by the Dean. It also repeated the accusation that our challenge was "racially inflected" and claimed that we "*staged* a walkout" (my emphasis), which suggests something orchestrated rather than the spontaneous decision of a series of individuals (who had been sitting in different parts of the room and who left at different times).[9]

The BAC statement obfuscated various matters. For example, it attempted to gloss over the Dean's attempt to alter the rules about who may vote at Faculty Board meetings, by referring to the Dean's "call to host an inclusive discussion (through Faculty Assembly or Special Faculty Board) on the ethics of diet at faculty events". In fact, the Dean had not proposed that the matter be discussed in a (future) Faculty Assembly. He said that that the matter would have been more appropriately discussed at the *previous* Faculty Assembly. In other words, it was not a practical suggestion about where to divert the proposal. In any event Faculty Assemblies are not decision-making fora, and the proposal was that a decision be made. The Dean did eventually agree to a Special Faculty Board meeting, but with his own alteration of the rules governing such meetings.

The BAC statement sought to view my interaction with the Dean through the lens of my views on transformation. As evidence of the latter, they cited the article that is republished as Chapter 3 in this book. In doing so, they sent a very clear message. If one expresses sceptical or critical views about transformation, this can then be used against one if, for example, one challenges rather than panders to a "black" dean who acts *ultra vires*.

In its statement, the BAC also took the opportunity to target me as (then) Head of the Department of Philosophy, asking the Vice-Chancellor for "clear direction" on whether heads of department's "performance assessment will be linked to their commitment to transformation". In other words, they sought to have heads of department judged, in part, on the level of their conformity to the BAC's agenda.

The BAC's statement characterized Professor Skotnes's accidental door slamming as a "micro-aggression" and her subsequent email of explanation to the Dean as "insulting". It asked the Vice-Chancellor whether he "intends to condemn the conduct of colleagues for actions that perpetuate an untransformed institutional culture" and "whether Professors Benatar and Skotnes will be asked to account for their conduct at the meeting".

I responded to the BAC's statement on 24 September. I said that I was quite happy to account for my conduct *without* any request to do so from the VC, and that the BAC should consider my response to be my accounting. I asked in return "whether signatories to the BAC statement will be required to reveal their identities and then held to account for their libellous accusations of racism". Of course, there was no such accountability from the nameless members of the BAC.

In making its statement, the BAC not only viewed the events of the Faculty Board meeting through its preferred lens, they also did so in ignorance of what had transpired in the lead-up to the meeting. Being ignorant of these facts was no impediment to their rushing to judgment. This is because the facts do not matter to the BAC. All that matters to them is their view of the racial identity of parties involved.

The facts did not matter to the Executive of the Academics' Union (AU) either. In a letter to the Vice-Chancellor on 18 September, the AU Executive placed on record its "support in principle for the sentiments expressed by the BAC". They conceded that they were not present at the Humanities Faculty Board meeting, but that did not stop them from saying that "to the extent that the events of that meeting ... imperilled the advancement of transformation, we would like to express our dismay" and that they supported the BAC's request "for a response from your office to the events at the Humanities Faculty Board".

The purpose of the AU is to represent its members, including against Management, when the former are in conflict with the latter. However, in this case the AU Executive did exactly the opposite. Instead of supporting those academics challenging a dean who was acting *ultra vires*, the AU Executive abandoned those academics and supported the Dean (along with those academics defending his high-handed behaviour). Nor was this the result of a careful investigation into which parties were deserving of support. The AU Executive never bothered to ask those of its members whom it was condemning, for *their* account of what had happened. Instead, the AU Executive rushed to judgement against us on the basis of the BAC's racialised account.

The UCT Students' Representative Council also rushed to judgement. In a statement on 21 September 2015, and signed by then SRC President Ramabina Mahapa, it said that it "supports the Black Academic Caucus's (BAC) condemnation of Professor David Benatar's behaviour as well as his consistent undermining of the decolonisation process at UCT". It quoted verbatim some of the BAC's allegations, including the claim that our challenge to the Dean was "racially inflected". The SRC also took aim at the Philosophy Department and my headship of it.

The SRC statement falsely claimed that Chumani Maxwele had been "suspended over racial allegations" and said that people like me "should be held accountable, as equals, rather than protected by their whiteness and Professorship". This is a ludicrous comparison. Chapter 21 of this book makes it clear just why the University attempted to suspend Mr Maxwele. It was not because of mere "racial allegations". He threatened, intimidated, assaulted and defamed people. In doing so, he never once elicited publicly expressed disapproval by the BAC or the SRC. By contrast, my colleagues and I were attempting to hold the Dean to the rules, and we were subjected to condemnation for doing so.

The SRC statement concluded by saying that:

> White people in this university and outside of it need to stop defending their power, whether directly through acts of supremacy, or indirectly through the silencing of black voices. Hiding behind the veil of liberalism and non-racialism will no longer shelter you from criticism - and nor will your academic positions.

The SRC was mistaken. When your proposal is, in contravention of the rules, kept off the agenda; when you are told to keep quiet and sit down; when your union supports management rather than you; when you are libelled and your correction of the record is dismissed on account of your purported race; then you are the one being silenced rather than the one doing the silencing.

THE SECOND MEETING

The Special Faculty Board meeting at which the proposal would be discussed was scheduled for 16 October 2015. By this point, the waters seemed to be poisoned. Given the resistance to getting the proposal on the agenda, and the way those opposed to its consideration had racialized it, it seemed unlikely that the proposal would enjoy open-minded consideration. The four initial proposers nonetheless decided to proceed. Our fears proved well-founded, which might explain why over half of the further fourteen co-proposers did not attend the meeting.

No sooner than the meeting had begun than Adam Haupt requested that "the behaviour of several of the proposers" at the previous meeting "be condemned". The Dean said that the Special Meeting had only one agenda item and that any members who wished to propose another item could do so for the next regular meeting.

The motivation for the proposal was presented by Dr Galgut and another colleague. The proposal itself was a modest one. The Faculty was asked to vote in favour of removing animal flesh and other products from official Faculty events. The resolution, if passed, would not apply to individual departments and, *a fortiori*, not to individuals within the Faculty. Instead it would apply only to Faculty-wide events. Nobody would be prohibited from eating meat or animal products that they purchased or were served elsewhere. If the proposal were adopted, the only upshot would be that such food would not be served at Faculty events. Accepting the proposal would thus be largely a symbolic stand against the mistreatment of animals in the production of food, although it was hoped that such a stand would serve as a moral example that others might choose to emulate.

In her presentation, Dr Galgut observed that there were many good reasons to support the proposal given that "animal agribusiness is ... complicit in many ills that befall our society, from impacting massively on global warming, land degradation, water usage and pollution".[10] She said that feeding grain to animals that are later killed and eaten is an inefficient way of feeding the poor, and that it was typically the poor, without alternative means of employment, who worked in abattoirs, with the attendant physical and psychological costs. In her talk, she quoted from a South African study in which abattoir workers complained of nightmares and feelings of guilt about being forced to slaughter animals. However, the focus of her presentation was on the vast amount of suffering and death inflicted on animals reared to provide food for humans.

Dr Galgut said that just as smokers could support a proposal to restrict where smokers may smoke, so too those who are not vegetarians or vegans could support the proposal before the Faculty Board. One of Dr Galgut's co-proposers then concluded the joint presentation by raising some possible objections to the proposal, and responding to them.

After the presentation, the Dean asked each of the other proposers who were present at the meeting if they wanted to make any additional comments. Most endorsed the proposal without further comment. However, one said that while she agreed with the proposal, she would no longer support it given the "manner in which the proposal had been brought to the Faculty". A second person offered a similar but less explicit comment. One wonders by what manner they would have liked it to have been brought to the Faculty, given that it was only by standing up to the Dean that the proposal made it on to the agenda at all.[11] It is the Dean who must bear responsibility for the fact that it took a conflict to get the proposal on the agenda. It is true that the proposers could have avoided the conflict, but only at the cost of abandoning the proposal by deferring to the Dean's exceeding of his authority.

The Dean then weighed in. He asked, *inter alia*, whether those who had made the proposal could guarantee that, if adopted, it would not violate any Constitutional or other legal rights. How the Dean thought that not being served meat or other products at UCT Faculty of Humanities events might violate anybody's legal rights beggars belief. Nobody has a constitutional or other legal right to be provided with *any* food by the Faculty of Humanities,[12] let alone any specific kind of food.

The Dean also expressed concern again that non-academic staff and students would be affected if the Faculty Board adopted the proposal. He was not similarly concerned about the animals who would be affected if it were *not* adopted. Nor did he express similar concerns when *other* proposals affecting administrative staff and students (both of which sectors have representatives on the Faculty Board) were discussed.

Finally, the Dean asked those present to consider what they would do if "another interest group"[13] were to bring another proposal to the Faculty Board for adoption. The answer to that question, I would have thought, is that they should evaluate any such proposal on its merits. Whether or not the UCT Humanities Faculty is capable of evaluating a proposal on its merits, that is what it *should* do.

When the proposal was opened to the floor for discussion, various desperate arguments were advanced against it. For example, one member said that violence could result from the Faculty endorsing a "dietary restriction". In support of this she cited the case of a Muslim in India who had been lynched for allegedly having eaten beef. The suggestion that the Faculty's adoption of the proposal might lead to violence strains credulity.[14]

The discussion rapidly became racialized by critics of the proposal. Paranoia was in evidence. For example, one member of the Faculty Board, ignoring all the arguments that had been presented and all the suffering and death that had been described and visually depicted, responded to a *cartoon* that had been included among the slides that accompanied the presentation of the proposal. The cartoon, by Joel Pett,[15] depicted a man in a coffee shop. He is looking at the wall-mounted menu and says to the person behind the counter: "I'm torn between the planet-wrecking factory-farmed energy-sucking cruelty burger and the fresh vegan wrap".

Those who had made the presentation were asked to comment "on the presentation of race" in the cartoon which, we were told, "depicted a middle-aged white man instructing black workers". However, there was manifestly no "instructing" going on. The customer was declaring his indecision to the worker (not workers) behind the counter.[16] If only one character is the butt of this cartoon, it is that customer. If he had instead been depicted as "black", then *that* would have been the basis for the objection. If *none* of the characters were "black", then the critique would have been that the cartoon was insufficiently diverse. If *all* of the characters were "black", then this would have been criticised for being racially insensitive. The point is that there is no winning in the face of paranoia.

By far the most racially inflammatory objections came from Adam Haupt. First, he characterised the conflict with the Dean in racial terms. He said that those attempting to get the proposal onto the agenda had engaged in a "direct challenge to a black dean". It is true that there was a direct challenge to the Dean, but the Dean's race was entirely irrelevant, except in the mind of Adam Haupt and his comrades.

Second, Adam Haupt said that I had attempted to "pit the black Registrar-designate against the Dean". He said this in ignorance of the background – namely that I had not chosen the Registrar-designate, Royston Pillay, to clarify whether our interpretation of the rules was correct. In fact, I had directed my initial inquiry to then current Registrar Hugh Amoore. I had directed my inquiry to him because the Registrar is the person to whom such inquiries should be directed. I then learned that Mr Amoore had been hospitalized. At that point I inquired whether my question would be answered by the Deputy Registrar, Dr Karen van Heerden, or by Mr Pillay. That decision was taken within the Registrar's office, and I was advised that Mr Pillay would respond, as described above. If it had been either Mr Amoore or Dr van Heerden who had dealt with my inquiry and attended the meeting, then I would probably have been accused of pitting a "black" dean against a "white" Registrar or Deputy Registrar. Accusations of racism are that malleable. Put another way, Adam Haupt's allegations are not made on the basis of the facts. Instead the facts are distorted to suit his preconceived conclusions.

Third, Adam Haupt claimed that we had made the proposal because we were unhappy about the extent to which the Faculty was and would still be "transformed". He made oblique refence to my criticism of the changes to promotion rules and processes in a then recently published piece.[17] He claimed that our proposal was a "Trojan horse for racism" and said that what he took to be our ulterior motives should be considered. He asserted that our proposal was about race and not about animal rights.[18]

There is much astounding about this speech. First, even if our motives had been ulterior, the proposal should have been evaluated on its merits. Second, our motives were not ulterior and the suggestion to the contrary is cynical opportunism. Our views on the treatment of animals are well-known in the University and have been for many years. If Adam Haupt were to be believed, our academic and other university work in this area, not to mention the decades-long exclusion of animals from our personal diets,[19] was all part of a devious racist plan. Third, he ignores the fact that if there had been no attempt to block our proposal from being placed on the agenda, and if it had then been discussed on its merits, it need not have occasioned any discussion of racial issues. It was our critics – not we – who turned this into a racial issue.

Associate Professor Sa'diyya Shaikh had a variant ideological tic. She said that if the proposal were accepted by the Faculty, she would bring a proposal to boycott Israeli universities.[20] Although three of the four core proposers were Jewish, we had the maturity not to respond to this with accusations of antisemitism.[21]

Sa'diyya Shaikh then moved that the matter be put to a vote without further discussion. There was no formal seconder to her motion. I objected to it on the grounds that those making a proposal should be given the opportunity to respond to objections. We had not yet had such an opportunity. The matter was put to a vote and by a narrow margin it was decided that the proposers be given the opportunity to reply. However, voting began, by secret ballot, before the response was completed – another lapse in chairing the meeting.

Eight members of the Board supported the motion, fifty opposed it and twenty-five abstained. In other words, the overwhelming majority of members of the Faculty of Humanities – or at least of those present at the meeting – were unwilling to oppose, even symbolically, the following sorts of practices that were clearly described to them and, in some case, visually illustrated:

- The slaughter, in South Africa, of well over a billion animals each year for food.

- Keeping sows in gestation crates so constraining that they are unable to turn around.
- Castration, tail docking, and teeth pulling of piglets – all without anaesthesia.
- Debeaking and declawing of chickens – also without anaesthesia.
- Cramming chickens into cages so tightly that they are unable to spread their wings.
- Killing, typically by gassing or maceration, of day-old male chicks that are useless to the egg industry.
- Dehorning of cattle without anaesthesia.
- Removing calves from their mothers, with the attendant psychological distress

It sounds more like the Faculty of *In*humanities. They may not see it now, but it is hard to imagine that future generations will not look back on this as an egregious moral failing. While they were worrying about the distress of people walking past the statue of a colonialist, they were indifferent to the much greater suffering being inflicted on billions of animals. Those who doubt that that the latter suffering is worse, should ask themselves whether they would rather walk past the statue of somebody they loathe, or have their finger, teeth or genitals excised without anaesthetic[22] (and later being butchered).

THE THIRD MEETING

The next meeting of the Humanities Faculty Board took place on 16 March 2016. Adam Haupt requested that a motion of censure be put on the agenda. This time, *four* of us were named, and others alluded to. He alleged that our behaviour:

> was disrespectful to all members of the Faculty Board, the Dean in his capacity as chair of the Board and as Dean of the Faculty of Humanities. The disrespectful manner in which the Dean was addressed and the

divisive manner in which the proposal had been brought to the Board set a dangerous precedent for the conduct of staff members at faculty boards. The aggressive engagement and staged walkout was a direct challenge to the Dean; this was further emphasised by the attempt to pit a black Registrar-designate against a black Dean. This action stands to polarise the Faculty along racial lines and should not be abided.[23]

At the meeting, two colleagues and I tabled a document that responded to this proposal. It contained the thread of communication that had preceded the Faculty Board meeting of 10 September 2015 (the "first meeting" described above), my response to the BAC's statement, as well as a number of comments in direct response to Adam Haupt's proposal.

We noted that when the Dean had refused to place on the Faculty Board agenda the proposal (from eighteen members of the Board) to remove animal products from Faculty events, he argued that the proposal "did not fall within the terms of reference of the Board",[24] which according to the Institutional Statute is *primarily* concerned with academic matters and resource allocation issues. He also argued that the proposal "could be divisive and cause alienation and a split within the Faculty".[25] It is thus unfortunate, we said, that a proposal (from a single member of Faculty Board) that is *explicitly* divisive and likely to cause alienation was now on the Faculty Board agenda without objection from the Dean.

We noted Adam Haupt's assertion that we were "disrespectful to all members of the Faculty Board, the Dean in his capacity as chair of the Board and as Dean of the Faculty of Humanities". We said that we had good reason to believe that the Dean was acting *ultra vires* in refusing to place the item on the Faculty Board agenda. We were not allowed to express our view that this was the case and were told to "sit down", in some cases mid-sentence. In these ways, *we* – and the Faculty Board –

were treated with disrespect. Our (staggered, not staged) walk out was not orchestrated but rather a response made individually by each of us to the manner in which we were treated. Some of us also felt that the atmosphere in the meeting was pointedly hostile, and had no wish to remain in the venue.[26]

We also responded to Adam Haupt's assertion that our "action stands to polarise the Faculty along racial lines and should not be abided." We said that alleging racial motivations where there are none is what is racially polarizing. A proposal to sanction members of the Board on the basis of groundless racial allegations is manifestly racially polarizing, and thus Adam Haupt's logic should result in the Faculty Board's censure of *him.*

We rejected as disingenuous his suggestion that I had attempted "to pit a black Registrar-designate against a black dean". He had made that allegation at the meeting on 10 September 2015 when he was ignorant of the background, and he had repeated it in his motion of censure even though he should by then have been aware of the background described above.

We reminded members of the Faculty Board that walking out is a standard way of registering some fundamental frustration or objection at a meeting, and should not attract censure. We noted that in the environment that then characterized UCT, staff had objected in more extreme ways than we had, without attracting a formal vote of censure from Adam Haupt or his associates. If those responsible for such actions were not censured for disrespect, then our own relatively milder action should not attract censure either.[27]

Finally, we observed that our proposal targeted no individual and focused on the arguments. By contrast, Adam Haupt was seeking a censure that was calculated to damage the reputations of named individuals and create further division in the faculty. He had again failed to engage the arguments, preferring to attack the individuals making them. We said that debate was critical to the health of the faculty, even, and in fact more importantly, where such debate revealed fault lines and differences of opinion. Adam Haupt's proposal was, in the light of this, misplaced, and counter to the values that we believe the board should uphold.

Adam Haupt presented his motion, which was then seconded.[28] One of our fellow proposers responded to it. He repeated a number of the points we had made in our tabled document, but also amplified on some of these. He argued that Adam Haupt's motion, if passed, would:

> have an ominous effect on debate in the faculty. If an authority takes actions that you believe are *ultra vires*, and you are prevented from explaining why, then expressing your opposition to the situation – rather than sitting down and being quiet – may well lead to censure and a racially-based smear. Once a precedent is set that members of the Faculty Board objecting to *ultra vires* actions can be silenced and censured, all (except the most compliant) become vulnerable.

A lengthy discussion followed. Some members of the Board thought that the motion ought to be rejected entirely, and spoke of its dangers. Others – whom the Dean clearly supported – either approved of the motion as it was, or expressed concern about the wording of the proposed motion but said that they might endorse a revised wording. As a result, and at the Dean's request, Adam Haupt drafted a new version of the motion, which was also much shorter. It said that the Faculty Board found the behaviour of four named individuals at the 10 September 2015 meeting "unacceptable" and requested an apology from them.

The vote was conducted by secret ballot. Of those who had not left the meeting by this point, thirty-seven supported the motion, thirty opposed it, and fourteen abstained. The motion was carried. At that point I asked to speak. I said that I had kept my silence during discussion of the motion because the well had been so poisoned that anything I would have said would have been used against me. However, with the resolution passed, I had nothing to lose. I said that when Alexander the Great died, Aristotle left Athens saying he would not let that city sin twice against philosophy. I suggested that the Faculty Board has sinned against philosophy – by which I said that I meant not the department, but the discipline in which conclusions followed from evidence rather than evidence being mustered to support pre-conceived conclusions.

I said the Faculty Board had acted like a kind of tribunal, but that many of those voting had rushed to judgement before knowing the background leading up to the September meeting. Many had not even been at the Faculty Board meeting in September and thus were not in a position to judge our conduct. Nor could they rely on the minutes which were not yet approved. (Moreover, we believed that the minutes misconstrued what had transpired in order to make the Dean appear more reasonable.[29] When the inaccurate minutes were eventually approved in our absence, at the meeting on 19 May 2016, our corrections were also adopted for the official record.)

I said that philosophy was also interested in consistency and that the reaction to our actions, where no rules were broken in the attempt to hold the Dean to account, was inconsistent with the absence of any condemnation of an array of blatantly illegal actions at UCT (during then recent protests). I compared the motion to a lynching, and indicated that I would leave the Faculty Board and not return until reason once again prevailed. (I have not returned,[30] and do not expect that I shall.)

While I was speaking, I was heckled by Dr Lwazi Lushaba, partly in English and partly in an African language. (It was Dr Lushaba's first Faculty Board meeting and thus he was among those who had not been at the earlier meetings.) The Dean attempted a few times to keep him quiet while I spoke, but Dr Lushaba persisted in his heckling. I pointed to that heckling as indicative of the lynching mentality to which I had referred. Despite Dr Lushaba's disruptive behaviour and his refusal to respect the Dean's attempts to silence his heckling, neither Adam Haupt, nor anybody else, sought to bring a motion of censure against Dr Lushaba. There was no objection that he had disrespected the Dean, the members of the Faculty Board, or me![31] This is because there was no principle underlying the censure of my colleagues and me. It was a mob behaving as mobs do.

When, during the meeting, my unnamed colleague had spoken against Adam Haupt's motion, he had said that his "worst fear is that some colleagues may take the chance to support this motion, to exercise a personal animosity towards some of us[32] or to support a political position. However, my colleague also expressed the hope and belief that most members of the Faculty Board would "see the unfairness of this, and the damage it will do not just to those targeted but to the Faculty as a whole." His worst fear materialized, while his hope was misplaced and his belief proved mistaken.

He was entirely correct, however, in thinking that the Faculty as a whole would be damaged. It was not only the Faculty, but also the University that would be damaged. UCT was already on a rapid descent into greater and greater toxicity, as many of the forthcoming chapters will demonstrate. The censure contributed significantly to that climate of increasing toxicity.

Chapter 5
A BLOW TO ACADEMIC FREEDOM

(Originally published: 22 July 2016)[1]

The irony should be lost on nobody. A speaker invited to give the annual academic freedom lecture at the University of Cape Town (UCT) has been prevented by the University Executive from giving that lecture.

In March 2015, the Academic Freedom Committee at UCT decided to invite Flemming Rose, a prominent defender of freedom of expression, to deliver the 2016 T.B. Davie Memorial Lecture, which was due to take place on 11 August.

As the culture editor of the Danish newspaper, the *Jyllands-Posten*, Mr Rose had published some drawings and cartoons depicting Mohammed. The purpose of this exercise was to establish the extent to which artists were self-censoring. The question had arisen following a number of European instances of self-censorship pertaining to Islam. One of these occurred when the author of a children's book about the life of Mohammed had had difficulty finding a willing illustrator because artists indicated they were fearful. Mr Rose wrote to members of the association of Danish cartoonists, asking them to "draw Mohammed as you see him". Twelve illustrations, not all of them depicting or targeting Mohammed, were published on 30 September 2005. Among those lampooned by the cartoons were the author of the children's book, the leader of a Danish anti-immigration party, and the *Jyllands-Posten* itself. Nevertheless, two Danish Muslim clerics used the publication of the cartoons to incite international violence in early 2006. These reactions galvanized Mr Rose, and he became a prominent advocate of free speech.

It is unsurprising that Mr Rose's unrepentant publication of the Mohammed illustrations makes him a controversial figure. However, it is precisely such a person who is a barometer of how much freedom of expression we enjoy. Everybody is willing to tolerate some speech. The real test of freedom of expression occurs when people are asked to tolerate the speech of those whose ideas they do not like. On that test, the University of Cape Town has shown that it does not have the robust commitment to freedom of expression that it says it has.

In explaining the University Executive's decision to override the Academic Freedom Committee's invitation to Mr Rose and to disinvite him, the Vice-Chancellor, Dr Max Price, makes the obligatory affirmation of "our commitment to the right to academic freedom and freedom of expression".[2]

As all those who seek to curtail freedom do, he is quick to qualify this commitment by noting that "[l]ike all fundamental rights ... the right to academic freedom is not unlimited". Of course, there is a sense in which academic freedom and freedom of expression are appropriately limited. Dr Price notes that according to section 16(2) of the South African constitution the right to free expression does not extend to "(a) propaganda for war; (b) incitement of imminent violence; or (c) advocacy of hatred that is based on race, ethnicity, gender or religion, and that constitutes incitement to cause harm".

These restrictions are reasonable, at least if we interpret them appropriately. Thus, what is ominous about a reminder that a right to freedom of expression is not unlimited is that it is commonly used to segue into a justification of an unjustifiable limitation. That is exactly what Dr Price does. He provides justifications that fail to meet any of the above criteria.

The justifications he provides are listed under three headings. One might presume that each heading would correspond to a different reason. However, he regularly slips from the titular reason to another. Irrespective of how they are classified his justifications fall short.

The first purported reason is that the lecture would provoke conflict on campus. It is not clear what Dr Price means by "conflict". In elaborating, he refers to "protest and disruption" and then to the likelihood that the lecture will "divide and inflame the campus".

Many events at UCT are protested against, and yet that has appropriately not been thought good reason to cancel them. The prospect of protest is not a reason – even under the South African Constitution – to limit freedom of expression. Instead, protest, on condition that it is peaceful and does not prevent the expression of those against whom the protest is being held, is itself a form of expression, and thus to be protected.

Nor does the prospect of disruption indicate that the potentially disrupted expression exceeds moral (or legal) limits. Disruption might be indicative merely of the disrupters' intolerance, and thus one has to show on other grounds that the limits are exceeded. If one cannot show this, then the disruption itself exceeds the limits of acceptable protest. UCT has proved very ineffective at prohibiting such forms of (illegal and immoral) protest, which makes the prohibition of (legally and morally) "protected" speech all the more curious.

Moreover, the campus is already divided – about all sorts of matters. If a view's likelihood to cause division were grounds for prohibiting it, then Dr Price's own letter should be prohibited for it too will divide the campus. If his letter does not *inflame* the campus, that is only because the people who disagree with him on this matter are unlikely to cause a conflagration.

The second reason for disinviting Mr Rose is "security". The Vice-Chancellor tells us that he and the University Executive are "convinced" that the lecture "would lead to vehement and possibly violent protest". The mere vehemence of the protest is beside the point, and thus we are left here with the conviction that there will *possibly* be violence.

There are two problems with this argument. First, we have been provided with no evidence that violence is likely to result from Mr Rose's lecture (even though the Academic Freedom Committee specifically requested such evidence). Second, if a lecture results in violence it does not follow that the lecture itself exceeds the moral or legal limits of freedom of expression. If it did follow, then those willing to respond violently will have a *de facto* veto on any ideas they dislike.

Put another way, there is a difference between "incitement" to violence and a violently intolerant response to a speaker or the expression of an idea. Speech constitutes incitement to violence when the speech aims to elicit the violent behaviour of those who then act violently. If the content of the speech does not seek violence, then it is not incitement. Your violent reaction to my expressing an idea does not mean that I have incited you. It means you have resorted to violence when you should not have done so.

The expectation of a violent reaction may sometimes require somebody to desist from expressing the idea that will be reacted to violently. However, in the rare cases that this is true, the reason for being silent is not that one's right to freedom of expression has exceeded its limits. Instead, one's right is being violated by those who threaten violence. Perhaps Dr Price and his colleagues have this position in mind. If that is the case, then they should unequivocally acknowledge that academic freedom and freedom of expression are being violated. Dr Price does gesture at such a possibility, but it is obscured by his more extensive (but flawed) implied argument that Mr Rose's lecture would fall foul of the Constitution's limits on freedom of expression.

When legitimate speech has to be curtailed because of a threat of violence, limiting the speech has to be seen as a temporary measure until the threat is neutralized. Dr Price's attempt to defend the position of those opposed to Mr Rose's speaking encourages rather than neutralizes that threat. Dr Price's energies should be focused on condemning those who threaten violence rather than on veiled condemnations of Mr Rose. He is thus ill-placed to invoke an "imminent violence" defence of the Executive's decision.

The third purported reason for disinviting Mr Rose is that bringing him to campus "might retard rather than advance academic freedom on campus". Here Dr Price's "doublespeak" reaches full-throttle. He wishes to restrict academic freedom in order to advance it.

He says that we "know that many within our universities don't feel safe to engage, which undermines the spirit of mutual tolerance and understanding". He asserts that this is "a deeply worrying situation which all adherents of academic freedom should find disconcerting, and ultimately unacceptable". However, he asks rhetorically whether progress will be made "by inviting somebody who represents a provocatively ... divisive view". Because the Academic Freedom Committee's brief is to defend academic freedom on campus, he implies that in sticking to its invitation to Mr Rose it is in breach of its brief.

Dr Price is not explicit about who "feel unsafe to engage". It is unlikely to be campus revolutionaries and those who will resort to violence, for their very actions suggest that they feel very safe. It is much more likely that Dr Price is referring to campus liberals who have either been cowering or, if outspoken, under constant attack – without a public word of support from the University Executive. (If Dr Price is referring to this group, then the fact that he does not identify them as such is another indication of just how politically dangerous it has become to express sympathy with them.)

Thus, it seems that we are being told that we must restrict the speech of those serious about freedom of speech in order to protect those same people's freedom of speech. That is exactly the wrong response. Instead, the University should be standing firm on freedom of speech and teaching those who do not already know, that this value extends (most crucially) to people with provocative and even divisive views.

There is a fourth reason running, as a thread, through Dr Price's argument for disinviting Mr Rose. This takes the form of impugning Mr Rose, although in a slippery way. Thus, Dr Price *refers* to accusations of bias and bigotry that are buttressed by the claim that "the *Jyllands-Posten* had previously refused to publish cartoons that mocked Christ, on the grounds that this would offend its readers, and also said that it would not publish cartoons about the Holocaust". In fact, the *Jyllands-Posten* has published several cartoons ridiculing Jesus. It has also published antisemitic and Holocaust-mocking cartoons – not because it endorsed them, but so that their readers could see for themselves what, for example, was being published in the Arab and Iranian press. Mr Rose is at pains to emphasize that publication does not constitute endorsement.

Dr Price also says that "Mr Rose is regarded by many around the world as right wing, Islamophobic, someone whose statements have been deliberately provocative, insulting and possibly amount to hate speech". Dr Price quickly adds that "[n]o doubt all these claims can be contested". This is exactly why it is not sufficient to trot out those accusations as a basis for disinviting. For example, there are those who have said that Edward Said, who in 1991 gave the TB Davie lecture without disruption, was an antisemite and terrorist sympathizer. It is easy to make such accusations but harder to make them stick. Anybody wanting to *disinvite* a speaker because they are not a suitable "chosen champion of the University of Cape Town to deliver its symbolic and prestigious TB Davie public lecture on academic freedom" will have to make the accusations stick. In fact, the accusations against Mr Rose, to which Dr Price refers, are utterly groundless. Mr Rose's commitment of freedom of expression is a deeply principled one and has resulted in his defending the anti-democratic speech of fundamentalist Muslims.[3]

Almost all of the arguments that Dr Price musters could be advanced, *mutatis mutandis*, against giving a platform for the many Israel-bashers who speak on campus. These speakers are typically selective in their moral outrage, cause division and hostility between different groups, and risk "diminishing, rather than bolstering, the opportunities for proper and mutually respectful intellectual and institutional engagement". Moreover, they occur against a background of millennia of antisemitism. This is not to say that anti-Israel speakers should be banned from campus, but rather that the selective application of the arguments to some speakers is revealing.

The one argument that does not apply to anti-Zionist speakers is the argument about violence. The University Executive have had grounds for confidence that campus Zionists will not engage in violent, disruptive protest. We can only hope that that remains the case and that other parties learn the bounds of acceptable protest. The University Executive should be helping them learn that rather than pandering.

The decision to disinvite Mr Rose is not the only way in which freedom of expression has been limited recently at the University of Cape Town. It is, however, the most obvious and the least deniable example. During the Apartheid era, the torch of academic freedom was extinguished. It was only rekindled with the advent of democracy. It is now time to extinguish it again, and to keep it extinguished at least until Mr Rose delivers the lecture he was invited to give.

POSTSCRIPT

The South African Institute of Race Relations, upon hearing of the disinvitation of Mr Rose, invited him to South Africa to deliver the annual Hoernlé lecture, which he did without incident in both Johannesburg and Cape Town in May 2017. While in South Africa, Mr Rose also spoke at the University of Cape Town, albeit unannounced and in a small class at my invitation. There he addressed and had a pleasant and respectful exchange with the students.

Chapter 6

THE TAMING OF THE ACADEMIC FREEDOM COMMITTEE?

(Written: 14 September 2016. Not published.)

It is now widely known that University of Cape Town's Executive disinvited Flemming Rose from giving the University's TB Davie Academic Freedom lecture. Mr Rose had been invited by the Academic Freedom Committee (AFC), which organizes the lecture. The University Executive initially asked the AFC to disinvite Mr Rose. When the AFC refused to do that, the Executive did so itself, over the protestations of the AFC.

That firm stand in defence of freedom, was taken by the Academic Freedom Committee that *was*. As fate would have it, the committee's four-year term of office expired in the middle of 2016, just after Mr Rose was disinvited. The committee's expression of outrage was its final act.

The process of constituting the new committee overlapped with the outgoing committee's struggle with the Executive and was completed only after the outgoing committee's term of office had ended. There is some reason to think that this committee's stand on the Flemming Rose matter galvanized the dominant regressive sector of the University in a way that influenced the way the committee was repopulated.

The AFC is constituted piecemeal. The Vice-Chancellor and up to two Deputy Vice-Chancellors are *ex officio* members. (It can easily be inferred that they were outvoted on the Flemming Rose matter.) University Council elects two members, the Senate elects three professors, the Academics' Union nominates two non-professorial members, and the Students' Representative Council nominates two members.

The Vice-Chancellor and Deputy Vice-Chancellor positions on the new committee remain unchanged. None of the professors who served on the outgoing committee are on the new committee. At least one of them – I – was nominated to serve again, but the University's Nominations Committee, the deliberations of which are confidential, decided not to put my nomination to a Senate vote, effectively vetoing my nomination. It is hard to know what the real basis for this decision was, and whether the desire for a more congenial academic freedom committee played a role.

One technicality that the Nominations Committee might have exploited is the principle, stipulated in its terms of reference that "no individual should *normally* serve more than two consecutive terms on a particular committee" (my emphasis). I had served more than two terms. Of course, "normally" indicates that there is not an absolute prohibition and thus this guideline would need to be weighed up against other considerations including the brief to "identify *suitable* people to fill all membership slots"[1] (my emphasis).

Continuity, although not explicitly mentioned in the terms of reference, seems like another important consideration. The new committee is almost entirely new. One representative of the Academics' Union remains on the committee, although she has not been on the committee very long. The two students' term of office ends in October. That leaves only the Vice-Chancellor and his Deputy, who attend AFC meetings only rarely.

The new professorial members of the committee are Haroon Bhorat (Economics), Rashida Manjoo (Public Law), and Pierre de Vos (Public Law). Professor de Vos,[2] while criticizing the disinvitation of Mr Rose, also criticized the initial invitation, suggesting that he will not be supporting the sort of nominations of TB Davie lecturers that will make the Executive uncomfortable. It remains to be seen where the other two professors will stand. Will they support only speakers who are congenial to the prevailing orthodoxy or will they support the invitation of speakers, such as Mr Rose, who have important but unpopular things to say?

The Council members on the previous incarnation of the Academic Freedom Committee were Judge Ian Farlam and Advocate Jeremy Gauntlett. Council considered three possible replacements for their two replacements. The candidate that Council did *not* elect was a defender of academic freedom. The two candidates that Council did elect are Associate Professor Elelwani Ramugondo (an occupational therapist who became Special Advisor to the Vice-Chancellor on Transformation) and Dr Shuaib Manjra (a medical doctor specializing in sports medicine and occupational health). Will an official transformation advisor support invitations of speakers and, more generally, take positions on academic freedom that the intolerant sector of the University will find uncongenial? Dr Manjra, commenting on the disinvitation of Flemming Rose, asserted that "human dignity and civility trumps" freedom of speech.[3] Because any view that is taken to be offensive can also be taken to violate dignity and be uncivil, Dr Manjra's position enables the shutting down rather than the protection of unpopular speech.

The Academics' Union also elected two candidates from three nominees. One of those elected was on the previous committee and is committed to academic freedom. Time will tell what position the other will take, but he obtained more votes than an outspoken defender of academic freedom,[4] which raises concerns about the general sentiment regarding academic freedom among the docile Academics' Union's membership.

Some threats to academic freedom and freedom of speech more generally, are overt and obvious. The disinvitation of Flemming Rose was one such case. It is thus concerning that at least some members of the (new) Academic Freedom Committee support such breaches.

However, most threats to freedom of speech are hidden from public view by their subtle or incipient nature. One such threat is that of self-censorship in the face of social pressure or the threat of violence. Ironically, it is this "tyranny of silence" that is the subject matter of Flemming Rose's excellent recent book by that title.[5] Those who read this book will find that Mr Rose, far from being the moral monster he has been portrayed as being, is rather a highly principled defender of freedom of expression. His message about the danger of self-censorship is an important one for South African universities, where a climate of intellectual intolerance is stifling freedom of expression. An Academic Freedom Committee that tows the orthodox line and is unwilling stand firm on freedom of speech and academic freedom, cannot be counted upon to highlight these threats. Instead, it masks them.

It remains to be seen whether the new Academic Freedom Committee will live up to its purpose – to "promote academic freedom ... within and outside UCT, and to take appropriate action when it is infringed" – or whether the recent transformation of the committee has also been its taming.

Chapter 7
THE UNIVERSITY OF
CAPITULATION

(Originally published: 21 September 2016)[1]

Once again, marauding thugs have disrupted normal activities at the University of Cape Town (and other universities in South Africa). Although they are fond of presenting themselves as victims and as a progressive vanguard, they are in fact the very opposite. They are perpetrators who violate the rights of others, and they are the agents of destruction, which, in the long run, is not good for anybody, least of all those whose interests they purport to represent.

In a rights-respecting democracy, we all have a very strong duty to respect the law. The social contract we have is that disagreements about what the law should be are sorted out via the designated political and legal processes. We then have a presumptive duty to respect the law on the understanding that that is the cost of expecting that others will respect the law when they disagree with it. You must obey the laws you don't like because otherwise you'll have no grounds for expecting me to obey those laws I don't like.

Yet the student protesters want things both ways. They expect the University to comply with the law while they themselves trample all over it. They are the first to demand their rights, while routinely violating the rights of those whose education they disrupt, those whom they intimidate and harass (sometimes with racist invective), and in some cases, those whom they physically assault.

In the face of this illegality, the University of Cape Town's Executive has repeatedly taken a soft path, attempting to negotiate and appease. There are, however, some serious problems with becoming the University of Capitulation.

First, the University becomes complicit in the protesters' violation of others' rights. We are repeatedly told that "UCT recognises the right to engage in legitimate and peaceful protest and urges protesters to respect the right of other members of the campus community to attend classes and arrive at work." However, *urging* protesters to respect the rights of others is simply not sufficient. One actually has to protect those rights.

Second, capitulation encourages those who seek to hold the University hostage to its growing list of demands.[2] One reason we are facing disruptions in 2016 is that the University surrendered in 2015. Had it conveyed a firm message last year that illegal behaviour would not be tolerated, it would have removed one incentive to the present (and potential future) disruptions.

Third, allowing chaos to reign on campus damages the University. In the short run, education cannot be delivered, researchers are distracted, and administrators have to spend time and energy on protest-related matters, diverting them from their actual work. In the medium and longer term such disruptions contribute to making UCT less attractive to donors and to prospective staff and students.

The latter include the significant "Semester Study Abroad" contingent of students who come from overseas for a semester and bring much-needed income for the University. However, it also includes prospective students from those families who could afford to send them abroad for their studies. UCT also stands to lose staff who seek more hospitable work conditions. The protesters may dismiss these concerns by saying "good riddance", but they, others like them, or their children will eventually suffer the consequences.

Finally, the University is passing up an opportunity to teach the protesting students an important life lesson, namely about the rule of law. Instead, the University has indulged a self-righteous narrative that puts the protesters above the law. We are all entitled to protest, but if one thinks that this is a licence to do as one pleases, one needs to be disabused of that idea – the sooner the better.

The University has been reluctant to enforce the law, and has instituted disciplinary proceedings against only a handful of students, despite many more students' having engaged in illegality. This, it seems, is because it wants to avoid a "heavier, hands-on security presence".[3] Indeed, we can be sure that the moment force is used against illegality, the protesters will call "foul". They will be supported by other sectors of the University, including some members of staff who have been egging on the disruptive protesters either explicitly or subtly. They will also be supported, or at least not opposed, by the campus's "useful idiots", who will earnestly condemn the "use of force".

What is lost on all of them is the fact that law is ultimately backed up by force. Many people comply with the law without the need for force to be used. However, the threat of force always lurks in the background and sometimes has to be exercised. For example, if one refuses to pay fines, one may be summoned to court. If one refuses to present oneself or to comply with the court's verdict, one may be arrested. If one resists arrest, force will be used to effect the arrest. If one uses force in return, then greater force will need to be used. That is the way it has to be, for otherwise there would be no sanction attached to breaking the law. Laws without teeth are not laws.

What should be done? First, the University Executive must recognize its responsibilities to the vast majority of members of the University who want to go about their work and studies. They must protect them from those who violate their rights by disrupting the functioning of the University. It must do so sooner rather than later.

Second, the remainder of the University should support the Executive if it acts in this way, and it should challenge those who would criticize the use of (necessary) force. (Many of those critics are, in any event, highly unprincipled. They don't sincerely object to illegal force but are quick to condemn legal force.)

Third, when the Students' Representative Council (SRC) elections finally take place – they have been postponed because a student interdicted from being on campus, and thus unable to campaign legally, is standing for election – students should vote in their droves for those candidates who will not indulge lawlessness. (Although the current SRC does not support a university shutdown "at this time",[4] its opposition to a shutdown seems more pragmatic than principled, and the next SRC could be worse.)

The SRC is typically elected by a small proportion of students, with the vast majority of potential voters not voting. The result is an SRC that, although filled with its own importance and purporting to speak on behalf of students, in fact only represents those students who take the SRC seriously enough to vote. Students who do not want their education, examinations and graduations disrupted or delayed, must take themselves to the polls and vote. A more representative SRC that opposes illegality would also provide a clearer contrast with the groups orchestrating the illegality and which are not elected student bodies.

What should be done and what will be done frequently diverge. I have no expectation that they will converge in this case. However, if they do not, then UCT – and South Africa – will pay the price.

Chapter 8
THE INSUFFICIENTLY "CONCERNED PHILOSOPHERS"

(Originally published: 10 October 2016)[1]

It is a sign of the times that a group identifying itself as "concerned philosophers" – current and former students and tutors in the UCT Philosophy Department – has seen fit to join the bandwagon of campus groupthink.

In a statement,[2] directed to the Philosophy Department they say that they are concerned "about 1) the increased militarisation of UCT including the presence of private security and the excessive use of force by private security and police on campus 2) the silence of the philosophy department on this issue and on the protests in general."

They think that the use of private security and police on campus is both "morally wrong" and "imprudent". They do not explain why it is wrong, but in support of the claim of imprudence they say that the "mere militarization of campus increases tensions and hostility, and creates an environment that is directly counterproductive to constructive engagement". They do not consider the medium- and longer-term imprudence of capitulating to illegal protest.

They argue that the Philosophy Department's silence is problematic because in the absence of a Department statement, a piece that I wrote in support of the enforcement of law on campus[3] "is perceived as the department's position". At the same time they say that the Department's silence, "perpetuates stereotypes about the department, its staff and its students" and makes the Department "seem untransformed and uncritical of current events".

In presenting this constellation of views, the "concerned philosophers" express no concern at all about the campus protesters' flagrantly illegal behaviour, including:

1. Blockading access to universities,[4] thereby preventing people from getting to their place of work and study.

2. Disrupting teaching and intimidating academic and administrative staff as well as students.[5]

3. Burning vehicles[6] and historic paintings.[7]

4. Causing nearly a billion rands worth of damage to universities around the country, evidently without a single person yet being convicted for these crimes.[8]

5. Threatening the completion of the academic year, with all the knock-on effects that this could have, including, but not limited to:

a. An extra year of study for thousands of students, which will impact most significantly on the poorest.

b. Preventing the qualification of final year health science students, thereby negatively impacting on the provision of healthcare in the public sector, on which the poor are reliant. (Similar points can be made about at least some other graduating professionals.)

c. A loss of fees to the universities that are already under financial pressure and will thus be even less adequately equipped to meet the expensive demands of the protesters.

6. Stone throwing[9] and other dangerous behaviour that appears to have resulted (although not at UCT) in the death of one person thus far.[10]

As unconcerned as the "concerned philosophers" are about the rampant illegality that seeks to cripple South African tertiary education and is likely to have very serious costs for the rest of the country, they are very concerned about any attempt to enforce the law.

Indeed, they take exception to my call for the law to be enforced. They say that my article "endorses violence against the protesters". This is a misrepresentation. What I actually said applies equally to them:

> What is lost on all of them is the fact that law is ultimately backed up by force. Many people comply with the law without the need for force to be used. However, the threat of force always lurks in the background and sometimes has to be exercised. For example, if one refuses to pay fines, one may be summoned to court. If one refuses to present oneself or to comply with the court's verdict, one may be arrested. If one resists arrest, force will be used to effect the arrest. If one uses force in return, then greater force will need to be used. That is the way it has to be, for otherwise there would be no sanction attached to breaking the law. Laws without teeth are not laws.[11]

There is a difference between *force* and *violence*. It is true that force can escalate into violence, but they are not the same. *Appropriate* law enforcement will often begin with words, proceed to force, and escalate into controlled and proportionate violence to the extent that those breaking the law refuse to yield to the lesser force.

It is a similarly sloppy use of language to say that the campus was "militarized". This is hyperbolic sloganeering. There is a difference between inviting private security or police onto campus and inviting the military. When the law is broken, at least in a legitimate state, it is entirely reasonable to call law enforcement agencies. A country's streets are not militarized merely because armed police are to be found patrolling them.

I would like the "concerned philosophers" to look me in the eye and tell me with a straight face that the claim I made about how law works is false. I would like them to similarly indicate whether they reject the concept of law enforcement. More specifically, would they want the law enforced should they become the victims of serious illegality? If somebody robs them, destroys their property, or blocks their access to their homes, would they be satisfied with "constructive engagement" with the criminals rather than have the police enforce the law? (If they think that the law should be enforced in such cases, they must explain why it should not be enforced in others.)

The "concerned philosophers" allege that when law enforcement was brought onto campus, excessive force was used and racial profiling employed. Insofar as that is true, it is a matter for legal redress. However, if the "concerned philosophers" are critical thinkers, they will recognize that sometimes perceptions and allegations can be inaccurate.

That is exactly why we have legal processes for dispassionately evaluating them and taking appropriate action. If security personnel have acted illegally then they should be subjected to sanction, but exactly the same should apply to protesters who have acted illegally. Asymmetric enforcement of the law would undermine the principle of equality before the law.

The "concerned philosophers" say that the presence of law

enforcement "on campus creates a climate of fear and uncertainty which is not conducive to academic activities". They fail to mention that the closure of the University and the intimidation of staff and students also "creates a climate of fear and uncertainty which is not conducive to academic activities". Nor do they mention that repeated negotiations with the protesters – who are not elected leaders – have failed to end the illegal behaviour and restore the "academic activities", the resumption of which they profess to want.

The "concerned philosophers" say that they "support the completion of the academic year in the context of a demilitarised negotiated settlement amongst UCT management and protesters". They must ask themselves the following questions: What if a negotiated settlement and thus the completion of the academic year is not possible? Would they then want full capitulation to whatever demands the unelected protesters make? Or are they prepared to countenance the ongoing closure of the University? Or do they think that there comes a time when illegality can no longer be tolerated?

The "concerned philosophers" say that as "a discipline centred around critical thinking and analysis, we feel that as philosophers we can't remain silent about events on campus" and they propose a "departmental mass meeting". However, it is absolutely clear that breaking the department silence will not satisfy them unless what is said concurs with the views they espouse.

Indeed, statements such as theirs, as well as the proposed mass meeting, further the intimidation that has pervaded campus. People espousing the views of the "concerned philosophers" are entirely comfortable expressing themselves. Those with opposing views are, with very few exceptions, too fearful to express their dissent. (What sort of university has ours become when the defenders of illegality seek to condemn those who want the law enforced?)

Those who are brave – or foolhardy – enough to speak out, are cut down by the zealots who signal their own virtue by "naming and shaming" the dissenters. (In our context the preferred form of the "heresy" accusation is the charge of insufficient commitment to "transformation".) Such denunciations are a recurring and noxious feature of human history. It would be good if the "concerned philosophers" were also concerned not to succumb to so familiar a vice.

Chapter 9

DR PANGLOSS AND THE BEST OF ALL ACTUAL AFRICAN UNIVERSITIES

(Originally published: 9 January 2017) [1]

It is bad enough that UCT, like other South African universities, was subjected to massive disruption in 2016 (and 2015). It is worse still that the costs of this are being glossed over by UCT's leadership. Both UCT's Vice-Chancellor, Dr Max Price, and UCT Council member Dianna Yach have suggested that Dr Price's strategy of "negotiating" has been vindicated.

Dr Price has claimed[2] that we "successfully concluded the year" and that he and his team "chose the right strategy which optimally served the interests of probably 90% of students and staff". Ms Yach said[3] that the agreement reached after weeks of discussions was intended in part "to create a quiet space ... to allow for the completion of final exams for students in November 2016 (in which it succeeded)".

The 2016 academic year may have been concluded (for most students so far), but it was concluded in a heavily truncated form in most of the University. One third of the semester was lost and students were, with limited exceptions, examined on only those two-thirds of course material covered before the disruptions and closure.

The costs so far are not merely the loss of a third of a semester. Morale in the institution has taken a massive hit. Staff members have begun to leave. It may be only a trickle so far, but many more are looking for alternative positions. Many of those who remain are withdrawing and no longer willing to contribute to the institution the way they did before. It is hard to know how many prospective students will seek their education at other institutions. The number of students visiting UCT on a Semester Study Abroad has begun to decline, and with it, much needed revenue has been lost. The University has also incurred massive financial loss on account of the costs of private security, damage to property, and various interventions to compensate for the disruptions.

You would not believe this if you listened to Dr Price. He says[4] that 2016 has been "one of our best years ever". In support of this he says that UCT "produced more research papers than ever before in our history", that research contracts "crossed the R1-billion mark and exceeded 2014/5's level by 30%", that the "impact of our research reached an all-time high", "pass rates of our first-year courses went up for all students", that "we have a vibrant debate going on in all faculties on curriculum change and what coloniality means", and that "we have retained our position as the best university in Africa and positioned in the top 1% globally". He says that these "are the criteria by which the performance of UCT management should be measured".

Here Dr Price has become positively Panglossian. First, as

any academic knows, there is typically a lag between when research is done and when it is published. What this means is that the publication count in 2016 is a reflection of work completed in prior years. It is an open question whether research productivity has been maintained in 2016 or whether the distractions of this *annus horribilis* have taken their toll.

Similar points can be made, *mutatis mutandis*, about research contracts and about the impact of research. Research contracts are the products of sustained effort rather than yield from a single year. Breaking records in 2016 is thus not an indication whether morale and research have taken a battering by the disruptions. Research *impact* is what happens *after* research has been done. Impacts in 2016 are typically the consequences of work done in the past.

It is hard to know how Dr Price can claim that "pass rates of our first-year courses went up for all students" when, by his own account, "about 25%" of students have not yet written their final examinations for 2016 because they have chosen to defer them to early 2017. Moreover, there is some reason to think that students deferring examinations under current circumstances perform less well on average than those who do not. Even if the pass rate were to increase in 2016 over past years, we do not know to what extent this is the result of (a) students being examined on only two-thirds of a regular semester's work, and (b) the widespread abandonment of Duly Performed requirements in the second semester of 2016, which is a reduced standard.

Nor is there a "vibrant debate going on in all faculties on curriculum change and what coloniality means". Indeed, anybody who dares to question what it means is ostracized. Not knowing what it means is taken as evidence that one is part of the problem. Instead, what we have are vocal ideologues pressing their "decolonizing" agenda, while others either cower or signal their "virtue" by mouthing the orthodoxy in some form or another.

Finally, while UCT may still be the best university in Africa it has dropped in world rankings, something UCT's Communication and Marketing Department has attempted to explain with a brave face.[5] University rankings should be treated with a great deal of skepticism, but if one *is* going to boast about one's rankings as a mark of one's success, one should not pretend that there has been no decline when there has in fact been a drop.

Perhaps the greatest cost to Dr Price's strategy of negotiated capitulation is that it will breed more disruptions, which will only fuel UCT's descent. Dr Price recognizes[6] that negotiations "may fail – in which case the securitized route will follow", but this, he says, should be "the last resort, not the first".

However, one wonders just what Dr Price counts as "failure". How many weeks of teaching must be lost and how many times must the campus be disrupted before he recognizes that negotiations have failed? Under the guise of "last resort" one can endlessly forestall the rule of law, because one can always try negotiations one more time. Negotiations went on for approximately six or seven weeks in late 2016. They failed to ensure that the final third of the semester be taught. (Examinations did take place without disruption but they may well have been able to take place if the law had been upheld from the start, and thus we do not know if the costs of the negotiations actually generated a benefit that would not otherwise have been enjoyed.)

If Dr Price and his Panglossian colleagues have many more of their Pyrrhic victories, there will not be much left of UCT.

POSTSCRIPT

Unsurprisingly, there *were* further protests and disruptions in 2017.[7]

Chapter 10

ACADEMIC CLIMATE CHANGE

(Originally published: 30 March 2017)[1]

Universities are all too frequently not the realms of critical thinking that they should be. Orthodoxies are prevalent and alternative views are often crowded out. University campuses can be unpleasant places for those who challenge the moral and political dogmas of the academy. This is true even in the freest societies.

It is in full cognizance of this disturbing baseline that I say, without exaggeration, that the climate at the University of Cape Town (UCT) has, in the past two years, become deeply toxic. Obviously, it could be worse – and it may yet become so. Nonetheless, the current situation is deeply disturbing in its own right. Unless the problem is addressed urgently, it does not augur well for the future of UCT. Because UCT is a leading university in South Africa, the implications for the country as a whole are also of concern.

The turning point was the dumping of human waste on the Cecil John Rhodes statue in March 2015. That act and the protests and disruptions that it inaugurated set a new poisonous tone. (Christopher Marlowe might say that it was "the waste that launched a thousand shits", for buckets more of excrement, both literal and figurative, have since been strewn. In one of the literal instances, an 8-month pregnant woman had to be virtually carried over the sewage to escape the foul odour, the stench causing her to vomit on the way.)

The campus toxicity is not attributable solely to the protests and disruptions. However, these and the University leadership's indulgent response to them have emboldened pre-existing and independent elements of campus intolerance.

The broad pathology affecting (and infecting) the campus is that of self-proclaimed "progressives" who are anything but that. Instead, they are deeply intolerant, closed-minded and unprincipled ideologues for whom particular conclusions and agendas come first, and then "arguments" and "evidence" are invoked selectively to support their preconceptions.

For example, the expression of views they do not like is characterized as "violence", while actual violence and real threats of it are perpetrated, championed or, at the very least, vigorously defended. Those who defend free speech and criticize real violence are denounced either as racists or as enemies of transformation, while those who seek to silence, not least through violence, are lauded as transformational progressives.

It is because UCT, despite ample opportunity, has not addressed, let alone corrected this pathology, that details of the problem must be made more widely known. UCT is a national resource and members of the public should know what is happening to it.

The culture of intimidation, intolerance, and bullying is so pervasive that a full accounting cannot be provided here. However, rather than merely speaking in generalities, I shall refer to a significant number of specific instances in order to give a taste of how prevalent the problem is. For this reason, and because I shall also provide some analysis, this essay provides quite a long account of what is happening.

I shall usually not name names or otherwise identify people. (The exceptions are cases where the details are already in the public domain.) This is both to protect those victims who are vulnerable to ongoing vilification, as well as not to sink towards the level of the perpetrators, who routinely engage in defamation of their adversaries – sometimes orally, and sometimes on so-called "social" media. (*Anti*-social media is often the more apt description.)

Some of the unpleasantness is already well known. On spurious grounds, the University Executive disinvited Flemming Rose,[2] who had been invited by the (previous) Academic Freedom Committee to deliver the TB Davie Memorial Lecture. Various self-styled "progressives" defended the disinvitation, while others merely criticized the initial invitation. This sort of intolerance is part of a more general trend. When the chairperson of a faculty "transformation committee" said (in another context) that we must not allow unacceptable views to be expressed, we should be left in no doubt about what that ever-slippery term "transformation" entails.

Protestors, whose list of demands keeps expanding, have shut down the University on a few occasions, the most recent instance resulting in the loss of a third of a semester. They have engaged in arson, and have burned vehicles,[3] historic paintings[4] and the Vice-Chancellor's office[5].

Artworks that offend have been censored by being removed[6] from, or covered up in[7] their places of exhibition, including the University library.[8] An exhibition – about Rhodes

Must Fall no less – was shut down[9] because it offended an intolerant splinter group. During the 2017 Orientation Week, students at a Pro-Life stall were forced to pack and leave after protesters who had been verbally abusing them then began dismantling the stall.

Protesters have inflicted personal violence, including vicious attacks on security officers[10] and a punching[11] of the Vice-Chancellor. A final-year law student was racially abused[12] and had his cellphone knocked out his hand by a sjambok-wielding protester, who then claimed that he wished he had "actually not been a good law abiding citizen & [had] whipped the white apartheid settler colonial entitlement out of the bastard".[13]

Protesters have threatened violence against many others to whom I have spoken but who, like this victimized law student, are fearful of being publicly identified. People can be intimidated even in the absence of threats of violence. One student reported that during protests she did not enter via the main entrance of one campus, for fear of being stopped and interrogated by protesters who wanted to know why those students continuing with their studies were not joining the protests.

The University leadership has repeatedly capitulated in the face of this appalling behaviour,[14] thereby emboldening the perpetrators. It was thus unsurprising that the 2016 Annual General Meeting of Convocation was disrupted.[15] When one academic rose to speak and complained that the University Executive had not consulted staff during negotiations with the protesters, one protester shouted repeatedly "Shut up you bitch".

In some cases, the threats are not directed at specific or named individuals, but the severity of the threat is alarming. For example, in a Facebook post it was said that "the slaughtering of the gusha [sheep] is symbolic of what is going to happen to all counter-revolutionary forces and those who stand in the way of free quality decolonized education in 2017".

Although it is difficult to prove, there is some evidence that endless concessions and manipulations have resulted in pass marks for some students who before the interventions had failed.

Another contaminant of the environment is authoritarianism from some people in leadership positions. In one faculty there has been a suspension of normal committee meetings in favour of centralized, *ad hoc* decision-making by a small group, which includes some people who do not hold formal positions of authority within that faculty.

Two deans have been described as authoritarian or mercurial, or both. One dean summarily suspended an academic staff member, causing that person untold trauma. Due process had not been followed, the suspension was eventually reversed, and the accusation that had prompted the Dean to act precipitously was found to be groundless. There were no repercussions for the Dean who proceeded to act with impunity in a string of other cases. One academic eventually laid a carefully documented complaint against this Dean for unprofessional behaviour, but the complaint was simply ignored.

A deputy director of a university-wide non-academic unit, who, in fewer than three years, lost at least two grievance complaints and a disciplinary hearing for bad behaviour against staff, was promoted to a directorship!

The poisonous environment is fuelled by naked racial politics. Anything can be contorted to be a racial grievance, which, in the contemporary South African context, has all the chilling effect of liquid nitrogen. It is quite common for students to respond to their own failings by attributing the consequences – such as refusal of "duly performed" certificates, failure of a course, or disciplinary action – to racism. One student went so far as to write to a "White Course Convenor at UCT" as follows:

> "This thing of you giving me low marks ever time I submit to you is becoming problematic, I'm starting to think that its personal motivated. On top of being dispossessed as a black child, you of all people you are continuously dispossessing my marks, knowing well we were not attending lectures due to the shutdown ... how on earth do you expect a protesting student to write an assignment same as the student who was studying during the protest receiving provisions from your Offices especially white students and you expect the same outcome. It is people like yourself who perpetuate black academic exclusion in UCT because you have a personal vendetta against black people, you hate the fact that we exist in this space, continue to fail me I will rise again no amount of hatred will demobilize me. We will continue to fight racism in these racist departments with whites masquerading as sympathizers of black people." (sic)

In other words, a student participated in shutting down the University, thereby preventing all students from accessing the usual teaching activities. That student failed to take advantage of the department's learning support and was aggrieved that other students did take advantage of it, but then believed that his or her resultant low marks were a manifestation of racism rather than poor academic performance. Welcome to UCT's Wonderland!

Charges of racism are infinitely malleable. When the mannequins on which medical students practise cardio-pulmonary resuscitation are all "white", this is attributed to racism. When the images of genitalia with sexually transmitted infections are "black", that is attributed to racism. It makes no difference to those laying the charges that the vast majority of people in the country and an even greater share of patients in the public sector are "black" and it would thus have been surprising if the clinical images gathered in this context did not reflect that. Moreover, if the images of genitals with sexually transmitted infections had been "white" that too would likely have been deemed racist – perhaps "Euro-uro-centric" – because such images would have been of less help in the local context.

Similarly, to the extent that the African experience is not included in the curriculum, there are calls for decolonizing the curriculum, but when "nonblack" academics do teach about "black ... practices and experiences" they are sometimes accused of "fetishizing, appropriating, and exotifying" those practices and experiences.

In at least one department, certain areas of research are perceived to be off limits to "white" students. Such students are expected, when making class interventions, to preface their comments with an acknowledgement of their (purported) privilege. Failure to do so can elicit accusations of "overt displays of whiteness", which in that environment is akin to being accused of "being a colonizer or a racist". If the "disclaimer [about purported privilege] is not made genuinely enough", one will similarly be put in one's place.

The charge of racism is wielded with paranoid – or cynical – abandon. It functions just as terms such as "kulak", "communist", "witch", and "heretic" have functioned in other contexts, namely as a tool for settling scores, persecuting, and silencing. It wields such power if directed at a pale(r)-skinned person and especially if leveled *by* a darker-skinned person.

Anything the purported "racist" says in response is taken as confirming evidence of that person's blindness to his or her own racism. The irony is that those wielding gratuitous charges of racism are real racists, although the context makes the counter accusation inert, and may even bolster the perceived force of the initial charge.

That same context explains the following recent incidents, which are but a small sample:

- A student protester ascended a stage, stood next to a visiting African academic and invited him to request that all "white" people leave the venue.[16]
- A student leader stated publicly that "white people are hectic".[17]
- Some students have told "white" classmates that on account of their "whiteness" they may not comment on certain issues in class.
- A student squelched a classmate's candidature for class representative by accusing him of having a "white saviour complex".
- In one faculty seeking a new Dean there is such a strong presumption that no "white" candidate could be successful, that some people from this demographic are not even bothering to apply.
- A small group of medical students objected that a patient invited to address the class about his personal experiences of illness was "white". They alleged, falsely, that this patient would not have benefited from therapy if he had been "black". They also said that in future a "black" patient should be invited so that students could better identify with the patient, even though there are patients of different "races" who are invited to speak to students in other teaching events. (The invited patient has spoken regularly to third year medical students for the past six to eight years. Feedback had always been immensely positive – until this occasion in 2016. The patient felt the objecting students had been angry and hostile.)

This is not to say that darker skinned people are immune to vilification if they express an "unorthodox" view. One alumna was labeled a "porch negro" for daring to "suggest that the agreement reached with a small group of students though with university-wide consequences was illegitimate".[18]

One senior academic went on extended leave following comparable personal attacks for insufficient fealty to the protesters' agenda. Various members of the University's senior leadership have been called "colonial administrators" on those occasions when they do not completely capitulate to the revolutionary agenda.

Race-baiting is not the preserve of students. The Black Academic Caucus (BAC) has an overt racial agenda, as its name suggests. The BAC has put racial solidarity ahead of principle, not least by targeting those melanin-deprived individuals who insist on the rule of law. Functioning like a contemporary Broederbond,[19] it had no formal standing within the University until January 2017. Yet it had deployed its cadres to "serve within key structures of the university"[20] and said that it has played a leading role in "initiatives that emerged directly from the demands of RMF, FMF, and other student groupings".

In January 2017 the BAC entered into a memorandum of understanding (MOU) with UCT even though UCT has not yet formulated the principles and criteria that will govern any other groups seeking official recognition. The MOU uncritically accepts the BAC's narrative, noting that the BAC was founded "with the purpose of challenging the slow pace of transformation that continues to maintain hegemonies and reproduce colonial relations of power". As part of the memorandum of understanding the BAC seems to be seeking formal representation on "university structures such as Council and Senate, and other university committees". Given that BAC members are already serving in other capacities in university governance, this is a bid for double (or treble) counting.

A senior academic and member of the BAC referred to a junior colleague as "just another fucking white woman". (A complaint was not lodged because the person about whom this was said "felt, rightly or wrongly, that the complaint of a white academic regarding racist remarks would not be considered in the same serious light as a reverse scenario".)

Given these sorts of academics and their fellow travellers, it should not be surprising that many classes have become hostile environments for those students not in the grip of the current orthodoxy. The situation may be worst in the Faculty of Humanities, where vast swathes of academics endlessly repeat tropes about race, gender, transformation and decolonization.

In one department a lecturer announced that "blacks" and "whites" cannot be friends. He then set an exam question that read as follows:

> Write detailed notes on race and racism. In your answer take care to specify the reasons for the impossibility of friendship between blacks and whites.

In other words, this ideologue gave students no option to disagree with him. His conclusion was assumed and then students were expected to trot out whatever explanation he gave them for this patently vicious claim.

It should not be surprising that the same lecturer also complained that there were "too many white females" in a postgraduate course of his. He also told students in an undergraduate course that rationality and reason are Western constructs and that if anybody tells them that they are being irrational or unreasonable, they should simply reply that they do not want to think "white".

With this sort of self-crippling drivel being peddled by academics, it should come as no surprise that at least some of those demanding the "decolonization" of the curriculum think that science and such phenomena as gravity are "products of western modernity" which should be scrapped, and that science should then be started from scratch from an "African perspective".[21]

Any attempt to contradict this is deemed a hostile intervention that has no place in the "progressive space". This is a stark illustration of how the insistence that some position is "progressive" does not make it so.

Similarly, the talk of "safe spaces" is disingenuous. What is typically being called for is a space in which the intolerant can safely intimidate without challenge. In other words, they want safety for those with approved views. They pay absolutely no attention to the "safety" of the space for those with whom they disagree. In this way the University becomes safe for the intolerant, and hostile to others.

Intolerant students demand that "action must be taken against staff members" who are alleged to "diminish the dignity and well-being of students in any manner", while those students defamed particular staff members, blocked access to their offices, humiliated them, posted aggressive notes on their office doors, and posted personal and derogatory drawings of individual staff members online.

After castigating one of their professors, protesting students responded to her resultant breakdown by saying that they did not care about her tears. Yet these same students were demanding "the right to protest without victimization", which would be a perfectly reasonable demand if by "protest" they did not include illegal activity, and by "victimization" they did not include enforcement of the law. On their view, real victimization of staff members is acceptable, but a disciplinary response to students' patently illegal behaviour is not.

In an environment in which an obsessional, delusional, and weaponized narrative of racial and other grievance predominates, various forms of psychopathology – including paranoia and narcissism – become adaptive. While I do not think that all or even most of those seeking to "transform" the University are mentally ill, there is certainly no shortage of disturbed people who have found a niche.

Given all this, it should come as no surprise that morale has plummeted – at least among those staff members who are not among the causes of the problem. Those causing the problems may well be in their element. They are riding the crest of a destructive wave. There are no hard data on the levels of morale, not least because no "institutional climate" survey has been conducted since things turned excremental.

I encourage the University leadership to conduct such a survey. (Here I assume, charitably, that the University leadership cares enough to find out what most people actually think. The leadership ignored earlier calls for a referendum on opening campus against the protesters' wishes.)

However, there is plenty of other evidence that morale has plummeted. Some staff have already resigned or taken early retirement. Others are looking for positions elsewhere. Those remaining have withdrawn. For example, some heads of department have stood down rather than deal with impossible deans, colleagues or students. Others are not making themselves available for leadership positions within their departments and faculties, preferring to keep a low profile. It should come as no surprise that a disproportionate number of those willing to fill the gaps are those most likely to make matters worse.

A number of proctors in the University's Disciplinary Tribunal system have resigned as they feel that their time and energies are wasted if those convicted are then granted clemency. The likely effects of this should be obvious to all but the most doctrinaire.

Many members of staff – along with students – are cowering. They know that if they speak up against those poisoning the campus atmosphere, they will be branded either as racists or as sell-outs. Given just how personally damaging these attacks are – and what a global reach they have as a result of the internet – most people keep their heads below the ramparts. The "progressive" staff members feel entirely comfortable writing under their own names,[22] but more often than not those disagreeing with them feel that they must write or speak anonymously for fear of victimization and retaliation. Similarly, students feel fearful of speaking out if they can be identified.[23] (I write under my own name despite the risks and the unpleasant experience of having already been targeted many times. I do so because I want to invite students and staff to share their unpleasant experiences with me. I shall not use any information without permission and will always protect the identities of informants.)

It should certainly be acknowledged that some of the pathology I have described above is rampant in South Africa more generally. For example, the resort to accusations of racism or betrayal is standard fare. Instead of engaging the arguments and positions of political opponents far too many South Africans will drop the dirty "R-bomb" (or the "Uncle-Tom bomb"). It might thus be suggested that UCT is not anomalous, given the national norm.

I certainly recognize the broader context within which UCT finds itself, but it is nonetheless the case that the University leadership could have done much to preserve academic freedom, ensure the rule of law, prevent intimidation, and counter the race-baiters.

For one thing, it would have been good if Max Price had followed his own advice. When he first arrived at UCT he expressed ideas that also found their way into his inaugural address on 19 August 2008:[24]

> The universities parted ways with the church and the two have continued in parallel partly because, with the rise of scientific rationalism it was a space which encouraged new ideas, controversy, argument, challenges to orthodoxy. This is the primary purpose of a university, and its success depends on a culture within the institution which is tolerant of heretical views (I use that term deliberately), which is *not* tolerant of attacks

on people based on their background, what they believe in or who they are, but insists on the debate being about ideas and their evidence and their logic. It means that a university requires that people respect each other and give them the benefit of the doubt that all are equally committed to seeking truth. It means that one may not call someone a racist as a way of challenging their views since this closes down the space for constructive debate and the expression of different opinions.

Of course, Dr Price did then draw a moral equivalence and added that "one may not label someone an affirmative action appointee since it communicates diminished respect for that individual and assumes their individual intellectual contribution and contribution to the institution to be less worthy without evaluating the substance of their views."

I won't engage that here, save to say that: (1) public charges of "affirmative action appointee" are vanishingly rare, if they exist at all, whereas charges of racism are ubiquitous, probably because there are powerful social forces militating against making the "affirmative action appointee" accusation publicly; (2) one cannot actively engage in strong forms of affirmative action and then think that there will not be affirmative action appointees; but (3) Dr Price is quite right that an accusation of "affirmative action appointee" is an inappropriate substitute for engaging that person's views or actions.

This is exactly why it is so surprising that, on more than one occasion, an academic has been told by members of the University's senior leadership that he has to speak differently to a "black" person than to a "white" one. Although a greater level of deference – or indulgence – was being recommended on both occasions, the implicit injunction was to patronize, which is *not* to treat people as equals.

I am not suggesting that Dr Price and his executive should have silenced anybody. Nobody committed to freedom of expression thinks that censorship is the appropriate response (although defamation is not protected by freedom of expression). However, what the University leadership could have done is to express itself quite clearly with speech of its own. For example, it could have *unequivocally* condemned those who defamed their colleagues or teachers and those who hurled appalling epithets.

In a statement issued on 13 March 2017 the Executive did condemn one academic who had defamed a colleague of his. The statement stated that the University "will not tolerate such behaviour", yet by refusing to take disciplinary action against the offender despite his refusal to "retract his allegations and to correct the public record", the Executive has shown that it *will* in fact tolerate such behaviour. Moreover, there are many other instances of abusive language that have not elicited any reproach from the University's leadership.

Curiously UCT's Council felt it needed to distance itself from one of its members who had expressed disdain for the crude racial politics, authoritarianism and intolerance of the Fallist protesters, but there has been no comparable distancing from real instances of harassment and intimidation, online and elsewhere.

The University leadership could also have stood firm on freedom of expression. It should have allowed Flemming Rose to speak and defended his right to do so. It should not have countenanced nor continued to permit the censorship of works of art. It should have responded forthrightly to lawlessness, drawing a clear line, and demonstrating that this sort of behaviour will not be tolerated. Similarly, it should not be fawning in the face of absurd and extremely dangerous rhetoric. (If it ever leads to bloodshed, probably against racial minorities, the University leadership, like the country's leadership, will have even more to answer for.)

In appointments, and especially senior ones, it could have

paid more attention to standard academic and leadership requirements, such as intellectual capacity and achievement, administrative and leadership experience and ability, and the absence of those personality problems that poison work environments. There are consequences to appointing comrades and commissars instead.

It gives me no pleasure to expose details of the toxic climate that currently prevails at UCT. I do this not to damage the institution, but to offer a very clear caution that unless these problems are taken in hand, what we should all expect is, if not a "great leap backwards" then an unrelenting series of steps in that direction.

Chapter 11

THE ACADEMIC FREEDOM
FARCE CONTINUES

(Originally published: 10 October 2017)[1]

One thing one should not do in an academic freedom lecture is defend the violation of academic freedom. Yet that is exactly what Mahmood Mamdani did when he delivered the 2017 TB Davie academic freedom lecture at the University of Cape Town in South Africa.

Curiously, Professor Mamdani's lecture itself, "Decolonizing the Post-Colonial University",[2] had nothing to do with academic freedom. However, in an (oral) addendum to his lecture [at 1:37:27 in the recording], he responded to those of us who had previously written to him.[3] We had requested that he refuse to give the TB Davie lecture until Flemming Rose had been permitted to deliver the TB Davie lecture he had been invited to give in 2016 before the invitation had been rescinded by the University's Executive.[4]

Professor Mamdani explicitly congratulated the University's administration for having disinvited Mr Rose, whom he portrayed as an Islamophobe (and whom he repeatedly called "Rose Flemming").

Flemming Rose had been the culture editor of the *Jyllands-Posten* newspaper when, in September 2005, it published twelve drawings and cartoons of the prophet Mohammed. Those who have read Mr Rose's *The Tyranny of Silence*[5] and other of his writings, will know that these cartoons were published not to single out Muslims but instead to treat them exactly the same as other members of Danish society. In that book, Mr Rose carefully lays out the developments that precipitated the decision to publish the cartoons. The *Jyllands-Posten* was responding to ample evidence that expression about Islam and Muslims was curtailed in ways in which expression about other religions and groups was not. Moreover, Mr Rose has defended the anti-democratic speech of fundamentalist Muslims,[6] hardly the action of an Islamophobe.

Professor Mamdani either ignored or was ignorant of all this. (I am not sure which of those alternatives is worse.) The only purported evidence he offered for his assertion that Mr Rose is an Islamophobe is the claim that the *Jyllands-Posten* had once refused to publish cartoons of Jesus on the grounds that this would have been offensive. However, as Mr Rose noted in his book, the rejected cartoons in question were those of a freelancer, and the reason they were rejected was that they were of poor quality. In any event, they had been rejected by another editor – not Mr Rose. Moreover, the *Jyllands-Posten* had repeatedly published cartoons that made fun of Christians and Jews. It is thus simply false that the *Jyllands-Posten* had singled out Islam.

Professor Mamdani offered no further evidence that Mr

Rose is an Islamophobe. Instead, he endorsed, without argument, Günter Grass's comparison of the Mohammed cartoons to antisemitic cartoons in the Nazi tabloid *Der Stürmer*, and compared the Mohammed cartoons, again without argument, to incitement that fomented the Rwandan genocide. The Rwandan trials, he said, were "the latest to bring out the dark side, the underbelly of free speech".

These comparisons are, of course, patently absurd, as is the suggestion that advocates of freedom of expression must also permit incitement to genocide. Anybody can *say* – as those who seek to curtail freedom of expression so often do – that speech they do not like amounts to incitement. It is quite another matter to have evidence for such claims. Denmark is neither Nazi Germany nor the Rwanda of 1993-1994. Flemming Rose is neither Julius Streicher nor Hassan Ngeze, Kantano Habimana, Valérie Bemeriki or Noël Hitimana. The suggestion to the contrary is as vicious as it is disingenuous.

Professor Mamdani also cited with approval, the actions of Allen Lane, co-founder of Penguin publishing, in response to complaints about the French cartoonist Sine's *Massacre*. That book, published in English by Penguin in 1966, contained anti-clerical and blasphemous cartoons that offended many Christians. Allen Lane, along with four accomplices, entered Penguin's warehouse, removed all the remaining copies, transported them away in a trailer, and burned them. The moral of this story, Professor Mamdani claimed, was that Allen Lane "a lifelong devotee of free speech ... when it came to upholding peaceful coexistence in a society with a history of religious conflict ... did not hesitate to set fire to a trailer full of books".

This is argument by anecdote. Principled defenders of the *Jyllands-Posten* cartoons will also disapprove of Allen Lane's bonfire of the blasphemies. Simply citing that earlier outrage and imputing some "moral" to it tells us much more about Mahmood Mamdani than it does about Flemming Rose and whether the University Executive was correct in disinviting him.

Professor Mamdani provided one other anecdote – about the long-running United States radio and then television show, *Amos 'n' Andy*. The lesson of this example, according to Professor Mamdani, is that despite years of objection by the NAACP against the racist character of the show, it was only cancelled after the Watts Riots of 1965 "taught CBS a lesson in how to recognize bigotry". This anecdote sheds no light on whether the *Jyllands-Posten* cartoons were like *Amos 'n' Andy* in relevant ways. Professor Mamdani offered no argument to this end. He merely assumed it.

Professor Mamdani was correct about one thing. There is no right to give the TB Davie lecture, at least if we interpret him charitably to mean that there is no right to be *invited* to deliver it. Once one has been invited one does have a right not to be stopped from doing so. Delivering such a lecture is, instead, an honour. Professor Mamdani's unsupported claim was that Flemming Rose was not worthy of that honour. Professor Mamdani's pastiche of anecdote and "alternative facts" in defence of Mr Rose's disinvitation and in favour of censorship, show that it is Mahmood Mamdani and not Flemming Rose who was undeserving of the honour of delivering an academic freedom lecture.

Chapter 12
IMPUGNING WITH IMPUNITY

On 19 January 2016 a student at the University of Cape Town began a systematic programme of defamation against me on social media (Facebook and Twitter). It had an international reach, causing me considerable reputational damage both in South Africa and abroad. The negative effects of this are ongoing. The student also invaded the Philosophy Department office, harassed the staff, and refused to leave. I lodged a disciplinary complaint with the University Student Disciplinary Tribunal for these serious infractions, as I had for an earlier instance of dishonesty.

The disciplinary process dragged on for three years, the delays caused partly by the student's manipulations and partly by the University's failures. During this time, I could not comment much in the public realm because the matter was *sub judice*, which meant that the defamatory remarks could spread unchecked. I repeatedly pushed for a completion of the disciplinary process, warning that "justice delayed is justice denied". In what has become a pattern at UCT, all charges against the student were eventually dropped, adding to the culture of impunity for the worst elements of the university, and betraying those who play by the rules.

INTRODUCING BUSISIWE MKHUMBUZI

In 2015, Busisiwe ("Busi") Mkhumbuzi registered for my introductory Ethics course. It was her second attempt at the course. (I did not teach it the first time she took it as I had been on sabbatical that year.) She, along with all other students in the class, signed a declaration indicating that she was aware of the "Duly Performed" (DP) requirements, without which students are not permitted to sit the examination ("Duly Performed Refused", or "DPR"). The DP requirements included regular lecture and tutorial attendance. In her declaration, Ms Mkhumbuzi affirmed, inter alia, that she was aware of the DP requirements, and "that (significant or repeated) absences from class must be explained timeously – *not* weeks later or at the end of the semester". She also affirmed this statement: "In the event that I do not meet the DP requirements, I undertake not to appeal my DPR status. (This does not preclude appealing a DPR that is honestly thought to be a mistake.)"

On 28 August, I entered the large lecture theatre in which the class takes place and gave the register to students at the back entrances, asking them to sign and begin circulating the register once the class began. Ms Mkhumbuzi was one of the students to whom I gave a register that morning. Just before the class began, I looked up and noticed that she was no longer present. Considering the possibility that she might have moved her seat within the venue, I called out her name to ask whether she was present. There was no answer. She had signed the register and then left before the class began.

She was subsequently asked, at my request, to come see me regarding her fraudulent signing of the register. In our meeting on 7 September, she admitted to signing the register and then leaving (to participate in an extra-curricular activity). She claimed that she did this because she was concerned that her lecture absences – five by this point in the semester – would compromise her DP. I explained that while full attendance was required, students would not be refused DP for reasonable absences, especially if they excused themselves in good time. The next day I laid a disciplinary complaint against her for fraudulently representing her presence at the lecture.

Ms Mkhumbuzi went on to miss a further eight lectures. She provided medical certificates that covered three of those missed lectures and was duly excused from them. However, because she had missed in excess of a third of lectures, she was refused DP.

She appealed the decision at the department level, but because we had made no error and she had not met the requirements, the DPR decision was not reversed. On 12 November, Ms Mkhumbuzi appealed the decision to the Dean. The matter was considered by the Dean's nominee, a deputy dean, and my decision was upheld. The following month, Ms Mkhumbuzi appealed the decision to the Vice-Chancellor. This was considered by the Vice-Chancellor's nominee, Deputy Vice-Chancellor Francis Petersen. He upheld the earlier decisions to refuse DP.

Although there are no appeals on an appeal to the Vice-Chancellor, Ms Mkhumbuzi nonetheless appealed to the Vice-Chancellor a second time. Professor Petersen considered the case and again upheld the earlier decisions. He conveyed this decision to her via SMS and email on 11 January 2016 after he had been unable to reach her telephonically.

The next day, in contravention of the university rule barring DPR students from writing the examination, Busi

Mkhumbuzi attended and wrote the examination. Because she was DPR, her script was set aside and not marked (graded). On 18 January, Professor Petersen provided her with a detailed explanation of his decision to uphold the earlier DPR decisions.

LET THE DEFAMATION BEGIN

On 19 January 2016, Ms Mkhumbuzi staged a sit-in at UCT's administrative building, blasting music. She began vilifying me on Facebook and Twitter. One Facebook post, entitled "Why am I staging a sit-in at Bremner Building?" included numerous falsehoods. For example, she claimed that she had been "signed off for 9 [lectures] by a medical practitioner", when in fact the medical certificates covered only three lectures. Instead of the 3.5 unexcused absences she claimed to have, she had eleven unexcused absences. She claimed that she had "met the course requirements for an exceptional case in terms of health", whereas this was not the case. She also misrepresented her coursework result by inflating it one grade (from a Lower Second to an Upper Second).

This all fed into her allegation, made at length, that she had been refused DP on account of her "race". She made out that she was, like other black students, the victim of racism from "white, male lecturers" in having been refused DP. Such allegations, the tired refuge of scoundrels, conveniently ignored the "white" students who had been refused DP and the fact that the decision to refuse her DP had been upheld by higher authorities within the university irrespective of their "race". They were not accused of racism, even though they found my decision entirely correct.

Professor Petersen contacted me on 20 January, requesting an urgent meeting. At that meeting he asked me to meet with him, the Registrar and Ms Mkhumbuzi. I agreed to meet. This was conveyed to Ms Mkhumbuzi, who responded that she would attend the meeting and that students and the media would be gathered outside "to see how the issue is resolved". Upon seeing that, I wrote to Professor Petersen, saying that this was an act of bad faith on Ms Mkhumbuzi's part and that I was not prepared to meet under these circumstances. Busi Mkhumbuzi then tweeted, falsely, that the "meeting was cancelled because Professor Benatar left".

Various attempts were then made to set up another meeting. I laid down some conditions for such a meeting. These included the absence of media or other students. Busi Mkhumbuzi falsely reported this on Twitter: "Professor Benatar refuses to speak to me because I've told students about my DP story", adding the hashtag #UCTisAntiBlack.

A meeting, subject to my conditions, was tentatively scheduled for 14h00 on 21 January. In an email of 10h56, Glynis Jethro, Francis Petersen's Personal Assistant, wrote to me saying: "Due to unavailability of some of the participants for this meeting, it will no longer take place at the suggested time of 14h00."

At approximately 13h15, Busi Mkhumbuzi arrived at the Philosophy Department reception asking about the meeting. She was advised by department administrators that the meeting had been cancelled. The following day, 22 January, she falsely tweeted: "Benatar lied yesterday and said the meeting was cancelled".

The meeting took place at 12h00 on 22 January. Ms Mkhumbuzi delivered a tirade and then stormed out of the room. As she was leaving, I noted that she had defamed me on social media. Her response was that I should sue her.

On 24 January, Ms Mkhumbuzi posted an essay on Facebook. It was headed "When Professor Benatar said that there is no hope for black students". I never said any such thing. In her Facebook post she misrepresented my views about affirmative action and "decolonization", alleging that I am a racist and concluded that she was refused DP because of this. Her words include: "Clearly the reason why Benatar has continued to refuse me DP is linked with his racial stereotypes as a grounding principle" and "The message is loud and clear, Professor Benatar is racist." No reference was made to the fact that the DPR decision was upheld by the Dean's nominee and twice by the Vice-Chancellor's nominee. Moreover, Ms Mkhumbuzi did not accuse *them* of racism.

Ms Mkhumbuzi's defamatory remarks resulted in an outpouring of condemnation of me. On 26 January, two of my colleagues in the Philosophy Department, Dr Elisa Galgut and Dr Greg Fried, made a public statement via the South African philosophical electronic mailing list, urging South Africa's philosophers not to rush to judgement when they are ignorant of all the relevant details.

A few days later, on 31 January, I made a statement correcting some of the falsehoods Busi Mkhumbuzi had expressed, noting that my statement had to be constrained by both civility and my duties not to disclose certain facts about her. As the charge of register fraud was still pending, I was unable to mention that at all.

On 4 February my statement was posted on the website of the course for which Ms Mkhumbuzi had been refused DP, because students in that class had been exposed to her defamatory remarks. About thirty minutes later, Busi Mkhumbuzi stormed into the Philosophy Department administrative office demanding to see me. I was not in at the time. She sat outside my locked door (which leads off from the administrative office), refusing to speak other than to demand that she speak to me. She began typing on her computer. Later she screamed in the face of a department administrator, spittle flying. Her volatile behaviour instilled fear and anxiety in the administrative staff, who remained traumatized for weeks afterwards. Ms Mkhumubzi refused to leave the office even when it came time for the administrators to leave at the end of the day. Campus Protection Services had to be called. As they were unwilling to forcibly remove her, Deputy Vice-Chancellor Anwar Mall and the Director of Student Wellness were called to persuade her to leave, which she eventually did.

Soon before or after arriving in the Philosophy Department administrative office, Busi Mkhumbuzi (falsely) tweeted that "Benatar has taken all my personal information about my mental health and published it for all students to read". This damaging falsehood gained traction and generated further hostility towards me. My statement made no reference at all to her mental health, although she herself had repeatedly referred to her purported mental health issues in social media prior to my statement. I referred to the medical certificates only to the extent of correcting her claims about the number of lectures these covered. I made no reference to any diagnosis. Nor would I have even mentioned the medical certificates at all if she had not made false claims about them in public.

On 8 February, a day on which Ms Mkhumbuzi made additional defamatory remarks about me on Twitter, I laid further disciplinary complaints against her. These pertained to her ongoing defamation, and her invasion of the Philosophy Department administrative office, and her harassment of the staff there.

Various people, ignorant of the details, fell for or uncritically reported Ms Mkhumbuzi's misrepresentations that I was seeking disciplinary action against her (merely) for calling me "racist". The label "racist" is, in the current climate, an immensely damaging one, with very material effects. However, even if there is some disagreement about whether falsely levelling it amounts to defamation or is instead merely the expression of an opinion, it is certainly defamatory to justify such an accusation with a collage of demonstrable falsehoods. This, even according to most liberal defenders of freedom of expression, falls beyond the scope of permissible expression. Freedom of expression does not protect demonstrably false defamatory claims about somebody. Nor were my disciplinary complaints restricted to her defamatory words. They included her dishonest and harassing behaviour, facts conveniently ignored by Ms Mkhumbuzi and those who swallowed her falsehoods.

These falsehoods were spread via social media. They also made their way into the local press[1] and were picked up by a prominent United States-based Philosophy blog, under the misleading headline "Student faces tribunal for calling Philosophy professor 'racist'".[2] In the comments section on that blog, many people opined about me in complete ignorance of the facts. Ms Mkhumbuzi's programme of defamation caused considerable reputational damage, with very material consequences.

Ms Mkhumbuzi made a *third* appeal to the Vice-Chancellor (even though the official procedures make allowance for only one such appeal). Given the brouhaha Ms Mkhumbuzi had caused, the then Vice Chancellor, Dr Max Price, agreed to a third review. Dr Price, who repeatedly capitulated to bad – even criminal – behaviour,[3] decided to overturn the earlier DPR decisions. In communicating his decision, he noted that all the previous decisions had been correct but that on the basis of purportedly new information, he was granting Busi Mkhumbuzi her DP. (His reasoning was actually a rationalization. The purportedly new information did not justify a reversal.) Nevertheless, he rejected "emphatically any suggestion that the original decision by Prof Benatar, or the subsequent appeal decisions, were in any way racist, as alleged by Ms Mkhumbuzi". In a covering email to Busi Mkhumbuzi (on 16 February 2016), Dr Price encouraged Busi Mkhumbuzi to apologise to me for her allegation that my refusal of her DP was racist.

Dr Price may have been naïve enough to think that this advice would be heeded, but I was not. On 10 March, Ms Mkhumbuzi announced on Facebook that Dr Price awarded her DP. She made no reference to his finding that the earlier decisions had all been correct. Nor did she apologize. Instead, she stated that "I refuse to retract the statements I have made about Prof Benatar", and then proceeded to renew the defamatory comments. In the same post she sought to mobilize students against me. She also wrote to a list of people, both within and outside of the University of Cape Town, renewing and intensifying her defamatory activity.

On 12 March, the Humanities Students' Council[4] wrote to the Dean of Humanities and others, indicating their support for Busi Mkhumbuzi and their intention to rally support for her. They did this without contacting me to hear the other side.

JUSTICE DELAYED

I lodged a request with the UCT Student Disciplinary Tribunal that Ms Mkhumbuzi be instructed to cease and desist from making any further defamatory remarks about me, and that she make no contact with those members of the Philosophy Department who want no contact with her. No such order was made.

On the same day, Miranda Rasehala,[5] an attorney acting for Busi Mkhumbuzi, wrote to me proposing "mediation" in order to avoid the disciplinary tribunal. I replied to Ms Rasehala on 21 March, indicating that I did not wish to meet with Busi Mkhumbuzi. I offered to drop some of the complaints (but not the one for register fraud) in exchange for (a) "a complete public retraction of every negative claim she has made" about me, (b) "a full and unequivocal apology" both for her defamation of me and for her harassment of staff in the Philosophy Department, and (c) an agreement to desist from any further comment about this matter and from any further harassment. A week later, Ms Rasehala conveyed Ms Mkhumbuzi's rejection of that offer.

On 5 April, Ms Mkhumbuzi announced on Facebook that she was selected to represent South Africa in the 2016 South-Africa Washington International Programme (SAWIP). In this post she again discussed her allegations against me and suggested that her selection for SAWIP constituted a kind of vindication. It is unclear how she was accepted into this programme, given her poor marks and the fact that there was a disciplinary case pending against her.

Eight days later, Ms Mkhumbuzi wrote to me requesting that I drop the charges against her. In this email she threatened that if the matter went to the tribunal, it would be bad for me, saying that I would "risk becoming the target, and the perceived face of racism in institutions of higher learning". She claimed that students and members of the "Alumni Advisory Board" were willing to testify in her favour and that the American Philosophical Association had offered her support. (I do not know whether that claim is true, but I do know that the American Philosophical Association never contacted me to ask what I had to say about this matter.) On 18 April, she posted further defamatory remarks on Facebook and Twitter.

After various attempts to fix a hearing date, it was set for 2 August 2016. On the day before the hearing, 1 August, Busi Mkhumbuzi advised the University Student Disciplinary Tribunal that she was taking a leave of absence from University and would be unavailable to attend the hearing. A few days later, she tweeted more defamatory remarks. Then, on 19 October, I was advised that she had (voluntarily) de-registered as a student. (This was a further step beyond the leave of absence.) However, the University Student Disciplinary Tribunal retained jurisdiction over actions while she was a student. This did not stop her making more disparaging comments about me in a Facebook post on 26 October 2016.

A hearing was set for 31 October 2016. Ms Mkhumbuzi was advised of this via emails to both her UCT and personal addresses. She did not respond. On 27 October she was informed that if she did not "respond or attend the hearing without any reasonable grounds, the hearing would proceed and judgement would be taken in her absence". She did not respond, and the hearing proceeded in her absence. She was found guilty on all counts. On the charge of falsifying the register, she was sentenced to R750 or 65 hours of community service. On the other charges, she was sentenced to rustication for twelve months, required to "post a full retraction of her claims about the integrity and character of Professor Benatar and an apology on her social media accounts" and write a personal letter of apology to me. The Tribunal also ruled that "the Registrar's office must issue a statement to be published on its home page that states the claims made against Professor Benatar by Ms Mkhumbuzi were without foundation and she has been sanctioned appropriately and required to apologise".

Ms Mkhumbuzi lodged an appeal against the judgement of the University Student Disciplinary Tribunal. In doing so, she wrote from one of the same addresses to which the summons to appear before the Tribunal had been sent. The Appeal Tribunal was scheduled for 23 February 2017. A few days before that date, Ms Mkhumbuzi issued a post inviting those who thought that I was racist to testify on her behalf at the appeal hearing. She repeated her accusations that I am racist in my "outlook and conduct".

At the Appeal Tribunal, Ms Mkhumbuzi was represented by a lawyer, Ashraf Mahomed. In the course of the hearing, the President of the Appeal Tribunal proposed that Ms Mkhumbuzi issue an apology in exchange for dropping the findings of guilt. I rejected this proposal because I feared that Busi Mkhumbuzi would later retract the apology and would have paid no cost for serious wrongdoing.

While the Appeal Tribunal was considering the matter, Ashraf Mahomed wrote to Vice-Chancellor Max Price asking that all charges against his client be dropped. Dr Price responded, saying that he did not believe it would be appropriate for him to intervene and that the appeal process should be completed.

The Appeal Tribunal issued its ruling on 13 August 2017. It noted that Busi Mkhumbuzi had offered no explanation for a number of matters, including why she had not responded to the notifications of the hearing on 31 October 2016. Nevertheless, it gave her the benefit of the doubt and ruled that the case must be heard *de novo*. Within days I proposed dates for the hearing for later that month and for September. Nothing came of that. Each month that followed, from September 2017 to February 2018, I wrote to propose dates for the following month, but no date was set. In the midst of that period, the Black Academic Caucus (BAC) repeated some of Ms Mkhumbuzi's defamatory remarks in a public post. It should go without saying that they did not seek my comment before they sided with her. Apparently, the only "facts" that matter to the BAC are the racial identities of parties to a conflict.

In February 2018, Registrar Royston Pillay communicated telephonically with me. He advised me that Mr Mohamed had proposed that UCT drop all charges in exchange for a full retraction and apology. I responded in writing, rejecting that proposal. I noted that I had "no guarantee that Ms Mkhumbuzi will not retract her retraction and apology once the charges have been dropped and she has completed her degree. She will then bear no consequences of her very harmful behaviour". I implored the Registrar to ensure that the hearing be held soon. I said that "the longer the matter is left unresolved, the more scope there is for justice never to be done".

In early March, Professor Danwood Chirwa, then Chief Proctor of the University Student Disciplinary Tribunal, met with me to convey a new proposal from Ashraf Mahomed on behalf of Busi Mkhumbuzi. The proposal was a plea bargain: Busi Mkhumbuzi would plead guilty to charges and offer a complete retraction and apology in exchange for a lesser sentence. I agreed to this on certain conditions, including that the apology be "proper and full".

When I asked Professor Chirwa, on 26 March, whether there had been any developments, he said that there had been none. I wrote to Registrar Pillay three more times over the following two months. He ignored the first two emails, but said, in response to the third, that a plea bargain was close to final. A month later, 28 June, I had still not heard anything and wrote to him again. This time I imposed a deadline of 29 July, saying that if the matter were not settled by then, my support for the plea bargain should be considered withdrawn.

On 17 July 2018, Busi Mkhumbuzi was the Master of Ceremonies for the Nelson Mandela Memorial Lecture delivered by former President Barack Obama. She clearly basked in the glory of national and even international attention and adulation. On her Twitter account, she placed a banner photograph of her and President Obama and tweeted: "15000 people attended & millions watched from their TV's & laptops." She also posted a glowing message from her "very first mentor, Eve Ensler".

In a radio interview subsequent to the lecture, the interviewer sang Ms Mkhumbuzi's praises and then mentioned the latter's difficulties with a professor discriminating against her at the University of Cape Town and how "relentless" she was in pursuing justice. Busi Mkhumbuzi did nothing to contradict this. Indeed, she advanced the narrative of "institutionalised racism" and falsely claimed that she had been suspended from UCT. In a tweet a few days later, she again claimed that she had been suspended by UCT, adding that she has "always told my story with authenticity", and that "backing me means backing black youth who are at the brunt of oppression". In another tweet she said that "many people have painted a dark picture of the student activist as being belligerent or a 'reverse racist' – as if the term exists. In reality, we are intelligent. We are active contributors to society. And we have been pushed out – I was fortunate to rebuild. Others weren't."

It was thus not surprising when, a few days later, Royston Pillay forwarded to me Ms Mkhumbuzi's proposed "apology" and "retraction". I found her letter to be grossly inadequate. For example, although she offered an "unconditional retraction" of social media posts, her proposed letter included one of her lies, namely that I "refused to acknowledge the medical certificate" she had provided. The letter made no mention of her fraudulent signing of the register or her invasion of the Philosophy department administrative office and the harassment of staff there.

I thus drafted a proper apology for her, which I conveyed to her via Mr Pillay. Given my past experience of delays, I stipulated that my support for the plea bargain would expire a week later. When that deadline arrived, I had received no reply, and thus I wrote to Mr Pillay for an update. He then advised me that my proposed letter was unacceptable to Ms Mkhumbuzi and that the disciplinary tribunal would proceed. If only it had!

JUSTICE DENIED

Each month, for the next four months, I proposed possible dates for the hearing. Nothing came of any of these suggestions. In late November 2018, Ashraf Mohamed wrote to the then new Vice-Chancellor, Professor Mamokgethi Phakeng, asking her to drop all the charges against his client. In mid-December, the Chief Proctor, Professor Danwood Chirwa recommended that Professor Phakeng oblige this request. He believed that the University would be liable to legal action by Ms Mkhumbuzi, on account of how long the disciplinary process had taken. I found this astounding, given that Ms Mkhumbuzi bore much of the responsibility for the delays. I asked whether the University was concerned that I might take legal action against them, but they were much more concerned about Ms Mkhumbuzi doing so.

I objected strenuously to Professor Chirwa's recommendation, and I sent the Vice-Chancellor ample documentation about the case. She then asked to meet with me, which we did on 11 January 2019. At this meeting she said that she had the interests of the University at heart and was concerned about its being sued. I had the sense that she wanted to communicate a decision to drop the charges. I told her that I too was concerned about the University but that we needed to take the long view of what was in the University's best interests. I was not convinced that Ms Mkhumbuzi would in fact sue UCT, but that if she did, UCT should finally take a stand and do what is right because otherwise it would damage itself in important ways in the longer run.

Among the numerous points I made were:

1. UCT has indulged appalling behaviour for far too long and it finally needed to show that students could not act with impunity.
2. UCT had to begin standing by staff who are maltreated for doing their jobs with integrity. I mentioned, multiple times, that staff morale had plummeted.
3. Students' long-term interests were not served if they were allowed to get away with bad behaviour.
4. I outlined some details of this case, including Ms Mkhumbuzi's repeated offences. (It was clear that Professor Phakeng was not familiar with important factual matters.)

By the end of the meeting, Professor Phakeng was in agreement that dropping the charges would not be acceptable, and that a plea bargain was a preferably route. However, she wrote to me on 31 January, advising me that she would be dropping all the charges in exchange for an apology (to her satisfaction rather than to mine). I responded, expressing dismay that she had reneged on our agreement that dropping the charges would be inappropriate. I asked her to provide me with the final apology, and I requested that the University issue a statement condemning Busi Mkhumbuzi's behaviour.

Ms Mkhumbuzi's apology was made to the "university community" and to Professor Phakeng rather than to me. Ms Mkhumbuzi provided an "unconditional retraction of the social media posts" that she "put in the public domain in 2016" and apologised for the "subsequent harassment" of "Department of Philosophy staff members" and for "contravening against the class attendance register requirements". Perhaps the latter claim was intended to cover the fraudulent signing of the register, but it certainly was not stated explicitly. There was no mention of defamatory statements made after 2016. Moreover, her letter of apology repeated one of her oft-repeated false claims – namely that I had "refused to acknowledge" her medical certificate.

This was all evidently acceptable to Professor Phakeng, who also twice ignored my requests for the University to make a statement clearing my name and condemning Ms Mkumbuzi's behaviour. After a further communication in which I said that I would assume that no such statement was forthcoming, Professor Phakeng confirmed that she was satisfied with Ms Mkhumbuzi's apology and saw "no further point in making a public statement".

DEMORALIZATION

I do *not* expect my university to stand by me, *come what may*. I *do* expect it to stand by me when I am in the right and a student behaves in the abysmal ways in which Ms Mkhumbuzi behaved. In failing to hold Ms Mkhumbuzi to proper account, the university became complicit in her maltreatment of me. It also rewarded her for her wrongs. However, the ramifications extend well beyond me and her. Through this saga, UCT has taught a number of lessons:

First, if you are teacher at UCT, then your decisions should *not* be made "without fear or favour". Instead, you should often be afraid – very afraid – if an unreasonable student (who belongs to a socially recognized "victim" demographic) wants special treatment (and especially if *you* are not a member of as protected a demographic). You should buckle, no matter how unfair that may be, and how bad a lesson that teaches. If you do not yield, you can fully expect to pay a significant price. You should also favour some students – at least if the favouring is of those who belong to a recognized "victim" demographic. It does not matter if they are actually perpetrators rather than victims. You should still favour them.

Second, if you are a student and you can avoid responsibility for your own actions by crying "racism" (or "sexism" or "ableism"), that is exactly what you should do. Feel free to cheat, lie, defame, and harass. Feel free to do that even in an *Ethics* class. Even if the lecturer does not tolerate this behaviour, the university will. Perhaps it will ask you to offer an incomplete and begrudging apology, but if you can delay justice long enough you can evade answering to the disciplinary tribunal. If you bleat about your purported victimization loud enough, you can advance your own career and reputation.

These two kinds of de*moral*ization are accompanied by demoralization of the more conventional kind – de-morale-ization. Although there are some demoralized students, staff are disproportionately affected. This is especially significant because staff tend to be, at least if the work environment does not drive them out, a much more enduring sector of the University than the students. Many students pass through in three or four years. Some are at university longer, but academic staff can remain for decades. Since I took up my post at UCT after returning to South African in 1997, I have seen four Vice-Chancellors and even more deans. They come and go. Those of us doing the core work of the university often stay for their entire careers.

When a university treats its staff as UCT has treated not only me but many others, then those staff who do not resign begin to care less. Why risk upholding any academic or moral standards if you will be made to suffer for it? Already a number of my colleagues have dropped DP requirements. The potential personal costs are too steep. That has inevitable implications for the quality of a UCT degree. Many staff also withdraw in all the ways that academia enables. I have spoken to dozens of people around the campus who are limiting themselves to their core duties (including their research), and are biding their time until retirement.

In my own case, I no longer teach the large introductory Ethics course that I taught for around twenty years. I used to do so in order to excite incoming students about Philosophy, many of whom went on to major in the discipline. I am no longer willing to teach a large introductory course, in which the chances of encountering a student such as Busi Mkhumbuzi are too high. It would be different if I could count on the University, but I cannot. Instead, I am teaching only more senior undergraduates (generally in smaller classes) and postgraduate students.

The University does not even know what it is losing because there is no visible contrast with the counterfactual scenario in which morale were high and the University were benefitting from more engaged staff – in classrooms, in committees, and in extra-curricular university activities.

On the surface, it appears as though there is a normally functioning university. The deep look reveals widespread demoralization and all the institutional costs attendant upon that.[6]

Chapter 13
GENOCIDAL TWEETS

(Co-authored with Anton Fagan.
Originally published: 13 November 2018)[1]

On the morning of Tuesday 6 November 2018, University of Cape Town student Masixole Mlandu tweeted the first few pages of his Political Studies Honours research project. The acknowledgements page ended with the words "ONE SETTLER, ONE BULLET!!" (Capitals in the original.) The following day, Wednesday 7 November, after significant indignation had been expressed in response, he expanded his point by tweeting as follows: "One Settler, One Bullet. Each bullet will take us closer to freedom."

Exactly what Mr Mlandu meant by his tweets is not clear. He may have meant them as a call for a genocide against millions of his fellow South Africans. Or he may have meant them only to express the view that such a genocide would be desirable or would be deserved by its victims. Either way, the tweeted words are morally repugnant. Reasonable people, whether or not they identify themselves as "settlers", will and should be outraged by them.

But should tweets like Mr Mlandu's be prohibited?

It is probable that his tweets are prohibited by section 10 of the Promotion of Equality and Prevention of Unfair Discrimination Act. Under the heading "Prohibition of Hate Speech", the section states that "no person may publish, propagate, advocate or communicate words based on [race, ethnic or social origin, colour, or culture] against any person, that could reasonably be construed to demonstrate a clear intention to – (a) be hurtful; (b) be harmful or incite harm; (c) promote or propagate hatred."

Relying on this section, the Equality Court found that a Facebook post by Penny Sparrow, which referred to "black" people as "monkeys", constituted hate speech and justified an award of damages against her of R150 000, to be paid to the Oliver and Adelaide Tambo Foundation. If, as is generally believed, the Equality Court's application of section 10 in the Sparrow matter cannot be faulted, it is hard to see how Mr Mlandu's tweets would not likewise constitute hate speech (as section 10 defines it) and would not also justify a substantial award of damages payable to a foundation promoting "non-racialism, tolerance, [and] reconciliation".

It is possible that tweets like Mr Mlandu's also are prohibited by UCT. UCT's "rules on conduct for students" include rule RCS7.6, which forbids students from acting or threatening to act "in a manner which interferes with the work or study of any member of staff or student ... in relation to the person's race ...", and rule RCS7.7, which forbids students from abusing "any member of the University community in any manner which contributes to the creation of an intimidating, hostile or demeaning environment ... in relation to the person's race ...". It might be said, not wholly implausibly, that Mr Mlandu's tweets constitute a threat of the kind prohibited by the first of these rules, as well as abusive behaviour of the kind prohibited by the second.

Even if tweets like Mr Mlandu's are prohibited by South African statute and by UCT's rules, they ought not to be – both constitutionally and morally. First, there is reason to believe that such prohibition is unconstitutional. Section 16(1) of the South African Constitution confers upon everyone a right to freedom of expression. However, according to section 16(2)(c), this right does not extend to "advocacy of hatred that is based on race [or] ethnicity ... *and* that constitutes incitement to cause harm" (our emphasis). Mr Mlandu's tweets almost certainly advocate hatred based on race or ethnicity. They almost certainly endorse the doing of harm by some to others. The intention behind them may have been to encourage such harm-doing. And it is possible that they might make such harm-doing more likely.

However, for Mr Mlandu's tweets to fall outside the ambit of the constitutional right to freedom of expression, because they fall within the exception created by section 16(2)(c), that is not enough. It is necessary, in addition, that the Tweets constituted "incitement to cause harm". As a number of legal philosophers have noted, the requirement of "incitement" sets a high threshold. For that threshold to be met, harm must not only be a probable consequence, it must be "imminent" or "in the very near future". There must be "a real threat to public safety", as there would be when – to borrow Joel Feinberg's metaphor – we have an "incendiary context" in which the audience is "tinder" and words advocating racial or ethnic hatred are intended as a "spark".

Mr Mlandu's tweets have constitutional protection, therefore, notwithstanding the likely intention behind them, which is reprehensible, and notwithstanding that they may contribute to appalling long term effects. The reason is their context. South Africa is not (yet?!) on the brink of genocide, and its citizens are not so resentful, nor so filled with hatred, nor so inclined to violence, that tweets like those of Mr Mlandu will tip them, almost unthinkingly, into the blood-letting that he possibly dreams of and hopes for.

If we are correct that Mr Mlandu's tweets are constitutionally protected, it remains an open question whether they *should* be. Put another way, why – morally speaking – should the Constitution protect hateful tweets? Words can have harmful consequences. Why should only *imminent* harms count as incitement? If an incendiary climate can be created by a steady accretion of hateful words, why should we not ban such words before there is tinder susceptible to a spark?

The answer is multifaceted. First, freedom of expression is a very important value. Second, it is often difficult, as we noted above, to differentiate the expression of a hateful opinion – for example, that all "whites" should be killed – from the intent to incite harmful action.

Third, and precisely because of this, freedom of expression can easily be eroded if one fails to maintain a high threshold for what counts as incitement. If merely contributing towards the creation of an incendiary climate counts as incitement, then the expression of many opinions could be counted as "incitement" and thus banned.

Fourth, this is unlikely to be done consistently, with those most vulnerable to violence from the creation of an incendiary environment also least likely to be able to curb the speech that would create such an environment.

Fifth, allowing hateful speech, morally repugnant though such speech is, has beneficial side-effects. About a year ago, a Berkeley university student newspaper published a cartoon of Harvard Law School Emeritus Professor Alan Dershowitz, which he subsequently criticised as antisemitic. Professor

Dershowitz nonetheless was "adamantly opposed" to "censoring the antisemitic cartoon". As Professor Dershowitz explained, "I want the world to see it and hold accountable those responsible for it".

The same applies to Mr Mlandu's tweets. Given his leading role in the UCT disruptions of the past few years, it is good that as many people as possible get to see the moral repugnance of his views. That he endorses a genocide of millions, or thinks that it would be desirable or deserved, is something that everyone with an interest in UCT should know. Among other things, it raises serious doubts about the process and findings of UCT's Institutional Reconciliation and Transformation Commission (IRTC).

Mr Mlandu was one of seven students granted amnesty[2] by UCT on the basis of the IRTC's recommendations. He must therefore have provided the IRTC with evidence of his contrition, or at least of an acknowledgement that he had done wrong. Mr Mlandu's tweets suggest that this evidence was provided without sincerity. And it suggests that the IRTC was naïve to accept it at face value.

Mr Mlandu's tweets, and the views they show him to hold, also have implications for the "diversion programme", managed by the National Institute for Crime Prevention and the Reintegration of Offenders (Nicro), that he reportedly was placed on earlier this year.[3] This was after he was charged with malicious damage to property, public violence, contempt of court, and contravention of the Intimidation Act, all in relation to an incident at UCT.

The aim of the diversion programme is rehabilitation, and those on the programme must provide proof that they have seen the error of their ways. Mr Mlandu's tweets suggest that he has not. It is good that we (and Nicro) know this. It would similarly be good to know how many of Mr Mlandu's comrades and their defenders hold genocidal views. If speech of this kind is prohibited we are less likely to find out who has such views.

This leads to a final reason for why the threshold for what counts as incitement should be kept high. There is a long causal chain between tweets such as Mr Mlandu's and the violence he would like to see. There are much better ways than restricting freedom of expression to prevent the former from resulting in the latter. These include holding people such as Mr Mlandu to account for their *actions* – rather than mere words. This is especially true when their actions are not only prohibited but also justifiably so.

Yet holding people such as Mr Mlandu to account for their actions is exactly what UCT has consistently *not* done. Worse still, following Mr Mlandu's initial tweet about his Honours project, UCT's Vice-Chancellor, Professor Mamokgethi Phakeng, replied on Twitter as follows: "Congratulations dear son on completing this paper! I would like to study it at some stage. In the meantime, let me be kliye: i am proud of you! Way more than you can imagine! Welldone!" (sic)

This was rightly met with widespread indignation by those who are opposed to genocide. Professor Phakeng responded by clarifying that "Of course I can never be proud of promises of bullets, what I am proud of is the fact that you did the paper and completed it". UCT also issued a statement noting that both Professor Phakeng and the institution distanced themselves from Mr Mlandu's "language".

But saying that one distances oneself is different from actually distancing oneself. (Think of Donald Trump's tepid condemnation of "white" supremacists.) We doubt that the Vice-Chancellor would publicly express pride in a student who, in the acknowledgements of his Honours project, called for the return of Apartheid, let alone a genocide of South Africa's indigenous peoples. And if she were to do so, subsequently distancing herself from such "language" would not be regarded as sufficient.

That she and others are fixated on a hateful slogan rather than on the underlying pathology of the institution is but another symptom of the deeply toxic environment that currently prevails at UCT.[4] It is that environment that should never have been allowed to develop and which should now be corrected. There is no evidence that it is being fixed. Indeed, the problem seems to be deepening. If that trajectory continues, there will be awful consequences whether or not the likes of Mr Mlandu advocate violence.

What is good for the goose is good for the gander. During the past few years, freedom of speech has been significantly eroded at UCT. The most notable infringements of this freedom were the de-platforming of Flemming Rose and the destruction, removal, and covering up of artworks on UCT campuses. If, as we have argued, the right to freedom of speech is sufficiently robust to protect Mr Mlandu's tweets, notwithstanding their moral repugnance, it is, *a fortiori*, robust enough to have protected Flemming Rose against being silenced and to protect the many notable South African artists whose artworks were removed or covered up from being rendered invisible.

This has a further implication. It shows that, even though (for the reasons we have given) UCT has done the right thing by not taking disciplinary action against Mr Mlandu for his reprehensible tweets, it has not done so because of a highly principled commitment to freedom of expression.

Chapter 14
A VERY STRANGE INVITATION

(Originally published: 5 August 2019)[1]

Consider the case of an American academic whose tweets include the following:

> "You may be too refined to say it, but I'm not: I wish all the fucking Mexicans would go missing." (Tweeted after three Hispanic teenagers in Texas, were abducted and murdered by members of a white supremacist group.)
>
> "At this point, if Mugabe appeared on TV with a necklace made from the teeth of white farmers, would anybody be surprised?"
>
> "The logic of 'racism' deployed by African nationalists, if applied in principle, would make pretty much everybody [who is] not a sociopath, 'racist'."

"African nationalists in South Africa: transforming racism from something horrible into something honorable since 1994."

Should this person have been invited to deliver the 2019 Steve Biko Memorial lecture, which he has entitled, "The inhumanity of liberation"? If you answer this question negatively, then be assured that this case is entirely fictional, as it could only be in the current context. Nobody with a track record like that would be invited to the University of Cape Town to deliver *any* lecture, let alone a Steve Biko Memorial lecture.

Now ask yourself whether an American academic who tweeted the following should have been invited to deliver the 2019 T.B. Davie Memorial Academic Freedom lecture at UCT?:

"You may be too refined to say it, but I'm not: I wish all the fucking West Bank settlers would go missing."[2] (Tweeted after three Jewish teenagers were abducted and then murdered by members of the demonstrably antisemitic[3] Hamas.)

"At this point, if Netanyahu appeared on TV with a necklace made from the teeth of Palestinian children, would anybody be surprised?"[4]

"The logic of 'antisemitism' deployed by Zionists, if applied in principle, would make pretty much everybody [who is] not a sociopath, 'antisemitic'."[5]

"Zionists: transforming anti-semitism from something horrible into something honorable since 1948."[6]

This case is entirely true. The UCT "Academic Freedom Committee" has invited Dr Steven Salaita to deliver the 2019 Academic Freedom lecture named in memory of Dr Thomas Benjamin Davie,[7] former UCT Principal who fought the imposition of Apartheid on UCT in 1950s. Dr Salaita's topic is "The Inhumanity of Academic Freedom".

It remains to be seen what Dr Salaita will say under that heading. *Whatever* it is, no matter how vile, he has a right to say it and I would oppose any call for him to be disinvited, heckled, or otherwise silenced. (I am not aware of any such calls, at least as yet.[8]) It does not follow, however, that he was a fitting invitee to deliver an academic freedom lecture in memory of Dr Davie, or that anybody should attend his lecture.

One reason for thinking this is to be found in considering the first (and fictional) case I presented. If such a person should not be invited to deliver the Steve Biko Memorial lecture, then Dr Salaita should probably not have been invited to deliver the T.B. Davie Memorial lecture.

Why might Dr Shuaib Manjra, who nominated Dr Salaita, and the UCT Academic Freedom Committee, which endorsed the nomination and issued the invitation, think that Dr Salaita would be a suitable speaker? The most charitable answer is that Dr Salaita's own academic freedom was threatened at one university and later infringed by another.

In 2013, while he was teaching at Virginia Tech, there were calls for his dismissal following his publication of an article in which he rejected the "Support Our Troops" slogan.[9] While Virginia Tech distanced itself from Dr Salaita's comments, it said that it supported his right to freedom of expression. Yet, some people found Virginia Tech's statement "wholly unsatisfactory" and "placing in doubt its commitment to academic freedom".[10]

Dr Salaita subsequently accepted an offer of a position at the University of Illinois at Urbana-Champaign. However, before his appointment was confirmed (and after he had already resigned his position at Virginia Tech), the offer of a position at the University of Illinois at Urbana-Champaign was rescinded following a series of tweets (including those above) that he made during the Gaza-Israel war of 2014.

After a settlement in which the University agreed to pay him $875 000,[11] he was left without a job. He was hired for a year at the American University of Beirut, but was not renewed in that position.[12] He has not found an academic position since then, and is now working as a school bus driver in Washington DC.[13]

The University of Illinois at Urbana-Champaign did indeed violate Dr Salaita's academic freedom, with momentous effects for him personally. It may well have had a chilling effect on others. However, if the UCT "Academic Freedom Committee" wanted to hear from somebody who had been silenced by a university, it should first have (re-)invited Flemming Rose, who was silenced by none other than UCT. (In addition to the other advantages, this would also be an act of redress, to which UCT purports to be committed.)

Mr Rose had been invited by the previous Academic Freedom Committee to deliver the T.B. Davie Memorial Lecture in 2016 and was subsequently disinvited by Dr Max Price and the then University Executive. Subsequent to that disinvitation, Mr Rose has been re-nominated by multiple people. One nominator, in justifying his nomination, said that in the face of Mr Rose's earlier disinvitation, "the very continuation of the T.B. Davie Academic Freedom lecture is a farce. The only way the lecture can be redeemed is by ensuring that Mr Rose is invited to give the lecture he had earlier been invited to give and was then barred from giving". Evidently the Academic Freedom Committee found this (and the rest of the motivation) "not convincing enough for the nomination to be reconsidered". Instead, it concluded that because Mr Rose "was previously regarded as an inappropriate speaker for the T.B. Davie Lecture, it would abide by that decision".

(It did not carry this logic through to Dr Salaita who has been regarded as inappropriate for an academic position. In this case the UCT Academic Freedom Committee had the "courage" to stand up to the University of Illinois. It just lacked the courage to stand up to the University of Cape Town.)

Nor is Flemming Rose the only person to have been silenced by or at UCT. His case may be the most ironic and the most explicit, but there are numerous other examples, overt and covert. Many artworks[14] have been covered up and removed to placate intolerant elements, without any protest from the current Academic Freedom Committee. Worse, two members of the committee – the Chair[15] and one other[16] – have actually defended the censorship.[17]

There are also innumerable other instances of academic freedom having been infringed upon, through intimidation, threats, disruption, violence, and vandalism. All of the worst offenders have been let off.[18] Others were never charged. The toxic climate at UCT has resulted in self-censorship. Many people are cowering, fearful of expressing their opinions. Those who have expressed their views have been threatened, shunned, censured, or otherwise victimized.

One such example is Dr Kenneth Hughes, a longstanding defender of academic freedom at UCT. After he published a letter, "Appeasing the UCT Taliban",[19] his next History of Economic Thought lecture was disrupted by protestors seeking his removal as course lecturer. [20] This is exactly what they achieved. The remaining lectures for the year had to be posted on the web and, by some contrivance, the course, long assigned to Dr Hughes, was conveniently assigned to somebody else from the following year onwards.

None of the threats to academic freedom at UCT come from reactionaries or conservatives (both vanishingly rare species at South African universities) or from liberals (a now endangered species.) *All* the threats to academic freedom at UCT come from the *regressive* left, whose views are the current orthodoxy. They champion the limitation of academic freedom, but only when that freedom is used for purposes *they* do not like. (Chillingly, the Chair of the Academic Freedom Committee has reminded her committee of the "context within which it was decided that academic freedom at this university needed to be reconsidered" – namely the "call for decolonization".)

In other words, those on the regressive left have no principled commitment to academic freedom. An Academic Freedom Committee worthy of its name would be testing and challenging that orthodoxy, not pandering to it by inviting one orthodox speaker[21] after another[22] into the echo chamber that UCT has become.

Instead, after re-inviting Mr Rose (who has stood up to threats to freedom of expression from both the left and the right[23]), a UCT Academic Freedom Committee worthy of its name would invite people who have stood up to the intolerance of the regressive left. There is no shortage of such people, but two outstanding examples are Professor Nicholas Christakis[24] and Dr Bret Weinstein.[25]

Both scholars are on the political left, but not its regressive strain. Both were harangued by intolerant, narrow-minded, cry-bullies, but admirably retained their composure and attempted to engage their persecutors. Both paid a high personal price. Dr Weinstein and his wife, Dr Heather Heying, were driven from their positions at Evergreen State University where campus police had told him that they were unable to protect him and advised him to remain off campus. Nicholas Christakis remains at Yale, but his wife, Dr Erika Christakis no longer teaches there. Both of them stepped down from their positions as Masters at Yale's Silliman College,[26] after months of pressure to do so.

The unfailing decency of Nicholas Christakis and Bret Weinstein stands in contrast to the intemperate, vituperative, and prejudicial comments of Steven Salaita. This is yet another reason why they rather than he would be much more fitting speakers for a lecture in memory of Dr Davie, who is recalled (by Benjamin Pogrund) as "a man of honour, integrity and commitment to academic freedom, and also a man who treated everyone with impeccable courtesy".

Finally, Dr Salaita has spoken of a "Palestinian exception to ... free speech"[27] in the United States, alleging that those expressing pro-Palestinian views are silenced in that country. Is that a reason to invite him? Whether or not there is an *element* of truth to that claim in the United States, it is certainly not true in South Africa, where there have been not only an endless stream of such speakers who have had no difficulty being heard and hired, and where the national government condemns and shuns Israel and cosies up to the Palestinian Authority and even Hamas. Whether (so-called) pro-Palestinian views[28] can be expressed is thus not a test of academic freedom in South Africa or at UCT. One test, instead, is whether pro-Israel views can be expressed.

Professor Elelwani Ramugondo, current Chair of the UCT Academic Freedom Committee has said that she does "not think that we can speak of academic freedom, and ever be certain that in inviting one speaker, and not another – we can avoid offending some members of our community". That may well be true. However, the question to ask her and her committee is why they are willing to offend again and again those with non-dominant views, and never offend those with the dominant ones. The test of freedom of expression and academic freedom is whether non-dominant views can be freely expressed. UCT has repeatedly failed that test. The current Academic Freedom Committee at UCT should start doing its job, which is to promote academic freedom and to take appropriate action when it is infringed.

Chapter 15
LIQUID BULLSHIT

People of principle follow the principle even when it is uncomfortable, or worse, for them to do so. For example, they tolerate the expression of not only the views they like but also the views they dislike. They apply the same standards in judging behaviour, irrespective of whether those behaving in a particular way are those with whom they agree or those with whom they disagree.

Then there are the unprincipled. Which standard they apply in a given situation, depends on what's good for them and those they like. Because being unprincipled is so obviously a vice, the unprincipled have to keep up a pretence that they are in fact acting in principled ways. This provides them with a strong incentive to be bullshitters. I use that term not in its vulgar, colloquial sense, but rather in two technical philosophical senses.

According to Harry Frankfurt's conception, bullshit is to be distinguished from lying. The bullshitter talks (or writes) without regard to whether what he (or she) is saying is true or not. The bullshitter is trying to "convey a certain impression of himself".[1] Thus, the "essence of bullshit is not that it is *false* but that it is *phony*". Jerry Cohen identifies a second variety of bullshit – what he calls "unclarifiable unclarity".[2] These are collections of words that are unclear, and which cannot be made clear.

Both these strategies are valuable to the unprincipled. The first helps them because they can talk as though they were committed to a principle when, in fact, they do not care what acting on principle requires. The second helps them because the obfuscation constitutes a kind of camouflage. If you are unprincipled, you can hide that fact by using obscure language. Indeed, the unclarity need not even be unclarifi*able* for it to serve that end. Even *clarifiable* unclarity, bullshit's half-sibling, can help. This is because the project of clarifying is so burdensome that few will expend the energy. Bullshit is liquid, in my terminology, when it seeps into and pervades the social "discourse", becoming an article of faith and a mantra.

AN UNPRINCIPLED DILEMMA

What is an unprincipled fellow to do when he supports the disinvitation of an academic freedom speaker[3] while claiming that "concerns about academic freedom are important" and that "concerns about the vice-chancellor vetoing the decisions of an academic committee are founded"?[4] And what is an unprincipled fellow to do when he does not wish to condemn criminal behaviour just because it is the behaviour of his ideological comrades? He can hardly say that criminal behaviour is acceptable either for anybody or only for his friends.

It should come as no surprise that one strategy for dealing

with such dilemmas is to distract people by levelling nasty accusations at those who think that the same rules apply to all. That is how Adam Haupt came to accuse Jacques Rousseau and me of "liquid racism" and "possessive investments in whiteness".

Adam Haupt's paper is ostensibly about a purported connection between these two concepts, on the one hand, and academic freedom, on the other hand. The specific case on which he focuses is the disinvitation of Flemming Rose from giving the 2016 TB Davie Academic Freedom Lecture[5] (although he regularly drifts into my criticism of student protests unrelated to Mr Rose). He endorsed that disinvitation, and takes aim first at Jacques Rousseau, even though Mr Rousseau actually expressed an *understanding* of the disinvitation (without explicitly endorsing it).[6] Adam Haupt's complaint is with Mr Rousseau's *rationale* for understanding the decision to disinvite Mr Rose.

Mr Rousseau had said that he thought that "the security threats were real" and that Mr Rose's appearance might have led to violence. He did not say *whom* he thought would have posed the security threat, although he did explicitly say that he did *not* think it would be the Muslim community.[7] Mr Rousseau said that the UCT Executive's decision to disinvite "should have started, and ended, with the simple acknowledgement that pragmatism is forcing us to grant the heckler's veto".

This, Adam Haupt opines, is an instance of liquid racism. Those without an advanced degree in racial paranoia might wonder how one reaches this conclusion from those premises. Here is how it is done:

Adam Haupt borrows the concept of liquid racism from Simon Weaver (whose paper on the Danish cartoons,[8] it must be said, is vastly more nuanced than Adam Haupt's). Dr Weaver defines liquid racism as "a racism generated by ambiguous cultural signs that encourages the development of entrenched socio-discursive positioning, alongside reactions to racism, when reading these signs."[9]

This is unclear and, based on what Dr Weaver says, only part of it is clarifiable. He is saying that "cultural signs" such as some of the cartoons published by Mr Rose in the *Jyllands-Posten* can be interpreted in different ways. On some of the interpretations, the cartoons are entirely reasonable, whereas on other interpretations they are racist – more specifically hostile to Muslims *qua* Muslims. Nothing that Dr Weaver says clarifies what we are meant to conclude from this. Is it the conclusion that racists will have a racist reading of the cartoons while reasonable people will have a reasonable reading? Is it that racists can hide behind the reasonable interpretations? Is it, instead, that the reasonable interpretation inevitably gets infected by the racist one? It is a pity that Dr Weaver does not make clear what he thinks we should infer from the fact that there are different interpretations of the cartoons.

What *is* clear is that Adam Haupt applies the concept of liquid racism not to "cultural signs" but to arguments. Adam Haupt alleges that the security concerns expressed by Mr Rousseau, at least in the context of the 2016 campus disruptions, invokes "the discourse of fear and racial stereotyping that is in line with hegemonic representations of black protesters and activists".[10] He concludes that student "activists are therefore framed as bullies and hecklers who shrink the space for debate and dissent through disruptions that may involve violence".[11]

Unlike Mr Rousseau, *I* was of the opinion that Mr Rose's lecture could proceed without disruption. Of course, I was not unaware of the widespread campus disruptions that were taking place at the time. I merely thought that Mr Rose's lecture would be of no interest to those causing the actual disruptions. (Moreover, when I asked members of the University Executive, before their disinvitation of Mr Rose, whether they had any evidence of potential disruptions of the lecture, they answered negatively.)

Of course, that did not stop Adam Haupt from characterizing me as a purveyor of liquid racism. This is because I had described *actual* (rather than imagined) disruptors who were shutting down the University for weeks as "marauding thugs".[12] This, he said, "is in line with Rousseau's characterisation of the students as hecklers who use threats or violence to win arguments, although it is more explicit in drawing on racialised stereotypes of black people".[13]

It is news to me that "marauding thugs" is a racialised stereotype of "blacks". The full gamut of human history is littered with marauding thugs – from every racial and ethnic group. In our own time, some are "black" nationalists, but others are "white" supremacists.[14] If protesters are blocking entrances to the University, wandering around the campus strewing human excrement, threatening and inflicting personal violence, torching vehicles, paintings, and the Vice-Chancellor's office, they *are* marauding thugs who are engaged in criminal conduct. That truth does not become ineffable merely because in this case they happen to be "black" (if they were indeed all "black"[15]).

The Western Cape High Court, in support of an interdict against the thugs, noted that the South African Constitution did not protect "hooliganism, vandalism or any other unlawful and illegitimate misconduct"[16] – a point then endorsed by South Africa's Constitutional Court in considering an appeal from the Fallists.[17] In referring to the criminal protesters to as "hooligans" and "vandals", the relevant judges were not "drawing on racialised stereotypes of black people". Instead, they were applying the law in an impartial manner.

Nor is the truth avoided by Hauptian double-speak. He says, for example, that "Benatar's call for the force of law to be used against activists therefore stands to undermine principles of academic freedom and constitutionally protected rights to peaceful protest."[18] It is not "peaceful" to assault people and threaten others with violence. Nor is it "peaceful" to engage in arson. Adam Haupt should be reminded that the South Africa's courts, including the Constitutional Court, agree with me and not with him about this.[19] I have not seen him accusing them of "liquid racism".

Moreover, not even all *peaceful* protest is consistent with academic freedom and constitutionally protected rights. A peaceful violation of the rights of others remains a violation of their rights. Accordingly, a peaceful violation of rights need not be protected. I have never called for – and would never call for – the force of law to be used against those engaged in protest that does not violate the rights of others.

You can be sure that if those engaged in criminal activity on campus were not Adam Haupt's ideological allies, he would have a very different view. Indeed, if you are in opposition to him, you do not need to be involved in *criminal* activity at all in order to elicit his condemnation. He has criticised those enforcing the law, even when law enforcement agents were not acting illegally.[20] He has also routinely lobbed the charge of racism – whether liquid or otherwise – at those expressing entirely reasonable views, because they differ from his own. Most glaringly in the current context, he condones those who perpetrate the criminal behaviour described above, but condemns (as racists) those who accurately describe it. He then gets credit for publishing such "research".

How does Adam Haupt justify his defence of the marauding thugs? He does so by saying that "subaltern polities create multiple publics to contest for attention to ensure that their concerns are addressed. They do so by engaging in contestation on their own terms, and not by criteria for deliberative modes of engagement".[21] Translated into English, this means that those who are unempowered cannot employ the usual deliberative processes for seeking change and thus they do so via other means. Of course, Adam Haupt understands power in racial terms. He speaks about "racialised privilege" and of "possessive investments in whiteness".

A few observations are in order. First, there is a difference between whether (purportedly) unempowered people *do* resort to violent and other criminal means to obtain what they want, and whether it is morally *permissible* for them to do so. If Adam Haupt is merely describing, then he is doing no normative work (and the descriptive claim is only sometimes true). If, by contrast, he is saying that violence by the powerless is permissible (even in a democracy), then he needs to argue for that conclusion – something he fails to do.

Second, there is a sense in which *everybody* who cannot get what they want is unempowered. They do not have the power to get what they want. Does that mean that everybody may resort to violence and criminality to obtain what they want? I doubt that Adam Haupt would assent to that. From his ramblings about the work of Homi Bhabha, Frantz Fanon and others,[22] it seems that he would say that even if there is some technical sense in which everybody is unempowered, the real power lies with "white privilege", while "blacks" remain unempowered.

Claims of who has power and who does not, are not *a priori* claims. We need to know something about the world, and specific places in the world, to know whether such claims are true. Moreover, what is true at one point in history may not be true at another point.

The one way in which "whites" in South Africa are still more powerful than "blacks" is economically. It is obviously true that the *average* "white" in South Africa has more economic power than the average "black" South African, and that South Africa's poor are overwhelmingly "black". It is also true that most of the richest people in South Africa are "white". There are some nuances, however. For example, there are now more middle class "blacks" than middle class "whites", even though the number of middle class "blacks" is still not proportionate to the proportion of South Africans who are "black".[23] Economic power impacts to some extent on other forms of power, but only to some extent. Moreover, other forms of power impact on economic power to some extent.

If we turn to political power, all adult citizens of South Africa have the vote, but because "whites" are a small minority of the total population, it is implausible to suggest that they hold the political power. Adam Haupt writes as though Apartheid never ended and that political power has not shifted from the "white" minority to the "black" majority. This political power manifests in many ways that impact on universities. These include but are not limited to ministerial appointments to university governing bodies,[24] funding priorities, and the government's legally imposed aggressive racial preferences.

There are also various forms of social power. This book contains many examples of such power. It explains how the marauding thugs were able to evade punishment. It explains how Busi Mkhumbuzi could engage in a long-standing campaign of defamation against me, pretend that she was the victim of discrimination, and evade the disciplinary tribunal, while earning national accolades. It is what explains how the University entered into a memorandum of recognition with the Black Academic Caucus (BAC) without having first determined the principles of such memoranda and without knowing the membership of the BAC.[25] It explains how Flemming Rose was disinvited because he offended the sensibilities of people like Adam Haupt, while there has been an endless parade of TB Davie speakers who are openly hostile to the State of Israel,[26] a position entirely congenial to many of those offended by the prospect of Mr Rose speaking.[27]

The social power also explains how the predominant South African press publishes pieces about UCT by Adam Haupt, the

BAC, and other race baiters, but places obstacles in my way,[28] or blocks me entirely.[29] It also explains why at the time (according to UCT's "melaninometers") 70% of UCT's governing body (Council) was "black".[30] To claim, in the face of all this and more, that "blacks" *as a group* are somehow unempowered at UCT is pure bullshit. Because that claim is so pervasive, the bullshit is liquid.

This is not to deny the obvious truth that individual "blacks" are unempowered in some ways. Economic disadvantage is a form of disadvantage suffered by many, but not all, individual "black" students. However, there are ways in which individual "whites" are disadvantaged. They cannot even *say* that they are disadvantaged in the ways in which they are disadvantaged, because *their* playing that card carries no positive power, and is regularly counter-productive.

GRASPING AT OTHER STRAWS

Adam Haupt offers other defences of the disinvitation of Mr Rose. These are familiar sloppy arguments. For example, he declares that

> under South African law, Rose's free speech rights are not limitless. Any individual's right to free speech has to be balanced with the public interest. Hate speech and incitement to violence are not in the public interest. Therefore, racist speech or representations would not be protected as free speech by Section 16 of the South African Constitution.[31]

If Adam Haupt had both read and understood Section 16 of the South African constitution, he would know that no reference is made there to the public interest and that hate speech *per se* is not prohibited by Section 16. What *is* prohibited, inter alia, is "advocacy of hatred that is based on race, ethnicity, gender or religion, *and that constitutes incitement to cause harm"* (my emphasis).

Publication of the cartoons did not constitute either the advocacy of hatred or incitement to cause harm. The cartoons did not call for violence against anybody. Indeed, some of them satirized those who do resort to violence. To think that the violent response of those offended by the cartoons constitutes incitement is to fail to understand what incitement is. If Adam – that is Adam of Eden, not Adam Haupt – is offended by Eve's expressing her opinion, and he therefore punches her, she has not incited violence. She is the victim of violent intolerance. Incitement is when one encourages somebody to act wrongly. For example, if Adam encourages Cain to kill Abel, then Adam has incited murder. There was no reason to think that Mr Rose was going to incite violence against anybody in his lecture.

In defence of his view that Mr Rose was a poor choice of speaker, Adam Haupt says: [32]

> The government has treated the call for state subsidization of university fees as a security threat, as opposed to engaging with student activists directly to resolve the problem that has been identified. This raises serious questions about the autonomy of universities and academic freedom, issues that neither Benatar nor Rousseau identify in their writing. In fact, the decision to invite a divisive editor to present a lecture on academic freedom is not merely ill-advised on the grounds of Rose's racism, but he is not a scholar and could hardly be expected to address the challenge that universities face.

There are at least three problems with this argument. First, it is highly unlikely that the government treated the call of student protesters for state subsidization of university fees as a security threat. It is much more likely that it saw the criminal protests as a security threat. If it saw the protests as a threat to the state, it would be guilty of exaggeration, but it was entirely reasonable to see the protests as a threat to the nation's universities.

Second, it is not clear how this fear raised a "serious question about the autonomy of universities and academic freedom". Is Adam Haupt suggesting that the state was interfering with university autonomy in some way? If so, he should provide evidence of this – evidence that could then be evaluated.

Third, let us set aside the conceit that Mr Rose "is not a scholar". He may not have a PhD or teach in a university,[33] but one does not need either of those to produce scholarship. (Sadly, the reverse is also true: having a PhD and teaching in a university is no guarantee that the work one produces will be scholarship.) The suggestion that Mr Rose "could hardly be expected to address the challenge that universities face" is deeply ironic. South African universities – and UCT in particular – face a very serious problem of silencing people with views that depart from those of the likes of Adam Haupt. The very fact that Mr Rose was disinvited vividly demonstrates that he had much to teach UCT about the "challenge that universities face".

WHO IS UNMASKED?

Adam Haupt argues that when people like me argue for free speech and academic freedom, we are using such concepts merely for what he takes to be racist purposes. For example, he says that "the decision to invite Rose is therefore both an expression of power and enabled by power, in essence it offers an example of the coloniality of power at work",[34] and that the "act of framing criticism of the invitation to Rose as a threat to academic freedom essentially points to the ways in which coloniality of power seeks to justify itself".[35] Even more explicitly, he says that "certain positions that are critical of the decision to withdraw the invitation to Rose have less to do with the principles of academic freedom and more to do with protecting racialised privilege; the concept of academic freedom is utilised to mask possessive investments in whiteness".[36]

One wonders how Adam Haupt presumes to know what is going on in my mind when I defend freedom of expression. Is he suggesting that *anybody* who criticizes the disinvitation of Mr Rose, is a racist who is cynically employing high-minded concepts such as freedom of expression? If that is the case, then presumably freedom of expression is not such a high-minded concept after all. But then why does Adam Haupt pay lip-service to it? Or is it only the sort of principle to which one should pay lip-service? Is a real commitment to it merely "white privilege" in disguise?

The problem with treating a principled commitment to freedom of expression as a covert way for anti-"black" racism, is that the principled defender of freedom of expression supports the freedom of expression of "blacks" even when they are engaged in anti-"white" racism. That is exactly what Professor Anton Fagan, the W.P. Schreiner Professor of Law at UCT, and I did in an opinion piece we co-authored. We argued that Masixole Mlandu should not face disciplinary action for using the racist expression "One settler, one bullet".[37]

I recognize that there *may* still be racial blood-letting in South Africa's future, with pale South Africans on the receiving end. Such an outcome would not be in our interests – or indeed in the long-term interests of any South African, no matter how much the likes of Mr Mlandu may believe otherwise. Even in the absence of such an outcome, the repeated expressions of hatred contribute to a hostile environment. Nevertheless, his vile, racist language does not reach the level of incitement to imminent violence or other harms, which we believe are among the very few sufficient conditions under which the law should restrict freedom of expression. Thus, we defended his right to say what he said. In doing so, is freedom of expression really being "utilised to mask possessive investments of whiteness"?[38] The only way Adam Haupt could provide a positive answer to that question is by generating even more bullshit.

Chapter 16
CRYBULLY MEDICAL STUDENTS

(Originally published: 12 November 2019)[1]

An "emergency class meeting" was recently called for the third year MBChB class at the University of Cape Town. It was called by some students in the class and was scheduled at a regular lecture time. It ended up displacing all the lectures that would otherwise have taken place that afternoon. The purpose of the meeting was not conveyed to the class, but in the course of it, some students were berated and humiliated for allegedly being insufficiently compassionate. In other words, the self-appointed guardians of compassion and sensitivity displayed the opposite of that in haranguing and shaming their classmates. This irony was lost on the former, but certainly not on the latter who, it turns out, were not guilty of the insensitivity attributed to them.

FIRST PRELUDES

Earlier in the year, one component group in the class were being taught about the aetiology of substance abuse. Some students in that class opined that the legacy of Apartheid was the main contributor to substance abuse. One of their classmates – I shall refer to him as Scott – who had read the relevant literature, disputed this. He acknowledged that it was a contributing factor but said that the evidence did not support the view that it was the dominant factor.

Scott fielded many challenges, but a handful of students in the class became steadily more personal, eventually accusing him of "white privilege". It turns out, as in this case, that one does not have to be "white" to be accused of "white privilege". Scott says that he can only speculate why they assumed that he was "Caucasian" rather than of "mixed race" background. Either way, they were making assumptions about him on the basis of his outward appearance, which he notes is exactly what prejudice is.

As is to be expected, these sorts of accusations had a silencing effect. Other students in the class were too intimidated to speak up. At least four of them called Scott afterwards to let him know that they agreed with him. One of them said that she agreed entirely, but that if Scott ever mentioned that she did, she would deny it.

Scott was a lone voice on other occasions too. When UCT first year Film and Media student, Uyinene Mrwetyana was raped and murdered, the name of the person accused of the crime was released before he had appeared in court and pleaded. This is in violation of South African law, but some medical students applauded the fact that the accused had been named prematurely. Scott expressed concern about flouting the law, and was taken to task for this.

He had previously rejected the idea, expressed by some of his fellow students, that #AllMenAreTrash. He noted, among other things, that this was a form of prejudice. This led to his being asked whether he was opposed to rape. In the minds of his interlocuters one must either accept their view of (all) men, or else one is an apologist for rape. Predictably, such engagement silenced the other men in his group – or at least those who did not offer apologies for male trashiness.

In a discussion about abortion in their first year, one student reproached a male pro-lifer by telling him that if one does not have a uterus one may not speak about this topic. Although not himself the target of this comment, Scott pointed out the problems with such a view.

Nor are these the only examples. Other students have spoken of multiple cases of silencing and self-censorship. These reached new levels in a developing further prelude to the "emergency class meeting".

FURTHER PRELUDE

When it became known that the aforementioned Uyinene Mrwetyana had been murdered, UCT's Vice-Chancellor announced that the University would be closed for a day. The closure was then extended for a further two days.

A few third-year medical students, feeling anxious about the impact of this closure on their studies, asked whether their small group could continue "if *everyone* is willing" (emphasis in the original). The student who initiated this request – I shall call her Davida – was subsequently subjected to substantial verbal and psychological abuse. Thus, it is important to be clear on exactly what she had said on the WhatsApp forum to which she had offered the comments. This WhatsApp forum was for her small group within the class, and not for the whole class. (The whole class is divided into small groups for various purposes.)

Davida spoke of the importance of being introduced to material in class, and of learning to "[d]eal with things while still doing our jobs". She immediately acknowledged that that comment might be "contentious". She also recognized that "obviously [the death of Uyinene] is very close to home for some people and they need a moment" but suggested that the appropriate response would be to "make a concession" for those students rather than "cancelling for everyone".

Another student, whom I shall call Camilla, also wanted to continue with work. She said that she was a financial aid student and could not afford to fail. She expressed the "hope that protests don't continue into [the] Clin[ical] skills [course] because some people get violent when you go to class and it's not pretty having to deal with that".

(Although the closure was not a result of protests, it is very likely that it was in order to *prevent* a forcible closure of the University. Moreover, there was some protest action aimed at forcing the University to close beyond the initial three days. It is certainly hard to see the closure as a matter of principle, given the high rate of rapes and murders in South Africa. The University does not close every time a student or staff member is raped or murdered. Indeed, when another first year student, Mhleli Cebo Mbatha, was stabbed to death on Clifton Beach less than a month later, UCT was not closed to protest his death. Murders of males, the vast majority of murders, do not fit into the orthodox "gender-based violence" rubric.)

Somebody else in the group responded: "I am disgusted by the insensitive commentary that is coming from all of you. I will not even make an attempt to educate you on how you have displayed your ignorance".

Davida responded as follows: "I don't think we doubt that any female has fears about these things and has them reinforced by this senseless violence. So let's try not to make it us and them. I guess we all just deal with it in different ways and are at different levels of sensitisation to it".

An uncharitable selection of Davida's and Camilla's posts

were then taken out of context and posted on the WhatsApp forum for the entire class of 232 students, along with the comment: "I hope that y'all know that this is shitty, and I hope that y'all change before you become shitty doctors". Because Davida's and Camilla's real names were displayed, everybody in the class knew exactly at whom this comment was directed.

A number of other people in the class then added, to the whole class WhatsApp forum, their own criticisms of Camilla and especially of Davida. One male wrote "that many of the things class members have said is very violent to womxn who have experienced these traumas, who have been (*TRIGGER WARNING*) harassed, assaulted and raped" and that "it is a frightening thought because these are people, many men especially, who will be interacting with people who have gone through these traumas as doctors ... their opinions will bleed into the way they speak and interact with their patients".

The author simply assumes that Davida and Camilla have not experienced any of these traumas he mentions. Perhaps this is because he assumes that anybody who has experienced them would share his own view. Is it inconceivable to him that different people could react in different ways? Then he pivots. He uses the words of female students to cast doubt on the suitability of male students in the class to interact protectively with patients who have suffered sexual assault.

This "kindly inquisitor" (as Jonathan Rauch would call him[2]) then ends: "I do not want to come across as being violent to any of you and if I have done so, I sincerely and wholeheartedly apologise". Perhaps there is a flicker of insight into his behaviour here, but it did not do his victims any good, because others then piled on (and he himself was later instrumental in arranging the emergency class meeting where the berating of Davida, Scott, and others became even worse).

A number of those scolding Davida on the WhatsApp group either misinterpreted her (perhaps because they rushed to judgment after seeing only some of her comments out of context) or they believe that it is "violence" if *they* (but not those with whom they disagree) are subjected to opinions they dislike.

Here were some of the comments:

> "When you make people feel like fighting for their right to feel safe is *such* an inconvenience to you, you are (in essence) making them question if they were better off suffering in silence".

> "Just because it's not personal to you doesn't give you the right to dismiss and belittle the movement."

> "If you can't relate then don't disregard other people's reality".

> "I hope that you don't have to deal with victims of sexual assault or other violent crimes because I'm afraid you might re-violate them".

> "I'm tired of the faux ignorance people employ here to victimize and silence".

> "The victims can't always be the ones making safe spaces!! We're tired."

> "We don't need safe spaces to educate violent people. Go read a flipping book and make every place safe. READ A FLIPPING BOOK."

> "We can['t?] always be educating you guys!! It's time you unlearn and relearn things yourself!!"

Contrary to these allegations, Davida never opposed anybody fighting for their safety. At most she questioned whether this was best done by shutting down the University for three days. She did not ask anybody to suffer in silence. She did not dismiss or belittle the movement for a safer South Africa. She did not disregard anybody's perception of reality. (There is a difference between "reality" and "perceptions of reality".)

She did not display any insensitivity to victims of violence. Instead, she displayed a strength to continue working in spite of the tragedy – a skill that doctors in training need to develop if they do not already have it. Saying such things is *not* violence. Anybody who doubts this, should read the relevant entry in *this* "flipping" book: *The Oxford English Dictionary*.

You are *not* a victim if somebody asks whether, by mutual consent, some students can continue their studies while those personally affected by the tragedy do not. You *are* a victim (albeit not of violence) if the response to that reasonable request is to shame you.

Some students who were uncomfortable with what was transpiring on the WhatsApp forum, started leaving it. In response, one student posted this: "And before anyone else decides to leave this group because it may be an inconvenience to you please fucking check yourself".

A few students did come to Davida's and Camilla's defence. One suggested that it was unfair to characterize their comments as "shitty" and to say that if they do not change they would become "shitty doctors". However, one student who thought that there was nothing unfair about these characterizations offered the following "double speak":

> It's actually a very compassionate statement to make, because I'm assuming (still am) they have the ability to change, and acknowledge the shitiness of their statements. That's more fair than necessary actually. (sic)

Another student noted that Camilla had said the following on the small group WhatsApp forum: "I'm sorry if my tone offended anyone", but this did not placate the crybullies. One responded: "It doesn't matter that they apologised afterwards the problem is that they made those statements in the first place".

Another said: "Even if they did apologize it would be nothing! Because I'm still waiting for [Davida] to apologize for saying FMF activism killed Mayosi".

To this another student responded: "As a person who was part of FMF 2016, I'm disgusted that she said that ... Fuck [Davida] actually".

In fact, Davida had not said that. She had once said that the protesting students had *played a role* in Professor Mayosi's suicide – a claim that Professor Mayosi's own family had made.[3] It is understandable that the Fees Must Fall activists are uncomfortable about their own culpability, but the appropriate response to this is not revisionist history. Instead, it is to learn the lesson that (cry-)bullying is much more harmful than hearing an opinion one does not like. That, it seems from the foregoing preludes and from the class meeting that followed, is not a lesson that has been learned.

DENOUEMENT: THE "EMERGENCY" (AND COMPULSORY) CLASS MEETING

On Friday 27 September 2019, the MBChB III class was advised in an email from their class representatives that a compulsory whole class meeting would be held on the following Monday, 30 September 2019. The class was not advised of the purpose of the meeting. However, at least some staff members had been told that:

> many black students" had spoken to one of the class representatives, "expressing their frustration and unhappiness towards the class and how many white students have said violent and racist remarks to them. This is a feeling that has been growing since first year and, as such, we as black students have been feeling very vulnerable and victimized by our fellow students.

The meeting, also attended by at least a dozen academic staff members, opened with a student facilitator from the UCT's

Office of Inclusivity and Change asking the class not to get defensive when they hear something that makes them uncomfortable. "Open your heart to that", he said, "engage empathetically, try and understand and imagine the pain that someone might be experiencing". (He and the other student facilitators left before the end of the meeting, evidently because their presence as facilitators was being ignored by those who organised the meeting.)

A class representative then read a statement, which included the following claims, among others:

- "As black students in this class, our struggles and experiences are constantly being erased", and that since 2017 their "class has been a toxic, violent environment and a hindrance to learning for us black students".
- During tutorials, "black" students' "voices are never heard" and their "explanations will always be second guessed", leading to their feeling "little" and "incompetent, even though we were all accepted into this degree because of our academic prowess".
- The "way our white colleagues speak to us black students is condescending", leading to the latter doubting themselves.
- That "white" students, when interacting with "black" patients, should understand that "raising your voice will not make the patient understand your English".
- "Black lecturers are constantly being disrespected".
- "Black" students "are ignored in the class by the lecturers" who "see the white hands above ours". Tutors "gravitate to the side of the class that has more white students, again cementing that this place is not welcoming to black bodies".

He then shifted from racism to mention "gender, transphobia, homophobia ... [and] fat phobia". He said that "it's really unsettling to be in this space" and asked everybody to be empathetic to those who were going to relate such experiences.

After he spoke, nine further students consecutively took the podium to express themselves. Many spoke about no longer having any confidence in themselves. One related how she "told somebody about something that I did and I thought it was pretty cool, it was quite great", but the person to whom she told this had a look of "shock of disbelief". The student said how hurtful non-verbal cues can be to one's self-esteem. Another student spoke about having been raped.

There is no reason to doubt their sincerity. Some struggled or failed to retain their composure. It was clear that these were young people in great pain. They called on their fellow students to take that pain seriously – to be compassionate.

The irony is that they were failing the very standards they were saying their classmates had failed. For example, one speaker had this to say:

> Even if you can't understand, how can it get to a point where, in the tutorial setting people are crying and within those tears you are seeing them cry, it doesn't make you think that maybe what I said was wrong, something happened that probably was wrong? It doesn't click. How does it not click? And yet you are taught empathy.

He said this after Davida had already been reduced to tears *twice* during the meeting in which she had been repeatedly criticized. A number of students had attributed to her a lack of compassion. Although she was not mentioned by name, it was obvious to the class from the earlier WhatsApp posts, who was being spoken about. Moreover, one speaker at the meeting, looking directly at Davida – who was seated only a few rows from the front – wailed: "Are you human? ... Huh?"

Nor was this the only time they questioned the humanity of those they believed had wronged them. One student related that she had told her mother that she had "never met people as fucked up as this group". "That's literally what I said to her", she told the class. She also mentioned that she calls them "Robocop".

Another student said: "So I want you all to know that whatever you say there are consequences. We can't keep it quiet. It is not our job to do so, and it is not right. But what we will do is hold you accountable to it, and do not – do not – play the victim when we do so."

Scott too was subjected to repeated criticism, mainly around his comments about the aetiology of substance abuse in the Mental Health block. He was criticised by one student for having suggested then that there should be no divisions between "blacks" and "whites". She thought that this was:

> ironic because many of us had to sit there for thirty minutes trying to refute, to show him that he must please understand that when your patient sits there she does not feel equal to you or as strong as you as you are in your white body.

She spoke also of "trying to convince this white man that our struggles are real". She assumed that Scott is "white" – a convenient way to dismiss his alternative perspective. She also assumed that his diligent note-taking during her presentation was a sign of disrespect, rather than the opposite – an effort to engage, not only in the moment but also afterwards, with the concerns being expressed. She rebuked him as follows: "And if you hear only one thing – and will you stop writing and hear my words, just for today – please have compassion."

Other students took issue with his referring to journal articles to support his views. Some joked about this. Others implied that their personal narratives were more authoritative than scientific studies. One suggested that "being human is not something you can look for in a journal".

Scott was also picked out for having written to a class representative in advance of the class meeting to say that the subject of the meeting should be made public so that students could decide whether or not they want to attend. (That email, to which he never received a response, was obviously shared by its recipient with selected others in the class.)

This speaker noted that Scott was sitting silently. She attributed this to his shame, and shortly after noted that he was turning red. Here and in many other times in the meeting there were either peals of laughter from the class or loud applause. One wonders how this fits with this same speaker's admonition that: "I would think that as a human being you would want everybody to feel inclusive, right?"

Immediately after her reference to Scott turning red, she ended her remarks with these words:

> I am smart guys. I run my ass off every single day and I never had anything given to me and I will be the first in my family to finish varsity and become a fucking doctor. An effing doctor! So who the fuck do you think you are to come and tell me I do not belong here. Who?! Who?!

But nobody – certainly not Scott – ever said that she did not belong at medical school. One definitely cannot read that into a fellow student's disagreement with one's view, his citing of academic studies, or his suggestion that people of different races should overcome their differences.

Some staff members, including some of those present, were also subjected to criticism. They, like most of the other staff appear to have been intimidated into silence. At least two staff members endorsed some of the grievances.

Those calling for compassion were showing none. Those declaring themselves victims, told those they were chastising not to "play the victim" – presumably because the former think that the latter are not victims. But this invites the obvious question: How can we determine who a real victim is?

The accusers in this meeting cannot use the subjective standard – according to which you are victim if you think you are – because then those they were scolding would be victims if they took themselves to be victims. At the same time, those doing the scolding were criticising their peers for not simply accepting their own victim narratives. In other words, they wanted to employ the subjective standard for themselves but not for others.

That may work as a political tool. The speakers at this meeting certainly managed to silence their opponents. *Nobody* with an alternative view felt that they could express it in the chilling climate of that class meeting. One staff member explicitly invited non-"black" students to speak, but the only ones who did so were those who bought into the narrative that had been presented to them. However, because something works politically does not mean that it is appropriate.

Anybody can claim to be a victim. It is precisely for that reason that it is not disrespectful to somebody who claims to be a victim to evaluate such claims. Evidence is what enables us to differentiate the real victims from those who mistakenly think that they are victims (and from those who know that they are not victims but cynically claim victim status for the advantages of doing so[4]).

ASSESSING THE GRIEVANCES

What are we to make of the complaints presented at the class meeting? Are "black" students' "voices never heard"? It seems unlikely. They were certainly heard in this meeting and, by their own accounts, they expressed themselves amply in earlier encounters too. Perhaps they are confusing "being heard" with "being agreed with". Alternatively, could it be that they are *often* not heard? If so, are they not heard because they are "black voices" or are they not heard because many people, irrespective of race, are often not heard?

Do "white" students speak in condescending ways to their "black" classmates or is this an inaccurate perception? (For example, it is not necessarily condescending for somebody to respond to one's dogmas about the aetiology of substance abuse with evidence from scientific journals.) If some students *are* condescending, is it a manifestation of racism or simply the fact that that some people are condescending to others, irrespective of their race? If it is racist condescension, how widespread is it?

Are "black" students' views "second guessed" any more than other students'? One student told me that in their "Problem Based Learning" module, they are taught not to take claims at face value but to seek the basis for them. She expressed the frustration of not knowing what was expected of "white" students. If they challenge their "black" fellow students as they challenge their "white" ones, they are liable to accusations of racism. If they do *not* challenge the "black" students but do challenge the "white" ones, then they will be guilty of racism.

Are "black" lecturers disrespected (more often than "white" ones)? Speaking at the class meeting, one of the Xhosa lecturers spoke of being respected on the main campus, but not by *some* students at medical school. Is that racism or is there some other explanation? There are lecturers whom (some) students respect and there are lecturers whom (some) students do not respect. Perhaps some students have less respect for those who teach the non-medical components of the curriculum. That is not an uncommon phenomenon. The organizers of the class meeting could plausibly be criticised for this. When they originally scheduled the meeting, their plan was to cancel only one lecture – bioethics – because *they* had decided, without consulting the lecturer, that that material could be covered in tutorials.

Do tutors gravitate to the side of the class that has more

"white" students? Some tell us that this is so. Other students insist that this is utterly false. Is it true in some cases, but false in others? If so, how often does it happen? How often does the opposite happen?

These are very difficult questions to answer, because we do not have all the necessary evidence. However, there is good reason to doubt that those making the complaints are always correct. This is because those accusations that we *can* evaluate, at least to a significant degree, seem to be instances of gross hypersensitivity and entitlement, as outlined above. If, for example, you feel hurt by somebody's suggestion that the University should not close down because somebody *you* knew was murdered or because *you* were traumatized, and you (and the murder victim, and most of the country) *happen to be* "black", it does not follow that those making the suggestion have created a "space" unsafe for "black bodies".

What explains why intelligent students can feel so earnestly aggrieved even when they have no cause to be? Part of the blame must go to the new climate on campuses in many (but not all) parts of the world, including South Africa. It is a climate of "identity politics", victimology, intolerance, and shaming. However, part of the problem is attributable to the especially toxic climate at UCT,[5] which UCT's leadership has done nothing to counter. Indeed, it reinforces this climate by consistently pandering to the most toxic elements and betraying decent people.

The problem is also reinforced by many of the "humanities" components of the MBChB curriculum. These modules have titles such as "Power, Privilege, and Intersecting Identities" or focus on topics such as race and gender – almost invariably from an orthodox "woke" perspective. The ideas and readings to which the students are exposed is certainly not *diverse*. You will not find a book like this on the reading list: *The Coddling of the American Mind.*[6]

It is thus no surprise that the crybullies kept referring back to such courses. They wondered why some of their classmates had learned nothing from them. (By "learned" they seem to have meant "came to accept the orthodox view".) It is also no surprise that the crybullies' speech and texts are peppered with references to "safe spaces", "trigger warnings", and "womxn", for example.

Some might want to add another (partial) explanation for why the "black" students might feel so victimized. They might say that it is not easy to be a minority. If that explanation has any force elsewhere or in other times, it does not in this case. UCT keeps detailed demographic data on its staff and students (using the bizarre Apartheid-era categories). An inquiry to the relevant office, yielded this information about the 2019 MBChB III class:

> 41.81% of the class is "African" (97 students)
> 21.55% of the class is "Coloured" (50 students)
> 11.64% of the class is "Indian" (27 students)
> 1.72% of the class is "Chinese" (4 students)
> 17.24% of the class is "White" (40 students)
> 6.03% of the class is "Other" (14 students)

In other words, at least 75% of the class is "black" in the expanded South African sense of that term. Only about 17% is "white". There are only thirteen "white" males in the class – the purported apex of privilege.

Earlier this year a class photograph was taken. Immediately thereafter, an informal "black" class photograph, which appeared to have been organised in advance, was taken. (When the photograph was posted online, one student added a note: "The beautiful melanin-popping future doctors".) Clearly not all the "black" students participated, but about 45 of them did. It is not clear whether the photograph was open to all "blacks" in the class or whether it was open only to the "Africans". In other words, it is not clear whether a minority was excluded or whether the largest single demographic was excluding all the others. Either way, it does not seem like a very good example of inclusivity (or diversity, for that matter).

Nobody is denying that some "black" students are disadvantaged. Some (but not others) are poor, for example. This makes life harder, despite the numerous forms of support provided by the University. However, it is not appropriate to read every hardship through the prism of race, or sex, sexuality, or any of the other standard categories.

When you look into the eyes of another human being, you do not know what hardships they have experienced. You do not know whether they suffer from a (physical or mental) chronic illness, whether they have been subjected to sexual or non-sexual assault, whether they have been bereaved, betrayed, or shamed, for example. You do not know their struggles or their torments. You are not entitled to make assumptions about them – one way or the other.

This does not entitle others to behave badly towards one, and it does not preclude one's taking people to task when they do behave badly. However, a narrative of one's own perpetual victimhood is likely to lead to the imputation of the least charitable – and sometimes outrightly vicious – motives and character traits to people who do not deserve to be so characterized. That is unfair to them, but it can also harm oneself. A university that encourages such narratives, as UCT continues to do, is failing everybody.

POSTSCRIPT

A few days after the above was first published on the website *Politicsweb*, the Health Sciences Students Council issued a response.[7] I replied[8] to this response as follows:

The response of the Health Sciences Students Council (HSSC) at the University of Cape Town to my article about bullying in the MBChB III class provides grist for my mill.

The members of the HSSC "reject the notion that black students are 'cry-bullies' for calling out people who victimize and discriminate against them". I too would reject that notion if they really were victimized and discriminated against. However, my article provided *evidence* to show that at least some of the purported instances of victimization and discrimination were nothing of the kind. It is noteworthy that the HSSC provides no evidence to counter my claims or to support their own. They are content with bald assertion of their own preconceived idea.

The HSSC claims that the article "is based on the experiences of just two non-black students". That claim is false. First, if they had read the article properly, they would have noticed that one of the two students to whom they referred has denied that he is "white". Does the HSSC claim to know better? Is it the arbiter of people's own (racial) identities?

Second, my article drew on comprehensive screenshots of comments by many students ("black" and "non-black"), corroborated reports of what transpired in some classes, and on what occurred in the "emergency" class meeting. The vast majority of those who spoke at the latter identified themselves as "black", and their experiences and words were quoted, often verbatim.

The HSSC claims that "[n]ot all interactions between these groups of students are accounted for in the article" but they do not fill in any of the purported gaps. If they had done so with the sort of detail I provided, we could have evaluated those claims too.

The HSSC believes that my "article is deepening the divide among students". This is an HSSC that was silent on the bullying that took place in the class meeting on which I reported. There was apparently no concern then or before about divisions in the class. It thus rings hollow when they say that they "recognize the need to have a safe space for all students to voice their opinions without being silenced and our role as the HSSC in creating that space".

The same goes for its request for "an official public response to the article" from the Faculty of Health Sciences Deanery. The HSSC sought no response from the Deanery to the bullying of a few students, but it seeks an official response to a public reporting of that bullying.

The HSSC response is also dripping with the usual "woke" slogans. For example, they say that "gas-lighting opinions from teaching staff have the potential to create a hostile learning environment for students who have to interact with those lecturers". Like the cry-bullies they are defending, they either don't know what "gas-lighting" is, or they cynically wield that charge to silence alternative views. It is not "gas-lighting" to provide a reasoned argument against an assertion. If it were, then the same would apply, *a fortiori*, to unreasoned responses to reasoned arguments, in which case they would be "gas-lighting" me.

Finally, they provide a "trigger warning" before the link to my article. Evidently the HSSC believes that their fellow students are so delicate that they require a trigger warning before reading an argument for a conclusion with which they might disagree. That is yet more evidence of the narrow-minded climate that currently prevails in the University.

The matter did not end here. As if to prove my point about

the pervasive intolerance and bullying at UCT, there was then an attempt to have me removed from the teaching of bioethics to the medical students on the grounds of my having written the article. I first learned about this when the Interim Dean of Health Sciences sent a request to the Dean of Humanities to deploy somebody else to teach bioethics to the medical students.

It then became apparent that the co-Chairs of the Faculty of Health Sciences Transformation and Equity Committee had written to the Interim Dean, insisting that I be replaced. They acknowledged that I was within my legal rights to express my views, although they mischaracterised my piece as stating that "white students were being victimised when some black students described their experience of exclusion during academic activities". They claimed, however, that my "opinion piece aggravated an already tenuous situation".[9] They then wrote about their (purported) dedication to "developing an institutional culture where all students and staff feel heard and acknowledged for the value they add".

It is hard to know how they wrote that with a straight face, because they then went on to write that "lectures by Prof Benatar to the 3rd and 4th year MBChB classes in 2020, and thereafter, will be counterproductive" because "his presence will not lend itself to a welcoming learning environment". They concluded that they "would not be fulfilling our mandate if we did not insist that Prof Benatar be replaced in his capacity as lecturer of Bioethics in the Faculty of Health Sciences".[10] So much for "developing an institutional culture where all students *and staff* feel heard and acknowledged for the value they add". Obviously if you stand up to bullying you do not add value and, far from being heard, you should be shut down.

If the environment in the Faculty of Health Sciences were not thoroughly toxic, one might be able to expect some leadership from the Interim Dean. She might have explained to those writing to her that there are these concepts called "academic freedom" and "freedom of expression", which just happen to be enshrined in the South African constitution. She would have noted the Faculty's collective failure to protect some students, especially minorities, from being bullied, and she would have told the Faculty Transformation and Equity Committee that their request was entirely inappropriate. That, however, is not what she did.

Instead, she wrote to the Dean of Humanities, asking her to attend to the problem. In her letter, the subject line "Request to find an alternative lecturer for MBChB 3rd and 4th year Ethics teaching",[11] she parroted the narrative of the HSSC and the Faculty Transformation and Equity Committee (TEC). She reported that they had labelled my article "as divisive and as detrimental to the development of good future relationships between different demographics in the class". She claimed that the HSSC and the TEC had "been approached by students from classes taught Ethics by Prof Benatar, requesting a different lecturer to be found to cover these lectures". She justified her writing to the Dean of Humanities by claiming that the teaching of ethics to these classes "is currently managed under a bilateral memorandum of understanding between the two faculties".

In fact, there is no such memorandum. Instead, the Bioethics Centre, of which I am the Director, is jointly located in the Faculty of Health Sciences and in the Department of Philosophy. As Director I co-ordinate (and participate in) bioethics teaching in the MBChB classes. Thus, if the Interim Dean of Health Sciences were to take up this matter with anybody, it should have been with me.

To the credit of the Dean of Humanities, she recognized that it would be highly inappropriate to act as requested. She handed the matter back to the Interim Dean of Health Sciences who, about ten days later (and a few days before she ended her term as Interim Dean), then wrote to me as follows:[12]

As you know, the meeting of the 3ʳᵈ year MBChB class last year exposed a fracture in the class along race lines that was traumatic for the class. Following your opinion piece ('Vindictive Victimhood at UCT') I received two formal complaints where firstly, it was felt that your opinion piece increased the divide in the class and, as such, will negatively affect how students (in this class) interact in the future; and secondly that your opinion piece could potentially create a hostile learning environment for students in your class. As the opinion piece was read by other students, these issues do not only pertain to the 2019 3ʳᵈ year class.

I am asking you consider how you could address narrowing this divide between students, and mitigate the potential hostile learning environment in the class.

I replied as follows:[13]

I am sorry to see that you have uncritically accepted the complaints you have received.

It's not clear to me that the "fracture in the class" is along race lines. One of the two students bullied in that class denies that he is "white". Those laying the complaints to you, seem to believe that they know better. Have we reached the point at UCT where people will be involuntarily reclassified along racial lines?

Moreover, while those complaining may feel that my "opinion piece increased the divide in the class and ... will negatively affect how students ... interact in the future" and that my piece "could potentially create a hostile learning environment for students" in my class, I believe that they are mistaken. The special class meeting (and its preludes) are what created the divide in the class. Staff sat by while students were bullied. I heard no response from the Deanery. All this is in keeping with the prevailing ethos at UCT. The class bullies did not like my calling them on their unacceptable behaviour and so they, and their allies, are now seeking to bully me (via the Deanery). Such behaviour and, worse still, it being indulged by those in leadership positions, can be expected to have a further chilling effect at UCT.

Narrowing the divide between the students is a massive undertaking. It requires, inter alia, intellectually honest discussion. I have started that discussion, but the Faculty will need to continue it. I would be happy to advise if my advice were sought. Intellectual honesty requires careful assessment of claims that people make, and a willingness to arrive at unpopular conclusions if that is where the evidence leads.

Those who have laid the complaints need to understand that while bullying makes an environment hostile, a learning environment is not hostile merely because students or lecturers express a well-reasoned, factually informed view that some people do not like. I have the ability to proceed with my teaching without letting the students' prior behaviour get in the way. I enter the class and treat all students equally, irrespective of whether I agree or disagree with them. If some students lack the maturity to interact decently with a lecturer (or other students) with whom they disagree, they need to learn to do so.

Not long after that Covid-19 hit South Africa. Most bioethics teaching was suspended or replaced with online readings. At the beginning of 2021 most of my Bioethics teaching proceeded without impediment. However, in one of the semesters, the course convener failed to respond to my inquiries about when my teaching had been scheduled. With some further prompting, she eventually replied that the MBChB programme convener had told her that the Faculty of

Health Sciences "would like to teach Bioethics internally".

I wrote to the MBChB convener on 16 February 2021, saying that it was not clear to me what that meant, but that I had my suspicions about what lay behind this development. I said that it would be best if she and I communicated directly about this matter and I asked her what was happening. When I had received no reply by 15 March, I wrote to her again asking for a reply. Again I received no reply, and thus I wrote to the Deputy Dean responsible for Undergraduate Education in the Faculty. She too did not reply. I then wrote to the Dean himself, but he also failed to respond.

On 5 April I lodged a grievance complaint to the Vice-Chancellor against the MBChB Convener, the Deputy Dean, and the Dean. The substance of my complaint was that they had failed to respond to entirely reasonable and collegial inquiries. I said that I had "good reason for believing that the failure to respond to my inquiries is part of an attempt to victimize me for having spoken out against the bullying of some medical students by others", but that I was suspending judgement on that matter for the moment. I sought two outcomes of my complaint:

i.   A prompt response to my inquiry, including communication regarding the dates and times at which the Bioethics teaching is scheduled for Semester 5 of the MBChB programme in 2021.

ii.   A written reassurance that that Faculty of Health Sciences was not seeking to remove me from any of the MBChB Bioethics teaching.

According to UCT's relevant policy, this grievance should have been adjudicated within five business days. That did not happen. After protracted communication, the matter was purportedly brought to a conclusion on 26 April by Deputy Vice-Chancellor Lis Lange, who had been nominated by the Vice-Chancellor to attend to my complaint.

Associate Professor Lange indicated to me that the colleagues in Health Sciences were in the wrong for failing to have responded "timeously" to my emails. (How long must one wait before a failure to reply loses the "timeous" qualification and becomes simply a failure to reply?) She said that the Deputy Dean would communicate with me about the dates and times that my teaching had been scheduled.[14]

Associate Professor Lange said that the second outcome I sought – a written reassurance that the Faculty of Health Sciences was not trying to remove me from Bioethics teaching – could not be provided because the MBChB curriculum was being revised.[15] This is clearly nonsense. I responded that because the inclusion of bioethics in the curriculum was a requirement of the South African Medical and Dental Council, whatever changes might be made to the curriculum, it would have to include bioethics.[16] For that reason, there had to be some *other* reason why the Faculty refused to provide a written reassurance. I said that I suspected that the reason was that they were in fact seeking to remove me from the teaching of bioethics.

At the time of concluding this postscript, it remains to be seen whether there will be an attempt, explicit or disguised, to remove me from Bioethics teaching. Even if that does not happen, the foregoing sends a clear message that those speaking out against (protected) bullies do so at their own peril.

Chapter 17
RACIAL PREFERENCES

Racial preferences seem to be an indelible part of South Africa. They have existed for centuries and reached their legal zenith, which was simultaneously their moral nadir, during the Apartheid period. They did not end with the demise of Apartheid. Instead, they were transformed. The preferences now work in the reverse racial direction. They are now *in favour* of "blacks" rather than against them. This is not to say that the new preferential practices are *as bad* as Apartheid-era racial preferences. However, they are still bad.

In contemporary South Africa (and a growing number of other places), there is widespread recognition that racial preference *against* "blacks" is wrong. However, the view that racial preferences are also wrong when they *favour* "blacks" borders on heresy. It is not easy to defend heresy even when the best arguments support the heretical view. This is because those arguments are not given a fair hearing. Given how much needs to be said to wear down the resistance, I cannot say it all here. I have argued much more extensively elsewhere against racial (and gender) preferences.[1] Here, I present only an outline of such arguments before considering UCT's practices.

THE CASE AGAINST RACIAL PREFERENCES

There are various arguments for the view opposing mine – namely, the view that racial preferences for "blacks" are entirely justified. Perhaps the most compelling of these, at least superficially, is the argument that such preferences are necessary in order to rectify historical injustices and their legacies. It is, of course, very important to rectify injustice. The question, however, is whether preferring some people on the basis of their race is the right way to rectify injustice.

Consider, for example, racial preferences in the context of university admissions. Favouring "black" applicants today will not rectify injustices done to those other people who were excluded from higher education for generations. Admitting one person on the basis of his race does not rectify the injustice to *another* person who, whether directly or indirectly, was excluded on the basis of his race, even if they are both of the same race. (Those who think otherwise should ask themselves whether, when conscription is next necessary, they would support conscripting women rather than men on the grounds that in the past it has almost always been men who have been conscripted.[2])

Of course, there are some contemporary applicants who have been disadvantaged by the consequences of past racial discrimination. "Black" children who have been educated in impoverished schools with inferior resources are the victims of past discrimination which has ongoing effects. There is excellent reason to grant some preference to such students. A school student who obtains 70% in deprived conditions may be as good or better than another child who obtains 80% in privileged conditions (even if the former is not as well prepared as the latter).

However, this is an argument for favouring those who are educationally disadvantaged. It is not an argument for favouring those who are "black". This is because there are some "black" students who are not suffering the legacy of past discrimination. These include applicants whose parents are professionals, or monied, or politically connected. They may have attended the same privileged schools and have the same parental and socio-economic advantages as many "non-black" South Africans. There is no reason to favour *them* in the name of rectifying injustice. (Moreover, those *most* educationally disadvantaged do not meet the basic requirements for university entrance and thus sadly cannot be considered at all.)

A similar point applies to racial preferences in (academic) staff appointments. Even though most of those who suffered educational disadvantage are "black", not all "black" applicants have suffered such disadvantage. Indeed, those being considered for academic positions are those who have received undergraduate and postgraduate degrees and, in virtue of this, are among the least educationally disadvantaged "blacks". If after their tertiary education they are at a point where they can compete on an even footing with other applicants for the same position, then favouring them does not rectify past injustice. If they had been the victims of a past educational injustice, it would already have been rectified. If some "black" candidates are as good or even better than other candidates, as is sometimes the case, one cannot invoke the rectification of injustice argument in order to justify favouring a candidate on the basis of his or her being "black".

Justifying the favouring of "black" candidates on the grounds that this will rectify injustice requires two assumptions: (a) that "black" candidates are weaker, and (b) that this is the result of injustice. One either has to think that this is true of all "black" candidates, or one has to think that we *need* to use being "black" as a proxy for being a less good applicant who has suffered injustice. ("Black" would be a necessary proxy only if we could not possibly determine in other ways whether somebody was less good on account of suffering injustice.) However, there is no good reason to think either of these things.

First, there are "black" candidates who are as good as or better than the other candidates for the same position. There is no reason why they should be favoured on account of their race or on account of being disadvantaged. On other occasions there are "black" candidates (just as there are "white" candidates) who are not as good as their competitors, but this is not the result of injustice. Racial preference to rectify injustice is inappropriate here too.

Second, where a "black" candidate *is* weaker on account of historical injustice there are better indicators of this than the fact that the candidate is "black". (Indeed, it is demeaning to assume that just because a candidate is "black", he or she is a weaker candidate. Operating on this assumption also reinforces rather than undermines stereotypes.) In appointments, selection committees make detailed evaluations and comparisons of individuals. They can make a determination of candidates' relative strengths and whether the differential is attributable to prior disadvantage (such as inferior educational opportunities). Given South Africa's history, we should fully expect there to be many more "blacks" than "whites" who have been disadvantaged, and thus many more "blacks" than "whites" who would benefit from preferential treatment for those who have been disadvantaged. However, expecting that *outcome* is not the same as using race as a *means* for determining which candidates are weaker on account of injustice.

Appointing weaker candidates has costs of various kinds. Those costs may or may not be worth the benefits. However, honest people will be willing to acknowledge when they are hiring a weaker candidate instead of pretending that they are not.

Unlike appointment decisions, undergraduate admission decisions are typically less individualized (at South African universities). However, even in such decisions, race is an inadequate proxy for disadvantage. Much better proxies of relative levels of advantage and disadvantage are factors such as the kind of school one attended, or parental wealth. Utilizing such proxies rather than race would not result in favouring of privileged "black" applicants. It would still result in favouring (mainly) people who are "black", but it would favour them because they are disadvantaged rather than because they are "black", which is surely the point of a policy of preference aimed at rectifying unfair disadvantage. (The policy would also favour those relatively few underprivileged applicants who are "white", but that too would be appropriate for a policy aimed at rectifying unfair disadvantage.)

It is interesting that for many years UCT was resistant to using other proxies for disadvantage in admissions decisions. This changed – or at least there was a pretence that it changed – in the mid 2010s. At that point there seems to have been increasing institutional discomfort at the use of "race" in admission decisions, not least because increasing "numbers of black applicants, often from wealthy families, are coming out of excellent schools with very good National Senior Certificate (NSC) results".[3] In May 2014, UCT Senate supported a policy that put more weight on proxies other than race. Under this policy, some students would still be admitted explicitly on the basis of racial preference, but other purported proxies for disadvantage were introduced. Council subsequently endorsed that policy and it came into effect for admissions for the 2016 academic year.

This was something of an advance, but not as much of an

advance as it might seem. In choosing the proxies for disadvantage, it became clear that at least some of them were actually proxies for "black" rather than proxies for disadvantage. For example, applicants would be counted as disadvantaged if the language spoken by their mother at home was "an indigenous SA [South African] language other than Afrikaans".[4] It is easy to see how one could be disadvantaged if one's mother tongue was not the language of instruction.[5] However, this would apply even if one's mother tongue were not an indigenous South African language other than Afrikaans. By contrast, one's mother's speaking an indigenous South African language (other than Afrikaans) is a very good (albeit not perfect) proxy for "black African". It is not difficult to see what game was being played.

Any policy giving preference to the disadvantaged would disproportionately favour "black" South Africans. That is entirely appropriate, given that "blacks" have been disproportionately disadvantaged. However, that is quite different from favouring "blacks" on the basis of their race or finding proxies for doing the same thing. The *aggregate* outcomes might be the same, but it does not follow that all means to the same aggregate outcome are just. For one thing, by favouring "blacks" rather than the disadvantaged, *advantaged* "blacks" are favoured over *disadvantaged* ones. One admits roughly the same number of "blacks" either way, but *which* ones are admitted differs.

Because the rectification of injustice argument fails to justify racial preferences, other arguments for such preferences are advanced. Most common among such arguments are those that defend the importance of "diversity". Diversity, in turn, is said to be valuable for various reasons. It is said to enhance the pursuit of truth, to undermine stereotypes, and to provide role models, for example.

However, the diversity arguments also run into difficulties

as a way to justify racial preferences, especially the way these are practised in South Africa. Consider, for example, the claim that diversity enhances the pursuit of truth. The idea here is that having different opinions and viewpoints aids the intellectual process of getting closer to the truth of a matter. Instead of an echo chamber, one has a productive clashing of ideas.

There are a number of problems with invoking this argument in support of racial preferences. First, it assumes that opinion (roughly) tracks race. It assumes that "blacks" think differently from "whites". Second, if diversity of opinion is really what one seeks, one would do better to pursue it directly rather than via a proxy such as race. In this regard, the diversity UCT desperately needs is an increase in the number of people with the kinds of views I defend in this book – irrespective of their race. Yet, these are the very sorts of people who are being excluded and silenced. What this suggests is that those defending diversity at UCT are not actually interested in diversity of opinion.

Consider, next, the suggestion that diversity undermines stereotypes. Interacting with people of different races (and sexes, nationalities, religious, and so forth) enables people to see that people from these groups do not conform to stereotypes. Instead, they are individuals with their own constellation of attributes.

There is a significant element of truth to this argument, but it is not clear that it justifies racial preferences, at least as they are practised at UCT and in South Africa more generally. In this country and increasingly elsewhere too, "diversity" really means "proportionality". Those advocating diversity are not seeking mere demographic variation in the student or staff population. Instead, they seek these populations to reflect, proportionally, the national demographics, or at least the working age national demographics. *That* conclusion is not justified by the desirability of breaking down of stereotypes, which requires only samples of different demographics rather than proportional samples.

If one thought that it *did* require proportionality, then one would think, for example, that males ought to be given preference in those disciplines in which they are have always been underrepresented – such as the allied-health professions.[6] It cannot be argued that males are different from "blacks", because the latter but not the former have been the victims of injustice. If for no other reason,[7] this is because the diversity argument (and its role model justification) is distinct from the rectification of injustice argument. If it is good to break down stereotypes by having all "races" proportionally represented, why is not also good to break down stereotypes about males by having them proportionally represented in nursing, physiotherapy, occupational therapy and audiology, for example? The fact that those advancing diversity arguments do not embrace their implications for these other cases[8] strongly suggests that the arguments are rationalizations of pre-existing conclusions and that it is those conclusions rather than the arguments for them that are genuinely believed.

There is a further problem. While diversity can undermine stereotypes, *strong* racial (and gender) preferences can reinforce them. Racial (and gender) preferences can be of varying strengths. They are weakest when race (or sex) serves as a tie-breaker: for example, two job candidates are equally good and then race (or sex) is used to break the tie. Stronger preferences favour marginally less-qualified candidates. Even stronger preferences favour significantly less-qualified candidates. The strongest preferences favour even unqualified candidates.

The stronger the preference required to appoint a particular candidate, the more the preference is likely to *reinforce* rather than undermine stereotypes. This is because those appointed as a result of such strong preferences are likely weaker, on average, than those who were appointed without racial preference and who thus had to meet a higher bar for appointment. I say "on average" because there are obviously cases of "whites" who meet only a lower bar. (The longer that strong preferences against "whites" have been in place, the fewer such cases there are, but there have certainly been cases of inferior "white" candidates being appointed.)

The same point can be made with regard to favouring males in nursing appointments. If one insisted that approximately fifty percent of nurses must be male and one aggressively pursued this outcome by giving strong preference to male candidates, one would find that, given the relatively small pool of male candidates, the average male nurse would be less good than the average female nurse. Thus, if one were *really* interested in undermining stereotypes, one would be opposed to strong racial (and gender) preferences, although one *could* still favour tie-breaking preferences.

UCT has very strong racial preferences. This is not to say that it routinely appoints people who are (entirely) unqualified. There are some such instances, but they are relatively few. Much more common is the appointment of people who are significantly weaker than the strongest competing candidate. The fact that strong preferences are in place does *not* mean that *every* "black" appointed is significantly weaker – or even weaker at all – than the strongest competing candidate. Where a "black" candidate is the strongest candidate in the pool, the racial preference is moot. Where a "black" candidate is only marginally weaker than the best competing candidate then the full extent of the racial preference is not necessary.

There is no way to determine precisely how often strong preferences are determining appointments at UCT. However, there is good reason to think that it is at least quite often. After all, there are quite a few cases, as I argue below and in other chapters, in which non-"black" candidates are not considered *at all*. Perhaps some of those ("black") people who are appointed under such circumstances would have been appointed even in open competition. In those cases, one does not help them by not having measured them against the competition. Such practices reinforce rather than undermine stereotypes.

A third argument for the importance of diversity is that it produces role models. The idea here is that "black" students will be empowered if they see "black" role models among their lecturers. There is certainly value in role models. The question is whether this value is sufficient to justify strong racial preferences. There are a few reasons to think that it does not.

First, it is not clear why role models have to share one's race (or sex, or nationality, or religion and so forth). Many people have had role models who do not share these characteristics with them. If one identifies people one admires,[9] one can aspire to be like them even if they do not *look* like oneself.

Second, while role models do have value, it is not clear how *much* difference they make. If one is sufficiently educationally deprived, role models will not magically compensate for that. If, by contrast, one is educationally competitive, it is unclear why one needs a role model (of the same race) in order to succeed. There have been plenty of examples of such success in the absence of demographically similar role models.[10]

Third, even if role models of the same race were necessary, such role models could be provided through diversity, in its more literal sense, rather than through proportionality. Finally, if strong racial preferences are used in hiring, the "role models" are less likely to be the best role models (for the reasons considered in evaluating the "destruction of stereotypes" argument). It is better to have fewer and better role models than to have more role models who are not worth modelling oneself after.

The arguments for racial preferences fail to justify the policies and practices that they purport to justify. Racial preferences are problematic for other reasons too.

First, systems of racial patronage (as well as some other forms of patronage) are bad for the countries that practise them. That was true of South Africa during the Apartheid era and it is also true of South Africa in the post-Apartheid era. South Africa is on a steep descent. Much of this (even though not all) is ultimately attributable to racial (and political) patronage. A country pays a price when people are appointed to positions based not on merit but rather on the basis of their racial or political connections.

Systems can tolerate a certain degree of this, because other parts of the system can compensate. However, when the patronage is as widespread as it is in South Africa, systems begin to break. That has been happening throughout South Africa. (We have a vivid example of this every time Eskom, the national power provider, "load-sheds" – a euphemism for fails – with massive implications for the economy and therefore for all South Africans, especially the poorest.) Some people may be in denial about this, but that does not make it any less true. The cumulative effects of appointing weaker academics in the humanities, for example, might be less obvious than the cumulative effects of hiring practices at Eskom, but they are no less real.

Second, the use of racial categories is absurd. People exist on a continuum of phenotypic features, not in discrete categories. There are plenty of fuzzy boundaries between so-called "Africans", "Coloureds", "Indians" and "whites". The Apartheid regime resorted to bizarre racial tests to assign people to different categories. Fortunately, the state no longer decides one's race. However, a policy of racial preference requires individual citizens to do the state's dirty work for it by self-classifying. This preserves the Apartheid mindset.

However, self-classification is often not accepted. There are instances where the purveyors of identity politics deem their own classification of somebody to be superior to that person's self-classification. Sometimes they do so even over the protestations of the person. We saw an example of that in Chapter 16, but there are others. I know of at least one staff member who was classified by the University as "white" even though he repeatedly asked not to be classified at all. Eventually he was listed as being of undeclared or unknown race, but it took some effort. Most staff and students, however, like most citizens more generally, are complicit in the perpetuation of these categories. The entire system would collapse if enough people rejected the Apartheid categories and refused to classify themselves.

Curiously, UCT's Council once rejected a proposal that people be assigned to racial categories on the basis of how they or their parents were classified by the Apartheid regime. It opted instead for self-classification, but then said that there would be serious repercussions for those "misclassifying" themselves! Clearly Council did not understand that if self-classification is the criterion, there can be no misclassification of oneself. One is what one says one is. To think that misclassification of oneself is possible, Council would have to believe that there are criteria independent of self-classification. Yet, it was understandably coy about stating those criteria.

The preservation of racial categories is not only absurd. It is also dangerous. If one keeps these categories alive, they could have very nasty and possibly even bloody consequences. There has been plenty of racially incendiary rhetoric from ANC and EFF politicians, as well as within UCT. This has not been good for the country or the University. It may still make the situation even worse.

RACIAL PREFERENCES AT UCT

South Africa has what has been described as the "world's most extreme affirmative action program".[11] It is so extreme that much of it would constitute illegal discrimination in other countries. What is rarely noticed, because it is kept well hidden, is that UCT exercises racial preferences that may possibly exceed legal permissibility even within South Africa. It is hard to know for sure whether some of UCT's practices are illegal until such a case is tried in the courts. Either way, it should become clear in what follows that at least some of the practices are dishonest (and also unfair).[12]

For years, advertisements for academic jobs at UCT included one of three possible "equity statements":

1. UCT is committed to the pursuit of excellence, diversity and redress in achieving its equity targets. Our Employment Equity Policy is available at www.uct.ac.za/downloads/uct.ac.za/about/policies/eepo licy.pdf
2. UCT is committed to the pursuit of excellence, diversity and redress in achieving its equity targets. Our Employment Equity Policy is available at www.uct.ac.za/downloads/uct.ac.za/about/policies/eepo licy.pdf. For this post we seek particularly to attract...... (target group) candidates.
3. UCT is committed to the pursuit of excellence, diversity and redress in achieving its equity targets. Our Employment Equity Policy is available at www.uct.ac.za/downloads/uct.ac.za/about/policies/eepo licy.pdf. Special funding has been provided for this post with the aim of advancing diversity, and for this post we seek particularly to attract.........(specify target group) candidates.

Selection committees had to decide, depending on the circumstances and conditions, which of these statements to include. In some circumstances, they were required to choose one particular statement. What should be clear is that these statements are not unambiguous and are thus prone to variable interpretation. Perhaps that was the plan. It is certainly the case that the statements have been interpreted in different ways.

The first possible statement is widely seen as the most flexible, even though it too gives preference to some candidates. At least sometimes the second possible statement has been understood as giving preference to candidates from the specified target group while still considering candidates from other groups. It has been understood this way both by applicants and by selection committees. We know the former because applicants who are not members of the "designated groups" have nonetheless applied for positions that include the second statement.

There is also good evidence that at least some selection committees have also interpreted this statement in this way. For example, on one occasion when the second equity statement was used, one member of the committee suggested that it be clarified with the addition of the words "but all applications will be seriously considered". This suggestion was rejected by the Chair of the committee who claimed that it did not need to be said because it was already implicit. Implicit or not, it made no difference. Under the Chair's direction, the committee then considered and interviewed only one candidate – a "black" candidate", who was then appointed. They did not even consider or interview any of the excellent non-"black" candidates.

In other cases, candidates who are not from "designated groups" have been strung along instead of immediately being told that they were not eligible for consideration. It is hard to understand why that would have happened if the selection committee had thought that the post was open only to "black" South Africans.

However, there have been many instances in which the following *modus operandi* has been in effect. A committee is instructed to use the second equity statement, with the "designated group" being "Black South Africans". The committee is then told that in shortlisting candidates it may not rank any "white" candidate, no matter how superb, higher than a "B" (in a taxonomy consisting of "A", "B", and "C" candidates). The shortlist of candidates for interview is then constructed from the list of candidates graded "A". If at least one of the A candidates is found to be "appointable" then an appointment is made. However, if none of those initially graded as "A" prove appointable, then the "B" list is *not* considered. Instead, the position is re-advertised.

In other words, "white" candidates were not genuinely considered, but were also not told that they were not considered. Under this *modus operandi*, no "white" candidate can be appointed, no matter how good he or she may be, and irrespective of whether there is *any* appointable "black" South African candidate. Yet, "white" candidates would sometimes be told, in the midst of the process, that it had been delayed, thereby reinforcing the impression that they were being considered.

It is one thing to say upfront that one is considering only "black" South Africans. It is quite another to pretend that all candidates are being considered while actually excluding some candidates on the basis of their purported race. The latter may possibly be illegal, even in South Africa.[13] If it is not, it should be.

Given the ambiguity and variable interpretation of the three equity statements, I sought some clarity on what the intended differences between them was. I put this question to UCT's Staff Recruitment Office, the office that coordinates and oversees all appointments. At first, I received no reply to my inquiry. When I asked again, my inquiry was forwarded to the Employment Equity office which, I was told "would be best placed" to answer my question. I found that curious. The Staff Recruitment Office works with these statements for every single appointment. How could they not know what the statements mean and what their practical implications were for which candidates may and may not be considered?

The Employment Equity office also did not respond immediately to my inquiry. After they were prompted I received a non-answer. Instead of telling me how the three statements were meant to differ, I was told what they had in common. I pointed that out to the relevant person in the Employment Equity office, asking again what the *differences* were. I received no answer. Thus, I put my question to the University Executive under a Senate agenda item allowing members of Senate to pose questions to the Executive.

Deputy Vice-Chancellor Professor Loretta Feris's response did not dispel all the ambiguity. For example, she had this to say about the second possible equity statement:

> This statement does not prevent anyone from applying and does not prevent the selection committee from appointing someone that is not from the designated groups. But it commits the selection committee to adopt a process that will allow it to meet the target of the Faculty of Department. It thus allows the committee to express a preference in line with the EE [Employment Equity] targets in the EE Plan and to make an appointment in line with that preference.[14]

Does this mean that all candidates *may* be considered but preference should be given to applicants from "designated groups"? Or does it mean that all candidates *must* be considered but that preference should be given to applicants from "designated groups"?

Professor Feris concluded her answer to my Senate questions by acknowledging that there had been "inconsistent practice across the university in respect of how these sentences are used" and that the relevant people were "currently developing a practice note that will provide guidance on how to use these EE sentences".[15]

Ambiguity in the equity statements has not been the only means by which selection committees have decided that no appointment is better than a "white" appointment. Sometimes this is done in a less programmatic way. Sometimes there is no formal bar to appointing a "white" candidate, but the committee simply passes up the opportunity to appoint an excellent "white" candidate even though there are no other appointable candidates, with the result that no appointment is made.

Although South African employment equity legislation does not treat non-South African "blacks" as a designated group, they are *de facto* often given preference over South African "whites" at UCT.[16] It is not uncommon in other countries for citizens to be prioritized over non-citizens in hiring decisions. Canada is one country that does this. At UCT, some non-citizens are actively favoured over some citizens.

On many other occasions a "white" applicant is passed over in favour of a much weaker applicant from a designated group. In one department, for example, an excellent "white" female candidate with a PhD, a number of publications and a book deal was not appointed. The selection committee appointed a "black" female without a PhD. It was stipulated that she would need to complete her PhD within three years. That deadline has come and gone, and, at the time of writing, she still did not have a PhD.

One academic expressed his frustration that top "white" students are never going to get jobs at UCT or in South Africa. "One knows that one is training them for abroad, while those who are hired are nowhere nearly as good". Of course, this is not true in every instance. Many excellent "black" candidates are appointed. However, when one has a system of explicit and weighty preferences, sometimes with rigged processes, it is inevitable that many of those appointed from favoured demographics are going to be much weaker than some of those who could have been appointed. That has implications not only for those appointed and those passed over, but also for students and for the University as a whole. This is especially so when affirmative action favours not a minority but rather a majority, as is the case in South Africa.

This is *not* a reflection on "black" ability. It's a function of how strong demographic preferences work, especially against the background realities of South Africa. (There would be the same effect if "whites" had been an oppressed majority in South Africa and then there were aggressive preferences in their favour.) The more weight one attaches to race or to sex or some other demographic variable, the proportionally less weight one attaches to other considerations, such as academic qualifications (and the absence of psychopathology). That is basic mathematics.

RACIAL PREFERENCES BECOME STRONGER

As of February 2021 a new Employment Equity policy has been in place at UCT. It is replete with "double-speak". For example, it acknowledges that "an employment policy can come across as simply a tick box compliance exercise. Especially when it utilizes the offensive racial and ethnic designations that characterised the apartheid system".[17] However, it continues, "not using these designations makes it very difficult to track the progress that is being made to undo the skewed racial profile of UCT's staff composition".[18] Yet, it is clear that the use of racial categories is not being used merely to "track the progress". They are being used to engineer particular racial outcomes. That use seems incompatible with another claim made by the policy namely that "using these designations does not mean an endorsement of them".[19]

According to the policy,[20] in keeping with South Africa's Employment Equity Act,[21] a "suitably qualified" candidate includes somebody with the "capacity to acquire, within a reasonable time, the ability to do the job". In other words, "suitably qualified" candidates include those who do not *currently* have the ability to do the job. Similarly, both the UCT policy and the Employment Equity Act stipulate that when "determining whether a person is suitably qualified for a job, …. an employer may not unfairly discriminate against a person solely on the grounds of that person's lack of relevant experience".[22] Such a provision can have far reaching implications. For example, a candidate for a deanship cannot be excluded on account of not having had any lower level administrative experience.

UCT's Employment Equity policy repeatedly refers to an attached "HR Practice Note" which, it says, must be adhered to. That Practice Note is, at least at the time of writing, still not attached to the policy. Moreover, unlike the policy, which went through a formal approval procedure, the Practice Note does not seem to have gone through the appropriate approval procedures before it was put into practice. For example, it was not attached to the policy when the policy was put to the University Senate for approval.[23] None of the Senators present at the meeting inquired about the Practice Note before they approved the policy *nem con.*[24] Yet the Practice Note is even more extreme than the Employment Equity Policy.

In May 2021, three and a half months after the Practice Note was introduced, it was suddenly suspended.[25] The relevant notice reported that it would be suspended for three months and that this decision followed "feedback from various faculties".[26] No further details were provided. It was thus initially difficult to determine which of the many problems with the document may have prompted the re-think. However, the re-think did not take the expected three months. Two *weeks* later, a revised Practice Note was distributed.[27] It contained almost all the problems of the earlier version, only avoiding a feature most easily open to legal challenge.[28] The revised version, like the first version, did not go through the usual approval processes.

The Practice Note stipulates that job advertisements should include a heading "requirements for the job" rather than "minimum requirements" in order "to ensure that people from the "designated groups" are not prohibited from applying for positions purely because they do not meet the minimum requirements".[29] This seems like a distinction without a difference. If something is a job requirement then it is, by definition, required. It is a (minimum) condition one must meet. However, even if one thought that there were a difference between a "job requirement" and a "minimum requirement", UCT would seem committed to the alarming view that people from "designated groups" are not ineligible to apply for positions even if they do not meet the job requirements.

The Practice Note also dispenses with the distinction between the three "equity statements" that I described. There is now only a single such statement:[30]

> UCT is a designated employer and is committed to the pursuit of excellence, diversity, and redress in achieving its equity targets in accordance with the Employment Equity Plan of the University and its Employment Equity goals and targets. Preference will be given to candidates from the under-represented designated groups. Our Employment Equity Policy is available at
> www.uct.ac.za/downloads/uct.ac.za/about/policies/eepolicy.pdf.

That statement is a misleading description of the process that the Practice Note then prescribes. It lays down a process that could have either one or two phases. The two phase process applies in situations in which the "identified and approved numerical goals and targets in a specific Occupational Level in the Faculty or PASS[31] Department have not been achieved".[32] It is somewhat inaccurate to describe this as a two-phase process, because in many instances, the process will not proceed beyond the first phase – because an appointment will be made in the first phase. In that first phase, candidates must be graded in the following way:[33]

A Applicants meeting **all** requirements as per the position advertisement, **and** matching Employment Equity targets for demographically under-represented employees at that specific occupational level.

B Applicants meeting **some** (not all) requirements as per the position advertisement, being applicants from a Designated Group who may be suitable qualified for the position in line with the provisions of (Section 20 (3) and (4) of the EEA.) *(Only Designated Groups can benefit from affirmative action measures as outlined in the provisions of section 20 (3) and (4) of the EEA.)*

C Applicants meeting **all** the requirements as per the position advertisement but who **do not** fall within the under-represented employees within the relevant Occupational Level as agreed in the Search Meeting.

D Applicants who **do not meet all or most** of the requirements as per the position advertisement.

The Practice Note says that only candidates from under-represented groups – candidates in categories A and B – may be shortlisted and interviewed.[34] If the first phase fails to produce a "suitable" candidate (from the designated group) then:

a) "communication may be sent to applicants indicating that the recruitment process has failed to find candidates suitably qualified for the job in keeping with the employment equity targets";[35]
b) there is a second phase in which category C candidates may also be considered, but in which preference will still be given to candidates from designated categories.

Indeed, the Practice Note states that the "Selection Committee may decide to invite only candidates from the under-represented employees for interview, and then only embark on a second round of interviews that would include candidates who fall outside of the under-represented employees".

It is hard to know whether those formulating the Practice Note had thought through the implications of the above. The second phase only occurs if *none* of the A and B candidates are thought to be suitable. Why would one then continue to consider and, *a fortiori*, to give preference to candidates one has just deemed unsuitable for appointment? Moreover, why would candidates be informed that the selection committee had failed to find a suitably qualified candidate from the designated group if the committee was continuing to consider candidates from designated categories. The Practice Note seems incoherent.

The Practice Note claims that the "assessment of the suitability of a candidate must consider the applicant against the position, and not against other candidates".[36]

Among the implications of the above processes are:

i.   Candidates who are not from "designated groups", no matter how superb they may be, and no matter how much better they may be than other candidates, cannot be ranked higher than C.

ii.   Candidates who are not from "designated groups", cannot be appointed in the first phase. They may not even be shortlisted or interviewed then. In this sense, there is an "absolute barrier" to their being appointed. The barrier is lifted only *if* the process extends into a second phase.

iii.   Even in a second phase, preference must be given to candidates from designated groups who meet the job requirements, even if other candidates are *much* better.

The racial preference is somewhat less extreme in the

titular "one phase" process, but this process applies when "identified numerical goals and targets in a specific Occupational Level have been met"[37] which, for the foreseeable future, will likely be only rarely. In such situations, candidates who are not from designated categories may also be considered in the first (and only) phase. However, those candidates may be considered only if they meet *all* the requirements for the position, whereas candidates from designated categories may also be considered if they meet only some of the requirements of the position as advertised.[38]

With very few exceptions, the response to the extreme racial preferences practised at UCT is a conspiracy of silence. Most academics will not speak out about rigged hiring practices. *A fortiori*, they will not speak out about weighty preferences that are clearly legally permissible. These preferences are socially acceptable. Criticizing them is not.[39] That results in widespread compliance and complicity. When significantly inferior candidates are appointed, as is often the case, there is a pretence that they are not inferior. Anybody who does not participate in this pretence is quickly condemned as hostile to transformation – an effective way of encouraging their or others' future silence. Given the scale of this subterfuge, both at UCT and in South Africa more generally, the adverse effects are monumental – and can be expected to become worse.

Chapter 18

SELECTING A DEAN: RACISTS V RACIST XENOPHOBES

It is not unusual for decanal appointments anywhere in the world to be suffused with university (and sometimes national) politics. However, the Humanities Faculty at the University of Cape Town is in a class of its own. The faltering process, punctuated with stops and starts, and managed incompetently, lasted over three years. It pitted (ordinary) racists against racist xenophobes, with one of the latter going so far as to disrupt a voting process by destroying ballot boxes and ballots. Their only common cause was that the new dean should not be "white": "better no dean than a pale one" seemed to be the guiding principle. Before the process had even begun, the climate in the Faculty (and the University) had already been so polluted, that anybody entertaining the idea that the Faculty should seek the best dean possible, irrespective of that person's race, sex, or national origin, had already been silenced.

THE FAT YEARS AND THE LEAN YEARS

For close on a decade until 2013, the Humanities Faculty had thrived under the deanship of Professor Paula Ensor. As with any leader, she had some detractors, but by any objective measure the Faculty flourished under her leadership. She devoted herself to her role, had her finger on the pulse of the Faculty, listened to (and did not demonize) those (including me, on many occasions) who disagreed with her, and nurtured a faculty administration that *worked*.

As she approached the end of her second term, the process for selecting a successor dean began. The best candidate was Professor David Attwell, a South African with an international reputation for his research. He had taught at three South African universities (including three years as Head of Department in each of two of them), before moving to the University of York in the United Kingdom. At the time that he was being considered for the deanship in the Humanities Faculty at UCT, he had completed a successful five-year term as Head of the Department of English and Related Literature, and had commenced a second term.

He was considered alongside a candidate who, there is good reason to believe, would not have been shortlisted had it not been for the very explicit and very aggressive racial preferences that have come to characterize appointment processes at UCT. This candidate had been an active researcher but had published largely, although not exclusively, in local publications. He did *not* have a proven track record in lower level administrative positions, which should be a requirement for a decanal appointment. He had served as head of department at another South African university for only one year. Some years later he was acting head of department in another South African university for six months. At the time of his application he had been a vice-dean for three months. There were other weaknesses in his candidacy too, but I shall remain silent here on these more personal issues that are also harder to prove.

The selection committee deemed both candidates appointable but proposed that the latter be offered the position (first). Professor Attwell was presented to the Faculty Board as a second candidate in the event that the first candidate either did not enjoy the support of the Faculty or decided not to take up the position.

At the Faculty Board meeting at which this proposal was discussed and put to the vote, I said, among other things, that given his track record of flitting from position to position, the selection committee's preferred candidate was unlikely to remain in the deanship very long. For this, I was – of course – accused of racism. That is how dissenters are either silenced or punished for not being silent.

This candidate was appointed and served three years – two years short of the initial five year term – before leaving, at three months' notice, for a yet more senior administrative position elsewhere in South Africa. (Curiously, academics at UCT are required to give six months' notice, but senior administrators, such as deans, are only required to give three months' notice, which says something about how readily the University can afford to lose somebody in these respective roles.)

In the three years that this dean spent at UCT, he transformed an extremely well-functioning faculty into a highly dysfunctional one. By the time he left, the academic administration was in a shambles and had begun haemorrhaging staff. The Faculty and individual academic departments within it, were riven. A number of heads of departments had resigned their headships under his regime. One department was functioning without an internal head of department and another had no head of department at all. The outgoing dean left with an open disciplinary complaint against him (not lodged by me!) – a complaint the University Executive had failed to act upon. While he evaded justice, he inflicted injustice on others. Just one of many examples: he suspended an academic (who was not the person who laid the aforementioned disciplinary complaint) on the basis of spurious allegations. An internal procedure overturned his precipitous decision, but the deleterious effects on the academic concerned were significant and lasting.

Not everybody in the Faculty was unhappy with his deanship. The Black Academic Caucus (BAC), for example, found an ally in him, and was an ally to him. Both engaged in the same racial and ideological politics, including aiding and abetting those students who engaged in the criminal behaviour that shut down the University for extended periods in 2015 and 2016. (Ironically, this dean had previously himself been involved, when he was a student, in shutting down Conor Cruise O'Brien's visit to UCT in 1986.[1] Thirty years later he was protecting a new generation of protestors.)

THE TORTUOUS PROCESS BEGINS

Supporters of the outgoing dean seemed to become jittery after he tendered his resignation in November 2016. They appeared to be concerned about losing the ground they had gained during his tenure. They called for an urgent Faculty Board Meeting, saying that "given the particular path of transformation that the faculty has embarked on" under the outgoing dean, "we believe that it is imperative that as a faculty, we are able to participate in setting the parameters for the appointment of any interim and incoming Dean."[2]

This request may have arisen from ignorance because there are very clear procedures for appointing a new dean, and these include constituting a selection committee that includes people elected from various sectors of the Faculty – professorial, non-professorial, administrative, students and "representatives of the faculty's Transformation Committee".[3] This was explained to them at the Special Faculty Board meeting on 22 November 2016. The process for appointing a new dean began. The selection committee was assembled and it met for the first time on 25 January 2017.

It is the Vice-Chancellor's prerogative to appoint an *interim* or *acting* dean, after consultation with the Dean's Advisory Committee (which is constituted mainly by heads of departments, along with deputy deans and a few others). In early 2017 Vice-Chancellor Dr Max Price appointed Associate Professor Harry Garuba, from the Centre for African Studies, who reluctantly agreed to take on the position for the remainder of that year.

At a Special Faculty Board meeting held on 13 July 2017, Dr Price reported on the selection process. The committee had decided that a "Black South African" candidate would be the first preference, and failing that another "equity candidate from the designated groups". (In some documentation this was interpreted as "other black equity groups".)

The selection committee had undertaken two rounds of search. In the first round, the committee identified four potential "black South African" candidates. The Chair of the selection committee contacted them and brought the advertisement to their attention, but none of them applied.

The first round yielded eleven candidates, of whom four were "black equity candidates". Only three candidates were thought to meet the minimum requirements of the position – "an International (Coloured) female, a Coloured male and a White male". (Yes, this is how the race-obsessed apparatchiks talk about applicants.)

Because the selection committee thought that this shortlist was "unsatisfactory and particularly weak with designated group candidates", a second round of recruitment was initiated. Professional "head-hunters" were engaged, but they failed to produce any applicants. There was a new application from a "white South African male". The committee agreed that this was a very strong application but was concerned about "employment equity" and whether "the targeted search was broad enough".

A sub-committee was formed "to conduct an extensive search of African and black candidates in South African institutions and Humanities departments". This yielded a list of 43 candidates that met the racial criterion. After an initial grading, ten of those were contacted and asked to apply. Nine of those were "black South Africans" and one was an "International Black". (The latter would satisfy the racists but not the racist xenophobes.) Only two of these ten candidates applied. In the course of the second round an "International black female" applicant withdrew her application.

The committee met to consider the new pool of applicants and decided to shortlist only two candidates – one "International Black male" and one "South African White male". The two candidates were interviewed, and also made presentations to the Faculty. Members of the Faculty provided feedback on these presentations to the selection committee.

Three members of the committee wanted to delay making a decision, while eleven wanted to make a decision. Moving to a second vote, eleven members of the committee voted for the candidacy of Professor David Attwell, while two opposed and one abstained. The selection committee thus presented Professor Attwell's candidacy to the Faculty Board for approval.

This is the same Professor Attwell who had been passed over for the deanship in 2013. The selection committee's proposal was discussed. Many members of the Faculty Board opposed Professor Attwell's appointment on the grounds of his "race", despite all the efforts that had been made by the racially diverse selection committee to identify a suitable "Black South African" candidate. When the matter was put to a vote, only 54% of members supported his appointment as Dean. This fell short of the required 60%, requiring the selection committee to reconvene.

It is noteworthy that when Professor Attwell had been considered in 2013 he had received support from over 70% of the Faculty Board. The fact that four years later he received support from only 54% is not attributable to any negative change in the candidate. Instead, it reflects either a change in membership of the Faculty Board (through retirements, resignations and new appointments) or a marked change in the climate of the Faculty and its tolerance for a "non-Black" dean, or a combination of the two.

It was then decided to put the process on hold because re-opening the search at that point would be unlikely to yield any further candidates. Professor David Wardle, a long-standing deputy dean, succeeded Harry Garuba as Interim Dean in early December 2017. To render this appointment more acceptable, at least two and possibly three of the proposed deputy deans were members of the Black Academic Caucus. (The uncertainty of the number results from its membership list not having been made public.) The proposed deputy deans were subject to a vetting process in which members of the Faculty were asked to indicate, via a poll, whether or not they would support each of the candidates. All four nominees were appointed.

When I asked, via a Faculty Board meeting, for the results of this poll to be made public, an evasive answer was provided, but the Faculty was assured that "[a]ll of the candidates received levels of support that justified their ... appointment as Deputy Deans". I then requested the information from the Registrar, under the Protection of Access to Information Act, and learned that one of the candidates, a BAC member and deeply divisive figure in the Faculty, had obtained only 49% support. The other nominees had received, respectively, 60%, 71% and 80% support. Forty-nine percent is ordinarily a failing grade, but evidently not in this case. Through a subsequent Faculty Board meeting, I put a follow-up question to the Interim Dean:

> I realise that the official procedures do not stipulate a minimum level of support required for the appointment of a deputy dean. However, Faculty Board draft minutes for the 13 March 2018 meeting, report the Interim Dean as saying that all the candidates "received levels of support that justified their candidacy and appointment as Deputy Deans". What are the levels of support that justify the appointment of a candidate as a deputy dean?

The minutes record the following "answer":

> The Dean answered the question, noting there were no rules prescribing the level of support required for the appointment of Deputy Deans and that it was thus a matter for the Dean's judgment. He had consulted with the Faculty Executive, which supported the appointments, deeming the level of support to be sufficient in the particular circumstances of this process.

BUMBLING

A new selection committee to appoint a permanent dean was constituted. It struggled to find suitable "blacks" who were willing to be nominated. Professor Mamokgethi Phakeng, the new Vice-Chancellor, who succeeded Max Price and was now chairing the committee, had asked a number of people whether they would apply, but they had refused.

Selection committees at UCT are required to include Employment Equity representatives, who are tasked with ensuring that the "employment equity" agenda is advanced. The two representatives on this committee were effectively excluding "white" candidates, none of whom were seriously considered. Another member of the committee concluded, quite reasonably, that the committee was only considering "equity candidates" and expressed this. The Vice-Chancellor expressed her dislike for that terminology, and preferred to say that they wanted to appoint people from particular "groups".

In other words, even though the *equity* representatives had just indicated the demographic attributes of the preferred candidate, the committee was now being asked not to refer to the preferred demographic as an equity demographic. There was a resistance to referring to the position as an "equity post". In other words, members of the committee were being discouraged from accurately describing what was transpiring. This suggests a desire to have strong racial preference and to hide it too.

The committee found only one suitable candidate – namely Professor Rose Boswell, who was then Executive Dean of Arts at Nelson Mandela University, a position she had held since 2015. She had previously been a Deputy Dean and Acting Dean of Humanities at Rhodes University. However, there seems to have been some reluctance to shortlist only one candidate. The Vice-Chancellor, looking around the room, then asked one of the members of the committee whether he would do her the honour of standing for the position.

This request was entirely irregular, as should have been obvious. The policy for appointment of deans *explicitly* says that "No member of the selection committee may apply for, or accept nominations for the position of Dean".[4] This did not stop the committee from shortlisting this person, who had now quickly switched from committee member to candidate.

The two short-listed candidates were scheduled to give presentations to the Faculty on 21 September 2018. Less than forty-eight hours before the presentations were due to take place, the Faculty was notified that the process was being suspended "following a procedural error". Details of the error were not provided, perhaps because such a disclosure would have been deeply embarrassing. It is difficult to understand how this error escaped the attention of the committee, its chair, equity representatives, and staff recruitment advisor, for as long as it did. Similarly difficult to understand is why the process was suspended in order to add a candidate who, as a deputy dean candidate, had obtained support from only 49% of the Faculty. Could it be that the single-minded fixation on the race of candidates led everybody involved to lose sight of all other considerations?

DECOLONIZING DEMOCRACY

A new selection committee was constituted, following the usual processes. First, various sectors of the Faculty (professorial, non-professorial, and administrative) were invited to nominate (including self-nominate) representatives to serve on the selection committee. Because nominations exceeded the eight slots, elections were held to elect representatives. The balance of the committee consisted of a further eleven people – the Vice-Chancellor, a deputy vice-chancellor, a dean from another Faculty, two Faculty Employment Equity representatives, two student representatives, two members of Council and two members "to provide balance to the composition of the committee". (The "balance" is always with regard to "race" and "sex", never "opinion", which is often heavily unbalanced towards the institutional orthodoxy.) Of the eighteen people on the full committee, the Vice-Chancellor reported much later, six were "Black South Africans", four were "Indian and Coloured" South Africans, and two were foreign nationals, including some who were "black African". Six were "white people".[5]

After the Faculty nominations and elections, one member of the Faculty, Dr Lwazi Lushaba, objected on 1 November 2018[6] to the composition of that component of the committee – namely the component elected by the Faculty. Dr Lushaba is flagrantly racist, but because his racial animosity is directed to the melanin-deprived, his racism is indulged. It is Dr Lushaba who told his students that "blacks" and "whites" cannot be friends and then set an examination question in which he asked students to "specify the reasons for the impossibility" of such friendships.[7] He is also the one who complained about the abundance of "white female" postgraduate students in his department. He has made a string of hateful remarks, including referring to "our enemies, white people" in a speech on campus on 31 May 2017.

Dr Lushaba's objection to the component of the selection committee elected by the Faculty is that it contained "not a single black South African". It is far from clear that that claim was true. The challenge for those of us who are not obsessed with the "race" (and nationality) of everybody we encounter, and who consequently lack the "expertise" to make flash racial (and national) classifications is that we cannot evaluate the claims of those who do. The latter are also inclined to use the phrase "black" in varying ways, depending on what suits them. Sometimes it is used narrowly to refer only to so-called "African blacks" and sometimes it is used broadly to refer to any "person of colour".

As I was unable to determine whether Dr Lushaba's claim was true, I decided to ask UCT, which obsessively records the "race" and other demographic information about all staff and students. Curiously, UCT proved very unwilling to answer this question. I first put the inquiry to Human Resources in the Humanities Faculty. They forwarded the question to the Staff Recruitment Office, which wanted to know in what capacity I was asking for that information. After some time, the question was referred to the Humanities Faculty Manager, who said that I should instead ask the Registrar. It would be an understatement to say that the Registrar was evasive.[8]

When Dr Lushaba objected to the composition of the Faculty's contribution to the selection committee, he indicated that instead of any legal challenge, "we shall protest, disrupt the interview process and ensure through political activism that the process does not proceed".[9] He later delivered on (only) part of that threat.

In his usual hyperbolic fashion, he added that the Faculty "may do well to start summoning state violence to come and shoot us as you always do when black people protest". "Death", he said", is better than being consigned into nothingness whilst alive". He signed his screed "I Remains, Cde Lwazi Lushaba" (sic).[10] This talk about UCT always shooting "black" people when they protest, was utter nonsense – but especially so against the backdrop of the University having utterly capitulated to criminal protests in 2015, 2016, and 2017. UCT, to the best of my knowledge, has never called on the state to shoot "blacks" or anybody else, whether they were protesting or not. There was once instance during the so-called Shackville protests in 2016, during which police shot rubber bullets, but this was not at the behest of UCT and I do not know the race of all those at whom these bullets were shot.[11]

"Comrade" Lushaba asked that his missive be sent to all members of the Faculty, who were then invited to comment. In a response, one of my colleagues in the Philosophy Department, Dr George Hull, opined that it would not be right "to re-open nominations – i.e. in effect discard the result of the nominations and ballot and re-run the process".[12] He said that there had been "a free nomination process, whereby anybody could nominate anyone for any reason, followed by a democratic vote. Several people who were approached declined to be nominated, several people nominated were not elected", adding that as far as he knew "the outcome cannot fairly be attributed to a will to reproduce exclusionary forces". What he did *not* say in that reply is that he himself had nominated a "black African South African", but that person had declined the nomination.[13] Dr Hull concluded his reply by saying that elections "stop being free and democratic when they are re-run until they deliver the 'right' result. And they especially do when their results are set aside because of a threat to stop the elected committee from doing its work."

This entirely reasonable comment on the nature of democratic elections was met with a scurrilous *ad hominem* attack from Comrade Lushaba. He accused Dr Hull of being one of the "beneficiaries of racial privilege ... [who] arrogate unto themselves to (sic) right to tell us victims of racial injustice how we ought to comport ourselves" and said that Dr Hull "can as best as whiteness does always summon institutions of British colonial violence and kill us".[14]

Dr Hull, who hails from Britain, rightly took these comments to be prejudicial. Comrade Lushaba was making assumptions about him on the basis of his "race" and nationality. While the Interim Dean *eventually* made a statement condemning prejudicial comments in Faculty discussions, the Faculty's Transformation Committee and its Chair refused to take a stand against Comrade Lushaba, and supported his view even if not for the precise way he expressed himself. The Chair of the Transformation Committee, Shose Kessi, said that Comrade Lushaba had been "calling out whiteness or racial privilege". Three months later, on 1 March 2019, Associate Professor Kessi was appointed Interim Dean after Professor Wardle stepped down from this position to begin a sabbatical.

The Transformation Committee had previously (in November 2018) written both to the Interim Dean and to the

Vice-Chancellor, Mamokgethi Phakeng, to endorse Comrade Lushaba's complaint, although they refined that complaint by noting that what that component of the committee lacked was a "black African South African" – not a "black", "African" or "South African" but a "black African South African". That the full committee of nineteen people contained a good number who have been identified as belonging to this demographic did not, in the mind of the Faculty Transformation Committee, minimize the problem that a *subset* of the committee purportedly lacked this demographic. They objected that this subset of the committee was "unrepresentative", "unfair", and "unjust given the existing structural inequities in the Faculty.

They did not explain what those purported structural inequities were. Some might wonder whether these structural inequities might be a paucity of "black" academics in the Faculty. However, according to UCT data for 2018, about 44% of the academics in the Faculty were "black". Although about 51% were "white" (and about 5% either "other" or "not declared"), this is hardly a faculty in which "blacks" do not exert considerable influence, including occupying most of the most senior positions. If one adds in the administrative staff (who also elect representatives to the selection committee), we find that "blacks" constitute 55% of the combined academic and administrative staff in the Faculty, while "whites" constitute only 40%.

The Transformation Committee also called for the "abandonment" (sic) of the current selection committee and a "new and alternative process for the appointment of the Dean's selection committee". The committee was *not* disbanded.

It should be said that Comrade Lushaba's opposition to democracy was selective. When one member of the Transformation Committee disagreed with that committee's position, Comrade Lushaba was quick to note that that disagreement "does not negate a collective decision taken at the meeting".[15] It is difficult to detect a principle (other than expediency) underlying Comrade Lushaba's views. He rejected democratic procedures when he disliked the outcome and endorsed democratic procedures when he liked the outcome. It did not seem to matter to him that the democratic procedures he rejected were the established procedures for electing a component of the selection committee and the democratic procedures he accepted had no jurisdiction over the constitution of the selection committee.

THE DEBACLE DEEPENS

On 27 May 2019, four shortlisted candidates made presentations to the Faculty. Two of these were the two candidates who would have presented on 21 September 2018 had the process not been suspended two days prior to that. The two additional candidates were the new Interim Dean, Associate Professor Shose Kessi, and Professor Grace Khunou from the University of Johannesburg. Unsurprisingly, all four candidates met the preferred racial criteria, but only Professor Khunou, the racial and citizenship experts noted, was a "black African South African".

Members of the Faculty were invited to submit their comments to the selection committee by midnight. The selection committee met on 28 May 2019 to interview the candidates, and a Faculty Board meeting at which the selection committee's choice would be presented, was scheduled for 29 May. However, that meeting was postponed and then rescheduled for 30 May. At that meeting, Professor Khunou was proposed as the new Dean.

During this meeting many concerns were raised about this choice of candidate, including her lack of experience and the fact that she had occupied her position as Vice-Dean at the University of Johannesburg for only two years. Vice-Chancellor

Phakeng was asked whether the committee had deemed any of the other candidates appointable. She replied that there were two other appointable candidates, but that the committee had decided only to propose Professor Khunou. The Vice-Chancellor noted that the other two appointable candidates were not South African citizens for the purpose of the employment equity requirements. It became clear that the reason why the Faculty Board meeting had been delayed by a day was in order to check *when* Professor Boswell, one of the candidates, had become a South African citizen – before or after 27 April 1994. Until then the question had not arisen. Once it was learned that she had become a citizen only after that date, the selection committee proposed Professor Khunou instead of Professor Boswell.

Facing a mounting wall of resistance from the Faculty Board, the Vice-Chancellor supported her call for a vote in favour of Professor Khunou by saying "that the university had committed to transformation and that this was a way to show commitment to the transformation process". It is very common for the transformation card to be played in trying to steer a UCT committee towards a particular conclusion. It usually works, but it did not on this occasion. (Perhaps this is because, as the Vice-Chancellor later noted,[16] all but two of those who spoke were "blacks", who are harder to silence with the transformation card.)

Also unsuccessful in winning over the Faculty Board, was the Vice-Chancellor's comment that if the committee ignored the appointability of Professor Khunou, UCT could face a legal challenge. (Just what "appointable" means at UCT has been hard to fathom. Although I have never received a satisfactory answer, it seems to include a candidate who would be minimally acceptable even if one had a *much* better alternative candidate. In other words, it is not a comparative judgement.) When Professor Khunou's candidacy was put to a vote, only 27%

of the Faculty supported her appointment. Therefore, the selection committee had to reconvene and further consider the matter.

On 7 June 2019 a Special Faculty Board meeting was called for 11 June. The Selection Committee planned to propose that Associate Professor Shose Kessi be appointed as Dean.

On 8 June, Comrade Lushaba, allegedly writing on behalf of the 27% who had voted for Professor Khunou, again railed at the outcome of a democratic process, claiming that the vote was "unjust and immoral".[17] He claimed that this was disrespectful to "the ably qualified African candidate" and "to VC Phakeng who headed the process".

Allegations of disrespect – this one is no exception – are cynically deployed at UCT. For an allegation to stick it matters not whether one has indeed been disrespectful but on where in the standing hierarchy of victimhood the accuser and the accused find themselves. Both Vice-Chancellor Phakeng and the BAC would later accuse Comrade Lushaba of not respecting her! The BAC claimed that his disrespect of the Vice-Chancellor demonstrated "that black women in positions of leadership continue to face relentless chauvinism".[18] Because "black woman" trumps "black man", this charge of disrespect had greater stickiness. The BAC seems not to have considered the more plausible explanation that Comrade Lushaba disrespects *anybody* who stands in his way.

In his letter, Comrade Lushaba also asked: "Why have a Selection Committee process if the Faculty members (with lesser information) can over-turn the process without clear and rational reasons for its rejection? Is it not about self-interested groups who want people they like or know to be Dean?"[19] Curiously one might ask exactly those questions about the Faculty's rejection of David Attwell in July 2017, when a selection committee had proposed him as Dean. However, Comrade Lushaba did not ask those questions then. Could it be that his concerns are not matters of principle, but of expediency?

On 10 June, Comrade Lushaba wrote to "Fellow Black People" but copied his rambling 1,592-word rant to everybody in the Faculty.[20] In it, he took aim at, among others, the Black Academic Caucus, which he referred to as a "cabal that has in the past few years consolidated its hold over the Faculty". He said that it is "a very amoral cabal that has a very unethical extractionist relationship or attitude towards the institution". He alleged that it "only becomes hyper-active, conniving and engaging in underhand activities aimed at advantaging their own nominated candidates when high paying positions become available". It had, he said, "fashioned itself into a patronage allocating clique". He took issue with those advocating "Pan-Africanism" which, he said, seems to include "everyone else other than us Black South Africans".

Here we see the racist xenophobic Comrade Lushaba who favours "black African South Africans" pitted against the racist BAC, that favours "blacks" of any nationality. Referring to Lenin by name, Comrade Lushaba asked "what is to be done?" His answer included: "we must ensure that the vote does not proceed".

The Black Academic Caucus responded, criticizing Dr Lushaba for making *ad hominem* attacks and accusing him of "dragging black scholars into conflict with each other". The BAC said that it "will not accept any rhetoric that divides us as black people". It rejected "the way in which 'black' is used in such a divisive, violating, homogenizing way, thrusting us into absurd apartheid-style compartments". The BAC declared that "we unapologetically support all black scholars".

The BAC statement is dripping with irony. First, it has regularly launched *ad hominem* attacks against those (typically "non-blacks") who disagree with them. Unlike Dr Lushaba, at least in his letter of 10 June, the BAC has directed ad hominem attacks against *named* individuals. Thus, the BAC's opposition to the *ad hominem* is not a principled one. Second, they too are in the business of divisiveness. They merely want to draw the divide in a different place from Dr Lushaba – along racial lines, rather than along the lines of both race and national origin.

Third, they accuse Dr Lushaba of homogenizing, but it is *they* rather than Dr Lushaba who are more liable to the criticism of homogenizing. They seek, at least when it is convenient, to homogenize all "blacks", whereas Dr Lushaba seeks to draw multiple distinctions within that category. That is not a point in favour of Dr Lushaba. The apartheid-style compartments are indeed absurd, but the BAC too preserves those categories. They may seek to unite all "blacks", itself one kind of apartheid category, but it is not beneath members of the BAC to draw the more fine-grained Apartheid distinctions. Indeed, that is exactly what those of them on the Faculty Transformation Committee did when they wrote that there was a "lack of black African South Africans"[21] among those elected by the Faculty to the selection committee for the Dean.

WANTING YOUR BALLOT AND EATING IT TOO

At the special Faculty Board meeting on 11 June 2019, Associate Professor Shose Kessi was presented as the selection committee's new choice for Dean. After the Vice-Chancellor had provided a motivation for this candidate, Dr Lushaba took the floor and spoke at length – at such great length that the Vice-Chancellor repeatedly asked him to conclude his point and allow others to speak. Dr Lushaba pressed on undeterred. He objected to the choice of Associate Professor Kessi over Professor Khunou. The former, a founder and former Chair of the BAC, identifies as "black" but is not an "African South African", while Professor Khunou is.

Eventually the Vice-Chancellor pulled victim-rank on Dr

Lushaba and said that as a "Black, South African woman" she "felt undermined by one of her own people in an argument that was meant to support her".[22] This did not have the desired effect. Dr Lushaba continued. The Vice-Chancellor again expressed her feeling of being undermined and spoke about the perception that "the Black South African woman could not manage a faculty Board meeting".[23] At this point Dr Lushaba began to read a section of the Employment Equity Act. He did eventually yield the floor and others asked various questions. Many of these questions revealed that there were members of the Faculty Board who had no understanding of the procedures. For example, some wanted to reconsider Professor Khunou even though her candidacy was no longer before the Faculty Board.

At some point the Vice-Chancellor noted that the meeting had exceeded its scheduled length and that the venue had been booked for another meeting. She asked members to cast their votes while the discussion continued. Dr Lushaba spoke further. One of his questions was pertinent: Why was the discussion continuing if voting had begun? Any discussion was now inconsequential. That was no excuse for what he did next: sabotage the vote counting.

He left the meeting room and entered the foyer where the votes were being tallied. He shouted that the vote would be stopped. He swept from the table the ballot boxes and the ballots that had already been removed from them. He began tearing up ballots, kicking ballot boxes, removing some ballots, and putting at least one in his mouth. He also "manhandled" two administrators when they tried to stop him.

The following day, 12 June 2019, the Vice-Chancellor sent an email to all members of the Humanities Faculty announcing that the meeting would be reconvened. She said that at the meeting, the Faculty "had robust discussion and proceeded to vote". "Unfortunately", she said, "the voting process started before the discussion was concluded". This makes it sound as though the voting spontaneously erupted before the discussion had finished, whereas, in fact, she had *instructed* the voting to begin and for the discussion to continue. She then added: "Moreover, the voting itself was disrupted". Note the passive tense and absence of any reference to who had done the disrupting.

She must have had further thoughts about that, because two days later she wrote again to the Faculty about the same meeting.[24] Once again she said that "We ran out of time in the venue and the discussions were proceeding whilst voting was taking place. This is certainly not optimal and the situation demands a new vote." However, this time she explicitly condemned the disruptive behaviour – although without mentioning Dr Lushaba by name. She said that it was "unacceptable, inappropriate and it nullified part of a legitimate governance process". She said she had "issued a letter of reprimand to the person involved in the incident" and that she was "considering the matter further". She announced that the Faculty Board had been scheduled to reconvene on 14 June in order to conclude the matter. That is exactly what should have happened. However, more bumbling followed.

MORE BUMBLING

The Faculty was advised that the "selection committee had requested" that it meet before the matter was brought back to the Faculty. The Faculty Board meeting was rescheduled for 18 June, but was postponed yet again.

On 25 June, the Vice-Chancellor wrote to the Faculty,[25] informing it that the selection committee has sought external legal opinion on whether it had followed the correct procedures in presenting Professor Khunou's candidacy to the Faculty.

Seeking external legal opinion was entirely unnecessary.

Anybody with a basic understanding of the University rules should have known that the processes had been in accordance with those rules. However, if there were any doubts, UCT's own experts in the Law Faculty could quickly have dispelled them. Seeking the external opinion complicated matters also because that opinion was flawed. According to the Vice-Chancellor, the legal opinion was that the selection committee "should have: a) requested the Faculty Board to provide the reasons why it did not give the necessary support to Prof Khunou; b) made a decision on this engagement".

The first part of this advice is incorrect. The rules say only that before the selection committee's recommendation of a candidate "can be taken forward, a 60% (sixty percent) majority of those voting must be in support of the candidate" and that if the candidate does "not receive the above majority vote, the selection committee must reconvene to make a decision on whether to submit its recommendation to the Institutional Forum (IF) and Council, or to return to the selection process". The rules also state that if "the selection committee decides to proceed with its recommendation, the Faculty Board will be entitled to submit a co-report containing the views of its members to the IF and Council".[26]

In other words, there is no reference in the rules to the selection committee having to garner the *reasons* why less than 60% of the Faculty supports a candidate. There is good reason for the rules not requiring this – namely, it may be impossible to determine. The vote is a secret ballot and those voting against, are not required to say why they vote as they do. The purpose of the vote is to determine *whether* the candidate enjoys the support of 60% of the Faculty, not *why* it does or does not. That said, discussion in Faculty Board can provide some insight into the concerns of members of the Faculty, and the selection committee certainly had access to this when it decided not to pursue Professor Khunou's candidacy. It was thus entirely unnecessary for the Vice-Chancellor to say that a special Faculty Board would be convened "to provide reasons for its lack of support for Prof Grace Khunou".[27]

That Faculty Board meeting was scheduled for 16 July. On 14 July, twenty-seven members of the Faculty Board wrote to the chair and members of the selection committee and to the chair and members of Council (the University's governing body), objecting to the meeting's agenda.[28] They correctly noted that all procedures had been followed with regard to Professor Khunou's candidacy. They correctly objected that the selection committee had rescinded its recommendation of Associate Professor Kessi and were revisiting the candidacy of Professor Khunou as a result of the "unlawful disruption of a faculty process" and that this in itself was in violation of the established procedures.

Towards the end of the letter, the authors criticized Dr Lushaba's behaviour which they said "*bordered* [on] harassment and aggression and has negatively impacted on staff morale in the Faculty" (my emphasis of their understatement). They stated that "the institution has a legal obligation to provide safe working spaces for its staff" and bemoaned the lack of accountability for misconduct. Without such accountability, they said, "the university is now setting precedent for future aggressive disruptions of university governance procedures".

What is curious about this, is its Rip van Winkle character. Many (but not all) of the signatories had been curiously silent during the criminal activity of student protesters from 2015 to 2017. Many of them had not spoken then of the institution's legal obligation to provide a safe working environment, of staff morale in the absence of such safety, and of the importance of "accountability for misconduct". They failed to notice that it was not the indulgence of Dr Lushaba's behaviour that was creating a precedent for future aggressive disruptions. That precedent had been created in 2015 and reinforced in 2016 and

2017. Dr Lushaba was merely acting on the well-established precedents.

The authors of this letter received no reply, but the special meeting scheduled for 16 July 2019 was cancelled earlier that day. On 17 July, the selection committee decided to abort the whole process (although this was not communicated to the Faculty until the following month). In other words, the selection committee had failed to appreciate the apt objections lodged by the twenty-seven members of the Faculty Board (who are not to be confused with the 27 *percent* on whose behalf Dr Lushaba purported to write).

A regular Faculty Board meeting took place on 8 August. The agenda included a question from the twenty-seven authors of the 14 July letter. Because they had not received a response to that letter, they specifically asked the University Executive to respond. However, before the Executive officer present could respond, Dr Lushaba took the floor.

He proceeded to read the questions that had been circulated and the list of names of those who had signed the letter. There were objections from the floor to his reading out the names (which were also on record) and Dr Lushaba was asked to state his own question about the questions. Undeterred, he focused on the first two names and proceeded to criticize those people, saying that they had been part of a staff disciplinary process (for another staff member) and thus understood that confidentiality was a requirement of such processes. The implication seems to have been that they should not have mentioned him by name in the letter they signed. One of them responded that his disruption of the Faculty Board had been a public act and was thus different from the disciplinary procedure to which Dr Lushaba was referring.

The Executive officer did eventually have the opportunity to reply. From her reply and a subsequent "communique" from the Vice-Chancellor (that bears no date, but which was sent on

14 August), it became apparent that Council Executive Committee had refused to accept the selection committee's decision to abort the process. The Council Executive Committee succumbed to the external legal opinion that the Faculty's reasons for rejecting Professor Khunou's application had to be considered. It went one step further by suggesting that the selection committee should possibly invite Professor Khunou to discuss with her the Faculty's concerns.

That is exactly what happened. The Selection Committee invited Professor Khunou back and engaged with her about the concerns that had been expressed about her candidacy. The Selection Committee reached the conclusion that she was not appointable. Its rationale, subsequently provided to the Faculty Board, is a mixture of vague references to her "disobedient personality" and of clear indications of her weaknesses as a candidate for Dean. So serious were the latter, that it may seem hard to understand how the Selection Committee could not have noticed these *before* it had recommended her to the Faculty Board. One possible explanation is that the Selection Committee was so obsessed with her *demographic* qualifications that it failed to notice the *crucial* qualifications, or rather the absence thereof. It would certainly not be the first time this had happened at UCT.[29]

The Selection Committee thus faced the decision whether to recommend no candidate to Council or to recommend a candidate who was a non-South African (or, in one case, at least not been a South African before 27 April 1994). They chose (by a vote of 12 to 2) to recommend a non-South African. They proposed Associate Professor Shose Kessi. Of the "black" candidates – the only ones shortlisted – she had evidently been their preferred candidate but had been pushed to third place because although reportedly meeting the racial criterion, she failed to meet the citizenship one.

Indeed the racial and national criteria had been dominant

(even if not decisive) throughout the Selection Committee's deliberations. Only "black" candidates were sought or considered. Of the "black" candidates, Professor Boswell had been the top candidate while she was thought to be a pre-27 April 1994 South African. Once it became clear that she became a South African only after that date, she fell to third place, and Professor Khunou, as the only "African black South African", was elevated to first place. For the racist xenophobes in the Faculty, no other candidate could be considered. However, the racists outnumbered the racist xenophobes and that is how a "non-South African black", Shose Kessi, came to be the Selection Committee's nomination for the deanship.

Associate Professor Kessi's candidacy was put to a vote in the Faculty Board and she received support from 86% of the Faculty. This seems like an impressive level of support but it is hard to know what to make of it. When she had been proposed as a *Deputy* Dean the previous year, her candidacy enjoyed the support of only 60% of the Faculty. What explains the surge in support from one year to the next? Could it be that she gained the confidence of more members of the Faculty in the six months she served as Acting Dean? Could it be that the Faculty was exhausted after the nearly three-year long process of searching for a new dean and was desperate to settle? It is impossible to know.

What we do know is that after the Humanities Faculty Board approved Associate Professor Kessi's candidacy on 18 September 2018, her appointment as Dean was only announced on 15 November, following final approval by the Institutional Forum and Council.

CONCLUSION

Components of the fiasco became public. For example, there were a few newspaper reports. At least some of this coverage resulted from a statement issued by Dr Lushaba's "27% Group" and focused on Professors Khunou and Kessi.[30] This was followed by another article that reported on Professor Boswell "breaking her silence".[31]

Some months earlier, a liberal student organization, Progress SA, had initiated a twitter campaign based on reports they received from "anonymous whistleblowers". In their tweets, the Vice-Chancellor was prodded to comment on the alleged xenophobia and the disruption of the voting. At one point Vice-Chancellor Phakeng tweeted back "Progress SA is acting on instruction to make me resign but I will not resign" and "Watch them engineer a shutdown. They want to agitate black students, and polarise an environment that is working hard at coming together".

In response to this paranoia, Progress SA tweeted: "All of the claims in these tweets are false. We have no personal gripe with Prof Phakeng (@FabAcademic). We just wanted to know what she (as VC) and her management team are doing to address a serious issue. There was no reason to turn to victimhood and racial conspiracies". There was also no reason for Professor Phakeng to block Progress SA's twitter account, along with the twitter accounts of "students raising similar concerns".[32]

The selection process has ended, but the story has not. At the time of writing, three of UCT's eight deans[33] are *associate* professors, a fourth is not even an associate professor, and a fifth was not a full professor when first appointed to a deanship. There is no reason to think that an associate professor (or senior lecturer) cannot be a good dean, just as there is no reason to think that every full professor would make a good dean. However, it does say something about a university if half its deans are not yet full professors (especially given the much laxer promotion standards that exist in some faculties now than a decade ago). It also says something when those elevated to deanships have had very little, if any, experience in lower level administrative leadership positions. A senior lecturer who has never been a head of department becomes a deputy dean when the position of Chair of the Transformation Committee is converted into a deputy deanship. That person is promoted to Associate Professor in January, is made Acting Dean two months later and Dean six months after that.

That does not happen in normal universities. When it happens at UCT, it is not because of a dearth of full professors (within UCT and further afield) with plenty of prior experience and success in administrative positions.[34] It is because the majority of those people are disqualified because they are of the wrong demographic.

UCT's policy on the appointment of deans, lists specific criteria that are used in the selection of deans.[35] According to this policy, the University should seek individuals who (i) "are scholars of note and have credibility among their academic peers", (ii) will offer academic leadership in the faculty" which includes "having proven leadership and management skills", and (iii) have a proven transformation skills record and will strive to transform the faculty in ways that achieve social justice in South Africa, which must include meeting staff and student equity targets". Of these three criteria, it is clear that the third weighs most heavily in practice. Weighing even more heavily is an unstated criterion, namely whether the candidate has the right demographic characteristics.

It is not in the University's interest to disqualify people on the basis of their nationality. It should seek the best talent from wherever it can. That is what the world's (better and) best universities do and it is *part* of what makes them as good as they are. Their hiring quarry is global and not merely local. (To its credit, UCT has made many international hires, including from elsewhere in Africa, but it is clear that there is increasing resistance to this.) The best universities also do not disqualify people on the basis of their race, even if some of them do give *some* preference on the basis of race, sex and citizenship.

Some forms of affirmative action can be justified on the grounds that special measures are needed to draw on the widest pool of talent. However, that justification is clearly shown to be an intellectually dishonest rationalization when opening up some parts of the pool is accompanied by closing down others. The larger the sections of the pool shut down the worse the problem is. The protracted process of selecting a new Dean of Humanities at UCT resulted from a deep pathology – an obsession with demographic characteristics, in this case primarily race and, to a lesser extent, citizenship. That pathology persists and will continue to do immense damage to UCT.

Chapter 19

MANUFACTURING THE NARRATIVE OF A RACIST UNIVERSITY

Central to the Fallist view is the claim that South African universities such as UCT are racist institutions that are hostile to "blacks". That narrative has become mainstream. There are a number of interconnected explanatory reasons for this, but among them is *not* the veracity of the narrative. Instead, it is a combination of historic, national and international resonance, endless repetition (encouraged in part by opportunistic considerations), as well as the silencing of opposing views.

The narrative was further entrenched with an official imprimatur by the reports issued by two commissions – the Institutional Reconciliation and Transformation Commission (IRTC) and an inquiry following the suicide of Faculty of Health Sciences Dean, Professor Bongani Mayosi. However, both these commissions made the same mistake – simply regurgitating as "findings" reports they had received, without subjecting those reports to critical scrutiny. This basic methodological requirement should be obvious to those running a university and to those working as academics in it.

NO RECONCILIATION

The IRTC grew out of an agreement – later referred to by some as the "November Agreement" – signed between four members of the "UCT Special Executive Task Team" and nine students, at least seven of whom, it was later noted, were affiliated with PASMA (the Pan Africanist Student Movement of Azania).[1] The latter referred to themselves and came to be known as "Shackville TRC".

According to the IRTC's "Background Document", the parties to the November agreement "expressed a commitment to establish a multi-stakeholder Steering Committee to oversee the proposed Institutional Reconciliation and Transformation Commission (IRTC) and other processes covered by the agreement".[2] The November Agreement itself makes no mention of a Steering Committee. It is thus unclear when or how it was agreed to establish such a committee. However, it was established.

The Steering Committee was composed largely of either Fallists or people sympathetic or pliant to them.[3] For example, the BAC, which had one position on the Steering Committee, was clearly in league with the Fallists. The "Shackville TRC" student grouping (one of three student groupings on the Steering Committee), had two places on the Steering Committee, and was alone in having the latitude to rotate its alternate member.[4] All other groupings had a designated alternate. The University Executive representatives and at least one of the Council representatives kowtowed to the Fallists.[5]

Fortunately, Senate's representative and alternate, respectively Professors Nicola Illing and Jeremy Seekings, were reasonable people who provided members of Senate with forthright, but disturbing reports of what was transpiring in the Steering Committee meetings.[6] It should come as no surprise that they were called to task for these critical reports by some of their fellow Steering Committee members.[7] Although the Senate representatives were conciliatory, they also noted that demanding that members of the Steering Committee "apologise for the tone of a report is too close to demanding an apology for the analysis itself, and that can only lead to the intimidation or silencing of dissenting voices".[8]

The Steering Committee meetings appear to have had a farcical quality. For example, when it was agreed that each group would submit documentation to be discussed at a meeting, the Senate representatives were the only ones who did so on time.[9] Students arrived very late for a Saturday workshop, resulting in the start of the workshop being delayed by an hour,[10] which was disrespectful to those who had arrived on time. The order of items on the agenda for that workshop was then shifted. The result of this was that those who had arrived on time were no longer present when a crucial matter was discussed after the originally scheduled end of the meeting and by which time they had to leave.[11] The status of this workshop then inexplicably acquired the status of a meeting, with the "agreements" at the end of the workshop being regarded as decisions of the Steering Committee.[12] The Senate representatives concluded that the workshop had been "successfully captured" by the Shackville TRC / BAC faction.[13]

The Senate representatives described the Steering Committee meetings as "highly theatrical".[14] They said that some of "the theatre is a diversion, and might even be intended to distract". They noted that the Shackville students had "repeatedly demanded postponements" and that "over three months, they have been unable to consult their 'constituents'".[15] Indeed, it seemed to the Senate representatives that the Shackville students were "implicitly presenting the rest of the university with a choice between rubber-stamping those parts of the November Agreement that suit them now ... or stalling indefinitely".[16]

One example of their selectivity pertained to whether the IRTC should "consider the boundaries of legitimate protest and the management of protest at the university". Consideration of this had been implied by the November 2016 Agreement, which had referred to the "recommendations of the IRTC/Shackville TRC on acceptable forms of protests and appropriate disciplinary procedures and sanctions by the University".[17] Yet, these students, along with the Alumni and BAC representatives, objected at a Steering Committee meeting[18] to the inclusion in the IRTC's Terms of Reference, of a stipulation that the IRTC should "consider the boundaries of legitimate protest and the management of protest at the university".[19] Similarly, a provision in the November Agreement allowing for "revoking clemency in the event that the signatories engage in further disruptions was omitted from the Terms of Reference.[20]

Both of these provisions were especially important because the farcical IRTC Steering Committee meetings were taking place against the backdrop of further criminal behaviour. For example, during one of the Steering Committee meetings, one of the Students' Representative Council (SRC) representatives raised a concern about the committee's continuing its business "while she was facing charges for events at the Sports Centre" the previous Thursday. When asked, at the meeting, why she was facing charges, she replied that "she had been caught on camera breaking down a locked door to Sports Centre, as well as marshalling the protesters who were disrupting the exams in the Sports Centre".[21] This makes a mockery of the idea that the IRTC was actually about reconciliation. One cannot be reconciling while one continues to offend.

Given what transpired in the Steering Committee, it is unsurprising that the representatives of Senate had "grave reservations" about the terms of reference formulated for the IRTC and about the composition of the Commission.[22] However, their objections were overruled[23] and the IRTC began its work.

Many members of the University distrusted the IRTC and were unwilling to make submissions. They either viewed it as a farce or they were fearful of making submissions. One of the Senate representatives was repeatedly told by members of Senate that "they feared sharing their experiences and impressions with the Commission because they viewed the Commissioners as basically hostile to their concerns".[24] Commenting on the IRTC's report, Professor Jeremy Seekings said that some of these members of Senate will surely read the IRTC's final report "as vindicating their scepticism about the Commission".[25]

The IRTC's conclusions were indeed predictable. Amnesty was granted to the eight affected students.[26] These students "were not required to express remorse or make an apology to be eligible for amnesty".[27] This requirement was abandoned even though the November Agreement included the provision that clemency would be conditional on "formally acknowledging wrong-doing and committing not to repeat such actions in the future".[28]

Equally predictable were the IRTC's purported "findings". It assigned much blame to then Vice-Chancellor Dr Max Price and his Executive for their handling of the protests. By contrast, it downplayed the wrongs perpetrated by the student protesters and largely excused them by suggesting that their grievances justified their behaviour. In these asymmetries, the IRTC displayed its partiality.

It also concluded that there was widespread (anti-"black")

racism at UCT. However, this finding was based on the reports of a highly selective sample, and these reports were not subjected to any critical scrutiny. Simply reporting that some people claim UCT to be pervaded by racism is not to find that it actually is. (One of the Commissioners, former Constitutional Court Judge Zak Yacoob, distanced himself from the Report's chapter on racism.[29])

By way of example, consider the following claim by Lwazi Lushaba and cited by the IRTC: "People like me are called black academics, but white academics are not called white academics. They are called academics."[30] The IRTC Report describes such alleged differential reference as a micro-aggression. However, they do not ask any of the questions that a good researcher (or Commissioner) should ask.

For example, they don't ask whether Dr Lushaba's claim is true. By this, I don't mean to suggest that Dr Lushaba has never been called a "black academic", or that "white" academics are not sometimes called "academics". Perhaps that is the case, and there are other times when "black" academics are called "academics" and "white" academics are called "white academics". There certainly times when Dr Lushaba himself has referred to "black academics" and to "white academics".[31] He does that a lot, which leads to a further question: How much of the reference to "black academics" is the result of the racial obsessions of Dr Lushaba and others who refer to themselves as "black academics"? At UCT, I most commonly hear the words "black academic" when these words are followed by the word "caucus". If one keeps calling oneself a "black academic" it is not a microaggression when others follow suit.[32]

The IRTC's Report was roundly criticised. One Senate representative on the Steering Committee reported that the feedback he received on the Report "was a tsunami of criticism" and that this was "echoed by the representative of the Deans".[33]

The administrative staff representatives on the Steering Committee also reported criticism from their constituency. These included the impression that there had been a "pre-determined outcome", that the IRTC's approach "appeared inquisitorial", was not ethical, and that its methodology was flawed.[34] There were also criticisms from individuals. For example, Professor Robert Morrell said that the Report "is unrepresentative, skewed and bears little resemblance to realities on the ground". He too pointed to its methodological flaws.[35]

Not everybody was unsatisfied. The Fallists and their allies – especially the BAC and the Alumni representative – were largely approving. This is probably because they liked the findings. They did not address the methodological concerns others had.

A DEAN'S DEATH

The IRTC's methodology of hearing narratives of anti-"black" racism and then presenting them as "findings" without interrogating them, was replicated by another panel – the one set up to investigate the suicide on 27 July 2018 of then Dean of the Faculty of Health Sciences, Professor Bongani Mayosi.[36] The latter panel (which consisted of Emeritus Professor Thandabantu Nhlapo, Dr Somadoda Fikeni, Professor Pumla Gobodo-Madikizela and Ms Nomfundo Walaza) explicitly stated in its report that it was "in a position to benefit from the work of the IRTC".[37]

Professor Mayosi had been a successful head of UCT's Department of Medicine for nearly a decade when the deanship of the Faculty of Health Sciences became available. He was encouraged to apply. Although he was originally reluctant to do so, once he took the decision to apply, he did so with enthusiasm.[38] It was no surprise that he was appointed.

He took up his new post in September 2016. About ten days later, the student protests that were wracking UCT flared in the Faculty of Health Sciences. A group of undergraduate students occupied the Dean's suite and became known as #OccupyFHS. Professor Mayosi's entry into the deanship was a baptism of fire – and the fire consumed him.

When I first wrote[39] about the then new toxic environment that had emerged at UCT, I made brief, anonymous reference to Professor Mayosi (as a "senior academic") and to the abysmal way he was being treated. (I did not name him then, in order to avoid his being further traumatized. Given that his maltreatment is now a matter of public record and that he is no longer alive to be further traumatized, I now write about him by name.)

Professor Mayosi was a conflict-averse person and was unaccustomed to the kind of resistance he met from the protesting students and from those members of staff who were aiding and abetting them. The panel's report on his brief tenure as dean recognized this. Indeed, it went so far as to acknowledge that the "panel had no hesitation in concluding ... that the eruption of the #FeesMustFall protests ... was the single most influential factor directly and indirectly affecting his Deanship".[40]

While the report includes repeated reference to the disrespectful way in which Professor Mayosi was treated by the protesters, it is somewhat coy about relating details. There were a few exceptions to this coyness. For example, it did note that he was called a "coconut" and a "sellout". It also related the following incident:

> He worked until late at night and at about 20h30, a group of students from the #OccupyFHS movement went to his office and really expressed their great disappointment with him ... they said they were not

going to leave until he sent out an email to faculty that students would be given a DP concession.[41]

He succumbed to that pressure, but almost immediately regretted doing so. The Dean's Advisory Committee had previously decided against this concession, and that decision had then been communicated to the Faculty. In capitulating to the student demand, Professor Mayosi felt, according to a colleague of his, that "he had severely compromised his integrity and that he has lost the confidence of both students and staff".[42] As a result, Professor Mayosi did not come to work the following day and submitted a letter of resignation to Dr Price. However, Dr Price persuaded him to withdraw this letter.

There were other instances in which Professor Mayosi was treated disrespectfully by the protesters. For example, on 28 September 2016, there was an open Faculty meeting which was held in the Frances Ames room but, because it was so amply attended, those present spilled out into the adjacent courtyard. The student protesters walked into the venue. Professor Mayosi was sitting at the front with some senior members of the Faculty. The students took the microphone from him and said that they would be running the meeting. He did not attempt to stop them. At the same meeting other staff members were treated dreadfully. One professor was so awfully treated that she broke down in tears. Perhaps because of his own condition, Professor Mayosi did not come to her defence. All this undermined others' sense of his authority and may well also have undermined his own sense of authority.

On another occasion Professor Mayosi was called to the New Learning Centre, which protesting students had just invaded. The protestors confronted him, accusing him of not assisting them with their cause. Some of them were shouting at him, with their faces close up to his. According to one report, epithets were hurled at him on this occasion.

It was not only student protesters who mistreated Professor

Mayosi. Those members of staff who were supporting and shielding these protesters were also complicit.

Any honest appraisal of what upended Professor Mayosi's life, would have given central place to the Fallists' treatment of him. Fallist viciousness felled him. At a memorial service for him shortly after his death, his sister, Advocate Ncumisa Mayosi said that:

> The vitriolic character of student engagements tore him apart. The abrasive, do-or-die, scorched earth approach adopted by students in navigating what was a legitimate cause, completely vandalised Bongani's soul. Put simply, this unravelled him. To be clear, Bongani believed in the students' cause but the personal insults and abuse that were hurled at him without any justification whatsoever, this cut him to the core. This matter of engaging was inimical to everything that Bongani was about. It was offensive to his core values , how he had lived his life up until that point, his vision as a leader. And so he became withdrawn, his personality changed, he spoke less.[43]

Professor Mayosi's widow, Professor Nonhlanhla Khumalo, wrote a letter to her late husband, which was read out at the funeral by a friend. In it she stated:

> During the protests, students sent you a list of demands and messages to your private cellphone at all hours. You cared so deeply for people who now treated you as the enemy.[44]

The then new Vice-Chancellor, Professor Mamokgethi Phakeng, had similarly identified the damaging effects of Fallist bullying on Professor Mayosi (and on others).[45] Her remarks, at least in my view, were a sensitive and mature response to the tragedy. She called on those who had insulted Professor Mayosi to express their contrition. She was subjected to criticism for this. In response, she issued an official statement attempting to clarify (and arguably soften) her earlier words. She nonetheless stuck to the view that "the protests were not kind to Professor Mayosi", that "some black students were angry with him" and "called him names" and "that things were said and actions were taken that caused serious harm to people".[46]

Obviously, Professor Mayosi's suicide and the fact that Fallist viciousness had played such a central role in his psychological unravelling, was intolerable to the Fallists and their sympathizers. For those who see themselves as the authoritative representatives of "black" interests and the vanguard of "black" liberation, bearing responsibility for ruining a leading "black" academic is too much to bear. It is thus unsurprising that they immediately sought to sow an alternative narrative.

According to this fictional narrative, it was UCT's anti-"black" racism that killed Professor Mayosi. For example, Phurah Jack, who describes himself as "a radical thinker in occupied Azania", complained that speakers at Professor Mayosi's funeral "ambushed students" by "blaming the students". According to him, the

> funeral was a space for those who do not care about Mayosi's struggle in the first place, a space for those who do not care about the well-being of black students at the university. This attack clearly was aimed at the activists who suffered and continued to suffer together with the black academics.[47]

It must have come as news to Professor Mayosi's family that they "do not care about [his] struggle in the first place".

Chumani Maxwele, who had initiated the #RhodesMustFall protest,[48] was another who attempted both to gloss over the damage done by Fallists to Professor Mayosi, and to pin the blame on UCT's purported anti-"black" racism.[49]

Xolela Mangcu, of "omelette-gate"[50] and "spinach-gate"[51] notoriety, published a piece under the heading "How many Mayosis must be martyred before UCT deals with its toxic racism".[52] He did not ignore the student's behaviour but he claimed that it is "disingenuous and cynical to use the conduct of the students to divert attention from UCT's underlying racist toxicity". UCT, he said, was a "racist hellhole". He was not speaking about the "racist hellhole" created by Fallists, their allies and fellow travellers. Nor was he speaking about his own contributions – such as his defamation of a colleague, which prompted a successful grievance complaint against him.[53] Instead, he was speaking about his old bogeyman. Bizarrely, he claimed that "Mayosi's death reminds me of Steve Biko's death" but that "unlike apartheid's brutal murderers, our tormentors greet us with an effusive smile in the morning, question our very humanity during the day, and bid us good night at the end of the day", which he referred to as "liberal duplicity".

A group calling itself "Concerned Academics", along with the Black Academic Caucus issued a joint statement in which they objected to "the mudslinging we have been witnessing over the last few days", claiming that it is "premature and not in keeping with the expressed wishes of the Mayosi family", who had conveyed their "need for privacy during this difficult time".[54] However, their statement then pivoted to framing their own preconceived narrative of Professor Mayosi's problems. In other words, they slung their preferred mud.

They proposed that immediately after the funeral, Council should establish an investigation into the "circumstances leading to Prof Mayosi's decision to terminate his life". They proposed "that this inquiry must be set up in consultation with especially black academics and students, who have on various occasions expressed their experiences of being marginalized at

UCT". Nor did they shy away from prejudging the outcome of such an inquiry. They said that it is their "firm view that the results of this inquiry will ... help us understand ... what is wrong with UCT structures and how these could be addressed to the benefit of especially the historically and currently marginalized groups, predominantly blacks". The confidence of this conclusion stands in ironic contrast to these groups' scepticism about the *facts*. They refer to the very real and extended occupation of Professor Mayosi's office by Fallists as "alleged".

Dr Lydia Cairncross, one of the Faculty of Health Sciences academic staff members at the forefront of supporting the Fallists,[55] did not doubt or deny the occupation of the Dean's offices. However, her spin on this and other Fallist activity was even more revisionist:

> Seldom have I seen political protest unfold so spontaneously, so respectfully, so democratically, so beautifully as that particular protest did. Having been lucky enough to be present in a few of those moments, I cannot recall an instance where Bongani Mayosi, the man, was disrespected, called names or denigrated in any way, though of course there may have been isolated instances of this. What I rather saw was principled political action to hold accountable the representatives of the structures of power in a flawed system.[56]

This revisionist history was effectively trashed by journalist Ed Herbst, who catalogued various protest actions – including arson, assault, and the strewing of human excrement – and remarked, facetiously, that they show "beautiful, respectful and principled commitment to democracy".[57]

When the panel investigating Professor Mayosi's deanship convened, it received testimony from those peddling the narrative of UCT as hostile to "blacks". The panel then regurgitated those narratives without subjecting them to critical evaluation. However, the narrative is without foundation. By all accounts, Professor Mayosi was flourishing at UCT (and more generally) until he ran up against the Fallist bullies and their allies. Before that, he was widely valued and lauded. He had been sought out to head the Department of Medicine and then later the Faculty of Health Sciences. It is thus unsurprising that the report acknowledges that according to members of the Mayosi family, "there were no detectable signs of any psychiatric problems prior to Professor Mayosi's ascension to the deanship".[58]

This is not to say that the University leadership could not have done more to help Professor Mayosi as he spiralled downwards. Most importantly, they should have stopped capitulating to the thugs who had been brutalizing not only him, but also innumerable others whose travails have elicited no institutional interest. This failing, however, was *not* one that made UCT especially hostile to "blacks". It was a failing that made UCT hostile to decency, principle, reasonableness, and the rule of law. This failure harmed some "blacks" and some "whites", and benefited some "blacks" and some "whites". Nor was Professor Mayosi's death the only suicide. Two months after he took his own life, a recently retired, long-standing and highly regarded senior administrator in the Faculty of Health Sciences took her own life. She too had suffered as a result of the Fallists' atrocious behaviour.

The University leadership did do *something* to assist Professor Mayosi. As his mental state declined, plans were being made for a dignified exit from the deanship into another senior university position – a pro-vice chancellorship. There were some failures in communicating with Professor Mayosi about this, and he took his life on the day that the position was due to be approved.[59] However, there is no evidence that these failures had anything to do with race, unless the paranoid would have us believe that Professor Mamokgethi Phakeng, who was leading this initiative,[60] was contributing to the allegedly anti-"black" institutional climate. The very fact that an alternative position was being sought for Professor Mayosi suggests otherwise. Comparable kindness has not been extended to innumerable others, including distinguished scholars, who have been mauled by the toxic climate at UCT. They may not have taken their own lives, but that does not mean that they have not been profoundly harmed.

DISTRACTING DISTORTIONS

Given that Professor Mayosi was thriving at UCT (and more generally) until the rise of the Fallists, the attempts to link his declining psychological state with UCT's purported hostility to "blacks" are, to put it gently, groundless. The report does not *demonstrate* any such connection, but it makes plenty of unsubstantiated assertions, the relevance of which is unclear. As a result, the subtitle of the panel's report – "Crucible for Senior Black Academic Staff?" – is sheer innuendo.[61]

Consider, for example, the report's claim that while the "demographic profiles of students and senior management have drastically changed since the 1990s ... the profile of the academic staff who are at the core of the academic enterprise has hardly changed".[62] This is manifestly false. In 1994, the year in which South Africa transitioned to a democracy, "blacks" (in the generic sense) constituted 7.75% of academic staff at UCT.[63] In 2019, 31% of academic staff were "black" South Africans.[64] The latter figure excludes non-South African "blacks"[65] and thus understates the demographic diversification. This can hardly be described as "hardly changed".[66]

The report also states that a "consistent refrain in the testimony of senior black staff, including deans, who appeared before the panel, was the issue of performance assessments.

Performance assessments of black deans or blacks in senior positions have generally been an issue because these staff members are reported as invariably achieving lower scores than their white counterparts".[67]

Here again the panel is repeating a claim rather than evaluating it. It is certainly not possible for *me* to evaluate it because the relevant information is neither presented nor available. However, there is good reason not to accept these claims uncritically. It seems unlikely these complaints came from the "line-managers" who conduct these performance appraisals (and who thus would most authoritatively be able to make the comparative claims), because they would hardly be in a position to *complain* about their own appraisals of these senior staff. If the complaints instead came from those appraised, then they are less likely to have all the comparative data.

Even if we assume that "black" deans, on average, have lower scores in performance assessments, there may be non-racist explanations for such a phenomenon. To the extent that race plays a part in dean selection processes, and other factors such as prior administrative and leadership experience are counted less, we should not be surprised if such appointees perform at lower levels – *on average*. Again, this is not a comment on "black ability". It is a consequence of the extent to which actual qualifications for a position are weighed. One would get the same result if historical circumstances were reversed and "whites" were being strongly preferred.

Because this consequence is an aggregate one, there could still be individual "black" deans who would perform as well and be assessed as highly as any other deans. Had it not been for Fallist toxicity, Professor Mayosi may well have been such a dean, not least because of his own prior success as a head of a large and complex department. However, he was personally ill-suited to the toxicity that had overtaken the Faculty of Health Sciences.

The report says that "Professor Mayosi was initially discussed as one of the deans 'not meeting' their key performance indicators" but that this "designation was ultimately discarded during the discussion".[68] It seems clear that Professor Mayosi was *not* coping as dean. This was not because he was "black". It was because he, as an individual, responded in entirely understandable ways to vile treatment by the Fallists. The initial designation as "not meeting" all his key performance indicators is thus unsurprising. The fact that this designation was ultimately discarded suggests that the final performance assessment was charitable to, rather than harsh on him.

Another aspect of the purportedly hostile environment cited by the report is the "sense elicited from the interviews with senior black staff, especially those boasting national and international research prominence, that in many ways they were more revered abroad than at UCT, their home."[69] I do not deny that there are "black" staff who feel this way, but this experience is not the preserve of "blacks". There are innumerable "non-blacks" who have exactly the same experience.

This is an excellent example of how some people interpret something bad as the product of racism when in fact it may have nothing to do with race. Of course, it may *seem* to them that others are revered in their home institution, but such impressions cannot just be accepted. Among the reasons for this is that it is so much easier to feel that one is not appreciated than it is to feel that others are not appreciated. Other people's lives often look better than one's own, but that is often because one simply does not know those lives from the inside.[70]

In any event, it is again not clear what any of this has to do with Professor Mayosi's decline. He was revered at UCT and thrived until he assumed the deanship. Then everything unravelled. There is no evidence that this is because he was suddenly unappreciated (or insufficiently appreciated) by UCT, the institution. Instead, it has everything to do with the toxic environment in which he found himself – an environment created by the protestors.

The report also referred to "informal networks" which are allegedly entrenched in UCT's institutional climate. It claimed that "blacks" felt as though they were not party to these networks.[71] Again, it is very difficult to evaluate such claims. It would be surprising if there were no informal networks. It would also be surprising if individuals – whether "black" or "white" – not embedded in those networks, did not feel a sense of disempowerment. However, the report provided no evidence that "blacks" were more excluded from such networks. Moreover, there is reason to think that informal networks connected with institutional power would be more important than those networks that are not connected with such power. Given the number of "blacks" in leadership positions, it would be surprising if informal networks connected to them were more marginalised. Thus, even those who think that the informal networks have a racial component to them, do not have reason for thinking that "blacks" are disadvantaged by informal networks – at least not without much more evidence and argument. In any event, the report provides no evidence that Professor *Mayosi* was unconnected or that this was a cause of his problems.

A final claim made by the report in support of the idea that the UCT environment is especially difficult for senior "black" academics is the claim that they are caught between competing expectations – for example, between the expectations of management to hold the official line and from "black staff and students [who] often see fellow blacks in leadership positions as allies to help fight their battles and advance transformation".[72] Applying this dynamic to Professor Mayosi, the panel said that during the "student protests it became clear that fellow staff members, mainly white, expected black leaders and Professor Mayosi in particular to be a buffer between protesting students and faculty members."[73]

The panel may well have been correct that Fallists had a greater expectation that "black" staff would be allies. However, while this would put some senior "black" academics in an invidious position, it would not be a uniquely invidious position. First, there were "black" deans who were unscathed by the Fallists. At least one such dean aided and abetted the protestors to such an extent that he was not subjected to the treatment to which Professor Mayosi was subjected. Second, any "white" dean or other senior university leader not capitulating adequately to the Fallists would be branded "racist" – which is at least as bad as being called a "coconut" or "sell-out".

Even Max Price himself, arguably the principal capitulator, was subjected to not only name-calling, but also fire-bombing of his office, and personal violence, with the threat of more. This was because although he capitulated, he did not capitulate enough (or quickly enough) to satisfy the insatiable Fallist appetite. He too was caught between competing expectations – those of student protesters and the staff who supported them, and those of vast swathes of the university who felt he was not taking a sufficiently strong stand against the protestors. The relevant difference between Bongani Mayosi and Max Price was not racial. It was that these two individual human beings had different personalities. It is a sign of the pathological environment that this cannot be recognized, and that everything has to be cast in terms of people's race.

The panel's report made a number of recommendations. Most disturbing among these is the following one:

> Given the recurring concerns about identity issues centring on race, gender, age group, religion, social class and nationality, it has become imperative to subject

staff, particularly those in leadership positions, to a deep, and compulsory, immersion programme of diversity sensitivity training. This must be more than the usual basic one- or two-day workshop that institutions often conduct. Such a programme should assist staff members to unlearn often subconscious identity-based prejudices and relearn new skills while embracing a new worldview on issues of diversity. The programme should be designed and driven by a credible institution or individual, with a proven track record of conducting transformative programmes of this nature which have demonstrated sustainable impact.[74]

Sensitivity is, of course, a good thing. However, it is possible to have too much of it. This is called hyper-sensitivity. When sensitivity training is blind to the possibility of hypersensitivity, as it surely is when it is driven by ideological pre-conceptions, then it becomes an instrument for *in*sensitivity to alternative views. Put another way, it becomes an instrument for ensuring (at least outward) conformity rather than recognizing and benefiting from a diversity of opinion.

Currently, the main purveyors of "identity-based prejudices" are those who see everything through the prism of identity issues. Instead of viewing human beings in their full array of individual characteristics and complexity, they reduce everybody to intersecting categories such as race, sex, gender, sexual orientation, religion, and class. Even at the intersection of these categories, individuals remain individuals. The last thing we need is to have ideologues with these pre-packaged conceptions of people lecturing us about "identity-based prejudices".

There are no prizes for anticipating that the Fallists would spin the report's findings to fit their own narrative. Fallist faeces-flinger, Chumani Maxwele, was quoted as saying:

> We are feeling happy that the students are exonerated by the very report of the university. The commissioners were clear that the university mishandled the communication about his death, and part of that was the blaming of students. And for us, we maintained that there is no black professor that can die as a result of being called names. Now that the inquiry exonerated students, they can apologise for accusing them, particularly black students, of contributing to his death while hiding the racists in health sciences.[75]

Anybody reading the report will see that the student protestors were certainly *not* exonerated.[76] The significant role they played is emphasised in the report. This is not to suggest that this was the sole factor, but it is the single biggest one. To suggest otherwise is wishful thinking on the part of Mr Maxwele. The same is true of his glib claim that "no black professor ... can die as a result of being called names".

CONCLUSION

The institutional climate at UCT is not hostile to "blacks" as "blacks". It is hostile to some "blacks", as it is to some "whites". There is much more evidence of an anti-"white" hostility than there is of an anti-"black" hostility, as this book shows. Yet, the narrative of UCT as a hotbed of anti-"black" racism is dominant. The IRTC and the inquiry into Bongani Mayosi's deanship have enabled this. By parroting the narrative without evaluating it, these panels have accorded a more official imprimatur to the narrative, which then becomes a backdrop through which other events are experienced. If everybody is telling you that UCT is "anti-black", then the next time you, as a "black" person, encounter some hardship at UCT, you are more likely to infer that it is the result of racism rather than, for example, the fact that life is filled with hardships. Even if you do not yourself believe that your hardship is the result of racism, there is a strong incentive to say that it is, because that narrative is more likely to bring you allies and relief.

Chapter 20
BENDING OVER BAC-WARDS

A TOXIC COCKTAIL

In the middle of 2020, an instance of UCT's institutional pathology made national headlines. This case, ignited by the Black Academic Caucus and then taken up also by the Vice-Chancellor and her executive team, was characterized by a toxic mix of racial paranoia, false accusations of racism, administrative overreach, threats to academic freedom, mobbing, and (attempted) silencing.

The Black Academic Caucus has some similarities to the Nationalist government of the Apartheid era. One of these similarities is that whereas the latter were paranoid about communists, finding them "under every bush", the BAC is paranoid about "racists", finding them under many a mortar board (and elsewhere). In early June 2020 they expressed their outrage at a commentary published in the *South African Journal of Science* by UCT economist Professor Nicoli Nattrass. They did so first in a public statement,[1] and then in an open letter[2] sent to the Minister and Deputy Minister of Higher Education, Science and Technology, to the Association of Science of South Africa, and to the *South African Journal of Science (SAJS)*. In the open letter they called for the retraction of Professor Nattrass's commentary by the journal. Professor Nattrass's commentary had presented some preliminary research on why "black" South African students were less likely than others to consider studying biological sciences.

Judging from the BAC's public statement and open letter, one would have thought that Professor Nattrass was a racist who had been peddling stereotypes about "blacks". The BAC accused her, inter alia, of making gross generalizations about "black" South African students, failing to acknowledge the structural and socio-economic inequalities that could underpin subject choice, presenting the "trope that black people are materialistic in their pursuits and lack respect for wildlife or the environment", and of providing material to be "used by white supremacists in promoting their agendas". The BAC said that the research fails to meet the basic requirements of scientific vigour. It called for the withdrawal of the publication and it called on "UCT to strongly condemn this research".

The intensity of the BAC outrage was, as usual, inversely proportional to its justification. Professor Nattrass is no racist and there was no good reason to be *outraged* by her commentary. (By contrast, as Professor Nattrass herself made clear, there may be plenty of room for *disagreement* with and *criticism* of her study.)

Consider the reason why the research was undertaken. UCT's Institute for Communities and Wildlife in Africa (iCWild), where Professor Nattrass is one of two directors, was scheduled for a review. iCWild had had difficulty attracting "black" South African students. iCWild decided to do some exploratory research to find out why this might be the case, in the hope of being able to attract more such students. Contrary to the claims of the BAC, Professor Nattrass had explicitly recognized structural and socio-economic inequalities as crucial. A questionnaire was constructed in consultation with students (of different "races"[3]). One objective was to test prevailing narratives, even though these narratives might arise from background inequalities. The narratives obviously did not include a narrative of innate racial difference, and the study found that the variable "black South African" was *not* statistically significant (when attitudinal variables were controlled for).

Other variables, however, were significant. The key differences, Professor Nattrass reported, "pertained to career aspirations, attitudes towards evolution and experience with, and attitudes to animals". Again, Professor Nattrass did not claim that these variables were innate. Instead, she suggested that they were likely explained by socio-economic inequalities. For example, students coming from more deprived backgrounds would be more likely to choose careers that provide more financial security than conservation biology does. Similarly, inequalities in education could explain why "black" South Africans were less likely to assent to the claim that "humans evolved from apes". Professor Nattrass hypothesized that wealthier people might have more experience of companion animals and that this might play some role in determining interest in a career involving animals.

She did *not* claim that these results were generalizable (as the BAC alleged that she had claimed). They were initial results from an exploratory survey and were intended to lay the foundation for further discussion and research. Instead of eliciting reasoned discussion, the commentary became the subject of a moral panic – as a result of the BAC's ignorant, incendiary statement.

The BAC failed to understand the research methodology it criticised. For example, it wrongly assumed that the study contained no control. Nor did it understand the findings, incorrectly claiming, for instance, that Professor Nattrass had claimed that "black" people have no respect for wildlife. To the contrary, the study found that there were high levels of support for conservation from "black" South Africans and other students. Therein lies one possible value in studying prevailing narratives about why South African "blacks" are less likely to study conservation biology. The study might find that a narrative is groundless, in which case one has some evidence rather than the bald assertion to which the BAC is prone.

Of course, one might also find that narratives have an element of truth to them, but there are both racist and non-racist ways of responding to such findings. Recognizing the limitations of a study, and that the findings are likely attributable to injustice and disadvantage, are among the non-racist ways of responding. Professor Nattrass met these conditions and certainly did not, as the BAC asserted, say that potential "black" South African students "are to blame" for not choosing conservation biology in greater numbers. She did not say that they are "morally and culturally indisposed to the field", nor did she jump from there "to the conclusion that black students have no desire to study biological sciences".

That said, it can be understandable if there are *sensitivities* when a study has findings that seem to reinforce preconceived ideas about a group. Imagine, for example, that somebody were investigating why, unlike in the past, there are so few (especially male) Jewish students studying medicine at UCT. Imagine further that a researcher acknowledged that strong racial preferences (in favour of "blacks") played a part, yet wanted to know what further factors might be playing a role. Imagine that it were found that (male) Jewish students were choosing other careers and perhaps were disproportionately found in the

Commerce Faculty.

Such a finding might be congenial to antisemites, and that might be a cause for Jewish sensitivity. However, would that mean that the research was antisemitic? Not necessarily. First, if it were *true* that Jewish students at UCT were currently disproportionately drawn to Commerce, there might be perfectly non-prejudicial explanations. The antisemite would suggest that Jews are genetically or culturally drawn to commerce. The unprejudiced person may recognize that what careers Jews enter into have varied with place and time, and that their choices (like those of "blacks" and everybody else) are influenced by their social circumstances in a given time and place. It would be a mistake to dismiss the research findings or the research itself as antisemitic.

Second, there might be entirely unprejudiced reasons why somebody might want to conduct such research. I am not aware of such research actually being done. However, the reason is likely that the dearth of Jewish medical students is not something that the Faculty of Health Sciences is constantly asked about and pressured to explain and "rectify". By contrast, iCWild was under considerable institutional and social pressure on account of the dearth of South African "blacks" in its programme. When there is such pressure, one must fully expect the matter to be investigated. The results will then be what they will be.

The BAC statement criticised Professor Nattrass for presenting "tropes" about "blacks". One of these tropes, they say, is that "blacks" do not care for wildlife and the environment. We have already seen that Professor Nattrass's study found that trope to be groundless, but her study did find some correlation between the number of companion animals one has had, and interest in biological sciences. The BAC's response to this was:

Apparently, judged from the vantage point of whiteness how can black people possibly care for wildlife and the environment if they don't fill their lives with pets? Because nothing shows care for an animal quite like owning it, restricting its movement, dominating its life and using it for emotional comfort.

"Black" South Africans do have proportionately fewer companion animals than "white" South Africans.[4] Professor Nattrass's socio-economic explanation is certainly more compelling and less noxious than former President Jacob Zuma's claim that having a "pet dog is part of 'white culture'" and that "blacks" should not try to emulate "whites".[5] Who needs tropes about "blacks" from "whites" when you can get them from former President Zuma?

What about the suggestion that "blacks" do not care about animals? Some of my Humanities colleagues and I unconsciously assumed that this suggestion was groundless. We made that assumption when, in 2015, we proposed that Faculty events not include animal products, in order to avoid complicity in abhorrent treatment of animals.[6] We assumed that those, irrespective of race, purporting to be interested in justice, would support a proposal to treat animals more justly. In response, race-baiters, including a number of BAC members, sought to characterise the proposal as a "trojan horse for racism" and as culturally insensitive to "blacks". (They seemed to assume that "blacks" are the only ones whose culture involves eating animals and their products, even though it is actually the case that the vast majority of human cultures involve these practices.) They then voted against the motion and censured those of us who had initiated it. The BAC issued a public statement in favour of those with regressive views about animals. In the light of this, the BAC's faux concern about the welfare of companion animals is deeply ironic.

None of the foregoing is to suggest that Professor Nattrass's study was without error or could not have been improved. She acknowledged this herself – even in her initial commentary in the *South African Journal of Science*. Of course, there is a difference between such an acknowledgement and thinking that the BAC's critique is correct. I have argued that the BAC is seriously mistaken. However, imagine for the sake of argument that there is much more to its critique than I have granted. There is still a problem with the way the BAC responded. If one disagrees with a published article, the appropriate response is to respond with another article. It is not to write to the Ministry of Higher Education, Science and Technology. It is not to whip up a Twitter storm with reckless accusations of racism – what we might call "*tropes* of white racism" – that ignore a person's *bona fides*.

Consider, for example, BAC member Adam Haupt's paper, "Liquid racism, possessive investments in whiteness and academic freedom at a post-apartheid university".[7] I believe that this piece of "research" is a display of inflammatory, intellectually dishonest, ideological drivel that is therefore unethical. I did not rush to Twitter to excoriate him and whip up outrage. I did not propose that he be censured. I did not call on the University Executive to distance itself from his article. I did not write to the Minister of Higher Education, or to the editor of the book in which the article was published.

Instead, I wrote a response[8] in which I analysed and evaluated Adam Haupt's argument. I examined what he actually said and offered reasoned arguments in response. Nothing in my argument relies on his (self-declared) racial identity (and *a fortiori* not on any racial identity others may attribute to him). The BAC lacks the maturity to respond in such a way. It is more a political caucus than an academic one.

When there is a brouhaha about something, there is a common human tendency to assume that anything causing that much outrage must be outrageous. Cool heads are needed to step back and ask whether or not the outrage is apt. I think that it is inapt in this case. Even when outrage is not *justified*, it might still be *explained*. Why was the BAC as outraged as it was? It is hard to know, but there are a number of (non-mutually exclusive) possibilities.

It is possible that they simply did not understand the research. Alternatively, or in addition, perhaps they did not like some of its findings. Among these might be the finding that a very small proportion of the South African "black" students had what were taken by the researchers as "Fallist" views. Another finding was that "black South African" was not a significant variable in a multi-variate analysis. An entity that puts as much store on the category "blacks" as the BAC does, might be discomforted by a finding that that category is not a good marker. If it is not a good marker in determining interest in biological sciences, it might also be a poor marker in the innumerable other instances where the BAC is happy to trade on racial markers.

THE EXECUTIVE AS ACADEMIC EXECUTIONER

It would have been bad enough if all that happened was that the BAC defamed and denounced Professor Nattrass. It was worse still that they wrote to the Academy of Science of South Africa, the editor of the *South African Journal of Science* (*SAJS*) and the Minister and Deputy Minister of Higher Education calling for the paper to be retracted. Professor Jonathan Jansen, the President of the Academy of Science of South Africa, which publishes the *SAJS*, described the act of writing to the Ministry with the call for retraction as a "stunt" that "not even apartheid's apparatchiks would pull".[9]

What makes matters worse is that when the BAC called on "UCT to strongly condemn the research", the UCT Executive snapped into action, doing exactly that. Instead of behaving like leaders, they leapt to do the bidding of the BAC. Without asking Professor Nattrass for her response to the criticism, the Executive acted precipitously in issuing a statement[10] that it tweeted to its more than 200 000 followers.

In this statement, they parroted the BAC's claim that the paper had methodological and conceptual flaws and that it was "constructed on unexamined assumptions about what black people think, feel, aspire to and are capable of". They pronounced that the "paper is offensive to black students at UCT; black people in general and to any academic who understands that the quality of research is inextricably linked to its ethical grounding". Ironically, *these* are unexamined assumptions about what black people (and others) think and feel, offered without conducting even any exploratory research of the Executive's own.

Lest we were in any doubt, the Executive went on to affirm its "commitment to dealing with any instances of racism, sexism, discrimination of any sort or any unethical behaviour" and renewed its "resolve to foster a university culture that is aligned with our values and that is sensitive, inclusive and free of racial prejudices". (This book shows just how selective that commitment and resolve are.) They distanced themselves from the content of Professor Nattrass's paper, and said that they were investigating the matter further.

The Vice-Chancellor telephoned Professor Jane Carruthers, the editor of the *South African Journal of Science* on 4 June 2020. What *exactly* happened during that conversation is the cause of some disagreement. Professor Nattrass reports[11] that Professor Carruthers had said that Professor Phakeng asked her to withdraw the paper, which she initially agreed to do. Professor Carruthers denies that she ever said that, claiming merely that Professor Phakeng had explained "the serious situation that had developed at UCT" as a result of the paper's publication, and that she, Professor Carruthers, "was able to include this information in further discussions with the *SAJS* Editorial Advisory Board".[12] Professor Phakeng herself has said that while she did not "demand" retraction, she did "advise" it.[13] Professor Jansen described the phone call to Professor Carruthers as "so chilling that it should send shivers down our democratic spines".[14]

It was subsequently decided that the Academy of Science of South Africa and its journal would not capitulate to the pressure brought to bear by Professor Phakeng. When the journal refused to withdraw the paper, the Vice-Chancellor and a Deputy Vice-Chancellor made attempts to have the Head of the Department of Economics as well as the co-Director of iCWild persuade Professor Nattrass to withdraw her own paper. Pressure was brought to bear during at least one of those conversations. In both cases the Vice-Chancellor or Deputy Vice-Chancellor were told to speak directly to Professor Nattrass.

Eventually Professor Phakeng *did* call Professor Nattrass and made it clear to her that she should withdraw her paper. When Professor Nattrass asked her why she must do so, Professor Phakeng responded that it contained conceptual and methodological flaws. When Professor Nattrass asked her what those were, she was unable to provide a satisfactory answer. At some point, Professor Phakeng said that she "did not want to debate" with Professor Nattrass.[15] There you have it: a vice-chancellor does not want to debate the merits of an academic paper that she seeks to have withdrawn and has already publicly condemned.

Professor Nattrass stood her ground. She responded to her critics in the press,[16] where the furore had already received widespread coverage, and had her lawyers send a letter to the University Executive. Among the contents of the latter was an objection to the investigation that the university had launched into an alleged breach of research ethics codes by Professor

Nattrass. The letter noted that such an investigation was *mala fide* because the Executive had already reached a conclusion about Professor Nattrass's study.

There was no shortage of people – many of the Twitterati, a number of academics, and the Psychological Society of South Africa[17] – willing to trash Professor Nattrass. In the *Sunday Times* she was labelled the "Mampara of the Week".[18] Muhammad Zakaria Asmal, a lecturer at UNISA (the University of South Africa), who is also a PhD student at UCT, wrote on Facebook that "Nicoli Natrass is a dumb ass white bitch who is uglier than her dog" and that he was not "sure whether Im [sic] more offended by the sickening ugliness of Natrass [sic] which is substantial .. or her dog ...".[19] He did preface and conclude his remarks (which also referred to "uncle Tom mandela" [sic], with the disclaimer that he was invoking his "right to satirical freedom",[20] but one can be sure that if a similar disclaimer accompanied a parallel claim about a "dumb ass black bitch who is uglier than her dog", the BAC and others would have been apoplectic. On the comment about Professor Nattrass they were silent.

Professor Nattrass also had a number of notable public defenders. They included then Democratic Alliance Member of Parliament (and Shadow Minister of Higher Education), Professor Belinda Bozzoli,[21] the "veterans" of the 1968 Archie Mafeje protest sit-in,[22] journalist and former political prisoner, Mr Paul Trewhela,[23] and a few former members of UCT academic staff.[24]

The Council of the Academy of Science of South Africa issued a brief statement, in which it affirmed editorial independence of the journal, the Academy's commitment to academic freedom, and its view that "the appropriate forum for criticism of published research is in the form of academic rebuttal by academic peers in and outside of the pages of the journal".[25] The *South African Journal of Science* then published a special issue devoted to Professor Nattrass's paper. It reprinted that paper, twelve responses (most, but not all of which were critical) as well as a robust response from Professor Nattrass.[26]

In the interim, Professor Jeremy Seekings, a colleague and also husband of Professor Nattrass, attempted to enter into negotiations with UCT's Executive on behalf of Professor Nattrass. Dr Russell Ally, UCT's Executive Director of Alumni and Development served as a mediator. The Executive was represented by Professor Loretta Feris and Associate Professor Lis Lange. Those negotiations, initially conducted via remote meetings (on account of the Covid-19 pandemic) were unsuccessful. However, a further attempt was made via email and eventually, on 22 July 2020, Dr Ally notified Professors Seekings and Nattrass that the (full) Executive had agreed to the following statement, which also met with Professor Nattrass's approval:

> Following discussion between the Executive and Professor Nicoli Nattrass, and noting that the South African Journal of Science recently published a special issue of responses to the Commentary by Prof Nattrass together with a rejoinder by Prof Nattrass, the Executive has decided to withdraw its statement of 5 June 2020 and apologizes for the hurt it caused to Prof Nattrass.
>
> The Executive acknowledges Prof Nattrass' rights as a scholar. Prof Nattrass has made a commitment to take on board constructive feedback on her Commentary. She appreciates that some colleagues and others may have been offended by her Commentary and regrets any hurt that she that she may have caused unintentionally.
>
> The university welcomes rigorous and respectful debate on all issues pertaining to transformation.

That same day, Dr Ally sent this statement through to Ms Gerda Kruger, UCT's Executive Director of Communication and Marketing for advice on publication. It was never published. Instead, Professor Nattrass received a letter from Vice-Chancellor Phakeng, dated 24 July 2020, effectively reneging on the agreement. Professor Phakeng advised Professor Nattrass "that the UCT Executive yesterday in its meeting did not agree to the draft combined statement prepared during the mediation process".

Professor Phakeng said that she wished "to affirm our respect for your academic freedom as a scholar, and your freedom to pursue any scholarly questions you deem important. Your standing as a respected academic at UCT is unquestioned. There was no intention to cause you harm".

But this was followed by a "but". Professor Phakeng said that "we are of the view that the executive has a right and obligation to speak out on matters that may concern the University" and that "we remain concerned that the Commentary has caused offense (intentionally or not), that it does not align with our transformational goals and values at UCT, and that ethical processes that lead the approval of the research may not have been followed correctly." Professor Phakeng claimed that it was their "obligation to look into these matters so as to ascertain whether our concerns are well founded or not".

She noted that Professor Nattrass had complained that the process the Executive had followed hitherto had been "flawed in the light of our statement on 5 June 2020". Professor Phakeng asserted that while she and her team believed that "our process so far was fair and independent, we have now suspended it" because of Professor Nattrass's concerns, and that "we will now proceed with a de novo process within the Commerce Faculty". She also wrote that although the *South African Journal of Science* had published the special issue, "it is important that consideration be given to host a university forum for further academic engagement on this".

ACADEMIC FREEDOM

There is much that is remarkable about this letter from the Vice-Chancellor, beyond the fact that it reneged on an agreement, and was thus a further display of bad faith. There may be rare occasions on which it is appropriate for university leadership to "comment" on how academics utilize their academic freedom and their freedom of expression. Imagine, for example, that a university is home to a (hypothetical) advocate of racial science and Aryan supremacy. I shall call him Professor Schicklgruber. In the face of Professor Schicklgruber's latest conspiracy theory, the university leadership might note that the university should not be taken to endorse his views just because he happens to be a professor in their university. They might even go so far as to say that they reject his theory. However, responsible university leadership would take the opportunity to remind those outraged by Professor Schicklgruber's theory that academic freedom and freedom of expression are important principles and it is not the place of university leaders to silence its professors even when they disagree with them. For precisely that reason, the right to "comment" on a professor's work does not include the right to take the various actions taken by the UCT Executive against Professor Nattrass who in any event, it must be said, is no Professor Schicklgruber.

Nor is it the case that university leaders should comment merely because an academic's research "offends" somebody or because it does "not align with ... transformational goals and values". A higher bar than "offence" is required. Moreover, expecting ideological conformity is antithetical to the very purpose of the university. Under no circumstances should disciplinary inquiries into suspected and purported breaches of research ethics be used as a cover for imposing viewpoint-conformity or for punishing those with unorthodox views. Obviously a university has a right and obligation to pursue *real* breaches of research ethics, but it is patently obvious that this is not what UCT's executive was doing.[27] Claiming that you are starting the process *de novo,* after you have poisoned the well, is wishful thinking at best, if not outright dishonesty.

Critics of Professor Nattrass might argue that it is absurd to argue that there has been an infringement of academic freedom in this case. After all, her paper was *not* withdrawn by the journal. Instead, it was republished in the special issue along with the various responses. She has not (yet) been subjected to any disciplinary action. She has not lost her job.

The premises of this argument may be true, but they do not support a reassuring conclusion about academic freedom. First, even if Professor Nattrass's academic freedom were not infringed, it would still be the case that there had been attempts to infringe upon it. The BAC and UCT's Executive may not have been successful in their attempts to have Professor Nattrass's paper withdrawn, but that does not mean that they did not try. Attempts at infringement of academic freedom are not justifiable merely because they fail.

Second, even though Professor Nattrass stood her ground, the collective action of those mobbing her – but most especially the actions of the BAC and the University Executive – can fully be expected to have a chilling effect, either on her or on others, or both on her and on others. Who would possibly investigate the paucity of "blacks" in any discipline after seeing the treatment to which Professor Nattrass was subjected? If they do ask such questions, the social incentives to find the "right" answers will be significant. That is not good for academia.

This is why the silence of UCT's (now so-called) Academic Freedom Committee (AFC) is so deafening. This silence provides yet more evidence that this committee has abrogated its responsibilities. This is not true of all its members. One temporary member did attempt to get the AFC to make a statement calling on the Vice-Chancellor and other members of the Executive to withdraw their statement of 5 June 2020 and to "issue a public apology to the university community for undermining academic freedom".[28] No such statement was ever made by the AFC, which is not surprising, given that 62.5% of its members denied that UCT's Executive had infringed upon academic freedom "in relation to Prof Nattrass and her paper published in by the SAJS".[29]

Instead of defending academic freedom, these members of the committee exercised themselves about another matter – whether the committee member who had proposed the statement had created the impression that he was writing on behalf of the full AFC when he wrote separately to Professor Carruthers and to the Vice-Chancellors' office to inquire whether the Vice-Chancellor had phoned Professor Carruthers in connection with Professor Nattrass's commentary. Professor Carruthers' answer was that she had.[30] The answer from the Vice-Chancellors office was that the "UCT Executive never phoned the Editor".[31]

Neither the allegation that the Vice-Chancellor had called the *SAJS* editor, nor the possibility that her office had now lied about this to a member of the AFC[32] were matters of concern to the majority of the AFC. Instead of defending academic freedom, they were criticizing one of their fellow AFC committee members who was bothering to investigate the violations of academic freedom.

It is not clear that Elelwani Ramugondo, the Chair of the Academic Freedom Committee, actually understands what academic freedom is. The Academy of Science of South Africa issued a statement in response to the controversy surrounding Professor Nattrass's commentary in the *SAJS*. In that statement, the Academy said, *inter alia*, that it "upholds the academic freedom of any author to submit for publication the results of research in a scholarly journal subject, of course, to editorial review processes and approval". Professor Ramugondo tweeted that statement and added the following comment: "There you have it ... Academic Freedom is not a blank cheque".[33]

Obviously, it is not a blank cheque. Academic freedom, just like other values, has its (justifiable) limits. However, the mistake made by many of those who inappropriately threaten academic freedom is to infer from this that the particular limitations *they* seek to impose are justifiable limitations. Merely noting that academic freedom has its limitations is insufficient to justify a particular limit. The chair of an academic freedom committee interpreted a statement in support of academic freedom as a check on academic freedom.

However, there is a vast difference between claiming that academic papers must be subjected to "editorial review processes and approval" and claiming that a university's management may, on ideological grounds, seek the withdrawal of a paper once it has met that approval and been published. Does the chair of an academic freedom committee not understand that difference?

Perhaps there is another difference that she cannot understand. This is evidenced in an earlier tweet, a few days after the BAC issued its statement condemning Professor Nattrass, and after the Vice-Chancellor had called Professor Carruthers. In this tweet Professor Ramugondo said that it "is not unusual for credible research journals to retract articles for flawed methodology or dubious data sources whenever this comes to light. Respectable journals do so because they are not confused about what academic freedom means".[34]

Respectable journals may not be confused, but Professor Ramugondo certainly is. Respectable journals do withdraw papers if there is evidence of serious scientific negligence or misconduct, such as data tampering or manufacture. They do not withdraw papers merely because other academics disagree with them or find fault with them. If that were the standard, then the vast majority of articles would be withdrawn.

Respectable journals do not withdraw papers merely because lobby groups take to Twitter with their ideologically laden accusations of flawed methodology. Respectable journals certainly do not withdraw a paper because the Vice-Chancellor calls the editor with such a request (or even to communicate "the serious situation that had developed" at her university as a result of the article having been published). It is clear that the chair of UCT's Academic Freedom Committee has little understanding of academic freedom, and seems more eager to limit it than to defend it.[35]

The failure of UCT's Academic Freedom Committee is evident even to people outside of UCT. The University of the Witwatersrand's Professor Nithaya Chetty, who had once fled the University of KwaZulu-Natal, noted as follows:

> The UCT Academic Freedom Committee of a decade ago stood by me in my time of need, but there seems to be an absence of their voice in Nattrass's time of need. Academic freedom is delicate and necessary at our universities. Let us protect it for future generations.[36]

That will not happen if the BAC and its fellow-travellers have their way.

Chapter 21
EXCREMENTAL BEHAVIOUR

The turning point at UCT, I have suggested, came when Chumani Maxwele poured human excrement on the statue of Cecil John Rhodes. That protest precipitated a torrent of excremental behaviour, including much more from Mr Maxwele himself. Some of his horrendous behaviour was part of his political protests, but some of it was not. Over the course of a few years, he engaged in intimidation, racial abuse, defamation, and assault.

UCT was far too indulgent of his outrageous behaviour, while repeatedly failing to give adequate support to his victims. Indeed, in one case, UCT actually prosecuted one of them (unsuccessfully) on the basis of his fabrications. This was another case in which the decent people were betrayed by a university pandering to its worst elements. Immeasurable damage was done.

Mr Maxwele first came to national attention when, on 10

February 2010, he was arrested by South African presidential bodyguards for allegedly "giving the finger" to then President Jacob Zuma's motorcade and then swearing at his bodyguards.[1] His hands were tied behind his back, he was hooded and bundled into a police VIP protection vehicle. He was kept in police custody for 24 hours, during which time he was interrogated and forced to write a letter of apology to President Zuma.[2]

There was widespread sympathy for him around this matter, not least because of the number of complaints that had been lodged by various people against the VIP protection unit and the pervasive sense of its high-handedness and impunity.[3]

The FW de Klerk Foundation's Centre for Constitutional Rights lodged a complaint on his behalf to the South African Human Rights Commission.[4] The irony of Mr Maxwele being assisted by this foundation became apparent only later with his regular invective against "whites".[5] Mr Maxwele then brought a civil suit against Police Minister Nathi Mthethwa for wrongful arrest. He sought R1.4 million and an apology. Before the matter went to court, he was offered a settlement of R80 000.[6] It seems that Mr Maxwele initially rejected that offer. He did eventually accept a settlement, although the quantum of the damages seems to have been the subject of a non-disclosure agreement.[7]

In 2011, while the above case was dragging on, Mr Maxwele registered at UCT for an undergraduate Humanities degree that should have taken three years to complete. His academic performance started out poorly and became steadily worse. By 2015 he was effectively (even if not officially) a very part-time student and a full-time protestor and troublemaker.

The protests began on 9 March 2015 with Mr Maxwele's strewing human excrement on a statue of Cecil John Rhodes that occupied a central place on UCT's main campus. It seems that Mr Maxwele had notified journalists in advance of his protest. When security guards attempted to stop a reporter from photographing the protest, Mr Maxwele is alleged to have assaulted at least one of those guards.[8]

Earlier that year, on 17 February, Mr Maxwele had entered the computer laboratory at the Hiddingh campus, without authorization. When he was asked to produce his student card, he refused to do so, and "directed verbal abuse in an aggressive manner" toward the part-time student employee who had asked to see his student card.[9] He shouted the words "fuck off" at her, "clenched his fists and banged on the computer table in a loud and aggressive manner".[10] The student employee called Campus Protections Services. The security officer's resultant presence did not cause Mr Maxwele to restrain himself. He continued pounding the desk and swearing at the student employee. The security officer asked the student employee to leave, which she did. Disciplinary charges were initiated against Mr Maxwele for this incident.

In the ensuing months and years, Mr Maxwele engaged in similar and worse behaviour. Some of this was in the course of "protests", but on other occasions it was not. For example, he ranted, assaulted people, intimidated them, and regularly spewed forth racial hatred and abuse. In this chapter, I shall focus on (some of) those incidents that were *not* part of the protests. It is those incidents that eventually resulted in his expulsion, although this was overturned on a procedural technicality by the Western Cape High Court. It is also those incidents that the people sympathetic to his protests will have the greatest difficulty defending. However, I shall mention some of his protest-related violations as well. I do so in order to provide context. Part of this context is the timeline of events, but part of it is the attitudinal and behavioural continuity between his protest-related and non-protest related behaviour.

Within a month of Mr Maxwele pouring poo on the statue of Cecil John Rhodes, the statue was removed. The process for reaching that decision was clearly expedited in response to the protests. Intimidation may also have played a role. On 8 April 2015, there was an invasion of a special meeting of Council that had been convened to discuss the matter of the statue. At least some of those who invaded the meeting were chanting the racist slogan, "One settler, one bullet".[11] At that meeting, Council (then chaired by Archbishop Njongonkulu Ndungane) authorized the removal of the statue. It was removed the following day, 9 April 2015.

MAY DAY MAYDAY

Less than a month later, on 1 May 2015, Mr Maxwele racially abused, intimidated and assaulted a lecturer in the Department of Mathematics and Applied Mathematics.[12] It was a public holiday, but the lecturer, whom I shall call Ms Mathematica, was at work, getting a head start on marking a large number of scripts along with two tutors.

At approximately 12h00, Ms Mathematica was leaving the Mathematics Building when a young man – whom she only later learned was Mr Maxwele – approached her and asked her to let him into the building. She responded by asking why he wanted access. He replied that he wanted a place to study. This time he did show his student card. Ms Mathematica replied that the building and all the venues inside the building were locked on account of the public holiday, and that students wishing to study had to use other, designated study venues on campus.

Mr Maxwele replied aggressively, claiming that it was his right to check that the venues were locked because he "pays fees to the institution". Ms Mathematica allowed him to enter the building and then escorted him as he went from venue to venue. When he found that the venues were indeed locked, he became increasingly aggressive, and shouted at Ms Mathematica, accusing her as a "white" woman, of taking away the rights of "black" students. Ms Mathematica then asked him to leave the building, at which time he shouted at her that "the statue fell; now it is time for all whites to go". She again asked him to leave to which he responded, in an aggressive tone, that he was not interested in the opinion of "white" people and that they should all be killed". He did not leave.

Ms Mathematica felt scared. On two previous occasions, in 2014, she had been attacked in her office by a young man claiming to be a student. This, combined with the memory of the killing of Professor Hahn, had led her to be especially aware of the access protocols. When she mentioned the killing of Professor Hahn, Mr Maxwele replied by asking "who cares, just because some Head of Department was killed is not a reason to lock the building and not give access to the students".

Given Ms Mathematica's fear, she sought help from the two tutors who were marking scripts in the department library. One of the tutors attempted to intervene and calm Mr Maxwele, but Mr Maxwele continued to shout and swear at Ms Mathematica and the two tutors. Ms Mathematica then ran to her office, locked the door, and attempted to call Campus Protection Services (CPS). Despite multiple calls to CPS, she was unable to reach them. Mr Maxwele followed her to her office and insisted on entering. She refused, which led him to bang on her office door aggressively (with his hand and body). She heard him shouting that "we must not listen to the whites, we do not need their apologies, they have to be removed from UCT and killed".

Ms Mathematica then became concerned that Mr Maxwele might harm the tutor who was outside her office. She thus opened her office door. Mr Maxwele pushed her into her office, causing her to retreat to behind her desk. Mr Maxwele remained at her office door, verbally abusing her.

The commotion caused another member of academic staff in the Department of Mathematics to leave his office and find out what was happening. He entered Ms Mathematica's office, assured her that she was safe, and asked her to put down the phone (to CPS). He managed to calm down Mr Maxwele and escort him from the building.

Ms Mathematica was left traumatized by the incident, which lasted about an hour. The following day, 2 May 2015, she laid a detailed complaint against Mr Maxwele. The complaint was investigated by Mr Steven Ganger, UCT's Investigations Manager at CPS. He took a statement from Ms Mathematica, as well as from the two tutors and from the other Mathematics academic. The latter three written statements all corroborated Ms Mathematica's account (from the point that they became witness to the encounter). Mr Ganger later found, also in support of Ms Mathematica's statement, that the CPS phone numbers had not been working at the time when she had been calling for assistance.

It should not be necessary to state this, but in an environment where the racial paranoia of Mr Maxwele is uncritically accepted, it may help to note that Ms Mathematica is the only "white" person in this episode. The two tutors, the other Mathematics academic, and the investigations manager were "black". This was not a "white" conspiracy against a poor persecuted "black" student. Instead, there were six people, of whom five people comported themselves with decency, honesty, and integrity, while the sixth behaved like a thug.

Mr Ganger attempted, by mobile phone and email, to contact Mr Maxwele to obtain a statement from him, but received no response at first. When Mr Maxwele did deign to reply, he told Mr Ganger that he would meet him a specific time at Mr Maxwele's home. Mr Ganger replied that he was not available to meet at that time. Mr Ganger suggested another time on 7 May, and said that he would meet Mr Maxwele at Mr Ganger's office. Mr Maxwele replied "I will not be able to see you in your office. This month, maybe next month".

On 7 May, Mr Ganger was asked to serve Mr Maxwele with a Provisional Suspension Order and notification to attend a suspension hearing. Mr Maxwele initially refused to accept the relevant documents, but eventually did, although he refused to sign for receipt.

On 11 May, Mr Maxwele arrived at Mr Ganger's office, presented him with a written statement, and said that he wanted to lay a complaint against Ms Mathematica who, he alleged, had racially abused *him*. Mr Ganger then opened a case against Ms Mathematica. He met with her, explained her rights, including the right to remain silent and to have a union representative present. However, she waived those rights, read Mr Maxwele's statement and responded that it was untrue. Mr Ganger then showed Mr Maxwele's statement to the witnesses from whom he had obtained statements and they all confirmed that Mr Maxwele's statement contained falsehoods.

On this basis, Mr Ganger concluded that there was insufficient evidence to support any charges against Ms Mathematica. Mr Ganger further noted that he found it very strange that Mr Maxwele only reported the alleged racial abuse so long – ten days – after it was alleged to have occurred, and four days after he had received the charge sheet against him.

On 12 May, the statement that Mr Maxwele had handed to Mr Ganger was published in full by the *Cape Times*. (For details about the cosy relationship that the *Cape Times* had with the Fallists and with Mr Maxwele in particular, see the Conclusion.[13]) Given that the statement mentioned Ms Mathematica by (her real) name, it defamed her by disseminating Mr Maxwele's false allegations about her.

On 13 May a hearing was held in order to determine whether the temporary suspension order against Mr Maxwele should be made final. The suspension decision was finalised. On the same day, but entirely independently, UCT granted amnesty to all those who had been involved in protests between 9 March 2015 and 12h00 on 18 May 2015.[14] While Mr Maxwele had been granted amnesty for his protests, the suspension remained in place because it was unconnected to the protests (other than in the mind of Mr Maxwele).

On 2 June, Mr Maxwele filed papers with South Africa's Equality Court.[15] He also appealed the suspension decision via UCT's internal appeal mechanism. This latter hearing was scheduled for 4 and 5 June 2015, but was postponed because Mr Maxwele's legal representatives submitted a medical certificate stating that Mr Maxwele was "indisposed" and could not present himself until 9 June 2015.[16] The UCT appeal hearing took place on 10 June and the suspension order was set aside[17] on the basis of a technicality.[18]

UCT then issued a second provisional suspension order on 16 June 2015. At the subsequent suspension hearing, on 18 June, a second final suspension order was issued. In response, Mr Maxwele then instituted proceedings against UCT in the Western Cape Division of the High Court of South Africa. Before that case was heard (on 25 August 2015), UCT altered the terms of the suspension, allowing Mr Maxwele to attend classes for which he was registered[19] and to use the library.[20]

On 18 August 2015, UCT entered into an agreement with Rhodes Must Fall, and granted a further amnesty.[21] One stipulation of the agreement was that UCT would "permanently withdraw disciplinary charges relating to continued occupation of Avenue House beyond 18 May 2015".[22]

This further latitude granted to the protestors stands in juxtaposition to an event that took place the same day.[23] Ms Mathematica was subjected to a "Preliminary Investigation Committee" in response to Mr Maxwele's allegations against Ms Mathematica. This was despite Mr Ganger's conclusion that there was insufficient evidence to support Mr Maxwele's allegations, and despite the fact that in public statements,[24] UCT had effectively accepted Ms Mathematica's rather than Mr Maxwele's account of what had happened.

UCT's policy on disciplinary procedures for academic staff

specifically states that "formal action must not be taken without prima facie evidence of misconduct" and that when "the Vice-Chancellor believes that there is an allegation of serious misconduct which requires formal investigation he/she must appoint a Preliminary Investigating Committee (PIC) to consider the application".[25]

In other words, while Max Price was repeatedly drawing and then erasing red lines for student protestors, he was convening a PIC to investigate Ms Mathematica despite the investigations manager having concluded, on very reasonable grounds, that there was insufficient evidence to prosecute a case against her.

However, whether or not one thinks that Mr Maxwele's allegations, even though contradicted by all the witnesses, constituted a *prima face* case against Ms Mathematica, the PIC should clearly have reached the conclusion that this case should not be pursued. Instead, it decided that Ms Mathematica should face the second stage of a disciplinary process for academic staff – a Committee of Inquiry (COI). Ms Mathematica was advised of this on 1 September 2015.

In the interim, on 20 August 2015, Mr Maxwele intimidated Ms Mathematica a second time. While she was speaking to a colleague outside the Mathematics Building, Mr Maxwele approached her from behind and said "You supposed to have security guards now, a?". Both Ms Mathematica and her colleague heard this, but her colleague, wanting Mr Maxwele to repeat what he had said, asked him what he had said. In response to this, Mr Maxwele said "Nothing, just greeting". When Ms Mathematica's colleague attempted to engage him further, Mr Maxwele said things such as "this woman ... she is a racist ... we will kill all your evidence". He then began speaking about "money, Marikana and politics".[26]

Within forty minutes of that event, Ms Mathematica wrote to the Vice-Chancellor, the Dean of Science, Mr Ganger and Ms

Mathematica's representative from the Academics' Union, to report the matter. She noted that the terms of Mr Maxwele's suspension prohibited him from approaching her or the Mathematics Building.

Following this incident, a Campus Protection Services officer was stationed outside Ms Mathematica's office[27] and accompanied her around campus.[28] At some point, a security gate was also installed across her office door.

This was not the last time that Mr Maxwele intimidated Ms Mathematica (and others). On 15 September 2015, the High Court of South Africa issued a judgement setting aside UCT's final suspension order against Mr Maxwele (again on various technical grounds). Mr Maxwele wasted no time. Within an hour or two of that High Court judgement having been issued, he was pacing up and down outside Ms Mathematica's office, loudly speaking (or pretending to speak) to somebody on his mobile telephone. Ms Mathematica's door was open because a colleague had come to see her. Ms Mathematica saw Mr Maxwele point at her and say "this racist, stupid lecturer". At that point, the security guard closed and locked her door. Ms Mathematica continued to hear the following sorts of phrases from Mr Maxwele: "all the people in this university are stupid", "stupid lecturers", "stupid security", "racists at UCT", and "the falling of the statue". This continued for about ten minutes before Mr Maxwele left.

Ms Mathematica was so traumatised by this incident that she was unable to teach that afternoon. Indeed, her series of experiences with Mr Maxwele up to this point and also later caused her deep anxiety and fear. She was put on paid leave for a month and prescribed medication.

The COI into Mr Maxwele's allegations against Ms Mathematica was scheduled for 2 November 2015. Mr Maxwele was advised, via his lawyers, of this date and asked to attend. (He had failed to attend the PIC hearing despite having been notified of that.) On 25 September, confirmation was received that Mr Maxwele would be present. However, on 12 October Mr Maxwele attempted to have the date changed on the grounds that he was due to write an examination that day. On investigation, it was found that his examination would be finished before the hearing was due to begin and thus the chair of the committee declined to change the date of the hearing. This was communicated to Mr Maxwele's lawyers.

It transpired that the examinations scheduled for that week did not take place at all on account of further protests. Nevertheless, neither Mr Maxwele nor his lawyers were present at the COI hearing. Mr Maxwele was photographed at a protest outside parliament a little later that day.

UCT had engaged Halton Cheadle, who is both a prominent attorney and a UCT Emeritus Professor, to prosecute the case. An advocate, Francois van Zyl, was engaged (at the expense of the Academics' Union) to defend Ms Mathematica. Both Ms Mathematica and one of the tutors were ready to give evidence. The other possible witnesses refused to give evidence because they feared retaliation from Mr Maxwele. In other words, they were intimidated. However, written statements from them (and Mr Maxwele) were available to the committee, but because these statements were unsworn and not subject to cross examination, their probative value as evidence was more limited than the sworn statements made by those present.

When neither Mr Maxwele nor his lawyers arrived at the hearing, the available evidence was presented and Ms Mathematics and the tutor confirmed the veracity of their affidavits. The committee deliberated for about an hour and then delivered its decision. The decision and justification was subsequently committed to writing on 11 November 2015 and conveyed to Ms Mathematica on 25 November.

Ms Mathematica was acquitted on all charges. The

Committee said that the fact that Mr Maxwele's statement was not sworn and he was not present to testify was sufficient to dismiss the charges. However, it cited further reasons in Ms Mathematica's favour. First, the sworn evidence of a witness corroborated Ms Mathematica's account and contradicted Mr Maxwele's. The timing of their respective complaints provided further support for Ms Mathematica's accounts. Finally, the motive that Mr Maxwele had imputed to Ms Mathematica – that she was trying to victimize him on account of his protests – was undermined by the fact that neither Ms Mathematica nor the two tutors knew Mr Maxwele's identity until he had been escorted from the Mathematics Building by Ms Mathematica's colleague who, when he returned, told them all who the student was. By all accounts (other than Mr Maxwele's) Ms Mathematica was motivated only by her fear for her physical safety.

By the end of 2015, Mr Maxwele's fabrications about Ms Mathematica had resulted in her being subjected to the full process of a disciplinary inquiry. Although she was eventually vindicated, this was not before she had been put through the mill. By contrast, the well-grounded cases against Mr Maxwele were far from resolved. Mr Maxwele, with his ample legal representation, was engaged in protracted lawfare. Incredibly, while he continued to seek legal recourse, he also continued to offend. His further public defamation of Ms Mathematica[29] after his allegations had been rejected by the Committee of Inquiry was only part of his ongoing offending.

"SHACKVILLE"

15 February 2016 saw the start of the new academic year and also the start of the new protest year. The latter began with what became known as the Shackville protests. These protests were ostensibly about a shortage of residential accommodation for

students, but the demands quickly multiplied. It was during these protests that their criminality was arguably at its peak. For example, it was then that artworks, university vehicles, and the Vice-Chancellor's office were torched. This arson was added to instances of assault and intimidation.

The Shackville protest began with the erection of a shack and the placement of an adjacent portable toilet on Residence Road, thus blocking a vehicular and pedestrian arterial route on campus. Tape was used to cordon off an area. When a (non-Shackville) student walked under that tape, Mr Maxwele pushed him. Mr Maxwele freely admitted this and justified it by alleging that this student sought "to provoke the protestors by ignoring the command to avoid the cordoned off area".[30]

Commenting on this in an interdict judgement, Judge Rosheni Allie, noted that Mr Maxwele "clearly does not appreciate, despite having legal representation, that when one person pushes another, it is most likely common assault".[31] When the interdicted students appealed to the Supreme Court of Appeal, the judgement in that case, reported that Mr Maxwele and another protestor, Slovo Magida, had done more than push the student. The student had been "grabbed, hit, pushed and scratched" and that this assault on him was "accompanied by racial abuse".[32] The judgement says that there was video footage of the incident.

Judge Allie noted that Mr Maxwele denied the other student "the right to counter protest without causing physical harm or danger to the 'Shackville' protestors".[33] She had the same disdain for Mr Maxwele's dismissing "altercations between protestors and other students as 'small scuffles of no significance'". She said that in "adopting this cavalier approach to physical altercations" Mr Maxwele "is treating with disdain the right of students not allied to his cause to protest".[34] Nor was this the only case of assault.[35]

Moreover, Mr Witbooi, the university's traffic manager

reported that when he was "attempting to remove dirt bins and rocks that were blocking Residence Road ... Mr Maxwele threatened him with physical assault and was involved in altercations with parents".[36] Mr Maxwele had also "lit bins that had been placed to block the entrance to P3 parking area and warned that anyone who came close to the area would be dealt with by him".[37] Mr Witbooi said that Mr Maxwele's "manner was aggressive and threatened violence".[38]

In UCT's application for an interdict against the Fallist protestors, it alleged that Mr Maxwele "was present when the [university] bus was torched and [that]he rolled drums into the road shortly before the bus was burned". Mr Maxwele denied this, but the interdict judgement noted that the university had "video footage to support its allegation".[39]

Mr Maxwele admitted to having been one of the protestors who entered a student residence and ate there.[40] This was food the protestors were not entitled to eat. As Judge Allie noted in connection with another protestor who had acted in the same way:

> There is a clear disconnect between a protestor who states that he or she is protesting for the benefit of other black students so that those students would be granted accommodation and food, but then appropriates for himself or herself, the food of other students.[41]

On 17 February 2016, two days after the Shackville protests began, UCT lodged the application in the Western Cape High Court for an interdict and restraint against various Fallists. The court granted the interim interdict, which was then confirmed, with some limitations, on 11 May 2016. Some of the Fallists later appealed this judgement, but the Supreme Court of Appeal upheld the final interdict, although it too restricted the scope. It awarded costs for the initial case to UCT.

Reading the judgments of the Western Cape High Court

and the Supreme Court of Appeal is both uplifting and demoralising. It is uplifting because one sees evidence of South Africa's courts judging impartially, yielding where there is reason to, but also standing firm against criminal behaviour. What is demoralising are the accounts of terrible behaviour. Still more demoralising is the knowledge that despite the interdicts, UCT's management kept indulging those who engaged in criminal behaviour. When the protestors crossed the line from legal to illegal forms of protest – from exercising their rights to violating those of others – the university should have instituted criminal charges and pursued them relentlessly. They would very likely have succeeded in the courts.

MORE ASSAULT AND INTIMIDATION

Mr Maxwele continued to assault and intimidate. On 5 April 2016, he was involved in a tussle with fellow Fallist, Thenjiwe Mswane, at the University of the Witwatersrand in Johannesburg (about 1300 kilometres from Cape Town). Ms Mswane had attempted to disrupt a Fees Must Fall protest because, she said, "political parties had hijacked the protest and had excluded feminist and queer members".[42] She claimed that she was then "surrounded by men, kicked, punched and dragged away from the protest".

According to a newspaper report, Mr Maxwele denied having assaulted Ms Mswane.[43] However, this could well be because, as Judge Allie had noted, Mr Maxwele does not seem to understand what assault is. The very article that reported his denial of assault also included a photograph of him grabbing Ms Mswane from behind, his left hand gripping her left breast.

On 5 May 2016, in a protest outside of Parliament, Mr Maxwele was arrested "for alleged incitement to commit a crime".[44] The previous day, 4 May 2016, Mr Maxwele assaulted Mr Ganger, UCT's Investigations Manager. This assault took place at a disciplinary hearing involving Mr Maxwele and two other students for Shackville related behaviour. Mr Ganger was present to serve as a witness. He had arrived early and was having a cup of coffee before the hearing began. Mr Maxwele walked into the room, saw Mr Ganger and became abusive towards and shouting at him. The verbal abuse included swearing and calling Mr Ganger a "nigger".[45] Mr Maxwele accused Mr Ganger of being a spy, and said that he would shoot and kill him. There were two witnesses to this outburst.

Mr Ganger remained calm and asked Mr Maxwele to step outside so that they could continue the conversation there (and not in the presence of the assessors who were present to hear the case against Mr Maxwele). Once they were outside Mr Maxwele continued to shout at Mr Ganger. He then pushed his finger into Mr Ganger's face, close to Mr Ganger's eye. The latter had to duck in order to avoid Mr Maxwele's finger harming him. Mr Ganger felt a scratch and began bleeding – "profusely" according to a witness – from under his right eye.

Mr Ganger was understandably scared by this interaction with Mr Maxwele. This was a clear case of intimidating and assaulting a witness. It is so brazen a case that it occurs at the venue of the disciplinary hearing, soon before it was scheduled to begin, and in the presence of two assessors who, together with the proctor, will make a decision in the disciplinary hearing. The assessors in this case against Mr Maxwele thus became witnesses in another case against him.

Mr Maxwele was now facing multiple charges. Despite the obvious temperamental and behavioural continuity between these, some of the charges pertained to his political activity, while others did not. Although the criminality of the former was no different from that of the latter, the university management treated them differently. Mr Maxwele, like other students engaged in political protests, was eventually granted amnesty. The journey to that outcome took the following route.

On 20 October 2016, the Supreme Court of Appeal issued a judgement upholding the final interdict against the Shackville protestors but, as noted above, restricting the scope of that interdict. It awarded costs to UCT.

On 25 October 2016 the Western Cape High Court issued a further interim interdict against "all those persons participating, or intending to participate, in unlawful conduct" at UCT. This interim interdict was modified on 27 October 2016. The South African Police Services and local law enforcement were directed to assist with the enforcement of this interdict (but to exercise "extreme restraint" in doing so).

On 6 November, UCT entered into the "November agreement" with nine students. Under the terms of this agreement, the students would be granted "clemency" under certain conditions. These included signing a declaration in which they acknowledged wrong-doing and committed to not offending beyond 6 November 2016.[46] While the declaration did include such provisions, it also included an alarming level of self-exculpation. (It was the latter that was more consistent with the Supreme Court of Appeal's observation that the "attitude that all of the appellants adopted in their affidavits was that they had done nothing wrong" and that there "was no expression of contrition".[47]) Another provision of the "November agreement" was that the establishment of an Institutional Reconciliation and Transformation Commission[48] that would determine whether the clemencies should become amnesties.

Before the IRTC process could be completed, five of the students lodged an appeal, on 17 November 2016,[49] to the Constitutional Court of South Africa. They were appealing the Supreme Court of Appeal's upholding of the High Court's interdict against them (and other students).

On 6 December 2016, charges against Mr Maxwele and two other students for their "Shackville" crimes, were withdrawn.[50] A little over a week later, on 15 December, Mr Maxwele was one of the students who invaded and disrupted the annual meeting of Convocation, a body of which Mr Maxwele was not then a member.[51] The protestors' disruptions caused the meeting to descend into chaos.[52] At some point, the meeting was adjourned because it could no longer continue. Mr Maxwele played a part in this. For instance, when Emeritus Professor Tim Crowe was speaking about a motion he had tabled, Mr Maxwele "repeatedly interrupted him"[53] and accusing him of being a racist. Similarly, when Gwen Ngwenya, a UCT alumna and then Chief Operating Officer of the South African Institute of Race Relations, attempted to speak in support of Professor Crowe's motion, she was "continuously interrupted" by Mr Maxwele.[54]

This behaviour was in breach of the "November agreement", which included the following provisions:[55]

iii)   accepting that if the student is in breach of the Student Code of Conduct after November 6 2016, the University shall be entitled to charge the student as provided for in the University's student discplinary (sic) procedures.

iv)   agreeing that if there are disruptions of … the normal functioning of the university, and where no clear evidence is demonstrated that concerted efforts were taken to prevent such actions, the University may approach the mediators to request revoking the clemency.

By now, it should come as no surprise that UCT's management did not invoke these provisions and take disciplinary action against any of those who had disrupted the meeting – and violated the agreement.

The February 2016 interdict against Mr Maxwele and other protesting students also remained in place, even though not enforced. On 12 April 2017, the Constitutional Court handed down its judgement about that interdict.[56] It ruled against the protestors, except for reversing the Supreme Court of Appeal's awarding of costs to UCT. In the interim, on 22 March 2017, the interdict of October 2016 had been discharged at the request of UCT, given that UCT was of the view that that interdict was no longer necessary.

UNFINISHED BUSINESS

By the beginning of December 2017, Mr Maxwele had still not been tried in the University Student Disciplinary Tribunal for his attacks in the Hiddingh library, on Ms Mathematica, and on Mr Ganger. This hearing had finally been scheduled for early that month. Proceedings began on 4 December. When Mr Maxwele arrived late, at around 10h00, he refused to allow the hearing to begin until he had had breakfast. He complained that the sandwiches and coffee available at the hearing was not proper food, and that he wanted cornflakes for breakfast, and meat and rice for lunch. The presiding proctor asked Mr Maxwele to be seated while the tribunal formally considered his "request". However, Mr Maxwele refused to co-operate and walked out of the room where the hearing was taking place.

He returned about ten minutes later. He had gone to ask Max Price for money and Dr Price had, according to one report, given him R100. Mr Maxwele announced that he was going to get breakfast and that he would return thereafter. It was apparent that he expected the proctor, assessors, and prosecutors to wait around for him.

When he returned, about an hour later, he initially spoke only Xhosa, which was taken to mean that he wanted a Xhosa interpreter. The proctor then considered that. In the process of doing so and engaging Mr Maxwele, the latter spoke in (fluent) English. There was much other evidence of Mr Maxwele's fluency in English. He offered no objection to a suggestion that the hearing proceed in English on the understanding that if there were any words he did not understand he could consult a dictionary that was provided to him or have the relevant words explained.

Mr Maxwele's next tactic was to request that one of the assessors recuse himself on the grounds that he "might be racist", that "white people" at the University "hate black people" and that the assessor in question "must accept that his parents killed [Mr Maxwele's] people". It was pointed out to Mr Maxwele that most of those on the disciplinary tribunal were "black". Mr Maxwele responded that he had no objection to them but he did object to the "white" person. He could provide no evidence for the claims he made about that person. The proctor ruled against the recusal request, but the "white" assessor voluntarily recused himself. He was not willing to remain, given the unsubstantiated false claims that were made about him and his family.

Mr Maxwele continued to conduct himself in an aggressive and disrespectful manner throughout the proceedings. He insulted people, levelled unfounded allegations of racism, interrupted people, asked questions the answers to which he then ignored, shouted, and refused to lower his voice when told to do so. He dismissed the process as "colonialist".

On 5 December, Ms Mathematica was entering the University's main administrative building, the Bremner building, in order to give evidence. Mr Maxwele entered just behind her and, according to Ms Mathematica, he said: "You will die soon, you white racist".[57] Ms Mathematica immediately reported this to the guard in the entrance foyer. He escorted her upstairs to where her staff representative was meeting her. That staff representative then immediately reported the matter to the university's legal counsellor, the Registrar and the prosecutor. Further guards were stationed in the foyer where Ms Mathematica and her representative were waiting to give evidence.

Inside, Mr Maxwele was indicating his intention to

withdraw from the hearing, purportedly for political reasons. He (falsely) alleged that witnesses had been bought and that "you are black people here, you will take instruction from the white people because you have to get paid". He said that he refused to "dignify this forum" with his presence! He was asked whether he was voluntarily withdrawing and he answered affirmatively. He was advised that the hearing would proceed if he left and that there could be a judgement against him. He responded that in that eventuality he would "happily" go to the High Court.

When Mr Maxwele marched out of the hearing, he saw Ms Mathematica, her staff representative and the guards. He asked the guards why they were "protecting white people".

The hearing concluded on 6 December 2017. The following day, Mr Maxwele emailed the proctor asking for a postponement of the hearing until February 2018 in order for him to obtain legal representation. He had not previously requested legal representation despite having been given the opportunity to do so. Because of this and because he had voluntarily and with full cognizance of the implications left the hearing, his request was seen as a stalling tactic and was denied.

At the end of the 2017 academic year, after seven years of study, Mr Maxwele finally completed all the requirements to graduate with his Bachelor's degree, a degree which should have taken three years to complete. When a student has an open disciplinary matter, they are standardly barred from graduating until the matter has been completed. However, Dr Price gave Mr Maxwele permission to graduate despite the fact that judgement had not yet been made. For this kindness – arguably weakness – Dr Price was treated to a bizarre in-your-face display at the graduation ceremony[58] which, on account of protests shutting down the university for part of 2017, only took place in April of 2018. Despite Mr Maxwele's dismal performance during his undergraduate degree, he was accepted for postgraduate studies in African Studies.

By 4 May 2018, the IRTC recommended amnesty for eight students,[59] including Mr Maxwele. On 23 June 2018, UCT's Council accepted this recommendation,[60] thus finalizing the amnesty. The scope of the amnesty extended only to protest-related wrongdoing. It did not extend to other UCT disciplinary charges that had been considered in December 2017. The proctor's judgement in that case was issued on 10 July 2018. Mr Maxwele was found guilty on all counts. He was subsequently sentenced to expulsion.

Mr Maxwele lodged an appeal. An Appeal Tribunal hearing that was scheduled for 16 November 2018 convened on that date, but was then postponed in order to give Mr Maxwele additional time in order to obtain legal representation and to file written submissions. Before it adjourned Mr Maxwele assaulted somebody in the hearing. The presiding proctor physically pulled Mr Maxwele off his victim.

When the hearing reconvened on 26 July 2019, Mr Maxwele was absent and the reasons for his absence were deemed inadequate. The hearing proceeded. The prosecution subsequently made some additional submissions, which were conveyed to Mr Maxwele. However, he failed to respond to them despite being given reasonable time to do so. On 9 October 2019, the Appeal Tribunal issued its judgement, dismissing Mr Maxwele's appeal.

Mr Maxwele lodged an urgent application with the Western Cape High Court on 21 November 2019. An interim order was granted that enabled him to continue with his studies, with some restrictions, pending a final adjudication on his application.[61] In a final ruling on 8 December 2020, Judge MJ Dolamo found in favour of Mr Maxwele, overturning the UCT tribunals' findings of guilt and the sentence of expulsion.

Mr Maxwele claimed vindication, and press coverage of the decision played to that narrative. An article in *Sowetan Live*[62] made no mention of the grounds – which were purely procedural – on which the High Court had reached its decision. More specifically the High Court had interpreted UCT's relevant procedural rule differently from the way in which the presiding proctor had interpreted it. Under the proctor's interpretation, the tribunal could continue once the student assessor had recused himself following Mr Maxwele's racially motivated impugning of him. Under the High Court's interpretation, a new student assessor should have been appointed at that time[63] and that the Tribunal's failure to do so rendered the entire process void.

Given the procedural fault, the High Court did not deal with the appropriateness of expulsion as the sanction. However, Judge Dolamo was at pains to emphasise that his "reluctance to deal with the appropriateness of the sanction must not be construed as an endorsement of Maxwele's conduct. The transcript of the proceedings and other documents portray Maxwele as a man who did not want to submit himself to authority."

Judge Dolamo described Mr Maxwele's behaviour as "outright rude, disrespectful, belligerent and defiant, even when it was not necessary" and said that his "bellicose attitude and unprovoked outbursts of anger are to be deprecated".[64]

Although Judge Dolamo awarded costs in Mr Maxwele's favour he did say that he had "agonised about" about this question" because "awarding him costs may appear to reward him for his unruly conduct", but eventually concluded that the award should be made in favour of the successful party.[65]

There are many instances in which procedural justice does not deliver substantive justice. Mr Maxwele has consistently avoided substantive justice. His atrocious and sometimes even criminal behaviour has resulted in no sanctions. After the High Court ruling, UCT could still do something about that. It could try the case *de novo*. I would be surprised if it did.

Chapter 22
COMMANDANTE LUSHABA AND THE FÜHRER

(Originally published: 15 April 2021)[1]

Dr Lwazi Lushaba, a lecturer in the Political Studies Department at the University of Cape Town, recently told his students in a pre-recorded lecture posted online that "Hitler committed no crime. All Hitler did was to do to white people what white people had reserved for us, black people."[2]

This comment has been greeted with outrage by some. There have also been calls for him to be removed from his position. The Democratic Alliance has indicated[3] its intention to report him to the South African Human Rights Commission, and has urged UCT's Vice-Chancellor, Mamokgethi Phakeng "to place him on suspension pending" an investigation.

Two questions need to be distinguished:

1. What did Dr Lushaba say?

2. What should our response to this be?

The answer to the first question might seem obvious – I have just quoted his very words. However, the President of UCT's Students' Representative Council, Declan Dyer, has been quoted as claiming that Dr Lushaba's views have been taken out of context.[4] This claim is only partly true.

Consider, first, the immediate context, even though this does not seem to be what Mr Dyer had in mind. Immediately after the quoted words above, Dr Lushaba said: "And so his [that is, Hitler's] crime, if he had a crime, was to do unto white people what white people had thought was right to do only to black people."

This statement is not the categorical one that Hitler committed no crime, but it is also not an acknowledgement that Hitler *did* commit the crime of genocide. In other words, the context makes his view less clear, but his view remains objectionable.

One possible charitable interpretation of Dr Lushaba's comment is that he understands the word "crime" quite literally to mean a legally proscribed, punishable offence and that he was claiming that under Nazi law it was not a crime to kill Jews.

However, it is quickly apparent that Dr Lushaba does not mean this, because then he would be committed to a conclusion that he does not accept – namely that many evils inflicted on "black" people were not "crimes". The maltreatment of "blacks" under Apartheid, for example, was not illegal under South African law, and thus could not have been a crime in that sense.

What about the broader context of Dr Lushaba's comments? His lecture was about the discipline of "Political Science". He argued that this discipline was unmoved by massacres of "black" people by "white" people. He cited two such massacres – the Herero genocide in Namibia from 1904 to 1907, and a 1921 massacre that he said took place in Queenstown,

South Africa (but which actually took place in Bulhoek, near Queenstown). It was, he said, "only when white people are killed by other white people – by Hitler – that Political Science is jolted back to its sensibility".

Even if one thought that this argument were compelling, this context would not explain why "Hitler committed no crime" in carrying out the Holocaust. Nor would it explain the need for the conditional "if he had a crime". Refusing to acknowledge the Holocaust as a crime is not necessary for Dr Lushaba's argument. It is a gratuitous and morally repugnant accessory.

Thus, the context does not exonerate or even extenuate Dr Lushaba's comments, which constitute a kind of Holocaust denial – not a denial that there was a Holocaust, but rather a denial that the Holocaust was a "crime".

Perhaps it will be suggested that Dr Lushaba did not mean what he said. If that is the case, he should both apologise for a sloppy formulation and clarify what he did mean. Alternatively, he might have been speaking in some benign figurative sense. It is difficult to fathom what that would be. This is especially so because part of the context is the speaker himself. What counts as a plausible interpretation of what somebody is saying, depends on their track record – both verbally and behaviourally.

Dr Lushaba has regularly engaged in racially inflammatory speech, targeting "whites". He has whipped up emotions with simplistic Manichean narratives about "white people" and "black people". He has told his students that "blacks" and "whites" cannot be friends and set an exam question in which he required students to "specify the reasons for the impossibility" of such friendships.

He has disrupted democratic elections[5] in the Faculty of Humanities and previously, while a PhD student at the University of the Witwatersrand, he was suspended[6] for "activities that were not conducive to free and fair elections and were intolerant to a democratic society". In the light of such behaviour, his repeated references to himself as "Comrade Lushaba" and his recent self-promotion to "Commandante Lushaba" are ominous.[7]

This context does not lend itself to a benign interpretation of words that, in their plain sense, minimize the wrongness of murdering people who Dr Lushaba determines to be "white". At the very least, the onus is on him to explain himself.

What should our response to Dr Lushaba's comments be? It should *not* be to seek his removal from his teaching post or his subjection to an official sanction. This is because he has a right to freedom of expression. Many people will say that while they endorse a right to freedom of expression, it must be limited, and that Dr Lushaba's comments fall outside the bounds of protected speech.

Understandable though that view is, it is a mistake. The limits on freedom of expression are themselves limited. It is not enough that views are "offensive" or ignorant or stupid or even malicious. They must constitute defamation or incitement to imminent violence or harm. Harm and offence, it needs to be emphasized, are not equivalent. (The South African Constitution adds a further explicit exception to the right to freedom of expression – namely "propaganda for war"). Dr Lushaba's comments, awful though they are, do not meet these conditions.

In taking this view, I do not underestimate the power of words. Even words that neither defame nor constitute incitement to *imminent* violence or harm can be part of a longer causal chain that can lead to future violence and harm. Dr Lushaba is a prime example of somebody whose words may very well be contributing to serious harm in the future.

The problem is that the more likely words are to contribute to longer term harm, the less likely they are to be restricted.

Consider Holocaust denial, for example. Where is such speech least likely to result in another genocide against the Jews? The answer is Israel, but that is a country in which Holocaust denial is legally prohibited.

By contrast, Iran is one of the countries in which Holocaust denial is most likely to contribute to another genocide against the Jews (through an attack on Israel, which Iranian leaders have sworn to wipe off the map). Yet Holocaust denial is not only legally permitted in Iran but also state sponsored.

None of this is surprising or accidental. In societies in which hateful words will not have traction, the hateful words are less dangerous. Those are not societies in which the hateful speech needs to be outlawed. The societies in which there could be some benefit from outlawing such speech are the very societies in which that speech is less likely to be outlawed – precisely because the hateful ideas have more traction in those societies.

Dr Lushaba's anti-"white" rhetoric is dangerous precisely because it has traction in South Africa. However, that is also why his speech is unlikely to be curbed (whether or not one thinks that it would be justifiable to do so). Comparable anti-"black" rhetoric in post-Apartheid South Africa is much less dangerous – because it is so widely condemned. Yet, a much harder line is taken against anti-"black" rhetoric in contemporary South Africa.

The South African Human Rights Commission's Priscilla Jana has been quoted[8] as saying that the Commission was intentionally more lenient to "black" offenders in racial incidents "because of the historical context". However, in terms of danger, it is not the historical context, but the present (and future) context that matters.

Even more worrying than the outlawing of hateful speech that, while offensive, is unlikely to harm, is the potential silencing of speech that is not hateful, but which is characterized as hateful by the majority in order to silence it.

Freedom of expression is needed not to protect speech of which a dominant majority approves. In a democracy such speech will be protected even without explicit legal provision. Instead, freedom of expression is needed in order to protect *unpopular* speech.

A vigorous defence of freedom of expression is thus not predicated on a naïve view that words can never contribute to harm. Instead, it is a matter of principle, but one rooted in, rather than divorced from, political reality. Another benefit of recognizing and respecting Dr Lushaba's right to freedom of expression is that the rest of us then know exactly who he is and what he stands for.

While he should not be removed from his position or officially sanctioned, he should be vigorously criticised for his vile comments – and especially because so many people have come to his defence. His defenders include the Executive of UCT's Faculty of Humanities which, like the SRC President, said that Dr Lushaba's "remarks were taken out of context".

We can be sure that the Faculty of Humanities Executive would have had a very different reaction if a "white" academic had made the claim that "Cecil John Rhodes committed no crime". The Black Academic Caucus would immediately have objected. Neither of these groups would have thought that context made any difference.

These defences are even more worrying given how academically impoverished Dr Lushaba's argument is. Dr Lushaba would have us believe that his discipline reconceived itself in response to the Holocaust only because it involved "white" people killing other "white" people. His supporting evidence consists of two prior massacres in which "white" people killed "black" people. These, he said, had not been sufficient to influence the course of political science.

This is an appallingly weak argument because it ignores the many massacres prior to the Holocaust in which "white" people killed "white" people. If the (purported) "whiteness" of the Holocaust's victims were the key factor, then the discipline of political science would, from its beginnings, have taken an alternative course. Massacres of "white" people by "white" people have been taking place since there were first "white" people (just as massacres of people by other people have been taking place for as long as there have been people). Dr Lushaba's fixation on race is so great that he is oblivious to other historical factors that must have played a role following the Holocaust.

Dr Lushaba's historical insensitivity and ignorance are not limited to this point. Here is another of many examples:

> And so we must see the Holocaust in exactly the same way that we must see the massacre of the Herero people, in exactly the same way we must see the Queenstown massacre and several other massacres that happened across the continent. We must not privilege one massacre over the others.

We should certainly be outraged by any massacre, but surely we must not see through *differences* between massacres by seeing them "in exactly the same way". Massacres differ and their various differences should be seen. For example, the Bulhoek massacre had 163 victims.[9] That is awful, but we should not see it in exactly same way we see the genocide of the Herero which resulted in the deaths of between 24 000 and 100 000 people.[10] We should also not see it in the same way that we see the Jewish Holocaust, which had nearly 6 000 000 victims.

Nor were the Jews Hitler's only victims. If we add Slavs, Roma, Sinti, homosexuals, the mentally disabled, prisoners of war, and others, the total is about 15 500 000. That is 15.5 million crimes for which Hitler was ultimately responsible.

The largest massacre of "black" people in what is now South Africa is believed to have taken the lives of between one and two million people (although some[11] have suggested that even a death toll of a million may be high). This is the Mfecane[12].

Perhaps Dr Lushaba overlooked this example because this was a case of "black" people killing "black" people, which does not fit his simplistic narrative. That perpetrators and victims were "black" should not detract from our outrage on behalf of the victims.

The relevant differences between massacres are not only numerical. Also relevant are the rate of killing, the methods of extermination, and, in genocides, the proportion of the targeted population that is killed. To recognise these differences is not to privilege one massacre over another.

Instead, it is to understand their commonalities and differences. That is the sort of nuance we should be able to expect from academics appointed at the University of Cape Town. When students are instead fed demagoguery, the University of Cape Town should feel a deep sense of embarrassment.

Chapter 23
AN ENDURING TOXIC CLIMATE

UCT has not been forcibly shut down by protesters since 2017. However, it was prophylactically closed, first for one day and then for a further two days in September 2019. This was precipitated by widespread anger about the rape and murder of a first-year student (off campus). There were fears that UCT would be shut down by protesters if a pre-emptive official closure were not declared. On at least one other occasion the University capitulated to demands to remove two staff members from a Faculty Readmission Committee, allegedly out of fear that the University would be shut down by student protestors if they did not.

There is ample talk on campus about mental health. This talk comes from students seeking (both reasonable and unreasonable) accommodations, from some staff (many of whom are virtue signalling), and from the University leadership generally saying what university leaders are expected to say (which is not to say that it is *all* insincere). However, the *talk* about mental health is not matched by the *actions* that would counter the toxic environment responsible for much misery and other mental ill-health. Indeed, much (but not all) of the talk about mental health is being used to protect the bullies rather than the bullied. This happens when the bullies' not getting their way is seen as injurious to their mental health.

FALLIST SCARS

Part – but only part – of the problem is that many decent people are still suffering the psychological sequelae of the Fallist-inflicted traumas.[1] Some staff members have disclosed having nightmares about Fallists. I have it on good authority (but without any breaches of confidentiality) that a number of psychiatrists in private practice have patients who are traumatised UCT staff.

An aggravating factor is that none of the perpetrators of serious crimes (including theft, assault, and arson) committed as part of the campus protests were punished. One wonders whether this outcome was calculated by the University leadership or whether they were out-manoeuvred by the wily student protesters. Either way, some[2] of this failure to hold students to account was the result of the Institutional Reconciliation and Transformation Commission (IRTC), which was discussed in Chapter 19.

Given the outrageous behaviour that went unpunished, a new environment has been created. It is an environment in which entitled students can refuse, with impunity, to abide by the rules. If they cannot intimidate the staff with whom they immediately interact, they can count on pliant senior administrators to pander to them. Of course, this is not true of *all* students. Many – perhaps even most – students comport themselves appropriately and abide by the rules. It does not take more than a few trouble-makers to poison the environment. Several staff members have commented on this.

One medical school lecturer described the students as a "generation of politicians" and noted that whereas in the past, complaints about student behaviour were rare, within the first month of the 2019 academic year there had already been seven complaints about final year medical students. Another staff member at the medical school said that some "students are rude and undisciplined", that attendance is poor, and that weak students are passing. Some of the future doctors fraudulently sign attendance registers for their classmates.[3] I reported one such case to the University Student Disciplinary Tribunal. A few years later, the case has still not been heard, making it less likely that it ever will be.

In October 2017, the bioethics oral examinations for the MBChB third year students were cancelled and the relevant lecturer notified less than twenty-four hours in advance of the scheduled examinations. This was in response to a student demand that they be cancelled. The oral bioethics examinations have not been held in the ensuing years (although there are a handful of multiple choice questions still in place in a written examination.) What kind of a university cancels examinations in response to student demands? What message about ethics does that send?

Most students whose applications for postgraduate funding or academic travel are unsuccessful, respond courteously. However, a minority are rude and demanding, sometimes using foul language and sometimes playing the race or transformation cards. (Not all of these are South Africans.) They, and their proxies, ignore that there are policies and protocols governing funding, and they are irate when the relevant people make their decisions in keeping with those policies and protocols. Similarly, one of the Faculty Readmission Committees that actually follows the rules in deciding on readmissions was accused of hating "black" students. It became clear that the students making these accusations had no idea what the criteria for readmission were. They were criticising the outcome – exclusion – because they did not like the outcome, which they attributed to the worst motives, without even realising just how lax the criteria already were.

Another case in point is that of former Students' Representative Council (SRC) President Rorisang Moseli who, years after he took a course, was given a pass, even though he did not actually pass the course. I name him here because he has made his complaints public, thus inviting a public correction of the record. Mr Moseli was a student in the same philosophy class as Busi Mkhumbuzi (discussed in Chapter 12). Like her, he failed to meet the Duly Performed (DP) requirements because he missed more than a third of the lectures. He and Ms Mkhumbuzi appealed the DP Refused (DPR) decision in tandem – first to the Dean, then to the Vice Chancellor – and were unsuccessful. Both then appealed a second time to the Vice-Chancellor. Although the rules specifically indicate that there "is no appeal from any decision by the Vice-Chancellor or Vice-Chancellor's nominee",[4] their appeals were considered again. The DPR decision was again upheld. Even though the rules specifically prohibited a student who has been refused DP from writing the examination, both Mr Moseli and Ms Mkhumbuzi attended and wrote the examination.

Mr Moseli made a few defamatory comments about me on social media, although nothing approaching the ferocity and extent of Ms Mkhumbuzi's campaign of defamation. Unlike her, he (initially) did not appeal a *third* time to the Vice-Chancellor. Ms Mkhumbuzi's third appeal was indulged because she protested more loudly and persistently than Mr Moseli. Vice-Chancellor Price capitulated, contorting himself to grant her DP.

Emboldened by Ms Mkhumbuzi's success, Mr Moseli lodged his third appeal to the Vice-Chancellor two *years* later! Vice-Chancellor Price nominated a senior law professor to consider the third appeal. She scrutinized various documents, but my input was not sought. The Vice-Chancellor's nominee explicitly compared Mr Moseli's case to Ms Mkhumbuzi's and found that it would be unfair to withhold DP from Mr Moseli given that Ms Mkhumbuzi had been granted DP. This fulfilled one of my earlier complaints about Dr Price's decision to grant Ms Mkhumbuzi DP – namely that it would create a dangerous precedent.

However, precedents can be less or more persuasive. They are more persuasive when the precedent is *really* like the later case in which the precedent is invoked. One crucial difference between Ms Mkhumbuzi's and Mr Moseli's cases is that Mr Moseli was appealing two years after the examination had been written. While there is no formal "period of prescription", there is a relevant practical problem. Departments are obligated to retain examination scripts for only a prescribed period, after which they may be destroyed. That period had long passed at the time that the Vice-Chancellor's nominee decided to overturn Mr Moseli's DPR and to instruct that his examination be marked. An examination script that no longer exists cannot be marked. That seems like an important difference between the cases of Ms Mkhumbuzi and Mr Moseli. It is not a difference that the Vice-Chancellor's nominee considered.

When Ms Mkhumbuzi's script had been marked (by an independent marker), it was found that she had failed the examination despite having had a reasonable coursework average. This is not surprising for a student who has missed a large proportion of the course. The coursework assignments are effectively open-book examinations, but with a much longer window for completion. Students are assigned a choice of topics. They choose which of these they wish to answer and then prepare and write essays on those topics. In the course that Ms Mkhumbuzi and Mr Moseli took, students wrote only two coursework essays. An examination is quite different. It tests one's command of the entire course, not merely two topics within the course, and it does so under examination conditions where one cannot make up for one's absence from class.

If there were no examination script to mark, Mr Moseli would need to sit a new examination. However, it "was deemed overly punitive to require Mr Moseli to rewrite the exam"[5] and the Interim Dean suggested that Mr Moseli should be awarded a mark equivalent to his coursework average. This required the Philosophy Department to sign off on the mark change. As I was not prepared to be complicit in granting a free pass, I refused to sign. The matter was subsequently taken to the Faculty Examinations Committee (FEC) in July 2018. That committee also refused to authorize a mark change. (It noted, among other things, that Mr Moseli had a string of other problems with his transcript.)

The matter was brought to the December 2018 meeting of the FEC, but for noting only. The committee was advised that the Registrar, Royston Pillay, had said that it "was not within the remit of the FEC to uphold the DPR once the VC's nominee had ruled on the matter". The Registrar was technically correct about that, but was mistaken about a second matter and silent on a third.

First, he responded to the FEC's objection that the third appeal to the VC was contrary to the rules. Mr Pillay attempted to claim that the VC's nominee had conducted a "review" of the earlier decisions rather than considered a new appeal. However, that is inconsistent with what the VC's nominee actually did. In a review, one checks whether the earlier decision was made correctly. One does not consider new evidence, which is exactly what happened in Mr Moseli's third appeal. The new evidence was the fact that Ms Mkhumbuzi had been granted a third appeal.[6] (*Her* third appeal also introduced new "evidence".)

Second, while it is not within the remit of the FEC to uphold a DPR once the VC's nominee has ruled on the matter, it is not within the remit of the VC, his nominee, or the Registrar to prescribe to the FEC that it pass a student who has not passed or to demand that the FEC do so. On this the Registrar was silent, despite advising the FEC that it was bound to implement the decision of the VC's nominee (even though he knew that it was too late to require the examination script to be marked).

By May 2020, Mr Moseli remained listed as DPR for this course. Although he had already completed his degree by this time, he wrote to various people, including the Vice-Chancellor, Registrar and Dean of Humanities, demanding that the decision of the previous Vice-Chancellor's nominee be implemented. The Registrar then wrote to the Dean of Humanities saying that the "decision of the VC's reviewer should have been implemented by the faculty". A few days later, Mr Moseli's mark was changed from DPR to an unqualified pass (50%).

In other words, Mr Moseli was reflected as passing a course he did not pass and which he may well have failed if he had rewritten the examination. Of course, Mr Moseli took this as vindication rather than a source of shame. When he took to Twitter to proclaim his vindication,[7] he paid no attention to the explicit statement of Dr Price's nominee that the purported unfairness of withholding DP from him was not attributable to me or to the Department of Philosophy. Furthermore, he claimed that he had missed classes because of the death of his sister, but he made no mention that her death had not impeded his campaigning for the SRC (and becoming its president), and that his campaigning explained some of his absences from class.

Occasional absences are to be expected, but Mr Moseli did not excuse himself from a single one of the twelve lectures he missed. Some other students excused themselves when they had personal problems or conflicting commitments, with the result that we could help them limit their absences and the deficits created by absences. Not Mr Moseli. He is one of those self-entitled students who demands that he must receive special treatment. That is bad enough. What is intolerable is that people like him find a university leadership ever willing to pander even if that involves bending or breaking the rules themselves.

At the height of the protests some lecturers received telephone calls from people in senior university management seeking concessions for various protest leaders in a bid to prevent them from failing to meet the academic progression requirements that would permit their continued registration as students. At least some of the academic staff who received these calls perceived them as inappropriate interferences.

One senior lecturer said that "since the protests, the relationship between the University leadership and the staff has deteriorated". He said that the University leadership seemed to have a "sneering contempt" for the staff, viewing them as a group that they have to manage rather than engage collegially.

UNHAPPINESS

The toxic climate at UCT has caused widespread unhappiness. Many staff members have expressed this in their (confidential) conversations with me. Many have said that they feel "miserable" and that they have stopped trusting people. One staff member at medical school said that she no longer engages in corridor chat, and she won't say anything unguarded, adding that "there is a fear about the BAC and who might be feeding back to them". She acknowledged that "it is hard to know whether this is paranoia or a well-grounded fear", but either way the fear is silencing people and contributing to an unhappy working environment.

Those who think that the unhappy ones are only disgruntled "whites" who cannot tolerate a "transforming university", should outgrow their apartheid-era racial thinking. Those who find the environment toxic include people of many hues. They report going to campus as little as possible (to teach, do necessary administration, and visit the library), preferring to work from home. One person – a "black" South African, for those for whom such categorization matters – reported locking himself in his office when he is at work rather than leaving the door open and "risk some of the toxicity entering". The same person remarked that the "culture of bullying is unbearable" and that it is "not tenable to remain". He said that many staff are looking to leave UCT.

Indeed, many staff have left. One staff member who was leaving UCT to take up a position abroad remarked that UCT is a "very unhappy, dysfunctional place".

Other staff are biding their time until retirement. One retiring staff member who described himself as "someone who has been massively committed to UCT [and] who has loved working" at UCT, said that "the toxic environment has finally become too much". When I wished him well for his forthcoming retirement, he replied "I will be retiring in 44 days' time and the good news is that tomorrow will be 43 days"!

Nor are staff the only unhappy people at UCT. Many students are unhappy too. In some departments in some faculties, students can expect to be subjected to an endless barrage of ideological claptrap. This is especially true in vast swathes of the Humanities Faculty, as well as in the "soft" components of the Faculty of Health Sciences' curricula. Insofar as opposing ideas are presented at all, they are caricatured to serve as a foil for the orthodox view.[8] This may suit the phalanxes of woke students, but it is deeply unsatisfying – not to mention disturbing – for those students with inquiring minds who actually want to explore ideas rather than imbibe received ones.

Some lecturers are so devoted to their political activism that they will insert it even when the topics – not to mention the activism about the topics – is inappropriate. For example, a number of students have complained that an ideologue has been teaching political theory and the politics of race in what is meant to be a research methods course. The result is that students are not learning what they should be learning about research methods. For these sorts of reasons there are students who would rather study elsewhere in South Africa or abroad.

What is clear from speaking to many people across the University is just how miserable everybody's life can be made by a single toxic character in a department. Sometimes there is more than one such character, or there is one main noxious figure who is aided and abetted by lesser venoms.

None of this is to say that those poisoning the environment are all happy. Given that they have an insatiable appetite, whatever gains they make are never sufficient. Thus, at least some of them believe that UCT is an inhospitable environment – because it has not bent sufficiently to their own wills. In other words, they are unhappy that they have not yet captured the institution to an even greater extent. Consider for example, the astounding level of racial entitlement of Elelwani Ramugondo and the BAC who took UCT to court for failing to appoint her to a Deputy Vice-Chancellor position and instead appointing a "white" woman. The court found against them and in favour of UCT. My concern, however, is not with the unhappiness of the bullies, but rather with the unhappiness of the bullied.

One fundamental problem with the 2019 Inclusivity Survey conducted on behalf of UCT, was that it was, at least in the quantitative questions, unable to distinguish between those who were unhappy on account of a purportedly anti-"black" environment and those were unhappy as a result of the bullying of those who claim that UCT is a hotbed of anti-"black" racism.

I drew these serious methodological problems to the attention of the company running the survey. For example, I said:

> Words like "inclusion" and "diversity" are used as code. Thus, the University Executive is obviously interested in these values as *they* understand them. I just don't think that they are really interested in those values as they should reasonably be interpreted. There is a deeply toxic atmosphere at UCT, which I have regularly pointed out. ... It has had a massive chilling effect on numerous decent people, while ideologues and the vicious have run rampant. The Executive is interested only in including some people, not others. If I answer that the Executive is not interested in inclusion, my answer will be indistinguishable from those who use that word in the same way as the Executive but who think that the Executive is not doing a good enough job at inclusion in *that* sense. If I say that the Executive *is* interested in inclusion, then my response is indistinguishable from those who think that the Executive is doing a great job with regard to inclusion in *their* sense.

I urged them to address these sorts of serious methodological problems. The problems were *not* addressed. Nor did the replies I received ameliorate my concerns. For example, I was told that terms like "inclusion" and "diversity" were defined. In response, I noted that there was code in the definitions themselves. For example, the survey indicated that "Diversity describes a workforce made up of a variety of people", but I know that some kinds of "variety" count at UCT, but others do not. For example, there is not much (if any) valuing of diversity of *opinion*, which is arguably one of the most important kinds of diversity for at least many sectors of a university to have.

The upshot of this is that I did not participate in the survey. If others in my position reacted similarly then there would have been selection bias in the survey.[9] It is interesting that this sloppy methodology elicited no public outrage – about poor methodology, weak social science, and unexamined assumptions. This stands in contrast to the complaints of this kind in the outpouring of criticism of Professor Nattrass's brief exploratory study.[10]

The survey was nonetheless revealing, although not always in ways intended. First, it included an offer of support and assistance. Those completing the survey were presented with this notice:

> The questionnaire made me feel uncomfortable and unsettled while / after completing it. Who can I contact for further support or counselling?

Details of whom to contact for assistance were then provided.

It is indeed ironic that there can be such concern about filling out a questionnaire when there was no concern for the traumatic effects on staff and students who have been witness to campus arson and the strewing of human excrement, subjected to taunts, harassment and bullying, and sometimes personal violence or threats of this. The psychological effects of a questionnaire about such events pale into insignificance in comparison with the events themselves.

Second, despite the shortcomings of the survey, its findings did reveal substantial unhappiness. For example, many staff are suffering from effects of trauma experienced during the period of protests (2015 to 2017),[11] and UCT was experienced as having a "culture of bullying". No surprises there.

For all his faults in capitulating to the worst elements of the

University, Vice Chancellor Price was not himself a bully. He pandered to bullies, but he did not engage in bullying behaviour himself. That is not true of his successor. In her UCT Ombud's report for the year 1 July 2018 to 30 June 2019, Zetu Makamandela-Mguqulwa, mentioned that her office had received "a number of work-related complaints ... about professional interactions with the VC where people felt bullied, silenced, undermined, rebuked and / or treated unfairly".[12] The Ombud reported that some "affected bystanders also came to express fear" and told her "how they were impacted individually by different incidents".[13] The Ombud said further that *none* of those who brought these issues wanted the Ombud to approach the VC "as they feared retaliation".[14] "The bystanders said that they would not want to experience what they saw first-hand happen to others."[15]

The Ombud contrasted the previous University leadership's openness to her in discussing issues, with a very different response from Professor Phakeng. The Ombud said that the "scrutiny and feedback no longer seemed welcome, at least from the highest office at UCT", adding that "in this reporting period, suddenly it seemed that I was not to be trusted".[16] Indeed, the Ombud alleged that Professor Phakeng explicitly uttered the words "I don't trust you" and "I don't trust your office".[17]

When, during a brief encounter with the new Vice-Chancellor, the Ombud suggested that they meet to discuss two cases, the Ombud reports that Professor Phakeng "became angry and made false assertions" about the office of the Ombud and its mandate.[18] The Ombud also said, but not in her initial report to Council, that the Vice-Chancellor had told her that she keeps a "black book in which she notes all the names of people who do not like or support her" and that the Ombud had been added to the black book.[19]

Professor Phakeng acknowledged that there were

disagreements between her and the Ombud but that this had nothing to do with her disrespect for the office. She also denied that she had bullied anybody.[20] There are questions about whether the Ombud acted appropriately in commenting as she did about the Vice-Chancellor in her report.[21] Nevertheless, a few things are clear. First, in the year covered by the Ombud's report there had been thirty-seven complaints about the Vice-Chancellor.[22] Second, there were significant tensions not only between the Vice-Chancellor and the Ombud, but also between the Vice-Chancellor and members of her executive team.[23] Indeed, the Chair and Deputy Chair of Council described the relations between members of the Executive as "dysfunctional".[24]

The complaints of bullying are consistent with reports of how the Vice-Chancellor has conducted Senate meetings. I ceased attending Senate *before* Professor Phakeng took over as Vice-Chancellor. I did so when it became apparent that I was wasting my time there. The reports I receive from other Senators is that meetings, which unsurprisingly now struggle to be quorate (and often fail to be), have become dysfunctional under Professor Phakeng. I am told that she is "prickly" with Senate and that meetings have now become a dialogue with her rather than between members of Senate. According to reports, the way that she responds to challenges, sometimes through ad hominem attacks, is silencing people. One Senator described Senate as "a mess, appallingly chaired, and generally awful".

None of this should come as a surprise. There were serious concerns about the appointment of Professor Phakeng as Vice-Chancellor. The selection committee that recommended her appointment was initially roughly evenly divided on whether she should be appointed. To win around those who had concerns, it was suggested that she be told that the committee would support her candidacy if she agreed to a programme of mentorship. That had the desired effect on the committee members who had concerns, but Professor Phakeng responded indignantly when the proposal was put to her. After that, her candidacy was not put to a formal (and secret) vote in the selection committee. She was characterised as a "transformation" candidate. Anybody opposed to her being appointed were implicitly expected to voice their opposition. Of course, there were powerful pressures against expressing opposition to a "transformation" candidate. This is how she came to be presented to Senate as the choice by "consensus".

At that Senate meeting, the Chair of the selection committee (who was also the Chair of Council) mentioned the committee's recognition of the areas in which Professor Phakeng needed development. These pertained mainly to perceptions of her personality. In response, one member of Senate asked who was going to oversee and monitor the development in a Vice-Chancellor, who is the most senior person in UCT Management.[25] (The Chancellor is a figurehead.) The answer to that pointed question was unsatisfactory, but included the claim that Council would perform that role. Clearly Council was not up to that task, although this might have been because it was far too optimistic in thinking that the shortcomings were remediable.

The Vice-Chancellor is not the only one bullying people at UCT. The Ombud also reported that there "is a growing use of public humiliation, manipulating and intimidating the seemingly powerless, using passive aggressive behaviours and flaunting power and authority".[26]

Such targeting of people does not even end with the death of those targeted. Steven Ganger, UCT's Investigations Manager, died on 27 December 2018, while still in service at UCT. He had been subjected to awful treatment,[27] which might have played some role in his death. After he died, vile comments were posted about him on Twitter. These included "I hope that he rots in hell",[28] "We celebrate Steven Ganger's death! He tormented many black students and I hope that he is enjoying 1000 Degrees Celcius"(sic),[29] and "this nigga ruined my life ... he was a poes ...".[30] UCT did call out these callous comments, but it was too little too late.

SILENCING

The intolerant bullies are silencing others at UCT – or attempting to do so. Some of this is obvious, such as a poster by Progress South Africa, a liberal student organization, being torn down[31] by those who cannot abide others having a say. However, much of it is not as readily apparent. This is because it is harder to notice when people are *not* saying something that they would say if it were not abundantly clear to them that saying it would come with a social cost. However, interviews with dozens of people across the University has revealed that many people feel silenced.

This is true in classrooms where, according to reports, radical students are intimidating non-radical and "white" students, who are consequently trying to keep their heads down. One professor told me that he now has much less discussion in his lectures than before. This, he said, is partly because of the climate at UCT. He is not prepared to take the risks that come with greater discussion. Various staff members are scared to speak up in response to their colleagues. Others were reluctant for me to disclose details which might identify them, given the backlash they could expect.

There used to be *some* debates at UCT – that is, real debates, in which people with different views would populate public platforms for discussion. That has ceased, if not entirely then almost entirely. Instead, there is an endless parade of the same orthodox themes and views. Consider the following few examples:

- A Sociology Department seminar entitled "Black and White Ways of Talking About Race: Shattering the Myth of a Post-Racial Consensus".[32]
- A public seminar series entitled "Citizenship and violence: Resilient colonialism, xenophobia, and femicide"[33] with included talks with titles such as "Race and Transformation in Higher Education", "Exclusive citizenship, masculinities and xenophobia", and "Performing Blackness in South Africa".
- A Film and Media Studies Seminar entitled "Liquid Racism, Possessive Investments in Whiteness and Academic Freedom at a Post-Apartheid University".[34]
- The "Hub for decolonial feminist psychologies in Africa".[35]
- A seminar entitled "Blackness Beyond White Supremacy: Race, Temporality and Agential Polyvalence".[36]
- The ironically named "Inclusive Practice: Speaker Series". An example of a talk in this series was entitled "Reason and unreason: Pedagogies of the oppressed in the twenty-first century: Gender, philosophy, education and the law". According to the blurb about this seminar, it drew "broadly on the work of Steve Biko, Frantz Fanon, Paolo Freire, Sylvia Tamale, Jacques Derrida, Lewis Gordon, Antonio Negri, Cheryl I Harris, Tembeka Ngcukaitobi and Leonard Harris, the latter who is one of the founding members of Philosophy Born of Struggle, in bringing together arguments and discussions which speak to the South African context of teaching and learning in the twenty-first century".[37]
- A webinar entitled "White Privilege: A critical dialogue on racism and inequality in a time of COVID-19".[38] This was the second time within the space of a few months at which Robin di Angelo, guru of "white fragility", spoke at a UCT-affiliated event.
- A webinar on "Decolonization and decoloniality",[39] with the following speakers: Shose Kessi, Floretta Boonzaier, Shadreck Chirikure, and Lwazi Lushaba.
- A "Decolonising Social Scientific Thought" seminar entitled "The Non-Identical Human. Ethnography and

Estrangement: Towards a Decolonial Anthropology", which was led by the ironically named Dr Hylton White.[40]

It is now vanishingly rare to find dissenting voices on panels or to encounter talks and panels (outside of the sciences, broadly construed) that do not fit the foregoing mould. Before 2015 I participated in a number of panel discussions at UCT, usually as a dissenting voice. I am no longer invited to do so. Even if I were, I would probably decline, given the levels of hostility that now prevail. I am still prepared to write. I am no longer willing to appear in person.

The sciences exception can be explained. First, it is much easier in the sciences than in other areas to tell the difference between fact and fiction (and to differentiate those from the middle ground where reasonable people can still disagree). Second, the harder the sciences (where the contrast to "hard science" is "soft science" rather than "easy science") the less overlap there is between their subject matter and that of leftist ideologues. There are exceptions, of course, and leftist ideologues (just like their counterparts on the right) have a knack for politicising even harder sciences.

There have been some instances at UCT where people have sought to politicise the sciences. One notorious case was the invitation of Professor CK Raju to speak at UCT about "decolonising science". He was invited by Professor Loretta Feris, the Deputy Vice-Chancellor for Transformation (who is a lawyer rather than a scientist) and the Curriculum Change Working Group.

Professor Raju was variably described by UCT professors as a "crank" and "conspiracy theorist".[41] While nobody was calling for Professor Raju to be silenced, many thought that it was inappropriate for a university to dignify his views with an official invitation to speak about them. Professor Feris attempted to defend the invitation. In response, Professor George Ellis, one of UCT's pre-eminent scientists, said that her distinction between western and other science was "pure rubbish". He said that "Third World Scientists adhere to the same international standards as Western scientists".[42] He also said that if UCT were to follow Professor Raju's suggestions, "we'd better close down the science and engineering faculties" because the "degrees we produce will be worthless".[43]

Nor was Professor Ellis alone in criticising the invitation. Then Dean of Science, Professor Anton le Roex declined to participate in a panel discussion with Professor Raju, and Associate Professor Jeff Murugan suggested that decolonising mathematics would "amount to a neo-bantu education that, implemented in South Africa, would see our students unable to compete in the global marketplace of ideas".[44]

It is clear that Professor Raju was invited to UCT because his message fitted well with the decolonization agenda. It is an embarrassment to the institution that he was invited, but at least there was forthright criticism from the Science Faculty. That is much harder to find in the humanities (including the medical humanities) and law. Those who are not silenced in those disciplines typically pay a price for daring to speak.

The silencing is also taking place in Senate, with even senior professors saying that they do not feel free to speak up. One such professor says that she is "nervous to say anything" and that "unless you follow a particular line, you can be ostracised". She described feeling intimidated, and she observed that "what one says is not judged on its merits but through the lens of one's racial or gender identity", a sentiment echoed by others.

Given this, it is "whites" (and more especially "white" males) who are disproportionately affected. However, it is certainly not *only* them. One person told me that a firebrand in his department assumed that he would share the firebrand's agenda, and that this assumption was made because my informant was also "black". When the firebrand found out that this was not the case, he berated his colleague, resulting in the latter's withdrawing. Another person told me that he has taken a conscious decision to remain largely silent in department meetings. He will make an occasional exception, if the matter is important enough, but in general it is not worth the risk of incurring the ire of the toxic characters in his department. Or consider the case of Professor Bongani Mayosi, the Dean of the Faculty of Health Sciences, who withdrew so much in response to the toxic environment at UCT that he took his own life.[45]

Nor is it the case that *all* "whites" are silenced. Those towing the orthodox line are entirely free to speak and to silence others. One professor at the medical school said that the clinicians and basic scientists there had "difficulty resisting the virtue signalling by woke elements" of the Faculty. The latter "speak in terms of caring and compassion". It is hard, I was told, for clinicians, who are committed to caring, to resist such talk even when it is persecutorial talk about caring and compassion. "Many of them are thus putting their heads into the sand or turning their attention to operational issues rather than political ones". This professor was not alone in saying that "it is extremely difficult to have rational conversations" about politically charged matters. In most cases such conversations are simply not happening.

This may explain why the Faculty of Health Sciences produced an ultra-woke *Transformation Framework*,[46] replete with the *de rigueur* misspelling of "woman" as "womxn"[47] and the predictable array of fashionable slogans. For example, the document commits the Faculty to challenging "intersectional forms of oppression such as patriarchy, privilege, 'whiteness', ableism, heteronormativity, Eurocentricity, and Judeo-Christianity". (Tell *that* to the Jews![48]) One of the Faculty's objectives is decolonization of the curriculum, and it will promote equality and inclusivity. We are not told that while all are equal, some are more equal than others,[49] or that inclusivity is not inclusivity for all. All staff and students, according to this framework, will be required to undergo mandatory "sensitivity training". For all the talk about non-discrimination, inclusion and sensitivity, there is no sign that those disagreeing with the orthodox line will evade discrimination, will be included, or will be dealt with sensitively. Indeed, as various chapters in this book make clear, they can expect the opposite.

Even more Orwellian is the *Health Sciences Students' Council Sensitisation Booklet: 2019*.[50] This booklet not only trots out all the aforementioned orthodox views but then characterizes these as critical thinking. Worse still, is that this booklet on sensitisation ends with a case study – the protests of 2016 and the occupation of the Dean's Suite under the #Occupy FHS banner, which it glorifies as an exercise in sensitizing. The booklet acknowledges that its recounting of events "obscures the often extremely antagonistic and conflictual nature of the interactions", but even that reference to obscuring obscures. It makes no mention of the callous treatment meted out by student protesters to then Dean, Professor Bongani Mayosi, and to others.[51] When a person has been driven to suicide, it takes a special insensitivity to obscure that and to present the scenario as a case study in sensitization.

Not all the silencing is around racial issues. There have been attempts to silence pro-life groups, which is unsurprising given how openly people express intolerance for such views. For example, one medical student wrote:

> It is extremely disappointing and disgusting how a university that claims to be a progressive institution continually allows violent anti-choice groups like 'Students for Life' to take up space on its campuses.

and

> This is not what a decolonised, intersectional feminist university looks like. I challenge UCT to remove anti-choice groups and shutdown this event; they should not be allowed to have room to exchange violent, unfounded ideas.[52]

It is a common woke ploy to characterise the expression of views with which one disagrees as violent. The mere expression of views is not violence. They may be disliked – even wrong – but if one is not prepared to tolerate views one dislikes or takes to be wrong, then one should not expect tolerance from those who dislike one's own views and take them to be wrong.

UCT has not shut down pro-life events. Unlike the medical student who authored the above words, UCT understands that such an action would violate the South African Constitution. Nor am I suggesting that, for this reason, this medical student should be prevented from expressing her intolerance. Understood correctly, freedom of expression also protects the expression of intolerant ideas. What it does not protect are intolerant *actions* (rather than mere words). However, it is noteworthy which words incur objection or backlash and which words do not. Students who express the above sorts of intolerance pay little or no price for their intolerance. By contrast, for example, some calls to protect academic freedom will bring down accusations of racism upon one's head. When intolerance passes without remark, but tolerance is condemned, one knows the climate is toxic.

Some might respond that the very fact that I am writing this book is an indication that people are not being silenced. Such a response would be a mistake. First, silencing comes in degrees. Obviously UCT is not a totalitarian regime. People are not being imprisoned, tortured, or executed for expressing unorthodox views. However, those who dare express such views do pay a serious price for doing so. They are targeted, censured, and marginalised. Their work environment becomes even more miserable. That may not silence *everybody*, but it does silence all those unwilling to take these risks.

ARTLESS DODGING

One distinctive form of "silencing" is not academic but rather artistic. During the Fallist period, twenty-four artworks on display in a few university buildings were irredeemably "silenced" – by being incinerated.[53] UCT briefly condemned this behaviour, correctly identifying it as "criminal" and saying that it "exceeded all possible limits of protest action"[54]. Of course, those words were not matched with appropriate actions to hold the arsonists to account. Moreover, UCT then either covered up or removed approximately seventy-five further artworks that had been on display in various parts of the University, including the library.[55]

Those with discernment immediately saw these coverings and removals for what they were – censorship. This is why noted anti-Apartheid photographer, David Goldblatt, decided to withdraw his collection of photographs from UCT's Special Collections[56] and to house it, instead, at Yale University.[57] It is also why poet, writer and artist, Breyten Breytenbach, who had been imprisoned for his anti-apartheid activities, wrote that he fully supported David Goldblatt's decision and that he would have done the same if he could have. Three of his paintings were among those removed. However, he did not own those paintings.[58] Two of them were on loan to UCT from the Hans Porer collection and were returned by UCT to the lender.[59] The third, it seems, was owned by UCT.[60]

Noted anti-apartheid photographer Paul Weinberg decided to withdraw from UCT an iconic photograph he had taken of Nelson Mandela casting his vote in South Africa's first democratic elections. This decision was taken partly in the light of UCT's general treatment of works of art, but also partly as a result of its treatment of this particular photograph of his.

The photograph had been part of an installation in the foyer of UCT's Special Collections and was removed the day before Mr Weinberg returned to the library after a two-year secondment to the Centre for African Studies. Mr Weinberg asked the head of Special Collections about the photograph's removal. He was told that it had been removed "due to the discussion with campus community regarding perceptions of accessibility and African studies and due to recalibration efforts".[61] Mr Weinberg said that the photograph was later "relocated ('recalibrated') to an obscure part of Special Collections, where it sat without is caption for about six months". UCT claimed that its new position might give it more prominence. However, this is clearly false. In the words of William Daniels, then a UCT librarian, who has photographs to prove it, it was moved "from the first landing of the main (and only public) staircase into the reading room, where it immediately confronted every visitor (emphatically not just some 'stairwell'!) to a corner alongside the microform machines behind an industrial fan!"[62] Mr Weinberg was not consulted on its relocation, which he found "not only strange but also disrespectful".[63]

More galling, however, was that Mr Weinberg's work had been identified by then Vice-Chancellor Max Price as contributing to "institutional racism" at UCT. Dr Price had written in a newspaper piece about a "body of photographic work intended to reveal the callousness of apartheid". He said that "Black people are shown in the wastelands of the Bantustans, in desolate squatter camps, and in the dehumanising grip of the migrant labour system" and that photographs of "white people, in the same collection, portray them as powerful, privileged overlords". He acknowledged that without any doubt, "the photographers involved – Peter Magubane, David Goldblatt, Paul Weinberg, Omar Badsha –

intended them as ammunition in the struggle against apartheid" but that "if you are a black student born well after 1994 what you see is a parade of black people stripped of their dignity and whites exuding wealth and success".[64]

Paul Weinberg said that he "found the manner in which the photographers were accused of contributing to 'institutional racism' totally unacceptable".[65] He had pointed out that neither Omar Badsha nor Peter Magubane had photographs on the walls of UCT, and that David Goldblatt's and his photographs were from the post-apartheid period. Max Price's response to this was that he was really referring to the digital photographic collections.[66] However, that would undermine the argument Dr Price had advanced in his original article, because digital collections, which are not on public display, do not contribute to the day to day experience of those inhabiting the university. One would have to specifically seek out those images which exist in UCT's collections alongside volumes of context. This seems like another case in which the conclusions come first, and the arguments are then mustered to support them.

When the offence comes first and the argument afterwards, it does not matter what the facts are. Imagine that art depicting "black" oppression were *not* displayed at UCT or if there were too little of it. We can expect that the complaint would then be that the history of oppression had been erased or minimized. In many countries around the world, the atrocities of the past are memorialized – and appropriately so – through artistic representations and historic photographs. If UCT had been different, *that* would have been a source of complaint.

Again, this is not to deny that impoverished students, especially those who are ill-prepared for university and who are not fluent in English feel – and have good reason for feeling – alienated in UCT's environment. Instead, it is to say that not everything cited in support of that claim is true. Moreover, many of those objecting to artworks at UCT are not part of such an underclass. Those objectors may be "black" but that is not equivalent to "disadvantaged". Indeed the substance of many of the objections to the artworks is precisely to undermine such an equivalence.

UCT, of course, denied that it had engaged in any censorship.[67] Two broad kinds of argument were offered – a custodial argument and a curatorial argument. The custodial argument was that following the Fallist bonfire, other artworks were not safe and needed to be temporarily removed in order to protect them. This, Dr Price said, "was necessarily in line with the primary custodial responsibility of the university for works of art in our care".[68] He acknowledged that it "is easy to see how removing these works would come across as censorship – but it was always made clear that they were removed temporarily for safe keeping".[69]

Define "temporarily"! Four years after the artworks were "temporarily" removed, they have not been returned to their places of exhibit. Perhaps it will be argued that the artworks are still in danger and will be so for quite some time. One problem with this argument is that if one allows people to burn art with impunity, as UCT did, one should fully expect the threat to remain. The university's custodial duty is not merely to hide threatened art. It is also to create the conditions under which the protected art can be taken out of storage and re-exhibited. That includes taking action against those who engage in criminal destruction of art that they find offensive. Either way, until the art is returned, we cannot know that the removal was temporary.

A second problem with the custodial argument is that it is in tension with the curatorial argument that other defenders of UCT's actions were advancing. Associate Professor Jay Pather, chair of the University's Works of Art Committee, offered an argument of this kind:

In any institution, be it a museum, art gallery or educational institution, artworks are routinely removed based on shifting contexts and themes. Some may emerge again later in a different context; others remain in storage. Any gallery or museum curator will tell you that some artworks in their collection have never been displayed. Other institutions also routinely allow the sale of works to make room for others.[70]

This is all true, but one cannot infer from this that removing artworks is *never* censorship – and therefore that it was not censorship in this case. It all depends on *why* the artworks are being removed. The custodial argument suggests that they are not being removed for the ordinary curatorial reasons. It was and remains clear that the mass removal was in response to the offence that some artworks were causing some people.

Here UCT might argue that its Artworks Task Team had offered curatorial reasons for removing some artworks – reasons that might be said to support the views of those offended. This task team's audit had established that the artists whose work was in the University's collection were disproportionately "white",[71] and that "black" and female history and achievements were underrepresented. A former Students' Representative Council President, Ramabina Mahapa, had earlier argued that "blacks" were disproportionately represented, in university art, in ways that were demeaning – such as being impoverished. There were too few artworks affirming "blacks".[72]

There is some merit to this critique. However, it is difficult to reconcile with the full list of artworks that were removed. Mr Mahapa did grant that "some of the portraits are not demeaning and humiliating in and of themselves, but concern is not necessarily with individual portraits but with the message the collective paintings are saying about someone of my pigmentation". Nevertheless, it is difficult to see how many of the artworks even contribute to some aggregate problem.

For example, how does Richard Keresemose Baholo's "Mandela receives honorary doctorate from UCT" possibly fit a curatorial policy aiming to rectify the aforementioned problems. He's a "black" artist painting "black" achievement. Similarly, how does Karina Turok's photograph of Nelson Mandela, feet-up in comfortable surroundings, reading the Sunday newspaper, contribute to the stated problem. The same might be asked of Sue Williamson's 1985 photograph of Mamphela Ramphele, who later became UCT's first "black" Vice-Chancellor.

Sometimes the offence is misplaced. For example, Mr Mahapa describes Breyten Breytenbach's "Hovering Dog" thus:

> a portrait of a naked white man, on his lap is a black woman, they seem to be having sexual intercourse. The white man has a black mask and the black woman has a white mask.

First, this is a poor description of the painting. Foregrounded is a dog suspended just above the ground by two ropes looped under him or her. Behind the dog there is a wall-mounted painting of a swimmer who appears to be emerging from the frame. To the swimmer's left, in the background, are the two naked figures. William Daniels had this to say:

> The nude figures might be slightly too far apart to be having coitus, but one is certainly sitting on the other's lap. In any case, the message is clear: a painting by Breyten Breytenbach depicting physical intimacy across the colour line cannot be displayed. In South Africa! In 2019. At the University of Cape Town.[73]

The treatment of Willie Bester's sculpture of Sarah Baartman provides more evidence of censorship. Sarah

Baartman was a Khoikhoi woman who was exhibited, on account of her steatopygia, as the "Hottentot Venus" at "freak shows" in England and France, dying in the latter country in her mid-twenties. Her body was then put on display. Her remains were eventually repatriated to South Africa, where she was interred on a hilltop overlooking Hankey in the Eastern Cape in 2002.

Mr Bester's sculpture of her arose, according to the artist, from his desire to understand his own suffering under Apartheid. He sought connections with others who have endured pain, which led him to Sarah Baartman.[74] He made the sculpture from pieces he collected from the junk yard. It was bought by UCT for its then new Chancellor Oppenheimer Library. Fifteen years later, in 2016, some students who were offended by her "nakedness", covered the sculpture in cloth.[75]

Mr Bester was "upset because it was not my intention to insult anybody by doing this sculpture. It was something about myself".[76] He said that what UCT is doing is "censorship at its worst" and he demanded the restoration of his work to its original state, saying that "I want it to be uncovered because it was not meant to be covered up".[77]

When librarian William Daniels and an unnamed colleague uncovered the statue two years after it had been covered, Dr Price instructed Gwenda Thomas, then Executive Director of the University libraries to arrange for the censorial coverings to be returned to the sculpture. With some encouragement from Mr Daniels, Ms Thomas refused to do so, noting that this would be in violation of her professional duties.[78]

Mr Daniels was denounced for having restored the sculpture to the artist's conception of its presentation. Professor Elelwani Ramugondo asked: "Why would a white man see the need to derobe a sculpture in order to expose a naked Sarah Baartman yet again?"[79] As Mr Daniels noted "using the term 'disrobe' fell 'victim to the pathetic fallacy' ... The word 'disrobed' implies that a person was deprived of clothing. But the sculpture is not a person, and it was not clothed, but covered up with cloth".[80]

In August 2018, the University announced that an exhibition, "Sarah Baartman – a Call to Respond" would be held at the Ritchie Gallery from 20 September to 4 October that year.[81] We were told that in "preparation, the sculpture has been moved from its position at the Chancellor Oppenheimer Library". That has been described as a "pretext" for removing it from the library because it was not returned there after the temporary exhibition.[82] This is despite the University's Works of Art Committee acknowledging that the "Sarah Baartman sculpture by Willie Bester is, in the words of committee member Professor Alta Steenkamp, 'one of the most important works in UCT's collection of art works right now".[83]

Thus, David Goldblatt was entirely correct in insisting "that the university's actions differ from the curatorship that takes place in museums around the world" and "that the administration is blatantly censoring selected works".[84] UCT's Works of Art Committee has been complicit in this censorship.[85] The "captured" Academic Freedom Committee[86] has offered no protest. There is no sign of any of this changing.

HYPOCRISY AND STUPIDITY

Sadly, it is not uncommon for universities to behave hypocritically and stupidly. For example, there are now many universities speaking endlessly about "inclusivity" but where this is a coded slogan rather than a principled commitment. Such universities, far from including those who are allergic to slogans, are hostile to such people. UCT has this in common with all too many contemporary universities, at least in the anglophone world. It is thus unsurprising that UCT's School of

Economics, following the onslaught on one of its own, Professor Nattrass,[87] decided to engage external facilitators. The conversations to be had were not about academic freedom or academic bullying, but "around race and more broadly institutional culture".[88] For the initial four (online) sessions, the School of Economics was willing to fork out R80 000.[89] UCT is not the only place where such madness can be found, but UCT seems to have more than its fair share of hypocrisy and stupidity.

For example, while UCT was censoring artworks, including in its library, the library unselfconsciously marked "Banned Books Week" with an exhibition of books, films, music and posters banned under Apartheid. Pointing to this absurdity, William Daniels wrote to "commend UCT Libraries for daring to mount an exhibition of materials that were banned under apartheid, even as the censorship of art continues within its own walls".[90] He said that in "order for the Libraries Banned Books Exhibition to have any credibility, and for it to remain free of a staggering degree of hypocrisy, it must present an honest account of the ongoing censorship of art inside the Libraries and elsewhere in the University".[91] It is easy to criticise censorship from a temporal or geographical distance or when it is others who are doing the censoring. It is much harder to criticise the censorship in which one is oneself currently complicit.

In 2020, UCT released "Vision 2030 Strategy". That, in itself, is a source of embarrassment, but an embarrassment shared with universities around the world. The grandiosity and vacuity of university "vision" and "mission" statements are notorious. They cost a lot to produce and are paraded around like the emperor without any clothes. However, UCT's "Vision 2030 Strategy" was especially embarrassing.

First, much fanfare was made of the fact that the document deliberately spells Africa with a "k" – Afrika. According to one report, this "is to reclaim the original spelling" and "also to retain Afrikan agency".[92] In the document itself, the alternative spelling was justified on the grounds that the "pre-colonial spelling is an invitation to reclaim Afrika's agency and use it to validate the global character of the local in the 21st century".[93]

The claim that "Afrika" is the original pre-colonial spelling is, as one UCT professor noted, "historical and philological nonsense". Both "c" and "k" are letters from the Latin alphabet, and neither was used in Africa before European colonization of this continent. It is unclear how asserting otherwise helps reclaim Africa's agency. That may explain why the agency claim was made again even when the claim about the purported pre-colonial spelling was dropped.[94] The suggestion that the reclaimed agency could be used "to validate the global character of the local in the 21st century" is a string of words in search of a meaning.

Even more embarrassing is that a UCT news item about Vision 2030, attributed to the Vice-Chancellor the claim that "the new University of Cape Town (UCT) will embrace inclusivity, *say no to non-racialism* and erase all traces of the past's injustices"[95] (my emphasis). UCT's Communications and Marketing Department was quickly questioned about this. There was an apologetic reply, and the article was corrected to read that UCT would "promote non-racialism". Some wondered[96] whether the initial wording was a Freudian slip. My own view was that if it was not a Freudian slip then the "correction" was either dishonest or ironic. UCT is dripping with racialism – everybody and everything is viewed through a racial lens. There is no sign of that changing, the correction notwithstanding.

Another, albeit lesser lens through which everybody at UCT is viewed is the gender lens. Here too there is no shortage of hypocrisy and stupidity. When UCT's Ombud released her report that referred to many instances of bullying by the Vice-

Chancellor and it subsequently came to light that the relationship between the Vice-Chancellor and her deputies was dysfunctional, UCT's response was to advertise that UCT has an "all-women executive academic leadership"[97] and is "women-led".[98] The Vice-Chancellor, three Deputy Vice-Chancellors and, since July 2020, the Chair and Deputy Chair of Council are all women. (The Chief Operating Officer is a man.)

If UCT were, in 2019 or 2020, men-led (perhaps with a female Chief Operating Officer), we would hear no end of complaints about the lack of gender diversity. When the leadership lacks gender diversity because the leadership is all-female, UCT's response is to trumpet this. I recognise that an all-female university leadership is a rarity, but if diversity is so valuable it is valuable even in such rare cases. The crowing about UCT leadership's gender homogeneity seems to suggest that gender diversity is not actually a principle but rather a cudgel. If it were a principle it would apply to both the goose and the gander.

I see no reason to complain about an all-female leadership (at least if that results from a gender-blind appointment process). However, unlike the starry-eyed, who think that female leadership is the solution to all problems, I take the view that we should expect no better and no worse from women than we get from men, even if there might be average differences in how each sex errs. It certainly seems to lack insight if one's response to the very public news of bullying by and dysfunctionality of the leadership is to harp on proudly about an (almost) all female leadership team.

Moreover, if an "all-male" team had been as dysfunctional as the VC and her DVCS, we would likely have heard about "toxic masculinity" or some variant thereof. If you want to understand just how insulting that stock diagnosis would be, think of comparable spin about the current team – perhaps talk about "cat fights". The point is that sometimes teams are dysfunctional and sometimes leaders are toxic. Attributing that to people's sex rather than to their individual characteristics is sloppy, prejudicial thinking.

FALSE ACCUSATIONS OF RACISM

One common way in which people are silenced is through false accusations of racism. Such false allegations are ubiquitous. I have provided detailed accounts of some of these instances elsewhere in this book. They are by no means the only cases.

Consider, for example, an Honours student in the Science Faculty who in the first semester of 2018 was not attending class or submitting required work. When he met with the programme convener, he disclosed that he was suffering from mental health problems. The convener said that if these were expected to continue, the student should consider requesting a leave of absence. In the middle of that year, the student failed to write all four examinations in his home department and at least one examination in another department. He requested permission from the programme convener to write make-up examinations for the four he missed in the department. He provided ambiguous medical certificates. The convener sought clarification from the medical practitioner and then granted permission for the student to write two make-up examinations. The other two absences, the convener said, were not covered by the medical certificates.

The student appealed the refused components of his requests, first to the Head of Department and then to the Dean. In both cases, the convener's decision was upheld. The Head of Department and the Dean also recommended that the student take a leave of absence. The student declined this advice, but he did begin to defame the course convener, whom he called a "racist with a smiling face". The student claimed that the decision to refuse him permission to write two of the examinations was racist. In support of this allegation, he offered various falsehoods, including the claim that he was the only student who had been refused a make-up examination.

The Dean instructed the student to cease and desist from defamatory remarks about the convener. The student did not obey this instruction, and instead doubled down on his defamatory remarks.

A different student, in a different Faculty, took to Twitter anonymously, posting the name and a picture of a lecturer. The student said that this lecturer "has been continuously victimizing black students and faced no consequences" and that the lecturer "vowed to weed them out and do all that is in his powers to ensure that they won't graduate". In a later tweet, the student invited "the people of South Africa to put pressure on UCT to ensure justice is pursued" against this staff member. Another student – or, more probably, the same one under a different Twitter pseudonym[99] – posted a picture of the lecturer's family and vehicle and repeated the claim that he "victimizes black students". Both tweeters tagged various well-known race-baiters and news media. UCT responded that it was looking into the matter, but the student tweeted that this was a lie, and that the University was "only saying this because we are exposing them on social media". This student then encouraged others to "expose whoever is abusing you in your faculty. NAME AND SHAME #EXPOSE_UCT".

The student's accusations about the lecturer were baseless. After a preliminary disciplinary investigation into the staff member's (purported) behaviour, he was officially exonerated. It seems that the perpetrator of the defamatory comments was a disgruntled student who had been found guilty of plagiarism, and had forged signatures, among other violations. The lecturer had not vowed to weed out "black" students, but instead to weed out dishonest ones. The student, not the lecturer, made the inference from the one category to the other. She was never brought to book for her defamatory activity despite UCT's having postured on Twitter about not accepting "bullying on our social media platforms" and about having reported to Twitter the student's posting of pictures of the staff member's minor children. This is another instance of defamation with impunity – although not as sustained and wide-reaching as Ms Mkhumbuzi's defamatory activity.

Another example is that of a person who applied to do a PhD at UCT. His academic transcript from another South African university was mediocre – dominated largely by Thirds and Lower Seconds, with the occasional Fail and low Upper Second. He had no mark above 70%. He subsequently completed a second Masters (this time by dissertation) at another, and significantly less reputable, South African university. It was examined by two academics from another academically weak university in the country. He obtained a First for this dissertation, but the relevant UCT department was not impressed with his writing sample or research proposal. Accordingly, the applicant was rejected. He responded that this decision was "plain racism".

Technically, this accusation came from outside UCT, but it is revealing of the broader national context, where false accusations of racism are so common that they can fairly be described as part of the national pathology. Consider, for example, former President Jacob Zuma who, in the face of charges of fraud, corruption and racketeering, complained that he was being victimized because he is "black".[100]

UCT's Vice-Chancellor, Mamokgethi Phakeng also played the race (and gender) card when she was openly criticised by UCT's Ombud (as recounted above). That the Ombud is a "black" woman was no impediment to Professor Phakeng ranting about the knives being out for successful "black women".[101] Others also advanced this narrative. One anonymous source claimed that "knives have been out for Phakeng since her first day in office" and that "the ombud's office was being weaponised to get rid of Phakeng".[102]

The Ombud hit back at the suggestion that she was part of a "white racist plot" and "that she was a member of a university faction with 'knives out' for the VC".[103] She asked, rhetorically, "why would I want to bring down the vice-chancellor? Why would I let myself be used by any race group?". She said that she "cannot be manipulated" and that the very narrative of "knives being out" is itself bullying.[104] She said that "[r]acialising feedback and changing standards and expectation (sic) based on race is irresponsible leadership. Black people should not protect each other like that. I wasn't going to bow to that pressure. If someone transgresses, notwithstanding their race, they should be called on it."[105] This forthright statement did not stop others from attempting to further the narrative.[106]

Another common way in which people are entrapped in an allegation of racism is by mispronouncing an African name (sometimes in an ever so miniscule a way). Those seeing racism in such mispronunciations fail to see their own inability to correctly pronounce the names of others. It is a common for people to be unable to accurately pronounce names in languages they do not speak. My own north African Jewish surname is regularly butchered – including, multiple times, by none other than Chumani Maxwele.[107] It would be bizarre, not to mention paranoid, if I leapt to the conclusion that this was a manifestation or indicator of antisemitism (or racism). Mature, mentally stable adults recognise that sometimes their names will be mispronounced, especially by those unfamiliar with them. It is reasonable to expect some effort be made to pronounce one's name correctly, but there may be a limit to how accurately some names will be pronounced by people in very different linguistic communities. To immediately infer prejudice is itself a prejudice.

There is a problem in the reverse direction. Sometimes native English speakers (in South Africa) complain of the "accents" of lecturers and students whose mother-tongue is an African language. They forget that *everybody* has an accent. It is sometimes very difficult to understand people with very different accents from our own, but we need to understand that they may have the same problem with us. The wrong way to respond to this is to assume the worst about others.

RACISM

The overt and covert racial preferences discussed in Chapter 17 are, in my view, instances of racism. I realise that some people argue that at least some racial preferences do not count as racism. I hope that most of those who argue for that view, would at least recognize many of the other instances of racism that pervade UCT.

The dominant narrative of racism at UCT today, would have us believe that "blacks" are its (only) victims. While I keep an open mind about there being some such manifestations of racism, this book shows that almost all the purported instances I have examined are not indeed instances of anti-"black" racism. The exceptions are instances in which "blacks" have been targeted by other "blacks" for not being what the latter regard as "real blacks". Being called a "coconut", "Uncle Tom", "colonial administrator", or "house negro", for example, is a racist technique for silencing or ostracising people who do not comply with one's own views.

I believe that I have also shown that there is plenty of anti-"white" racism. Some staff and students have been discriminated against or (at least in part) targeted because they have been identified as "white". (See, for example, Chapters 4, 10, 12, 15, 16, 17, 20 and 21.) Here are some further examples.

Consider, for example, the "Decolonial School" event

organized at UCT in 2018. It included a supper that was originally billed as for "POC only". ("POC" standardly refers to "People of Colour".) The consequent backlash led UCT to indicate that no such restriction may be placed on UCT events. This resulted in the organizers reluctantly dropping that restriction, but not without saying that "if a white person comes through, we can't kick them out but we have made it clear that we would prefer that white people respect there is a preference"[108] and that "although the school is not segregationist, we think it is high time that white people now become comfortable with being excluded" and signed off "Warmest, Decol School Team".

Given this, it is unsurprising that "no white people attended the supper" and that "white attendees at the Decolonial School organised among themselves to remain absent from the supper out of respect for the space and its intended purpose".[109]

Organizers and defenders of the racially exclusive dinner obviously had to rationalize their racism. Thus, responding to the backlash, Elelwani Ramugondo tweeted: "As we have noted before. Empire always over-reacts. POC could easily be 'People of the Continent'."[110] This is disingenuous, because she well knows that that was not what "POC" meant here. In any event, who are "People of the Continent"? They obviously were not including non-"black" people of the continent, which means that under either interpretation of "POC", the goal was a racially exclusive event.

Nor was this the only response that sought to portray non-racialist objections to the racially exclusive event as a moral flaw. There was the inevitable reference to "white tears".[111] Another commentator opined that part

> of the decolonial project is about recognising how colonialism centred whiteness in every aspect of life. The decentring of that and allowing unapologetic space for black people to openly and honestly reflect on their

experiences should be a given. The outrage at the thought of not being included in everything demonstrates how some white people are refuse (sic) to place others' struggles beyond their discomfort.[112]

Similarly, the Decolonial School described the racially exclusive dinner as "a space where black people can come together to communicate their experiences of the day without having to shelter white fragility"[113] and "a space to debrief, reflect and exist outside of the white gaze".[114]

All this in a country (and, to a lesser extent, a university) where "whites" are a shrinking minority of people. Although there was a backlash (in some quarters – and not only "white" quarters) to the racially exclusive dinner, it is impossible even to imagine an exclusively "white" dinner being proposed (in 2018!) and then defended with reference to "black tears", a space in which to communicate experiences "outside the black gaze" and without having to shelter "black fragility". The naked racism – not to mention childishness – of such an endeavour would be readily apparent to the Decolonial School, who would certainly not respect the expressed preference for a "safe space".

Media coverage of this event led journalist Ed Herbst to relate an incident in which a UCT student – the daughter of a "white" friend – attended a UCT poetry reading with her "black" boyfriend, a fellow UCT student. At the door she was told that "she was to be separated from her boyfriend" and "told to go to the back of the room so as to create a 'safe space' at the front for black students".[115]

Consider too the case of a student who was failing her courses and confronted the head of department in his office, insisting that "you fucking whites" can't do this to her. She refused to leave his office when requested to do so. She insisted that "no white man" would tell her what to do. This case drew zero attention in the media (including social media), most likely because it was never publicly revealed. That, in itself, is revealing about the climate. If a "white" student had spoken to a "black" professor in comparable ways (*mutatis mutandis*), there is every likelihood that it would have made it into the public domain and elicited widespread condemnation.

There was one public report, in the UCT student newspaper, of a Black Land First member telling a Jewish student that "Hitler should have killed all of you, you thieves".[116] That seems not to have elicited any outrage from the Fallists and their apologists. Nor are they silent only on references to *past* genocides. The same applies to potential future racial blood-letting. For example, a Pan Africanist Student Movement of Azania (PASMA) poster at medical school contained the racist slogan, "#OneSettlerOneBullet".[117] A few days later a member of the administrative staff reported hearing a student with a PASMA t-shirt "talking the one-settler-one-bullet rhetoric".[118] Somebody else reported in 2019 that a young relative, who was then a first year UCT student had been on a university bus in which she was one of only two "whites". The bus was full of Economic Freedom Front (EFF) supporters who sang this slogan to the two "whites".[119] Those who doubt whether "One Settler, One Bullet" really is racist or who suggest, disingenuously, that it is "only" a metaphor, should ask what they would say about the use of the phrase "One Native, One Bullet" in comparable situations and ways.

The problem is not just words, but also deeds. One head of department was concerned that a lecturer in his department was marking with a racist agenda – marking students down if they were "white", and up if they were "black". It should not be necessary to say that this head of department is "black", but it is worth noting for those who interpret all motives through a racial prism. The head of department raised his concerns with the Dean who asked him to lodge a formal complaint. This did not happen because the head of department was too fearful of doing so.

Consider too the department in which postgraduate admissions decisions were sometimes being made on explicitly racial grounds, with "white" applicants who were on the Dean's Merit List being turned away, while "black" students with failing marks, or with no background in the discipline, were admitted. In some but not all cases, these initial decisions were countermanded.

Compounding the evils of such racism is the common mantra that "blacks" cannot be racist (or "whites" the victims of racism). Consider, for example, the words of Ntokozo Qwabe. This was the UCT student, Rhodes Scholar to Oxford (and, ironically, a leader there of Rhodes Must Fall) who threatened a "white" student with a sjambok, knocking the latter's mobile phone out of his hand, and who later said that he wished he had "whipped the white apartheid settler colonial entitlement out of the bastard". He was also among the group of people, who when dining out and served by a "white" waitress, left the following note where the gratuity amount would be inserted: "WE WILL GIVE TIP WHEN YOU RETURN THE LAND" (capitals in the original). When Mr Qwabe was asked about anti-white racism, he answered: "There can never be racism against white people".[120]

When advocates of this view bother to justify it, they typically do so by appealing to power structures or systemic considerations. They argue that prejudice or discrimination does not amount to racism unless it is part of a system in which power lies with those doing the victimization.

This argument is convenient for "black" racists (and their "useful idiots"[121]) in countries in which "blacks" are an unempowered minority. It becomes vacuous in those countries where "blacks" are dominant. There must be at least some such countries. While "blacks" are not dominant in *every* way in South Africa, they are dominant in many important ways, including politically. Prejudice and discrimination against "blacks" is certainly treated much more seriously, both legally and socially, than are prejudice and discrimination in the reverse direction. Some of the discrimination in the reverse direction is legally required. Hate speech against "blacks" has resulted in more severe repercussions for the speaker than is the case when "whites" are the victims of hate speech.[122] One commissioner at the South African Human Rights Commission has been reported as saying that the Commission "was purposefully lenient to black offenders in racial incidents".[123]

Even those who think that "blacks" in South Africa are not yet sufficiently dominant for any of their anti-"white" prejudice or discrimination to count as racism, they must acknowledge that this is not a necessary, *a priori* truth. There must be at least some possible conditions under which "blacks" *can* be racist. (It might be productive if those espousing the dominance view of racism could stipulate what those conditions would be. To consider an extreme case, would ethnic cleansing of "whites" from South Africa, constitute anti-"white" racism?) Thus, even on the dominance view of racism "blacks" *can* be racist.

The range of conditions in which they can be racist increases if one accepts, as I argue elsewhere we should, that while systemic and power considerations often do exacerbate sexism or racism they are not necessary conditions for it.[124] Racism is ultimately a form of tribalism – roughly a favouring of (perceived) fellow group members over outsiders. (This is not to deny more complex derivatives – such as those who internalise dominant negative views about their own group. This often does result from power relations.)

Tribalism is not the preserve of any one human group. All human groupings are prone to it, and there is good evolutionary explanation for why this is the case. Explanation, of course, is not the same as justification. For many people – of all "races" and other groupings – the moral circle has expanded to varying degrees. They recognize that we are not justified in thinking and feeling some things that our evolutionary psychology might incline us to think and feel. Many others, however, still indulge their human proclivity to favour perceived fellows over outsiders. Again, people who do this are to be found in all "races" (and religions, ethnicities, and so forth). To suggest otherwise, is to defy the evidence. Such a propensity is also a familiar human failing. This is deeply regrettable whenever it occurs, but is even more so when it becomes programmatic in a university.

Chapter 24
CONCLUSION

UCT has degenerated. It lost much lustre in the lustrum following the start of the Rhodes Must Fall protests. Nor is it only lustre that has been lost. The institution has become badly osteoporotic. Although I feared this sort of decline back in 2015, it was not inevitable. The current situation could have been different if earlier warnings had been heeded, and if a more principled path had been pursued.

The future is also not inevitable. What will happen will depend on choices that are made. Perhaps UCT can still be saved. My sense is that it will not be. If it has not already passed a tipping point, which I suspect it has, it is sufficiently far down a path of toxicity that it has become that much harder to reverse. The more the worst elements of the University are indulged, the more difficult it becomes to change the course that the University is taking.

Much of this book describes specific problems and how

they arose. However, I have also provided more general descriptions and diagnoses. Much of the blame for the current situation must be apportioned to those who have acted criminally or unethically, and to those who have aided and abetted them. Chief among those who have enabled the criminal and unethical behaviour, is UCT's leadership.

I do not minimize the challenges the leadership faced. As I acknowledged back in June 2015,[1] they were in an unenviable position. However, it was a mistake to capitulate to criminality and to indulge vicious elements of the University. Moreover, they capitulated not only in circumstances in which they sought to placate people who might otherwise have resorted to even more violence, but also in many circumstances in which they could clearly have held the line without such risks.[2] They were manifestly employing double standards – different standards for people of different purported races, and different standards for the reasonable and for the unreasonable. Where race and degree of reasonableness or unreasonableness overlapped, the double standard was enhanced.

UCT purports to be committed to a series of values that include:[3]

- Truth, fairness, consistency and integrity in both academic and other work, and in all personal and institutional relationships.
- Compassion, generosity and concern for the needs and aspirations of others ...
- Respect and tolerance for cultural, religious, political and other differences ...
- Intellectual honesty, vigour in debate, openness to alternative ideas ...
- High standards, personal fulfilment and the pursuit of excellence.
- The protection and responsible use of the University's assets and resources.

It asks its members to undertake, individually and collectively, *inter alia*:[4]

- To promote and protect academic freedom.
- To oppose and take steps to prevent racial, gender or other forms of unfair discrimination.
- To refrain from speech or conduct that demeans or humiliates others.
- To advance the principle of open governance and to be fully accountable for our actions.

These are words – noble words – but they are, all too often, not reflected in the institutional deeds. The proof of a commitment is not in its utterance but rather in its manifestation through actions. The commitment has yet to be proved.

BLACK ACADEMIC CAUCUS

The Black Academic Caucus (BAC) has played an outsized roll in fostering and facilitating the toxic climate that currently pervades UCT. It was founded in 2012[5] "with the purpose of challenging the slow pace of transformation that continues to maintain hegemonies and reproduce colonial relations of power"[6] – a purpose that could easily have been produced by the algorithms of the postmodern generator.[7]

According to its constitution, which was adopted in late 2015,[8] membership is not explicitly restricted by "race", but all applications for membership "shall be lodged with the BAC Executive Committee who has the right to decide on membership". All members must meet the requirement of supporting and upholding the purposes and objectives of the BAC.

These include the "transformation and decolonization of UCT" and the "higher education landscape in South Africa", "transforming the curriculum and research scholarship so that it is linked to social justice and the experience of black people", "increased number/s of black academic staff employed in the university, particularly in the professoriate and an increase in South African black staff", "increased representation of black academics in the governance of the university", recognizing and "mainstreaming of disability issues in academia", and challenging "traditions of patriarchy".

The Management of UCT, acting on behalf of the University, entered into a memorandum of understanding (MoU) with the BAC on 26 January 2017.[9] Under this agreement, the BAC received "formal recognition ... as an Independent Interest Group at the University of Cape Town". The MoU also stated that both parties "commit to consultation and cooperation with respect to policies and decisions related to transformation at UCT", and to "cooperation and consultation when making submissions on Higher Education policy". Another significant provision of the MoU is that "the representation of the BAC on university structures such as Council and Senate, and other university committees will enjoy further attention".

It is remarkable that UCT entered into this MoU with the BAC before UCT formulated the principles that would govern its entering into memoranda of understanding with independent interest groups. (To the best of my knowledge it *still* has no such policy.) Even more remarkable is that UCT entered into this particular MoU without knowing either *who* the members of the BAC were[10] or even how *many* members it has.[11] How does one enter into an agreement with an interest group, agreeing to consult with it and to consider according it representation on key committees, without knowing just how many people it represents? To the extent that the BAC represents a small group of people, including a small proportion of "black" academics, it is unclear why it (over other small groups) should be accorded special status. To the extent that the BAC represents a large group of people, they already have a voice through the regular governance structures.

Indeed, the BAC itself has claimed that "[m]any of our members currently serve within key structures of the university including council, senate, and university and faculty committees" and that its "members are also leading strategic initiatives around transformation".[12] This has become even more true since that statement was made.

The BAC presents itself as a progressive organization. There is little evidence of that – unless one understands "progressive" as a slogan. By contrast, there is strong evidence that this is an organization devoid of (impartially applied) moral principles. Consider the two columns on the next page, each referring to (examples of) behaviour at UCT in the years since the founding of the BAC:

Column 1	Column 2
Punching the Vice-Chancellor.[13]	Verbally challenging a dean who was excluding from a Faculty Board agenda an item that it was not within his rights to exclude.[14]
Blocking entrances to and shutting down the university for weeks.[15]	Walking out of a meeting in protest.[16]
Strewing excrement in university buildings.[17]	Fair application of DP requirements.[18]
Assaulting security guards.[19]	Writing a commentary in the *South African Journal of Science*, reporting on preliminary findings about why there are disproportionately few "black" students in UCT's conservation biology programme.[20]
Arson – Historic paintings.[21]	
Arson – University vehicles.[22]	
Arson – Vice-Chancellor's office.[23]	
Students defaming staff members.[24]	
Staff member defaming a colleague.[25]	
Failure of the Dean and University executive to sanction that staff member.[26]	
Racially abusing a fellow student and knocking the cell phone out of his hand with a sjambok.[27]	
Wearing a T-shirt on campus with the words "Kill all Whites".[28]	
Requesting all "white" people to leave a public lecture.[29]	
Stating that "white people are hectic".[30]	
Opposing the appointment of a dean on the grounds of his race.[31]	
Referring to a junior colleague (in her absence) as "just another fucking white woman".[32]	
Setting the following exam question: "Write detailed notes on race and racism. In your answer take care to specify the reasons for the impossibility of friendship between blacks and whites."[33]	
Calling for "One settler, one bullet".[34]	
Defacing the campus World War Memorial with the words "Fuck White People".[35]	
Students reducing a professor to tears and then telling her that they do not care about her tears.[36]	
Censorship of artworks.[37]	
Disinvitation of Academic Freedom lecturer.[38]	

Which behaviour – that in Column 1 or that in Column 2 – would a group motivated by moral considerations support, and which would it condemn? Which conduct is "disrespectful" – that in Column 1 or that in Column 2? In some cases, a reader might want further information. This book has provided much of that information (within the limits of protecting my sources from retribution). It is difficult to imagine a world in which *all* of the items in Column 1 would be acceptable and all the items in Column 2 would be worthy of denunciation. Once one has familiarised oneself with the facts of the specific cases, it is impossible to defend the record of the BAC – tolerating and even defending actions in Column 1 and denouncing those responsible for the actions in Column 2.

The only way to explain the BAC's record is by understanding the racial identities of the players in the various scenarios. Whenever a "black" student or staff member is in conflict with UCT or with a "white" person, the BAC can be expected to take the side of the "black" person. The facts do not matter, and the BAC does not investigate them before it pronounces on the situation.[39]

There is one possible scenario in which I could at least imagine the BAC supporting a "white" over a "black". That is if the "white" were their ideological ally and the "black" were espousing a view that the BAC takes not to be in the interests of "blacks". Under such a circumstance, the BAC might well be sufficiently uncomfortable to remain silent, but I suspect that if it did not remain silent, it would support the "white". I am not aware of any such instances thus far.

It might be suggested that the BAC *has* condemned some of the behaviour in the left column. In a statement, they did say that they "do not support or encourage ... any form of violence, destruction of property or intimidation by any group or individual".[40] However, those words are empty. In the same statement they said that "we do not support or encourage ... the arrest ... of our students". These are the students who were engaging in violence, destruction of property and intimidation. It would be fascinating to know when the BAC thinks that people who inflict personal violence, property destruction and intimidation should be arrested.

Thus, what we have here is a passing and unconvincing rejection, in very general terms, of criminal behaviour (in a democratic state). There has been no condemnation by the BAC of any of the specific behaviour in the left column, whether illegal or "merely" immoral, nor any attempt to hold those responsible to account. This stands in contrast to the specific public condemnations of those responsible for the actions in the right-hand column.

The BAC remained silent when, for example, the Vice-Chancellor, Dr Price, was punched and when security guards were assaulted – one beaten and another hospitalised in a serious condition after a rock was dropped from a height onto his head. However, the BAC condemned those who verbally challenged a dean for acting *ultra vires*. The BAC tolerated the entire university's being shut down by protesters for weeks, but it condemned those who walked out of a meeting in protest. It was silent in the face of censorship, but denounced an academic who required substantial (at least two-thirds) lecture attendance. It remained silent about multiple instances of explicit, overt, and unequivocal racial hatred (against "whites"), but then condemned a published study that it implausibly claimed was racist (against "blacks), demanding that action be taken against its author.

The BAC, as I noted in Chapter 10, is a Broederbond-like organization. Of course it is not like that erstwhile Afrikaner secret society in *all* ways. For example, it serves the purported interests of "blacks" rather than of Afrikaners, and it is not restricted to men. However, it is racially self-serving organization. It is also, in an important sense, a secret society.

Although it has members, its membership list has not been made public despite repeated requests for this.

For example, I wrote to the then Chair of the BAC, Dr Phoebe Kisubi-Mbasalaki, on 4 May 2020, asking for the BAC's membership list. I did so on the basis of the BAC having defamed me. I provided evidence that the claims against me had been false. Dr Kisubi-Mbasalaki ignored my email. I wrote again on 11 May 2020 to remind her about my request. This too was ignored. I wrote again on 18 May 2020, this time filing an official Protection of Access to Information ACT (PAIA) request for the information. Under South African law, this obliged Dr Kisubi-Mbasalaki to provide me with the information (unless she could show that the requested information was exempt). Despite this legal obligation, Dr Kisubi-Mbasalaki ignored this request too.

This impunity was further entrenched by UCT. On 25 June 2020, I lodged a grievance complaint against Dr Kisubi-Mbasalaki. Her head of department simply refused to deal with it. I thus escalated the matter to the relevant deputy vice-chancellor, Professor Sue Harrison, on 27 June 2020. She acknowledged receipt on 1 July 2020, but failed to follow up, despite reminders on 6 July and 13 July.

According to UCT's policy on grievance complaints, my complaint should have been dealt with by Professor Harrison within five busines days. When twenty-five business days had elapsed without a response from her, I reported the matter to the UCT Ombud, Zetu Makamandela-Mguqulwa. On 12 August 2020, she wrote to Professor Harrison, who responded in a way that led Ms Makamandela-Mguqulwa to believe that Professor Harrison would contact me directly. By 20 August I had still heard nothing further from Professor Harrison. I notified the Ombud of this and she make a further overture to Professor Harrison. On 11 September Professor Harrison wrote to let me know that she was attending to the matter. On 15 September she handed over the matter to an employee relations specialist in Human Resources. He and I had some communication about the matter and he followed up on it. However, by 1 October he handed the matter back to Professor Harrison because Dr Kisubi-Mbasalaki's status as a post-doctoral student rather than a staff member put her beyond his remit.[41]

Given that UCT failed to deal with this matter, I took the only action open to those whose PAIA applications to private bodies such as the BAC are either ignored or refused. I lodged High Court Action. I did this in December 2020. The case has yet to be resolved.

Not only is the general membership kept secret, but at any time it was not easy to determine who the office bearers of the BAC were. Until I lodged my High Court action the BAC did not seem to maintain any public record of this (on their Facebook page, for example). Whenever I wanted to contact the BAC, I had to ask who the current chair was. When I put this question to the Registrar, Royston Pillay, on 2 May 2020, even he did not know! He referred me to the Deputy Dean for Transformation in the Humanities Faculty, who then provided me with the name and contact details for the then current Chair. This changed around 30 January 2021 when the BAC suddenly posted the names of their office bearers on their Facebook page.

The secrecy of the BAC's membership (and former obscurity of its office bearers) is pertinent because of the way the BAC operates. It periodically makes public statements denouncing named individuals, initiating or feeding a moral panic. It does so under the banner of the BAC, but the people behind that mask remain obscured. Their victims are in the public spotlight, but the accusers are shielded from public view. UCT, in turn, has protected the BAC, its office bearers and members, from accountability and transparency. For the BAC to suggest that old "hegemonies" and "colonial relations of power"[42] are still operative is sheer balderdash.

METASTATIC DEFAMATION

Those who question the orthodoxy that is prevalent at UCT, and those who speak up against intolerance, bullying, extreme racial preferences, as well as criminality of various kinds, pay a heavy price. There are many mechanisms by which this occurs, but one of them is the metastasizing of defamation. My own case is a good illustration of how this happens.

My critique of strong race-based affirmative action has long elicited *ad hominem* critics, but it was not until 2015 that the defamation moved into high gear. It arguably began with Xolela Mangcu's intemperate response to an opinion piece that I had published about decolonization and transformation.[43] He referred to my piece as a "racially offensive diatribe". His reply was published online, while my article and subsequent response were for a long time, restricted to the print edition of the *Cape Times*. (See Appendix 1.) The defamation therefore spread much further.

When Busi Mkhumbuzi was refused DP for failing to meet the course requirements, she cited Xolela Mangcu's critique as "evidence" that I am racist. She then intensified the defamation, both in how much she said and how far it spread.[44]

When Adam Haupt accused me and others of racism for seeking to put the vegan proposal on the Faculty Board agenda, this accusation was very likely viewed through the prism of the earlier allegations. At the time that Adam Haupt proposed a censure of us, Ms Mkhumbuzi's allegations were swirling around and very likely fed into the mob's frenzy.[45]

INADEQUATE COUNTERWEIGHT

UCT has gone mad. Some of the madness is not unique to UCT and is found in many universities around the world.[46] However, I have a sense that the problem is even more pervasive at UCT than it is in countries such as the United States, the United Kingdom, Canada, and Australia. As I mentioned in the introductory chapter, a more definitive evaluation would require a comparison, in the similar detail, with other universities that are purported to be as bad.

There are explanations for why UCT (and South African universities) would be manifesting more madness. Part of the explanation for this is specific to UCT and to its (weak) leadership in recent years, a period during which strong, principled leadership was required to rescue the institution.

Another explanatory factor is the national context (which also affects other South African universities). In South African universities those claiming to be the victims of university racism are not a minority but rather a majority – and they are a majority with political and social power. Related to this, is the absence of a significant national counterweight to the excesses of the regressive left within the academic context.

In other countries there is such a counterweight. Sometimes this counterweight is, in itself, no better than what it is counterweighting. Nor is it the case that madness of a regressive right somehow balances out the madness of a regressive left, producing a sane outcome. Instead, the difference is that South Africa's politics is heavily skewed towards a dangerous left. The dangers are already apparent, and I fear that they will become even more so as South Africa continues its descent.[47]

This is not to say that there are no liberals trying to moderate towards the centre. However, there are not many of them, and South Africa is a one-party dominant democracy. There has been no change of national government since the democratic transition in 1994. The racial narrative of the ANC is congruent with that of UCT and other South African universities. If the ANC's dominance is fractured, the country will likely lurch further to the left rather than to the centre.

South Africa is not a country in which either the centre holds or in which there are periodic swings between left of centre and right of centre.

State power thus consistently reinforces the narratives that are dominant within the university. For example, the *Report of the Ministerial Task Team on the Recruitment, Retention and Progression of Black South African Academics* includes the following recommendation:

> Perhaps the most important recommendation to be made in this report is the need to tackle institutional and individual racism and sexism in direct and visible ways, including through penalising perpetrators, but also in ways that assist to build institutional cultures that embrace diversity and that are anti-racist and anti-sexist. This means moving from hoping that this will happen naturally to actually putting measures in place to ensure it happens. Universities must interrogate how institutional cultures and traditional practices may be creating alienating environments that intentionally or unintentionally work to exclude, and put proactive measures in place to address this. University leadership and management must lead in this regard and must receive training in how to do so where this is needed.[48]

This may all sound very noble, until we know that the opposition to "racism" and "sexism" is code that (often) refers to delusional perceptions of these evils, and that excludes many real instances of them. There is no concern here about South Africa's institutions of higher education being welcoming to those who deviate from orthodox views. There is no embrace of *intellectual* diversity. The "training" to be provided to university leadership and management sounds like shades of Maoist re-education. The "perpetrators" who will be "penalised" may not (yet?) be required to stare at the sun, but it will be their tormentors and not they who wield the power – power endorsed by the state.

In some cases, the state has become a refuge for those who are too toxic even for UCT. For example, when Paul Ngobeni left UCT under a cloud, after it was revealed that he was a fugitive from justice in the United States,[49] he was promptly hired as a special adviser to Minister Lindiwe Sisulu in the Department of Defence and Military Veterans.[50] When the Minister was challenged for hiring Mr Ngobeni, she defended him,[51] a defence eventually rejected by the Public Protector.[52] Some years later, Lindiwe Sisulu, then Minister of Human Settlements, Water and Sanitation, hired Chumani Maxwele,[53] a serial intimidator, assaulter and defamer.[54]

Ntokozo Qwabe, a Fallist who (i) used a sjambok to knock a mobile phone out of a fellow-student's hand, (ii) later expressed the wish that he had "whipped the white apartheid settler colonial entitlement out of the bastard", and (iii) was one member of the dining party that provided a nasty note rather than a tip to a "white" waitress,[55] subsequently became a clerk in South Africa's Constitutional Court. It is hard to imagine that somebody expressing racial animus in the opposite direction would have been appointed to such a position. As one of my former students observed, it "seems that the Fallists are only capable of falling upwards".

The problem of deficient counterweight is to be found not only at the level of the state. A similar problem has come to exist in the media. Consider, for example, what happened to the Argus Group, the largest group of newspapers at the time of South Africa's democratic transition. It was purchased by the Dublin-based Independent News and Media group, after that group had been "handpicked by ANC President Nelson Mandela" to do so.[56] One consequence of this is that it shifted from its historic liberal orientation to become more pro-ANC.[57]

In 2013, the Irish group sold its South African holdings, the (so-called) Independent Media SA ("INMSA", "Independent Group" or "Independent Newspapers"). Sekunjalo Investments, headed by Dr Iqbal Survé, purchased a controlling share of this media group, with much of the funding coming from the Public Investment Corporation, a government agency.[58] At that time Dr Survé was the Chair of UCT's Graduate School of Business's advisory board. However, he was asked to step down from the latter position after repeated scandals surrounding his business.[59] These included the firing of *Cape Times* editor, Alide Dasnois, immediately after she gave front-page coverage, in December 2013, to the findings of the Public Protector that a tender given to Sekunjalo Marine, part of the Sekunjalo Group, "amounted to maladministration".[60] Dr Survé claimed that her dismissal had nothing to do with this editorial decision, but that claim, especially given the timing of the dismissal, is not credible.[61]

Dr Survé seems to have been aggrieved by the request to resign as chair of the advisory board of UCT's Graduate School of Business. He did not resign at the meeting in November 2014 at which he was expected to do so. Before Vice Chancellor Price could confront him about this, Dr Survé attended his daughter's graduation in December 2014. The speaker at that graduation ceremony was none other than Alide Dasnois. This was entirely coincidental,[62] as Dr Price wrote that night to tell Dr Survé,[63] but the latter evidently perceived it as a calculated attempt to humiliate him and his family.[64] He then did resign from his position as chair of the advisory board, citing the University's "lack of transformation" as his reason.[65] He continued that theme in comments he made at a meeting of the UCT Association of Black Alumni. He claimed (to applause) that UCT is a "racist institution" and that the leadership needed to change.[66]

It is well documented that the Independent Newspapers, and especially the *Cape Times* in Cape Town became deeply antagonistic towards UCT from early 2015.[67] The Fallist era was ushered in on 9 March that year, when Chumani Maxwele poured excrement on the statue of Cecil John Rhodes. Mr Maxwele had invited the *Cape Times* and eTV to be present.

The *Cape Times* flouted the press code in various ways, reporting in a flagrantly biased and unfair way. It presented Dr Price and the University as "villains" who were "anti-transformation, anti-student activism and anti-change", and the Fallists as "an intersection between victims of the university's lack of transformation and heroes of the revolution".[68] Much more space was given to the Fallist narrative[69] and crucial information provided by UCT was routinely ignored. There was "little indication that the reporters fact-checked or engaged with multiple sources if claims were made" by the Fallists.[70]

Lest it be thought that this was all a coincidence, Ramabina Mahapa, one of the Fallist leaders and the 2015 SRC President has spoken of a close, symbiotic relationship between the Fallists on the one hand, and Iqbal Survé and the *Cape Times*, on the other:

> We noticed there was some kind of a scuffle between Iqbal and the University and from then on... [there] ... was the negative representation [of the university] in the Cape Times... that was... looked at as an opportunity for us. Whenever something happened we got some sort of coverage.
>
> There was certainly communication between the movement and Carlo Peterson... we would allow to some extent unrestricted access of the Cape Times into what the movement was doing and we would inform them regularly as to what was happening with #RMF.
>
> It would work toward both party's parties' (sic) benefits, we wanted... to ensure that the movement issues were circulated within the media and they wanted

to know what happened at UCT so that they could report on it.

Yes, I would say that there was an element of wanting stories that would humiliate the University, again one of the movements (sic) tactics was to create as much negative publicity for the university so that they would act... it certainly might have been the case that Iqbal was issuing directives to people in the Cape Times.[71]

While Mr Mahapa was not personally present, he confirmed that at the Cape Town Jazz Festival 2015, Dr Survé (a sponsor of the event) had invited Rhodes Must Fall members to his private suite, where they had a meeting.[72]

Both Dr Price and former Cape Times opinions page editor, Tony Weaver, have "confirmed unequivocally" that they know lawyers who had been approached by Dr Survé with an offer to cover all their costs if they represented Chumani Maxwele. None of the lawyers who were the source of this information accepted the offer, but it is not unreasonable to extrapolate that eventually some lawyer did accept the offer.[73] Mr Maxwele certainly did not suffer a shortage of legal representation.

The bias of the Independent Newspapers was manifest not only in its coverage of Fallism. I had personal experience of such bias and its damaging effects. For example, the *Cape Times* included an article[74] about Busi Mkhumbuzi's allegations of racism against me.[75] It appeared in a section themed "StopRacism.iol – Racism stops with me". Almost the entire article consisted of her unsubstantiated claims. Although I was approached for comment, my response was covered in only the final two sentences of the article and was uncharitably presented. For example, I had told the journalist that I could not discuss the matter in detail because the student was facing disciplinary charges and the matter was *sub judice*. His article omitted reference to my explanation *why* I could not discuss all the details. He said only that "Benatar said the facts were not as Mkhumbuzi alleged and cannot be discussed".[76] Nor was this my first experience with the bias of the Independent Newspapers. The previous year I had published a piece in *Politicsweb*[77] detailing another example of inexcusable bias. This is all consistent with the precipitous decline of the Independent Newspapers, which has been amply documented.[78]

There are media in South Africa that are critical of the governing ANC and that are not as obviously fawning to Fallists as the Independent Newspapers. However, with rare exceptions that also have a more limited readership, there is a clear favouring by South Africa's media of the BAC's narrative over alternatives that, to put it bluntly, are more informed by the facts. The *Mail&Guardian*, for example, has repeatedly given space to the BAC's views, but when the Philosophy Department at UCT submitted a statement correcting the BAC's misinformation, that statement was not published.[79]

It is not only the state and the fourth estate that fail to provide a counterweight to the climate at UCT. The problem pervades society. This very book is an example. None of the major presses in South Africa would publish it. In some cases, the explanations may be innocuous, but it is curious that while publishers saw no interest in a book such as this, they are themselves interested in or see a market for Fallist drivel.[80]

South Africa's philosophical "community" is, sadly, another illustration of the lack of counterweight in the broader South African society. For example, when Busi Mkhumbuzi was engaged in her campaign of defamation against me,[81] many philosophers exercised none of the critical thinking skills that are required for their profession. There were many who simply assumed that the claims being made about me were true. This led two of my colleagues, Dr Elisa Galgut and Dr Greg Fried, to issue a statement in support of me. They distributed it via the South African philosophical electronic mailing list (ZAPhil).

Four *years* later, when I was finally at liberty to speak about Ms Mkhumbuzi without the *sub judice* constraints, Dr Galgut distributed a brief statement of my own via the same electronic mailing list.[82] In it, I pointed to an article[83] and a timeline[84] of events (both of which clearly demonstrated Ms Mkhumbuzi's fabrications and why what she had said about me was defamatory). In my six-sentence statement, I asked those who had believed Ms Mkhumbuzi to familiarize themselves with the facts.

That was too much for some of those calling themselves philosophers. This is how Dr John Lamola responded on the electronic mailing list, four days later:

> This latest episode of the Benatar versus Mkhumbuzi saga as now resuscitated by Professor Benatar and his supporters on ZAPhil and *Daily Nous* is laden with multiple folds, and it will not be buried as abruptly as its protagonists wish. This matter cannot just dissipate into such an unconscious collective orgy of white power and a parade of a disregard of the sensibilities pertaining to the intersectionality of antiblack racism, gender and class in a South African and Euro-American academy, as presented in the propaganda of *Politics Web* and in the latest commentaries in *Daily Nous*. Nor will it be buried by the silence it is being greeted with by the ZAPhil community. In the least, it will remain as a case study on the import of the power dynamics at play in the professional space inhabited by academically successful white male and senior teachers, and young socially vulnerable black women seeking to make a career in Philosophy.[85]

Two of my colleagues, Professor Bernhard Weiss and Dr Elisa Galgut replied to Dr Lamola on the electronic mailing list.

They said that anybody should be free to respond to damaging accusations against them, that I had presented the facts, and that the facts allowed only one reading – namely that I and the Philosophy Department administrators had been the abused parties. They observed that it was a "sad indictment of the current climate that Dr Lamola feels no shame in broadcasting such baseless accusations". They concluded that there was "indeed an orgy of power at work in this episode and surrounding commentary" but that it was not the one that Dr Lamola imagined.[86]

What followed, demonstrated just how correct they were about whose orgy of power it was. Although there were *some* messages of support for me on the electronic mailing list, they were overwhelmed by other messages. Some of these had the character of John Lamola's comment. Another called into question my right to defend myself. Others sat carefully on the fence. Most overwhelming, however, was the silence. The worst elements of South Africa's philosophical community had succeeded in silencing the vast majority of their colleagues who had been shown – not only by this event but also earlier ones – what they could expect if they stuck their necks out and dared challenge the hegemonic narrative.

When Ms Mkhumbuzi's allegations were finally publicly debunked, most of those at UCT who had previously accepted her claims remained silent.[87] When the facts were presented to them, they did not, with one exception, apologise or retract. That one exception[88] was willing to apologise to a handful of individuals within the University to whom she had previously written, but she did not issue an apology on Facebook for a message that she had posted there and had asked to be distributed widely.[89] False narratives are created but not corrected.

Consider a further example. PEN South Africa is, according to its website, a centre of PEN International, a "worldwide, politically non-aligned organizations of writers" that, *inter alia*, is "dedicated to promoting freedom of expression".[90] For all that dedication, PEN South Africa has not condemned the censorship of works of art at UCT. It did call for comments from its members, but it did not make an unequivocal statement itself. This is despite repeated requests that it do so.[91]

It cannot be said that the visual arts fall beyond PEN's scope because its charter explicitly says that in "all circumstances ... works of art, the patrimony of humanity at large, should be left untouched by national or political passion".[92] At one stage, PEN SA suggested that it had not responded because of "serious overstretch within the organization".[93] However, it did find time, soon thereafter, to issue a statement about the reclassification of *Inxeba* ("The Wound") as a result of criticism of that film.[94] Moreover, when it did eventually comment on the removal of artworks at UCT, it said that this was a matter that it "deems too complex and nuanced to distil into an unequivocal statement".[95]

The claim that there is insufficient counterweight to what has been happening at UCT is not the claim that there is *no* criticism. PEN SA, for example, did at least condemn the burning of artworks at UCT,[96] even though it took them over two years to do so. The Library and Information Association of South Africa (LIASA) issued a statement on the censorship of Willie Bester's sculpture of Sarah Baartman[97] but not explicitly, it seems, about other censored art works at UCT. LIASA made its statement three *years* after the sculpture was first covered.[98] Moreover, it is curious that this statement, unlike other statements by LIASA, is not available on its website.[99]

There were critics of capitulation, although their voices were drowned out. When Professor Nattrass was denounced by the BAC, there were *some* important people who came to her defence although – of course! – they were in turn dismissed as "white liberals".[100] The support, welcome though it is, is rarely as helpful as the denunciation is damaging.

The narrative of "black" victims and "white" oppressors in South Africa has resonance not only within South Africa, but also well beyond it. That narrative was entirely appropriate during the apartheid era (even if it often lacked nuance, by failing to recognise those "whites" who were appalled by the widespread and legalised racism). The problem is that many people abroad have failed to recognise that 1994's transition to democracy is now decades in the past. They continue to cling to the narrative. Some are either so ill-informed or in the grip of pre-packaged thoughts that they unreflectively refer to "black" South Africans as "minorities". In excess of 90 percent is not a minority, although there are some groups – "Coloureds" and more especially "Indians" – partially constituent of that majority that, like "whites", are minorities.

This might explain why the play, *The Fall*,[101] written by and performed by Fallists, received such accolades abroad,[102] despite its having been a one-sided justification for and glorification of Fallism. Its only nuance was to capture the fractures within the movement. Beyond that, the Fallist narrative was presented uncritically. For example, the play included a *cri de coeur* about the unbearable whiteness of the paintings that were burned, but no mention that the incinerated paintings included those of a "black" artist. Similarly, the protesters demanded the insourcing of workers, but there was no recognition that they had only been outsourced in the *post-Apartheid* era during the tenure of UCT's first "black" (and first female) Vice-Chancellor. That does not fit the narrative of oppressive "whites".

Nor does the play make more than passing reference to the inexcusable ways in which the protesters behaved. To be fair, its focus was on the initial *Rhodes* Must Fall period. The worst excesses occurred after that, during the *Fees* Must Fall period – but well before the play was written and first performed, and thus the writers and performers must have been fully aware of what happened later. Moreover, at least some of the Fees Must Fall period *is* covered in the play, but is highly sanitized.

Journalist Olivia Goldhill is another example of the international affinity for the narrative of fragile, racist "whites" oblivious to their own purported privilege, creating a hostile environment for long-suffering oppressed "black" students". In an article in *Quartz*,[103] Ms Goldhill focused on two "black" South African postgraduate philosophy students (including one from UCT) who, she reported, were dismayed not to find more African philosophy in their curriculum. The thesis of the article was predicated on clear factual errors (not to mention considerable spin). When the errors were pointed out, they were corrected but without revising the conclusion drawn from them.[104] Again, the narrative came first, and the "evidence" was mustered, or manufactured, to buttress the narrative.

An even more significant example of international journalistic disposition towards the motif of "black" victims and "white oppressors" is to be found in Linda Nordling's news report in that pre-eminent scientific journal, *Nature*,[105] about the findings of the Institutional Reconciliation and Transformation Commission. Her report uncritically presented the findings of that deeply flawed commission.[106] *Nature* received a few letters in response to Ms Nordling's report. Two of them were published. The author of one of them told me that his letter had been "shortened to the point of losing its substance". The other letter was also significantly truncated. The edits all seemed to be in service of *Nature*'s image, which might explain why it did not publish my even more forthright letter at all:

> It is a pity that *Nature* does not apply to its news items, the kind of rigour it requires of the science it publishes. Linda Nordling (*Nature* **568**, 151-152; 2019) uncritically parrots the "findings" of a commission that

the University of Cape Town is rife with (anti-black) racism.

To her credit, she does quote one professor who questioned the size of the university sample that testified before the commission. However, she makes no mention of the self-selection of that small sample. The relevant commission, from its inception, has been regarded by many at the University of Cape Town as a farce, orchestrated in order to justify the criminal behaviour (including intimidation, theft, arson and assault) of a small group of protesters who shut down the University for extended periods from 2015 to 2017. That is one reason why those with different views never testified before the commission. Another is the culture of intimidation against those questioning the narrative that the commission report has predictably peddled.

Nor does Ms Nordling mention that the "findings" of the commission are merely reports of what it was told by those who testified. The commission did not actually test the testimony against the facts. Neither does Ms Nordling. For example, she quotes, without question, the claim that "Black staff members remain underrepresented in the university's senior decision-making bodies" and that until "the structures change, there won't be significant change". The reality is more complex. According to the University's website, 70% of Council (the governing body) are "black". Most of the senior executive and Deans appear to identify as "black". The racial composition of Senate (the highest academic decision-making body) is not stated, but the structure of Senate was changed many years ago precisely to increase the representation of "blacks" and women.

In other words, a major scientific journal imbibed a familiar narrative and further disseminated it. It then silenced a full-throated correction. Worse still, Ms Nordling, unchastened, subsequently repeated the same narrative in another piece in *Nature*.[107]

WHERE ARE THEY NOW?

Responsibility for the toxic climate that now prevails at UCT is shared not only by student protestors and the likes of the BAC, who have fomented much of the poison, and by UCT's leadership that has repeatedly kowtowed to them, but also by a larger group of people. The latter are transformation's "useful idiots".[108] Many of them have not put their money where their woke mouths are. They might talk the transformation talk but they are not walking the transformation walk.

Consider, for example, the student who wrote that *Sax Appeal*, the student humour magazine sold annually in aid of UCT's student-run charity (SHAWCO[109]) that assists underprivileged communities in the Cape metropolitan area, "must be stripped of all undue supremacist influence and chronic liberal saviour elitism".[110] What *Sax Appeal* has certainly been stripped of since 2015 is *humour*. In 2015 and the following few years it was thoroughly unfunny.

The same student criticized those who engaged in what might have been the sole (and peaceful) counter protest by those objecting to the Fallists' shutting down of the campus with all the associated criminality. She wrote:

> To those who sat on Jammie stairs today, I implore you to think about the incredible irony of your 'struggle'. These past two weeks have only been a taste of what poor students of colour experience daily and indefinitely at UCT. Before trying to drag your 'brown friends' to a silent protest, consider the way you and the

system have been silencing the cries of black pain for years.[III]

However, "poor students of colour", until the protests began, had not been experiencing what the counter-protestors were opposing: threats for attempting to enter campus, the cancellation of their classes, arson and assault, for example. When they did start experiencing these things, it was with almost everybody else at UCT – of all races and economic backgrounds. The irony is that poorer students often had more to lose from cancelled classes and delayed exams.

The same student who chastened the counter-protestors, also came to the support of Busi Mkhumbuzi, when she was defaming me. Commenting on Facebook beneath one of Ms Mkhumbuzi's defamatory rants, she wrote "Here to support in any way that I can".[112]

Where is this former student now? Working at a "firm of entrepreneurs" in London, of all places. Rather than remaining in South Africa – the former colony purportedly still in need of decolonization – she has decamped to the heart of the colonialist metropole. She is not having to live with the consequences of what she helped create here. She has not tied her fate to South Africa, earning her living in the ever-devaluing currency of the rand and facing the country's violent crime and worrying future. It is pounds sterling and the relative security of the United *Kingdom* for her.

Indeed, London (and England more generally) is a popular destination for those who, during their sojourn at UCT, were polluting the environment here. Among those is a former UCT student who came to study at UCT from elsewhere in Africa. I shall call this student Neil. One of Neil's lecturers was seeking nominations or volunteers for a representative on the department's Student Council. When a "white" student volunteered, Neil "suggested" that the representative should be "black". Although Neil was not volunteering in her place, the immediate response of the person who had volunteered was to agree with Neil and to withdraw her candidacy. Neil was also involved in defacing a photographic exhibition on campus, and publicly praised the BAC. Neil is now a trainee solicitor at one of the most prestigious British law firms.

It is also curious how many of those calling for the purported decolonization of UCT, go on to postgraduate study in places like Oxford (sometimes on *Rhodes* Scholarships), Cambridge, and Kings College London. One wonders why they are not seeking their doctoral and other postgraduate degrees from universities in countries like Uganda, Nigeria, and Kenya. The curricula and certainly the academic staffing profile are considerably more "decolonized" in these places than they are in the UK. Why will they not hitch their academic futures and their careers to the ideals they were seeking to spread to UCT?

Even while at UCT, their curricular choices are often at odds with their calls for decolonization and Africanization. One obvious way to decolonize and Africanize one's own curriculum at UCT is to study an African language, which a fraction of one percent of students at UCT do.[113] There is an abundance of talk, plenty of protest, and copious bullying of the "ideologically impure", but very little personal commitment.

THE PRESENT AND THE FUTURE

UCT's future is bound up with that of South Africa. If South Africa fails, UCT will suffer as a result. There is a limit to what a university can do to guard against national failures such as corruption, state capture, power outages, a weakening currency, economic decline, growing unemployment, and significant emigration of those most able to leave. However, South Africa's future is also bound up with that of its universities, and especially its best universities. Failed (and failing) universities contribute to a country's failure.

I have painted a grim picture of UCT. I conclude with two qualifications and a caution. First, UCT is obviously not all bad. There are still some decent people, although almost all of them have been silenced. UCT still has some outstanding students, teachers, academics, and administrators – from diverse backgrounds. There are parts of the University that function very well. There are also some local cases of improvement since the depths of the Fallist period. For example, the Faculty of Law is a much happier place under the deanship of Professor Danwood Chirwa than it was under his predecessor. This is not to say that the Law Faculty is unaffected by the broader currents at UCT, but having good people in leadership positions can make a significant positive difference. That does mean that there can be another turn for the worse with the next change of leadership. As the broader institution breaks, it becomes more likely that bad appointments will be made.[114]

Second, as bad as UCT currently is, it could be worse. For all the misery, UCT in 2021 is not the University of KwaZulu-Natal (UKZN) during the Vice-Chancellorship of Professor Malegapuru William Makgoba (2004 to 2014). UKZN then had much in common with UCT now. Writing about those *anni horribili* at UKZN, Nithiya Chetty and Christopher Merrett, noted that there was a McCarthyist culture:

> McCarthy worked to a cynical, but effective, plan. He set up a popular cause and a supposed bogeyman; and then set about fabricating evidence to show that one was going to destroy the other. At UKZN the ideal is transformation, a conveniently elastic concept that has yet to be properly defined. The threat is alleged racism practised by 'old cliques' (liberals), 'misfits' (upholders of standards), those with 'conflicting interests' (members of staff associations and unions), 'settler intellectuals' (Indian and white staff), the 'compromised' (those who criticise political and personal agendas); and various

individuals described by a variety of pejorative zoological tags. The intention, and the effect, has been to delegitimise certain opinions through allegations of bias. Both McCarthyism and the condition of UKZN arose out of paranoia and insecurity thriving on imprecision and lack of substance. The inevitable result is conformity and the requirement that intellectual activity should genuflect before institutional power as a test of loyalty. And just as individuals were effectively erased from American public life, so they were removed from the official UKZN community.[115]

UKZN haemorrhaged talent. Many academics, especially many of the best, either jumped or were pushed. In some cases, their academic careers ended prematurely. In other cases, they found new homes elsewhere, including other South African universities that were more hospitable (or less inhospitable) than UKZN. UCT was a beneficiary of a number of such exiles.

There has been one important difference between UCT (since 2015) and UKZN (in the decade following 2004). At UCT, the leadership, at least under Dr Price, did not itself engage in persecution of those expressing dissident views. They capitulated to lawlessness, and failed to protect people from persecution. In a few cases they pursued disciplinary complaints against staff when they should not have, but the University leadership was generally not in the business of persecuting dissidents itself.

The situation was quite different at UKZN, where the Vice-Chancellor required complete fealty to him, his views and his increasingly autocratic methods. Anybody daring to dissent paid a heavy price, including disciplinary proceedings, sometimes resulting in dismissal. All the fears of managerial power were realised. This has not been true at UCT. However, there have recently been some indications that UCT might be heading more in that direction. The University Executive's precipitous response to the BAC's complaint about Professor Nicoli Nattrass is one such instance.[116] It is heartening that the Executive subsequently backed off (even though only after poisoning the well).

Even more disturbing is Council's treatment of UCT Ombud Zetu Makamandela-Mguqulwa. In her annual report Ms Makamandela-Mguqulwa notified Council that she had received numerous complaints of bullying by the Vice-Chancellor, Professor Phakeng. The Vice-Chancellor, who was shown this report, demanded that it be "withdrawn unconditionally so that all offensive parts are removed", that the "revised report must meet my approval before it is submitted to Council" and that the Ombud issue a written apology.[117] As a result, the Ombud's report was withdrawn from the agenda of the March 2020 meeting of Council.[118] The Deputy Chair of Council objected to this decision and resigned in protest.[119]

The report was discussed at Council's April 2020 meeting. Council resolved to "note" the first part of the Ombud's report – the "message from the Ombud". This is the part in which the Ombud had raised the complaints about the Vice-Chancellor. Council resolved that only the second (and anodyne) part of the Ombud's report may be published. The Ombud was dismayed by this and requested that she be permitted to re-write the initial part. She was refused permission to do so.

Council recognised that relations between members of the University Executive were dysfunctional. Council also recognised that there were concerns about the Vice-Chancellor's leadership dating back to the selection process following which she was appointed, and that the interventions made since then did not seem to have worked.[120] However, they were concerned not to make the Vice-Chancellor "a lame duck' or worse still ... to have reduced her to a female black token leader".[121]

In July the Ombud took the decision to publish her full report unilaterally. At the end of June, Council's term of office ended. The new Chair of Council seems to have supported the Vice-Chancellor over the Ombud. Attempts were made to rein in the Ombud. However, Ms Makamandela-Mguqulwa refused to amend her report. She was then served with a notice of suspension and asked to attend a meeting at which her alleged misconduct would be discussed.[122]

In other words, UCT Council's response to the Ombud's calling out bullying by the Vice-Chancellor, was to bully the Ombud. That is exactly the wrong response. If UCT were really opposed to bullying it would take very seriously the Ombud's report that she had received many complaints of bullying by the Vice-Chancellor. Instead to bully the Ombud is not merely to show no commitment to opposing bullying, but to send the reverse message very clearly. If the Ombud is not safe, nobody is.

One test of whether UCT is headed down the path of UKZN is how it reacts to the publication of this book. Will it respond in a high-handed, punitive way or will it not? The current situation is bad enough. If UCT's leadership seeks to emulate Professor Makgoba's reign at UKZN, it will intensify and hasten UCT's own decline. Whether UCT takes this route or merely remains on its current path, great damage will (continue to) be done. Sadly, those responsible will be unlikely to recognize this. If they were capable of recognizing the damage, they would be less likely to bring it about.

I have not written this book because I believe that it will make a difference to UCT's future. It has been some time since I ceased trying to preserve what is good in UCT and change what is not. I have no confidence that what I say or do will effect either. All I have sought to do in his book is to document and analyse what has been happening, and to offer caution about what is likely to result. Nobody at UCT can later claim that they were not warned.

Appendix 1:
INDEPENDENT ONLINE, OUT OF LINE: WHAT READERS OF INDEPENDENT ONLINE (IOL) SHOULD KNOW

(Originally published: 12 August 2015)[1]

According to a basic principle of justice, *"Audi alteram partem"*, one should hear from both sides of a dispute, and not from one side only. It is a crucial ingredient for reaching an informed judgment about which side has the stronger case. The principle is most commonly applied in legal contexts, but it is applicable also to the press. We should have no confidence in a medium that presents only one side of a debate. In disrespecting this principle, Independent Online (IOL) has demonstrated that it might more accurately be known as Partiality Online (POL).

On Monday 29 June 2015 I published a piece in the *Cape Times* under the heading "Those who seek changes must show that they are desirable".[2] In this piece I indicated that terms like "transformation" and "decolonization" had been bandied about as slogans at universities and that it was crucial to gain clarity on exactly what they mean, in order to evaluate whether the changes they stood for were desirable ones.

My article was, I thought, a measured piece. It recognized the ways in which the curriculum has already been "decolonized" and "Africanized" and the ways in which this project might proceed. However, it also criticized some notions of "transformation" and "decolonization", and attempted to allay some of the concerns of those who find universities "foreign".

Three days later, a response by Xolela Mangcu appeared in the *Cape Times* under the inflammatory heading "Racially offensive diatribe has no place" and a subtitle which read "Benatar's ideas 'unacceptable'". (Newspapers almost always impose their own titles on opinion pieces and letters and thus I presume that the title was the newspaper's rather than the author's.) To be fair to the *Cape Times*, the title was in keeping with the content of Professor Mangcu's intemperate, *ad hominem* response.

However, IOL proceeded to post Professor Mangcu's article online without making my original piece available to the much larger online readership. The many online readers who had not seen the print paper were thus unable readily to locate and read my contribution and see for themselves that it was not the "racially offensive diatribe" it was (libelously) alleged to be.

I responded to Xolela Mangcu in the following day's print issue of the *Cape Times* ("Not enough space to address all Mangcu's mistakes, but here's a summary", Friday 3 July 2015),[3] but that reply too was kept from the online readership.

By this time, I was receiving requests from a number of

acquaintances for my original article, which they were unable to find online. They too were struck by the unfairness and thus I wrote to IOL (on 3 July) to complain about the selectivity of the online opinion content, and requesting that they post my original piece as well as my reply to Xolela Mangcu.

I received no response and my request was not obliged. Yet, when Associate Professor Mangcu shot back with another volley of invective ("Professor dangerously blind to his own racial double standards", *Cape Times*, Monday 6 July 2015), that was published not only in the print edition but also online.

At this point (6 July 2015), I wrote to the Press Ombudsman. I complained about the bias and requested various remedial actions, including the publication online of all my contributions to this "debate" as well as a public apology from those responsible for this display of partiality. I received a swift response from the office of the Press Ombudsman, indicating that the matter had been referred to the legal department of Independent Newspapers for their comment. (The Ombudsman, at least, was interested in *Audi alteram partem*!)

Despite this, my rejoinder to Professor Mangcu the next day ("Personal attacks not the answer, stick to the facts", *Cape Times*, 7 July 2015) was not posted to IOL. Nor were any of my earlier pieces.

I wrote to the Press Ombudsman again on 13 July and 15 July indicating that five further contributions to this "debate" had been published online, but none of these were pieces by me. Two – including a letter – were by Xolela Mangcu. One was an "op-ed" open letter to me by Zubeida Jaffer ("Mangcu has a point, Professor Benatar", *Cape Times*, 9 July 2015). [Bizarrely, when this piece was placed on IOL the author was listed as Mansoor (rather than Zubeida) Jaffer.] It came as no surprise that my reply to Ms. Jaffer was not posted on IOL.

Finally, on 17 July, IOL posted my original piece and my initial reply to Xolela Mangcu online (with links inserted between those two items and his first response to me). This was between two and three weeks after they first appeared in the print edition, and one can reasonably suppose that most of those who had previously searched for these pieces would not now do so again. Thus, while those two pieces are now available to the wider online readership, they were not available at the most crucial time. No explanation was provided for the late posting. Moreover, none of my other responses have been made available online.

The same is true of those letters that defended me against personal attacks. Even in the print version of one of these letters a sinister edit was made. After Xolela Mangcu accused me of racism, my colleague, Dr. Elisa Galgut, wrote a letter in my defence. The editors saw fit to edit out her claim that "Professor Benatar opposes unfair discrimination of all kinds" – the only deletion they made to her letter. In other words, after allowing article upon article to make scurrilous accusations against me (sometimes highlighted in the articles' headings), they deleted the few words to the contrary from somebody who actually knows me.

The last I heard from the Press Ombudsman's office (on 24 July 2015), they were trying to establish whether Independent Newspapers would publish an apology. I have heard nothing further and am not aware of any public apology having been made.

One final curious fact: When I submitted my original piece to the *Cape Times* it was around 1850 words long. That is longer than most opinion articles in that newspaper, but I provided a motivation for accepting it at that length. The editor replied, saying that they would consider it if I could reduce it to 1200 words, which I did. Yet, in the midst of the subsequent debate, the *Cape Times* published a 1866-word piece by Xolela Mangcu ("Always space for firm courage", 13 July 2015), in which he ranted about an email – a document not in the public domain –

that he had received from David Bullard. Professor Mangcu complained that "racists can get away with their words and actions without any prospect of going to jail", and that this "speaks ... to black powerlessness ... and shows who is aligning with whom at UCT".

Many of those calling for "transformation" and "decolonization" have complained about traditional "hegemonies" continuing to operate in South Africa. However, in the case of Independent Newspapers and especially its online division, it is absolutely clear that the views of people complaining about these purported hegemonies have now become hegemonic.

Appendix 2:
WHAT *MAIL&GUARDIAN* READERS NEED TO KNOW

(Originally published: 13 November 2017)[1]

In August 2015, I provided explicit evidence of Independent Online's egregious bias. While this bias was widely known, it was (and remains) important to document clear instances of it. Without this sort of evidence all one has, are unsubstantiated impressions.

I noted in that article[2] that according to a basic principle of justice, *"Audi alteram partem"*, one should hear from both sides of a dispute, and not from one side only. Without doing so, one cannot reach an informed judgement about which side is correct (or more correct). Although the principle is most commonly used in legal contexts it also relevant to the press. A medium that presents only side of a debate is not to be trusted.

I now present evidence of bias at the *Mail&Guardian Online*.

This medium has regularly published statements by the University of Cape Town's Black Academic Caucus (BAC).[3] Although it did not publish the BAC's statement of 1 October 2017 which was headed "Parading White Privilege",[4] it did republish a News24 piece with the sensationalist title "UCT test concession for Rocking the Daisies festival is 'parade of white privilege'", that not only quoted the BAC statement but also incorporated that statement's title into the article's heading.[5]

The concession in question, which was granted by one of my colleagues in the Philosophy Department, led to an uninformed and hysterical moral panic and a flurry of reports and references in various media. This eventually resulted in the University leadership taking the unusual step of effectively directing a course convener to withdraw a concession.

Nearly a fifth of the article republished on the *Mail&Guardian* website was devoted to conveying the BAC's view, as expressed in its statement. The report said:

> The UCT Black Academic Caucus (BAC) said it was "humiliating and traumatising" that black students were made to be an "unwilling audience to exhibitions of privilege".
>
> The caucus said in a statement that racialised class disparities were highlighted in the inconsistent approach to handling the different needs of students.
>
> "It's not enough that black students have to silently carry the burden of disadvantage, or think twice before approaching some of their white lecturers when they are in distress; they now even have to watch as racialised privilege is paraded before them."

The article also referred to a student who had "said on Facebook that the concession was a 'joke', as Muslim students had to write exams during Eid". This could create the utterly false impression that the same course convener or even department had granted a concession in the case of a music festival but not in the case of a major religious holiday.

Ten days later, on 13 October 2017, the *Mail&Guardian Online* published another statement by the BAC in which the Rocking the Daisies concession was again mentioned.[6]

Following the widespread and misplaced outrage at the concession that my colleague had granted, the Philosophy Department issued a public statement in response.[7] I forwarded that statement to the editor of the *Mail&Guardian Online*, with the request that they publish it there.

I received no reply and the statement never appeared on the *Mail&Guardian*'s website. (This is in keeping with my earlier personal experience with the *Mail&Guardian*, which has simply ignored submissions from me, and thus it is unlikely that this was a single email that went astray.) Of course, editors are not duty bound to publish everything that is sent to them. However, when a newspaper publishes a sloppy one-sided report and gives substantial coverage to one side of a controversy, it does have something of an obligation to let the other side be heard. At the very least it could explain why it did not do so.

The fact that the *Mail&Guardian* publishes numerous ideologically saturated and factually phony statements from the BAC, but will not publish a single reasoned and substantiated response from the UCT Philosophy Department is another indication of a third-rate fourth estate in South Africa. Such a press does not augur well for the country's fragile democracy.

Appendix 3:

PHILOSOPHY AND SOUTH AFRICA'S "BATTLE AGAINST COLONIALISM"

(Originally published: 8 October 2018)[1]

The narrative is familiar: Fragile racist "whites", oblivious to their own purported privilege, creating a hostile environment for long-suffering oppressed "black" students. If there is some truth in that narrative, there is none in Olivia Goldhill's version of it,[2] or in the situation she purports to describe.

Ms Goldhill focuses on two "black" South African postgraduate philosophy students who, she reports, are dismayed not to find more African philosophy in their curriculum. The situation is said to be especially bad in the Philosophy Department at the University of Cape Town (UCT), where I work.

The article begins inauspiciously with the claim that to "study philosophy in South Africa today is to study a series of pronouncements from white, European men". If one knows anything about academic philosophy, and especially its analytic branch, one knows that it is not the study of anybody's "pronouncements". Instead it is the critical evaluation of arguments. This and other features of the opening paragraph set the tone for her entire piece, which is replete with factual errors, as well as spin.

For example, we are told that Olerato Mogomotsi is the only black postgraduate student in the Philosophy Department at the University of Cape Town (false), that he took the Department's Philosophy of Race course (false), that "the vast majority of students in the class of 40 were ... white" (false), and that "they quickly came to a consensus that race was inconsequential" (also false).

These are not inconsequential mistakes. Once they are corrected, Ms Goldhill's entire thesis collapses. She would have her readers believe that our curriculum is entirely "Eurocentric" and indifferent to the interests of "black" students in matters of race. For example, she quotes Mr Mogomotsi – whether accurately or not, I do not know – as saying that "he doesn't think about race within his field of philosophy; everyone around him ignores the subject, and so he feels he has no choice but to do the same". She quotes him as saying that he is "on autopilot mode" and that his "black experience is increasingly detached from the discipline".

The very existence of the Philosophy of Race course refutes the suggestion that everybody around him ignores the subject. Nor is the existence of this course the only refutation of the suggestion that everybody around him ignores the subject. There are other courses in the Department that also touch on these issues, as well as on African thinkers. Contrary to the impression conveyed in Ms Goldhill's article, some curricular attention *is* paid to what we should think about philosophers who held abhorrent – including racist – views.

Ms Goldhill not only gets the demonstrable facts wrong. She also misrepresents and spins things to fit her narrative. For example, she says that the situation at the University of Cape Town "reflects the broader racism of the city". Cape Town's purported racism is an old canard, which she swallows whole and then regurgitates in order to frame her depiction of the city's university and its Philosophy Department.

Similarly, she says that Professor Thaddeus Metz, an exponent of African philosophy at the University of Johannesburg, "faced some dismissal from colleagues who seemed to devalue African philosophy". Ms Goldhill then immediately refers to an occasion when "he gave a talk at UCT, drawing on ideas in the African tradition".

The clear implication here is that Professor Metz attempted to talk about African philosophy to the UCT Philosophy Department, only to be met with dismissal of the very idea of African Philosophy. In fact, his talk was part of a series, "Philosophy in Africa, Africa in Philosophy", co-convened by the Philosophy Department and the Centre for African Studies at UCT. Professor Metz's arguments met with robust challenges, which is just what one would and should expect. The criticisms did not take the form of rejecting the very idea of African philosophy.

Ms Goldhill also spins her narrative by contrasting her sympathetic portrayals of the students with an uncharitable portrayal of me. She says of Tony Shabangu that he has "none of the pretension or buttoned-up demeanor typical of academics. When he's not smiling, he looks on the verge of a grin, the corners of his mouth tugging upwards in easy humor". Olerato Mogomotisi is said to have "a gentle demeanor" and that his face is "slightly reminiscent of a wise, calm owl".

In her depiction of me, on the other hand, she speaks of my

"steady gaze" and says that "he's convinced by the validity of his arguments" – are the two students not? – and "repeatedly emphasizes ways in which he feels he has been oppressed or slighted".

"Oppressed" and "slighted" are her words, not mine. She seems dismissive of my claim that the environment at the University of Cape Town has become toxic. I shall leave it for readers to peruse my account of this toxicity[3] – an account that makes no mention of my own personal experiences – to decide whether the environment is indeed toxic.

Suffice it to say here that one dean, mentioned anonymously in my account, has subsequently and recently taken his own life. He was accused of being a "coconut" and "sell-out" by protesting students who shut down the University for weeks[4] and who objected to his insufficient fealty to their cause. His family,[5] among others,[6] have attributed his descent into depression and eventually suicide to this sort of treatment.

Ms Goldhill opines that I show "great concern for those who wish to resist aspects of decolonization" but that I show "comparatively little empathy for those who feel oppressed by the existing system". In fact, I show great concern for those who are silenced and much less for those who are either doing the silencing or abetting it. And I have great empathy for students with *real* problems, which is why we have introduced so much support for students, especially disadvantaged ones.

My care for students is one reason why I am resistant to the insatiable appetite for "de-colonization", which I take to be not merely misguided but self-crippling. I have argued elsewhere[7] for such claims and responded[8] to other critics[9] who have misrepresented my views. I shall not rehearse those arguments here.

However, it should be noted that the complaints continually shift. To the extent that African philosophy is not taught, the curriculum is said to be "colonised". If one teaches some African philosophy, one is not teaching enough, and if one teaches it while "white", one risks other charges, including that of cultural appropriation, as Professor Metz has found. Similarly, students say that they want more philosophy of race and African philosophy but then do not avail themselves of the opportunities to engage these areas when they are offered.

This is entirely consistent with experience elsewhere at the University of Cape Town. Consider, for example, the African Languages section in the School of Languages and Literatures. Only about twenty-two students take first language Xhosa in first year. The numbers drop to about eleven in second year and only five in third year. The enrolments are somewhat better for second-language Xhosa, which is taken by about 100 students in first year. The enrolments slip to about 15 in second year and five in third year.

About 100 students take second-language Sotho in first year, but only 18 in the second year. These numbers are a negligible proportion – less than 0.04% – of the approximately 6600 students enrolled in the Humanities Faculty in a given year. For all the student talk about wanting more African content, very few of them are actually drawn to it when it is offered. That, however, does not fit the narrative Ms Goldhill eagerly advances.

ADDENDUM

(Originally published: 10 October 2018)[10]

Before writing my response to Olivia Goldhill's article, I wrote to the editor at *Quartz* to point out that it contained "a number of factual errors as well as features that I believe violate *Quartz*'s professed values".[11] I asked for an opportunity to reply. In response I was asked to advise them of the factual errors, which they would then review. I was told that they "don't typically publish letters to the editor or pieces that function as direct responses to stories", but that if I were to submit an opinion piece it would be reviewed.

I responded as follows:

> I agreed to an interview with Olivia Goldhill in good faith, largely because her earlier essays suggested to me that she would be fair and willing to consider an unpopular view. I told her as much. The piece she has produced has broken that trust. The entire thesis of the piece comes crashing down if the serious factual errors are corrected. However, I now have no confidence that if I were to point out the factual errors, the article's thesis would be revised accordingly. I'm thus reluctant to help you fix the most demonstrable errors while more insidious ones remain. I wish that I could have more confidence. Since you don't allow direct responses, I may have to publish my response elsewhere.

The reply I received did not reassure me, as it only repeated the request to provide the factual errors, and provided no undertaking to revise the narrative if that is what the facts warranted.

Accordingly, I sent my response piece to *Politicsweb*. Subsequent to its publication, *Quartz* corrected some of the clear factual errors, not all of which are explicitly noted in the correction notice appended at the end of Olivia Goldhill's piece. Unsurprisingly, the central narrative of the piece has not been altered. This supports my contention that the narrative preceded the facts and was not rooted in them.

TIMELINE

2015

February

17: Chumani Maxwele enters Hiddingh campus computer laboratory without authorization and intimidates a student employee.

March

9: Rhodes Must Fall protests begin when Chumani Maxwele strews human excrement on Cecil John Rhodes's statue.

April

9: Statue of Cecil John Rhodes is removed.

May

1: Chumani Maxwele harasses staff in the Mathematics Building.

August

18: UCT enters into an agreement with Rhodes Must Fall and grants an amnesty.

20: Chumani Maxwele intimidates Mathematics lecturer again.

September

15: Chumani Maxwele intimidates Mathematics lecturer yet again.

October

Fees Must Fall protests begin.

2016

January

19: Busisiswe Mkhumbuzi begins her campaign of defamation against me.

February

15: Shackville protests begin.

17: UCT seeks and obtains provisional interdict against protesters.

March

9: Sculpture of Sarah Baartman covered up.

16: Four members of the Faculty of Humanities censured.

April

5: Chumani Maxwele assaults a fellow Fallist at the University of the Witwatersrand.

May

4: Chumani Maxwele assaults Steven Ganger, UCT's Head of Investigations.

5: Chumani Maxwele arrested at a protest outside of Parliament.

July

17: UCT Executive announces that it is withdrawing the Academic Freedom Committee's invitation to Flemming Rose to deliver the 2016 TB Davie Memorial Academic Freedom Lecture.

August

New Academic Freedom Committee takes office.

September

1: Bongani Mayosi assumes office at Dean of the Faculty of Health Sciences.

23: A group of undergraduate students occupies the Dean's suite and became known as #OccupyFHS.

October

4: #OccupyFHS ceases occupation of Dean's Suite.

31: Busi Mkhumbuzi Disciplinary Tribunal hearing.

November

6: UCT enters into "November agreement" with nine students.

Dean of Humanities resigns to take a more senior position elsewhere in South Africa.

December

15: Chumani Maxwele is among those who disrupt the annual meeting of Convocation.

2017

February

23: Busi Mkhumbuzi Appeal Tribunal hearing

July

13: Professor David Attwell presented to the Humanities Faculty as the Selection Committee's choice at the new Dean. This proposal does not meet the required 60% approval.

August

13: Appeal Tribunal rules that Busi Mkhumbuzi hearing must be heard *de novo*.

22: Mahmood Mamdani delivers TB David Memorial Lecture.

2018

March

The Final Report by the Institutional Reconciliation and Transformation Commission of the University of Cape Town (IRTC) issued.

June

24-30: Decolonial School, Dinners initially billed as for "People of Colour" only.

July

1: Professor Mamokgethi Phakeng assumes office as UCT's Vice-Chancellor

27: Professor Bongani Mayosi's suicide.

31: "Concerned Academics" and the UCT Black Academic Caucus call for Council to establish an investigation into the circumstances leading to Professor Mayosi's death.

August

Statue of Sarah Baartman removed from the Chancellor Oppenheimer Library.

November

6: Masixole Mlandu tweets the first few pages of his Political Studies research page, which includes the words "One settler, one bullet".

2019

January

31: Professor Phakeng advises me that she will be dropping charges against Busi Mkhumbuzi

May

30: Humanities Faculty Board votes against the proposal that Professor Grace Khunou be appointed as Dean.

June

11: Associate Professor Shose Kessi is proposed as the Selection Committee's new choice to be Dean of Humanities. Dr Lwazi Lushaba disrupts the voting.

August

7: Steven Salaita delivers the TB Davie Memorial Lecture.

September

18: Associate Professor Shose Kessi is, for the second time, proposed as the Selection Committee's new choice to be Dean of Humanities. Faculty Board approves the selection.

27: MBChB III meeting held, at which some students are berated and humiliated for allegedly being insufficiently compassionate.

November

15: Associate Professor Shose Kessi's Deanship is announced following approval from Council.

2020

June

c4: BAC issues a statement condemning a commentary article in the *South African Journal of Science* authored by Professor Nicoli Nattrass, and calls on UCT to condemn it too.

5: UCT Executive issues a statement criticizing Professor Nattrass's article.

16: The report, *Enquiry into the Circumstances Surrounding Professor Bongani's Tenure: Crucible for Senior Black Staff?*, is released.

July

UCT Ombud releases a report in which Vice-Chancellor Mamokgethi Phakeng is accused of bullying behaviour.

2021

February

1: New Employment Equity Policy and associated "Practice Note" take effect.

April

Dr Lwazi Lushaba tells his first year Political Science students that "Hitler committed no crime".

May

13: Employment Equity "Practice Note" suspended "for three months".

27: Revised "Practice Note" issued, but with effect from 20 May 2021.

NOTES

Preface

[1] *101 ways (and more) to end apartheid*, Johannesburg: Five Freedoms Forum, 1989, p. 4.

[2] I recognize the possibility of a liberal nationalism, but that is not what I am speaking about here.

[3] The argument for my alternative practice, can be found here: David Benatar, "Why don't academics address each other politely?" in *Times Higher Education*, 31 January 2019.
https://www.timeshighereducation.com/opinion/why-dont-academics-address-each-other-politely

(A somewhat longer version of this essay was published in *What's Wrong?*, 4 February 2019
https://whatswrongcvsp.com/2019/02/04/toward-more-respectful-academic-reference-practices/)

[4] https://www.politicsweb.co.za/home

Chapter 1

[1] Times Higher Education (2020), Quacquarelli Symonds (2020), US News Best Global Universities (2020), Center for World University Rankings (2019-2020), and Academic Ranking of World Universities (2019). "World Rankings",

https://www.uct.ac.za/main/research/rankings (Accessed 13 May 2020).

[2] In 2020, UCT slipped to second place in Academic Ranking of World Universities, with the University of the Witwatersrand in Johannesburg edging up to first place. "These are the 9 best universities in South Africa for academic performance", *Business Tech*, 16 August 2020, https://businesstech.co.za/news/lifestyle/425416/these-are-the-9-best-universities-in-south-africa-for-academic-performance/ (Accessed 30 September 2020).

[3] Greg Lukianoff and Jonathan Haidt, *The Coddling of the American Mind*, Penguin Books, 2019, p. 6

[4] Ibid.

[5] Ibid, p. 125.

[6] @ Ms Wakkiey, https://twitter.com/Ms_Wakkiey/status/1057741394431934473 .

[7] "UCT apologises for ghoulish exam invigilators on Halloween", Dispatch Live, 5 November 2018, https://www.dispatchlive.co.za/news/2018-11-05-uct-apologises-for-ghoulish-exam-invigilators-on-halloween/# (Accessed 5 November 2018).

[8] Lindsay Anderson, Twitter, 5 November 2018.

[9] Anthea Jeffery, *Unite the Middle*, South African Institute of Race Relations, April 2019.

[10] Identified as the top priority by 26% of all South Africans, by 27% of "Black" (African) South Africans, by 32% of "Coloureds", 19% of "Indians" and 13% of "Whites", Ibid, p. 4.

[11] Identified as a priority by 14% of all South Africans, by 10% of "Black" (African) South Africans, by 19% of "Coloureds", 31% of "Indians" and 34% of "Whites", Ibid.

[12] Identified as a priority by 11% of all South Africans, by 10% of "Black" (African) South Africans, by 9% of "Coloureds", 19% of "Indians" and 18% of "Whites", Ibid.

[13] Identified as a priority by 10% of all South Africans, by 9% of "Black" (African) South Africans, by 18% of "Coloureds", 0% of "Indians" and 11% of "Whites", Ibid.

[14] Anthea Jeffery, *Unite the Middle*, South African Institute of Race Relations, April 2019, p. 4.

[15] Ibid.

[16] Ibid, p. 6.

[17] Ibid, p. 9.

[18] Ibid, pp. 9-10.

[19] Initial enrolment in school has increased since 1994. However, about half of all children drop out before completing the final year of schooling. Only 12% of those who start school complete it with a qualification that renders them eligible to enter university. The proportion of students taking mathematics reduced from 56% in 2008 to 45% in 2011, with an increase in the proportion of students taking the easier mathematics literacy option. (Nicholas Spaull, "South Africa's Education Crisis: The quality of education in South Africa 1994-2011", Report commissioned by the Centre for Development and Enterprise, October 2013.)

[20] Nicholas Spaull, "South Africa's Education Crisis: The quality of education in South Africa 1994-2011", Report commissioned by the Centre for Development and Enterprise, October 2013, p. 3.

[21] Kate Wilkinson, "Are 80% of South African schools dysfunctional?", *Africa Check*, 25 March 2015, https://africacheck.org/reports/are-80-of-south-african-schools-dysfunctional/ (Accessed 22 June 2015).

[22] David Benatar, *Better Never to Have Been: The Harm of Coming into Existence*, Oxford: Oxford University Press, 2006, Chapter 3; David Benatar, *The Human Predicament: Candid Answers to Life's Biggest Questions*, New York: Oxford University Press, 2017, Chapter 4.

[23] In 2019 (the most recent year for which there was data at the time of writing) 19% of students at UCT were "white" South Africans. A further 1% were international "whites". "Black" South Africans (in the broad sense of "black") constituted 42% of students. A further 6% of students were international "blacks". 32% of students were racially unclassified.

[24] In 2019, 77% of all staff at UCT were "black" (in the broad sense). This includes South Africans and non-South Africans, but the vast majority of those were South Africans. 22% of all staff were "white". Those members of staff for whom there was no racial information constituted 1% of all staff.

[25] In 2019, 41% of academic staff at UCT were "black" (in the broad sense of this term). This includes South Africans and non-South Africans. In the same year 56% of academic staff were (South African and non-South African) "whites". There was no racial information on 3% of academic staff.

[26] Even before Chumani Maxwele hurled human excrement on the statue of Cecil John Rhodes and demanded its removal, UCT had already scheduled a series of discussions about "the issue of symbols in a wider context of transformation at the university", the first of which was on "Heritage, Signage and Symbolism". (Sandra Klopper, "UCT: Professor Sandra Klopper Rhodes on statue protest incident at UCT on 9 March 2015" (sic), *Polity*, 12 March 2015, https://www.polity.org.za/article/uct-professor-sandra-klopper-rhodes-on-statue-protest-incident-at-uct-on-9-march-2015-2015-03-12 (Accessed 11 August 2020).

[27] Indeed, the leading exponent of "white fragility", Robin diAngelo, has been invited to speak at UCT events on more than one occasion. Robin diAngelo, *White Fragility: Why it is so Hard for White People to Speak about Racism*, Boston: Beacon Press, 2018.

[28] It is not clear that facts matter at UCT. At a meeting scheduled before the Rhodes Must Fall protests began but which took place after they had begun, one student said that protestors were being intimidated and treated like criminals by the University and that the University's security guards would beat him up. Then Deputy-Vice Chancellor Crain Soudien took him to task and said that this was simply not true. The response of Russell Ally, Executive Director of Alumni and Development, to Professor Soudien was that "whether it is true or not actually is not the issue" ("UCT Talks: Heritage, Signage and Symbolism", 16 March 2015, https://www.youtube.com/watch?v=4NgpJooM5Ho . Student starts speaking at 44:45. Professor Soudien replies at 46:30. Dr Ally makes his comment at 47:12.)

[29] For an example, see Chapter 16.

30 The resultant dissonance is resolved by pretending (whether it be to themselves or others) that those who hold "blacks" to the same standard are actually holding them to *higher* standards. We often hear that argument. We cannot assume that these claims are always false. The claims have to be evaluated and, again, the evidence matters. I consider a number of examples in this book. See, for example, Chapter 12,

31 That joke may very well offend some people with speech impediments (and some of those who take vicarious offence). That too is a hypersensitivity. For more on the ethics of humour see David Benatar, "Taking Humour (Ethics) Seriously, but not too Seriously", *Journal of Practical Ethics*, Vol. 2, No. 1, June 2014, pp. 24-43, http://www.jpe.ox.ac.uk/papers/taking-humour-ethics-seriously-but-not-too-seriously/ .

32 Until June 2021, Smuts Hall was another example. One wonders how many of the other names on this list will still be removed, but most of them will be replaced by other gentiles.

33 Nor need all "white" gentiles identify with those after whom UCT's buildings were once predominately named. There may be many reasons why people might not identify with those with whom they share some characteristics.

34 The Ben Beinart room, Otto Beit, and the (Alfred) Beit half of the Wernher-Beit, for example. Harry Oppenheimer of the Chancellor Oppenheimer Library converted to Christianity.

35 AJ Jordan, Steve Biko Students' Union, Chris Hani, Sarah Baartman Hall, Neville Alexander, Dullah Omar Hall, and Graça Machel. Beyond buildings, there is Cissie Gool Plaza and Madiba Circle. There are also a number of buildings with African names, including Hoerikwaggo, Hlanganani, and Masingene.

36 Mr Maxwele took seven years to complete a three-year degree. His excremental protest took place at the beginning of his fifth year of study.

37 I do not pretend that this triggering occurred in a vacuum. There are no doubt historical explanations for why such a protest had the effect that it did when it did.

38 http://www.uct.ac.za/usr/news/downloads/2016/2016-09-19_Demands.pdf (Accessed 12 May 2020).

39 Shackville TRC, "Current Demands to UCT Management", 30 March 2017. (Document was misdated as 2009, but the filename and the historical context suggest that the year was 2017.)

40 Ilanit Chernik, Olivia Exstrum and Botho Molosankwe, "#FeesMustFall damages bill: R300 302 848.58", *Independent Online*, 13 April 2016, https://www.iol.co.za/news/south-africa/feesmustfall-damages-bill-r300-302-84858-2008936 (Accessed 14 May 2020).

41 Adam Habib, *Rebels and Rage: Reflecting on #FeesMustFall*, Johannesburg: Jonathan Ball Publishers, 2019.

42 "Questionnaire on resumption of lectures", Friday 23 September 2016.

43 See Chapter 19.

44 "Breaking the Academic Boycott", *UCT News*, 20 April 2015, https://www.news.uct.ac.za/article/-2015-04-20-breaking-the-academic-boycott

(Accessed 14 May 2020).

[45] The late David Brooks, a philosopher at UCT, mused at the time that this argument had a dangerous logic. It could justify the banning of fruit and vegetables on the grounds of "no healthy food in an unhealthy society".

[46] The information about the assault is drawn from sworn eyewitness statements and from an interview with one of the eyewitnesses.

[47] "Post-It" notes.

[48] At least in the case of the Academics' Association, this was done without consulting the members of the Association. In other words, the (majority of the) Executive abused their position to issue the statement. Although they technically spoke only for the Executive, they had no regard for whether the rank and file members of the Association would endorse their statement.

[49] "Open Letter to VC for public debate on transformation at UCT", in *Academics Association Newsletter*, March 2005, pp. 3-4.

[50] The Chair of the Academics' Association was even more explicit in his message to members, when he said "We have asked whether perhaps this loss could have been avoided" before talking about "institutional culture". Sam Muradzikwa, "From the Chair", *Academics' Association Newsletter*, March 2005, p. 1.

[51] I lampooned the Open Letter to the VC by imagining another open letter in which the signatories called for an examination of the domestic arrangements that may have resulted in this act of violence. "Another Open Letter", *Not the Monday Paper*, Vol 2, No. 1, May 2006, p. 4.

[52] He started working at UCT on 14 August 2007. It is possible that the appointment *offer* was made in 2006, but Mr Ngobeni's legal problems in the United States were already well advanced by then.

[53] Disciplinary Hearing Finding, *University of Cape Town and Paul Ngobeni*, 25 February 2009, p. 6.

[54] Ibid.

[55] He was originally suspended and later disbarred from legal practice in the state of Connecticut. By reciprocal arrangements he was suspended from practice in Massachusetts and New York. He was later also suspended by the US Department of Justice and by the US Supreme Court.

[56] Douglas Malan, "Lawyer accused of forgery", *The Connecticut Law Tribune*, 23 October 2006.

[57] Paul Ngobeni was regularly referred to at UCT as *Dr* Ngobeni. He has a JD degree, which is the United States equivalent of an LLB. The JD is a "professional doctorate" rather than a "research doctorate". Opinion is divided on whether it is ethical to represent oneself as "Doctor" if one holds a JD (and no higher degree). However, those holding a JD are not typically referred to as Doctor. Given its equivalence to the LLB, I see no reason, especially in the South African context, to refer to him as *Dr* Ngobeni.

[58] There was an attempt by Mr Ngobeni's subsequent employer to deny this, but the Public Protector found that this is what he was. See Thuli Madonsela, "Report on an investigation into the alleged irregular appointment of the special advisor to the

Minister of Defence and Military Veterans", *Politicsweb*, 26 April 2012, https://www.politicsweb.co.za/documents/paul-ngobeni-what-the-public-protector-found (Accessed 26 April 2012).

[59] Paul Ngobeni, "Why Hlophe Should Remain as Judge President", *Cape Times*, 17 October 2007, p. 11.

[60] Not all the professors signing the letter were "white". Those who were, included noted opponents of Apartheid. In a subsequent disciplinary hearing at UCT, Mr Ngobeni, denied claiming that the professors who authored the letter were racist, but they are the only scholars mentioned in his letter and thus it is hard to conclude that they were not in fact among those he was writing about. However, whether or not he was speaking about them, he was imputing the worst (and highly implausible) motives to those calling for the removal or resignation of Judge Hlophe.

[61] UCT Disciplinary Hearing Finding in case against Paul Ngobeni, p. 2.

[62] Ibid, p. 3.

[63] Ibid.

[64] Michelle Jones, "UCT Pays out ex-Deputy Registrar R2.5 million", *Cape Times*, 18 August 2010, p. 1.

[65] Max Price, "Conclusion of disciplinary case" (Message to all staff and others), 21 June 2009.

[66] Some of this resulted from "strong attacks on UCT ... following the separation agreement" which, according to Max Price were "quite contrary to the terms of the agreement". (Max Price, "Paul Ngobeni and related issues", message to all staff, 19 August 2009).

[67] Max Price, "Conclusion of disciplinary case", message to all staff and others, 21 June 2009

[68] Max Price, "Paul Ngobeni and related issues", message to all staff, 19 August 2009.

[69] For reasons I shall not discuss here, I am less averse now to naming perpetrators than I was when I first wrote about UCT.

[70] The same phenomenon can be found in the United States. See, for example, Benjamin Ginsberg, *The Fall of the Faculty: The Rise of the All-Administrative University and Why it Matters*, New York: Oxford University Press, 2011, pp. 99-102.

[71] In some of these chapters I have made *very* minor changes or corrections.

[72] "TB Davie: Champion of Academic Freedom",

https://www.news.uct.ac.za/news/lecturesandspeeches/tbdavie/history/ (Accessed 4 August 2020).

[73] Technically the inquiry was into his brief deanship before he took his own life, but the inquiry was precipitated by his suicide.

Chapter 2

[1] David Benatar, "Those who seek changes must show they are desirable", *Cape Times*, 29 June 2015, p. 11.

[2] David Benatar, "Not enough space to address all Mangcu's mistakes, but here's a summary", *Cape Times*, Friday 3 July 2015, p. 9.

[3] Xolela Mangcu, "Racially offensive diatribe has no place", *Cape Times*, 2 July 2015, p. 9.

Chapter 3

[1] David Benatar, "Must UCT now fall?", *Politicsweb*, 30 June 2015, https://www.politicsweb.co.za/news-and-analysis/must-uct-also-now-fall .

Chapter 4

[1] David Benatar, Elisa Galgut, "Putting our principles where our mouth is", *Monday Monthly*, October 2014, p. 8.

[2] Ibid

[3] Victoria Braithwaite, *Do fish feel pain?*, Oxford: Oxford University Press, 2010.

[4] Coincidentally this took place about a week after Chumani Maxwele poured human excrement on the statue of Cecil John Rhodes.

[5] Minutes, Humanities Faculty Board Meeting, 17 March 2015, p. 3.

[6] By "Faculty events" we meant "any event or meeting that is arranged either by or on behalf of the Humanities Faculty itself, but does not include departments, schools and units within the Faculty, which are encouraged to follow this example but which would not be bound by the resolution for Faculty functions."

[7] Professor Sakhela Buhlungu.

[8] I have already made reference to Xolela Mangcu's tendency to level the charge of racism. I shall say more later in this chapter and this book about Adam Haupt's tendency to do the same.

[9] We would have been entirely within our rights to protest through an organized walkout. However, it was not organized. Each of us who left, left as an individual protest. It is possible that some people's walkout set an example which others then followed, but that too is fully within one's rights – unlike many of the protest activities that were to wrack the campus in the following years and to which the BAC did not object. For more on this, see Chapter 24.

[10] Elisa Galgut, presentation to Humanities Faculty Board, 16 October 2015.

[11] Moreover, it is hard to imagine those same people refusing to support more trendy proposals because of the manner in which they reached the agenda.

[12] Of course, there might be ancillary rights such as a right against having food withheld from one on the basis of such characteristics as one's race or sex.

[13] It is telling that those seeking to defend animal rights are an "interest group", while those who seek to defend human rights are not.

[14] Much more likely to lead to violence is the race-baiting that has come to permeate UCT. Also, if one is opposed to violence (and not only to violence against humans) then, as Dr Galgut noted, one should *support* the proposal.

[15] It can be seen here: https://www.cartoonistgroup.com/cartoon/Joel+Pett%27s+Editorial+Cartoons/2008-08-04/25748 (Accessed 29 October 2020).

[16] There are two other figures in the cartoon, one of whom appears to be a "black" woman and the other a "white" man. They both seem to be additional customers, although one cannot be sure about some of these appearances.

[17] Republished in Chapter 3 in this book.

[18] On social media he had previously described it as "a beef about beef, which was really a beef about race" (Facebook, 10 September 2015 at 18h52).

[19] In the case of one of us, it was well over four decades.

[20] Such a proposal was brought to UCT's Senate in 2019. At first it passed, but Council returned the matter to Senate for further consideration. In the second round, the decision was reversed.

[21] When Adam Haupt had previously stated on social media with regard to our proposal that "meat was the side dish", Antoinette Stafford Cloete responded "Wassitie kosher nie?" (which means "Was it not kosher?") Facebook, 10 September 2015 at 19h57.

[22] My detractors are very likely, given their track record, to respond that I care more about animals than about "black" people. That is sheer nonsense. I think that severe animal pain is worse than the discomfort for *anybody,* irrespective of their race, of walking past a statue of somebody they loathe.

[23] UCT Faculty of Humanities Board Meeting Agenda, 16 March 2016, Item 5.3, pp. 1-2.

[24] Faculty Board Minutes, Thursday 10 September 2015, p. 5.

[25] Ibid.

[26] This text is minimally adapted from our tabled document, and was also used in the verbal response at the meeting by one of our number.

[27] This text is minimally adapted from our tabled document, and was also used in the verbal response at the meeting by one of our number.

[28] According to the minutes of the meeting, the motion was seconded by "Dr Musawenkosi". This is presumably a reference to Dr Musawenkosi Ndlovu. However, my own notes suggest that the motion had been seconded by two other people – Mantoa Rose Smouse and Nomusa Makhubu.

[29] This was not the first time that the minutes were an exercise in revisionist history. Indeed, the Dean's Advisory Committee (DAC) minutes for the meeting on 25 August 2015 falsely recorded that because "there was insufficient time to discuss the matter, the matter was deferred to the next meeting." This was challenged at the next meeting. The Dean would not relent and most members of the DAC either genuinely did not remember or were intimidated into silence. Thus the final minute simply records the disagreement between the Dean and me. One piece of independent evidence for my account is that when the Dean wrote to me on 4 September 2015 to say that he would not put the item on the agenda, I noted (in my reply on the same date) that this was a reversal of what he had said before. He did

not write back to dispute that. Yet, when the minutes were subsequently presented, the Dean's revised narrative was included.) From then we began recording meetings in case of disputes about the minutes.

[30] Except to cast a vote on two important occasions. On those occasions, I voted and then then left immediately afterwards.

[31] Dr Lushaba's behaviour would become even more disrespectful later. See Chapter 18.

[32] This is not implausible. Busi Mkhumbuzi's programme of defamation against me had begun in January 2016 – see Chapter 12 – and was widely disseminated and believed, including by those who were involved in the censure. I would be surprised if that had not played some role in influencing sentiment against me.

Chapter 5

[1] David Benatar, "UCT: A blow to academic freedom", *Politicsweb*, 22 July 2016, https://www.politicsweb.co.za/opinion/uct-a-blow-against-academic-freedom .

[2] Max Price's letter to Academic Freedom Committee, 12 July 2016.

[3] Flemming Rose, "Denmark sacrifices free speech in the name of fighting terror", *Politico*, 12 May 2016, https://www.politico.eu/article/denmark-sacrifices-free-speech-in-the-name-of-fighting-terror-muslim-religion-europe-integration-imams/ (Accessed 19 July 2016).

Chapter 6

[1] Nominations Committee Terms of Reference. § 9.1.5

[2] Pierre de Vos, "UCT's Dis-Invitation: Who has the power to speak and to be heard?" *Constitutionally Speaking*, 25 July 2016, https://constitutionallyspeaking.co.za/ucts-dis-invitation-who-has-the-power-to-speak-and-to-be-heard/ (Accessed 25 July 2016).

[3] Shuaib Manjra, "When freedom of expression becomes a weapon against the underclass and oppressed", *The Daily Maverick*, 27 January 2015, https://www.dailymaverick.co.za/opinionista/2015-01-27-when-freedom-of-expression-becomes-a-weapon-against-the-underclass-and-oppressed/#.V9moFWMZzww (Accessed, 20 August 2016).

[4] Elisa Galgut, "How free is UCT?", *Politicsweb*, 25 July 2016, https://www.politicsweb.co.za/opinion/how-free-is-uct (Accessed 25 July 2016).

[5] Flemming Rose, *The Tyranny of Silence*, Washington DC: Cato Institute, 2014.

Chapter 7

[1] David Benatar, "The University of Capitulation", *Politicsweb*, 21 September 2016, https://www.politicsweb.co.za/opinion/uct-capitulation-isnt-working .

[2] http://www.uct.ac.za/usr/news/downloads/2016/2016-09-19_Demands.pdf (Accessed 12 May 2020).

3 Max Price, "Message to Campus", 19 September 2016, https://www.news.uct.ac.za/article/-2016-09-19-message-to-campus (Accessed 12 May 2020).

4 Rorisang Moseli, SRC President, Letter to UCT students, 17 August 2016, http://www.uct.ac.za/usr/news/downloads/2016/2016-08-17_SRCStatement.PDF (Accessed 12 May 2020).

Chapter 8

1 David Benatar, "If only the 'concerned philosophers' were more concerned", *Politicsweb*, 10 October 2016, https://www.politicsweb.co.za/opinion/a-reply-to-the-concerned-philosophers .

2 UCT: Concerned Philosophers, Statement, 6 October 2016, https://www.facebook.com/uct.concernedphilosophers/posts/1853666571531584 .

3 David Benatar, "The University of Capitulation", *Politicsweb*, 21 September 2016, https://www.politicsweb.co.za/opinion/uct-capitulation-isnt-working (Chapter 7 in this book).

4 Lauren Isaacs, "Protesters block main entrances to UCT", *Eyewitness News*, 19 September 2016, https://ewn.co.za/2016/09/19/North-and-South-entrances-to-UCT-Upper-Campus-blocked-by-protesters (Accessed 24 August 2020).

5 "Stick-wielding protester whips at UCT student", *News24*, 20 September 2016, https://www.news24.com/news24/video/southafrica/news/watch-stick-wielding-protester-whips-at-uct-student-20160920 (Accessed 24 August 2020).

6 Ilze-Marie Le Roux, "Protesting UCT students burn historic paintings, refuse to leave", *Eyewitness News*, 16 February 2016, https://ewn.co.za/2016/02/16/Chaos-erupts-at-UCT (Accessed 24 August 2020).

7 Marelise van der Merwe, "#RhodesMustFall: UCT's Days of Mayhem", 16 February 2016, https://www.dailymaverick.co.za/article/2016-02-16-rhodesmustfall-ucts-day-of-mayhem/#.V-oxJWMZzww (Accessed 24 August 2020).

8 Lizeka Tandwa, "Some students want their own Marikana – Adam Habib", *News24*, 3 October 2016, https://www.news24.com/news24/southafrica/news/some-students-want-their-own-marikana-adam-habib-20161003 (Accessed 24 August 2020).

9 "Wits students stone the Great Hall", *eNCA*, 20 September 2016, https://www.enca.com/south-africa/video-wits-students-stone-the-great-hall (Accessed 24 August 2020).

10 "Wits contract worker dies after exposure to fire extinguisher fumes", *eNCA*, 26 September 2016, https://www.enca.com/south-africa/wits-contract-worker-dies-after-exposure-to-fire-extinguisher-fumes (Accessed 24 August 2020).

11 David Benatar, "The University of Capitulation", *Politicsweb*, 21 September 2016, https://www.politicsweb.co.za/opinion/uct-capitulation-isnt-working (Chapter 7 in this book).

Chapter 9

[1] David Benatar, "Dr Pangloss and the best of all actual African universities", *Politicsweb*, 9 January 2017, http://www.politicsweb.co.za/opinion/dr-pangloss-and-the-best-of-all-actual-african-uni .

[2] Andrew Brown, "Q&A: Max Price on UCT's year of living on the edge", *Daily Maverick*, 14 December 2016, https://www.dailymaverick.co.za/article/2016-12-14-qa-max-price-on-ucts-year-of-living-on-the-edge/ (Accessed 13 November 2020).

[3] Diana Yach, "Max Price's deal with the Fallists upholds UCT's core values", *Politicsweb*, 7 December 2016, https://www.politicsweb.co.za/opinion/max-prices-deal-with-the-fallists-upholds-ucts-cor (Accessed 20 November 2020).

[4] Andrew Brown, "Q&A: Max Price on UCT's year of living on the edge", *Daily Maverick*, 14 December 2016, https://www.dailymaverick.co.za/article/2016-12-14-qa-max-price-on-ucts-year-of-living-on-the-edge/ (Accessed 13 November 2020).

[5] "UCT still ranked first in Africa despite drop on overall QS rankings", Communication and Marketing Department, University of Cape Town, 7 September 2016, https://www.news.uct.ac.za/images/archive/releases/2016/2016-09-07_QSRankings_EM.pdf (Accessed 13 November 2020).

[6] Andrew Brown, "Q&A: Max Price on UCT's year of living on the edge", *Daily Maverick*, 14 December 2016, https://www.dailymaverick.co.za/article/2016-12-14-qa-max-price-on-ucts-year-of-living-on-the-edge/ (Accessed 13 November 2020).

[7] Among the targets were "laboratories that typically house dangerous materials". "Developments regarding attempted shutdown of UCT", Communication and Marketing Department, University of Cape Town, 25 October 2017, https://www.news.uct.ac.za/article/-2017-10-25-developments-regarding-attempted-shutdown-of-uct (Accessed 13 November 2020); "Update on protests and disruption", Communication and Marketing Department, University of Cape Town, 6 November 2017, https://www.news.uct.ac.za/article/-2017-11-06-update-on-protests-and-disruption (Accessed 13 November 2020).

Chapter 10

[1] David Benatar, "Academic Climate Change at UCT: An Inconvenient Truth", *Politicsweb*, 30 March 2017, https://www.politicsweb.co.za/opinion/ucts-climate-turns-toxic .

[2] See Chapter 5.

[3] Ilze-Marie Le Roux, "Protesting UCT Students Burn Historic Paintings, Refuse to Leave", *Eyewitness News*, 16 February 2020, https://ewn.co.za/2016/02/16/Chaos-erupts-at-UCT (Accessed 4 August 2020).

[4] Marelise van der Merwe, "#RhodesMustFall: UCT's Day of Mayhem", *Daily Maverick*, 16 February 2016, https://www.dailymaverick.co.za/article/2016-02-16-rhodesmustfall-ucts-day-of-mayhem/#.V-oxJWMZzww (Accessed 4 August 2020).

[5] Siyabonga Sesant and Lauren Isaacs, "#UCT: Vice-Chancellor's Office Petrol Bombed in Overnight Protests", *Eyewitness News*, 17 February 2016,

https://ewn.co.za/2016/02/17/Protesting-students-arrested-as-UCT-vice-chancellor-condemns-violence (Accessed 17 February 2016).

⁶ Brent Meersman, "Is UCT a safe space for art?", *GroundUp*, 4 April 2016, https://www.groundup.org.za/article/uct-safe-space-art/ (Accessed 4 August 2020).

⁷ Nathan Geffen, "Art and UCT: an opportunity to encourage debate", *GroundUp*, 14 April 2016, https://www.groundup.org.za/article/art-and-uct-opportunity-encourage-debate/ (Accessed 4 August 2020).

⁸ Ashleigh Furlong, "Prominent Artwork Covered up at UCT", *GroundUp*, 8 April 2016, https://www.groundup.org.za/article/prominent-artwork-covered-uct/ (Accessed 9 April 2016).

⁹ Ashraf Hendricks, "Rhodes Must Fall exhibition vandalized in UCT process", *GroundUp*, 10 March 2016, https://www.groundup.org.za/article/rhodes-must-fall-exhibition-vandalised-uct-protest/ (Accessed 10 March 2016).

¹⁰ Elijah Moholola, "Fallist dropped rock on security guard's head – UCT", *Politicsweb*, 20 October 2016, https://www.politicsweb.co.za/news-and-analysis/fallist-dropped-rock-on-security-guards-head--uct (Accessed 1 October 2020); "Security guard attacked at UCT during #FeesMustFall protests", Multimedia Live, Youtube, 19 October 2016, https://www.youtube.com/watch?v=qMmolu8f--s (Accessed 1 October 2020).

¹¹ Gerda Kruger, "Max Price punched by Fallist protesters – UCT", *Politicsweb*, 14 October 2016, https://www.politicsweb.co.za/politics/max-price-punched-by-fallist-protesters--uct (Accessed 4 August 2020).

¹² Daneesha Pillay, "'UCT protests have nothing to do with #FeesMustFall' says student attacked by stick-wielding activist", *Times Live*, 22 September 2016, https://www.timeslive.co.za/news/south-africa/2016-09-22-uct-protests-have-nothing-to-do-with-feesmustfall-says-student-attacked-by-stick-wielding-activist/ (Accessed 22 September 2016).

¹³ Ezra Claymore, "'I should have whipped the bastard', Ntokozo Qwabe says of white UCT student", *The South African*, 22 September 2016, https://www.thesouthafrican.com/news/i-should-have-whipped-the-bastard-ntokozo-qwabe-says-of-white-uct-student/ (Access date unknown.)

¹⁴ See Chapter 7.

¹⁵ Nathan Geffen, "UCT Convocation Descends into Chaos", *GroundUp*, 16 December 2016, https://www.groundup.org.za/article/uct-convocation-descends-chaos/ (Accessed 16 December 2016).

¹⁶ Mohammed Jameel Abdulla, "Should Ngũgĩ wa Thiong'o have asked white people to leave his UCT public lecture", *The Daily Vox*, 4 March 2017, https://www.thedailyvox.co.za/ngugi-wa-thiongo-white-people-uct-jameel-abdulla/ (Accessed 4 March 2017).

¹⁷ Rorisang Moseli, Tweet, 7:33am, 28 February 2017.

¹⁸ Gwen Ngwenya, "Fall in line with the Fallists, or else", *Politicsweb*, 6 January 2017, https://www.politicsweb.co.za/opinion/fall-in-line-with-the-fallists-or-else (Accessed 4 August 2020).

¹⁹ The (Afrikaner) Broederbond, was a secret society of "white" Afrikaans Calvinist

males devoted to the advancement of Afrikaner interests.

[20] UCT Black Academic Caucus Statement, 21 October 2016, https://thoughtleader.co.za/blackacademiccaucus/2016/10/23/uct-black-academic-caucus-statement/ (Accessed 4 August 2020).

[21] Science Must Fall? *YouTube*, 13 October 2016, https://www.youtube.com/watch?v=C9SiRNibD14

[22] Leslie London, "Stampede for securitization of UCT clouds logical argument", *GroundUp*, 8 November 2016, https://www.groundup.org.za/article/stampede-securitisation-uct-clouds-logical-argument/ (Accessed 8 November 2016).

[23] Deneesha Pillay, "Students against varsity shutdowns – in their own words", *TimesLive,* 20 September 2016, https://www.timeslive.co.za/news/south-africa/2016-09-20-students-against-varsity-shutdowns---in-their-own-words/ (Accessed 21 September 2016).

[24] Max Price, "Installation Address by Dr Max Price", University of Cape Town, 19 August 2008.

Chapter 11

[1] This chapter was originally published under a different heading. David Benatar, "Mahmood Mamdani continues the academic freedom farce", *Politicsweb*, 10 October 2017, http://www.politicsweb.co.za/opinion/uct-the-academic-freedom-farce-continues .

[2] "Mamdani delivers rousing TB Davie Memorial Lecture", *YouTube*, 23 August 2017, https://www.youtube.com/watch?v=vKFAYXf05No .

[3] David Benatar email to Mahmood Mamdani, 2 April 2017. Published in *Index on Censorship*, 7 August 2017, https://www.indexoncensorship.org/2017/08/tb-davie-memorial-lecture-david-benatar-writes-mahmood-mamdani/ (Accessed 4 August 2020).

[4] David Benatar, "The Academic Freedom Farce at the University of Cape Town", *Index on Censorship,* 7 August 2017, https://www.indexoncensorship.org/2017/08/academic-freedom-farce-university-cape-town/ .

[5] Flemming Rose, *The Tyranny of Silence*, Washington DC: Cato Institute, 2014.

[6] Flemming Rose, "Denmark sacrifices free speech in the name of fighting terror", *Politico*, 12 May 2016, https://www.politico.eu/article/denmark-sacrifices-free-speech-in-the-name-of-fighting-terror-muslim-religion-europe-integration-imams/ (Accessed 19 July 2016).

Chapter 12

[1] Carlo Petersen, "UCT student in hot water over social media slurs", *Independent Online*, 14 March 2016, http://www.iol.co.za/capetimes/uct-student-in-hot-water-over-social-media-slurs-1997740 (Accessed, 15 March 2016; Carlo Petersen, "Disciplinary action over 'racist, defamatory' remarks between student, lecturer", *Cape Times*, Tuesday 15 March 2016, p. 3; Ezra Claymore, "UCT student in trouble

over racist comments", *The South African*, 16 March 2016, https://www.thesouthafrican.com/news/uct-student-in-trouble-over-racist-comments/ (Accessed 16 March 2016).

[2] Justin Weinberg, "Student faces tribunal for calling Philosophy professor 'racist'", *Daily Nous*, 11 March 2016, http://dailynous.com/2016/03/11/student-faces-tribunal-for-calling-philosophy-professor-racist/ (Accessed 19 March 2016.)

[3] See Chapter 7.

[4] The Humanities Students' Council in 2016 was constituted by the following: Nickita Maesela (Chairperson), Precious Bikitsha, Reon van der Merwe, Priyanka Naidoo, Nonkululeko "Mickey" Moyo, Nandi Ntshiliza, Aphelele Mjana, Tandie Nkosi, Ally Dlamini, and Sakhile Tembe.

[5] Although she wrote to me under the name "Miranda Rasehala", she works under the name "Miranda Mkhumbuzi-Rasehala". See http://soonderinc.co.za/miranda-mkhumbuzi-rasehala/ (Accessed 5 May 2020).

[6] Here is one example from my own experience: During the Covid-19 pandemic, when most on-campus teaching was suspended and teaching had to be done remotely, the Faculty of Humanities issued a directive that, with a few exceptions, no synchronous teaching would be permitted in undergraduate courses. Academics were permitted to place teaching materials online for download later, but were not permitted to interact synchronously with students online. This, we were told, also precluded online consultation meetings between lecturer and individual students. The rationale for this was to prevent those without stable internet connections from being disadvantaged. That rationale may have been well-meaning, but it was stupid. There were better ways to prevent disadvantaged students from being further disadvantaged. Indeed, those most in need of interactive teaching are socio-economically disadvantaged students. In a different time or place, I would have objected to the directive and fought it. I would have proposed a better solution. In a work environment in which one has been ground down and from which one has subsequently disengaged, one does not bother.

Chapter 13

[1] David Benatar and Anton Fagan, "On the genocidal fantasies of Masixole Mlandu", 13 November 2018, https://www.politicsweb.co.za/opinion/on-the-genocidal-fantasies-of-masixole-mlandu .

[2] Sara Gon, "UCT lets the Fallists go Free", *Politicsweb*, 18 July 2018, https://www.politicsweb.co.za/opinion/uct-lets-the-fallists-go-free .

[3] Jenni Evans, "UCT #FeesMustFall activist to do community service, attend counselling", *News24*, 15 August 2018, https://www.news24.com/news24/SouthAfrica/News/uct-feesmustfall-activist-to-do-community-service-attend-counselling-20180815 (Accessed 16 August 2018).

[4] David Benatar, "Academic Climate Change at UCT: An inconvenient truth", *Politicsweb*, 30 March 2017, https://www.politicsweb.co.za/opinion/ucts-climate-turns-toxic , Chapter 10 in this book.

Chapter 14

[1] David Benatar, "A very strange invitation", *Politicsweb*, 5 August 2019, https://www.politicsweb.co.za/opinion/a-very-strange-invitation .

[2] Steven Salaita Tweet, 20 June 2014, https://twitter.com/stevesalaita/status/479805591401922561 .

[3] "The Charter of Allah: The Platform of the Islamic Resistance Movement (Hamas)", https://fas.org/irp/world/para/docs/880818.htm (Accessed 4 August 2020).

[4] Steven Salaita Tweet, 20 July 2014, https://twitter.com/stevesalaita/status/490683700116738048 .

[5] Steven Salaita Tweet, 17 July 2014, https://twitter.com/stevesalaita/status/489636061099089920 .

[6] Steven Salaita Tweet, 20 July 2014, https://twitter.com/stevesalaita/status/490651053101441025 .

[7] "TB Davie: champion of academic freedom", https://www.news.uct.ac.za/news/lecturesandspeeches/tbdavie/history/ (Accessed 4 August 2020).

[8] There were no such calls after this paper, republished here, was originally written.

[9] Steven Salaita, "No, thanks: Stop saying 'support the troops'", *Salon*, 25 August 2013, https://www.salon.com/2013/08/25/no_thanks_i_wont_support_the_troops/ (Access date unknown).

[10] Peter Schmidt, "Virginia Tech Professors Fault University Over Tepid Defense of Colleague", *Chronicle of Higher Education,* 20 November 2013.

[11] Scott Jaschik, "Another Lost Job for Salaita", *Inside HigherEd*, 14 April 2016.

[12] Ibid.

[13] Steven Salaita, "An Honest Living", *Steve Salaita*, 17 February 2019, https://stevesalaita.com/an-honest-living/ (Accessed 2 March 2019).

[14] "South Africa: Art destroyed and censored at University of Cape Town", *Free Muse,* 21 July 2017, https://freemuse.org/news/south-africa-art-destroyed-censored-university-cape-town/ (Accessed 4 August 2020).

[15] Natalie Pertsovsky and GroundUp Staff, "Quarrel over Sarah Baartman sculpture at UCT", *GroundUp*, 2 March 2018, https://www.groundup.org.za/article/quarrel-over-sarah-baartman-sculpture-uct/ (Accessed 4 August 2020).

[16] Pierre de Vos, "Art at UCT: Why claims of censorship may be anti-intellectual", *Daily Maverick*, 11 January 2019, https://www.dailymaverick.co.za/opinionista/2019-01-11-art-at-uct-why-claims-of-censorship-may-be-anti-intellectual/ (Accessed 4 August 2020).

[17] Elisa Galgut and William Daniels, "The Art of Bullshit at UCT", *Politicsweb,* 1 November 2018.

[18] "Withdrawn student cases and other updates", 19 July 2019, https://www.news.uct.ac.za/article/-2019-07-19-withdrawn-student-cases-and-other-updates (Accessed 4 August 2020).

[19] Kenneth Hughes, "Appeasing the UCT Taliban", *Daily Maverick*, 22 April 2016,

https://www.dailymaverick.co.za/article/2016-04-22-letter-to-the-editor-appeasing-the-uct-taliban/#.VyMQWnqH9Qs (Accessed 30 April 2016).

[20] Stephanie Kelly, "Students call for lecturer to be removed" *GroundUp*, 29 April 2016, https://www.groundup.org.za/article/students-call-uct-lecturer-be-removed/ (Accessed 30 April 2016).

[21] David Benatar, "Mahmood Mamdani continues the academic freedom farce", *Politicsweb*, 10 October 2017, http://www.politicsweb.co.za/opinion/uct-the-academic-freedom-farce-continues, Chapter 11 in this book.

[22] "The 2018 TB Davie Memorial Lecture delivered by Professor Pumla Dineo Gqola", https://www.news.uct.ac.za/article/-2018-08-16-2018-tb-davie-memorial-lecture .

[23] Flemming Rose, *The Tyranny of Silence*, Washington DC: Cato Institute, 2014; Flemming Rose, "Denmark sacrifices free speech in the name of fighting terror", *Politico*, 12 May 2016, https://www.politico.eu/article/denmark-sacrifices-free-speech-in-the-name-of-fighting-terror-muslim-religion-europe-integration-imams/ (Accessed 19 July 2016).

[24] "Yale University Students Protest Halloween Costume Email (VIDEO 3)" *YouTube*, 6 November 2015, https://www.youtube.com/watch?v=9IEFD_JVYdo&feature=youtu.be ; "Part I: Yale Students and Nicholas Kristachis" [sic], *YouTube*, 13 November 2015, https://www.youtube.com/watch?v=ELzUfKWTvIo

[25] "EvergreenStateCollege01", *YouTube*, 5 October 2017, https://www.youtube.com/watch?v=2fDm5fXzrQQ&feature=youtu.be .

[26] Conor Friedersdorf, "The Perils of Writing a Provocative Email at Yale", 26 May 2016, https://www.theatlantic.com/politics/archive/2016/05/the-peril-of-writing-a-provocative-email-at-yale/484418/ (Accessed 5 August 2020).

[27] Robert Mackey, "Professor's Angry Tweets on Gaza Cost Him a Job", *New York Times*, 12 September 2014, https://www.nytimes.com/2014/09/13/world/middleeast/professors-angry-tweets-on-gaza-cost-him-a-job.html (Accessed 14 September 2014).

[28] I say "so-called" because so many of those professing support for the Palestinian people, devote zero attention to the serious ways in which Palestinians are oppressed by both the Palestinian Authority and Hamas. (For some details of this oppression see: "Palestine: Authorities Crush Dissent", Human Rights Watch, 23 October 2018, https://www.hrw.org/news/2018/10/23/palestine-authorities-crush-dissent .)

Chapter 15

[1] Harry Frankfurt, "On Bullshit", in *The Importance of What We Care About* ,New York: Cambridge University Press, 1988, p. 121.

[2] G.A. Cohen, "Deeper Into Bullshit", in Sarah Buss and Lee Overton (Eds.), *Contours of Agency: Essays on Themes from Harry Frankfurt,* Cambridge MA: MIT Press, 2002, pp. 332-333.

[3] Adam Haupt, "UCT's Max Price was right to disinvite Flemming Rose, but he

insulted students", *Mail & Guardian*, 25 July 2016 , https://mg.co.za/article/2016-07-25-ucts-max-price-was-right-to-disinvite-flemming-rose-but-he-insulted-students/ (Accessed 7 May 2020).

[4] Adam Haupt, "Liquid racism, possessive investments in whiteness and academic freedom at a post-apartheid university", in Evangelina Kindinger and Mark Schmitt (Eds.), *The Intersections of Whiteness*, Abingdon, Oxon: Routledge, 2019, p. 88.

[5] This was discussed in Chapter 5.

[6] Jacques Rousseau, "Jacques Rousseau on UCT's Disinvitation of Femming Rose", *PEN South Africa*, 17 August 2016, http://pensouthafrica.co.za/jacques-rousseau-on-ucts-disinvitation-of-flemming-rose/ (Accessed 7 May 2020).

[7] This does not stop Adam Haupt from accusing Jacques Rousseau of peddling "Islamophobic stereotypes". Mr Rousseau, in making an unrelated point, had referred to ISIS and Boko Haram. Adam Haupt responded that these are "Islamophobic stereotypes". Of course, it is a reprehensible stereotype to think that all Muslims are in the mould of ISIS and Boko Haram – something Mr Rousseau did not do. However, it is not Islamophobic to criticise groups such as these. Amusingly, Adam Haupt says in manifest ignorance that "Boko Haram" means "books are forbidden", adding "(presumably except for the Quran and related Islamic text themselves), a statement that goes against the Islamic imperative to 'seek knowledge'" (p. 95). Was he reading "Boko Haram" as "Book Haram"? "Boko Haram" is widely translated as "Western education is forbidden" although evidently the literal (Hausa) meaning of "Boko" is "fake", a term used in reference to Western education. While Boko Haram's methods differ significantly from those seeking decolonization of the curriculum in South Africa and elsewhere, there are striking similarities between these insular worldviews. Indeed, among the Fallists there was evidently a group known as Boko Haram!

[8] Simon Weaver, "Liquid Racism and the Danish Prophet Muhammad Cartoons", *Current Sociology*, Vol. 58, No. 5, September 2010, pp. 675-692.

[9] Ibid, p. 678. (p. 88 in Adam Haupt, "Liquid racism, possessive investments in whiteness and academic freedom at a post-apartheid university".)

[10] Adam Haupt, "Liquid racism, possessive investments in whiteness and academic freedom at a post-apartheid university", p. 91.

[11] Ibid.

[12] David Benatar, "UCT: Capitulation Isn't Working." PoliticsWeb, 21 September 2016, http://www.politicsweb.co.za/opinion/uct-capitulation-isnt-working, See Chapter 7 in this book.

[13] Adam Haupt, "Liquid racism, possessive investments in whiteness and academic freedom at a post-apartheid university", p. 92.

[14] I am inserting this note after 6 January 2021, the day on which right-wing, Donald Trump-supporting thugs violently invaded the US Congress building, posing a threat to lawmakers who were ratifying the election of Joseph Biden as President and Kamala Harris as Vice-President. The New York Times repeatedly referred to the invaders as a "mob", as well as variants such as "violent mob" and "mobsters". It would be patently absurd to suggest that the New York Times was drawing on stereotypes of Sicilians and was thus guilty of liquid racism. See, for example, Peter Baker, "A Mob and the Breach of Democracy: The Violent End of the Trump Era",

New York Times, 6 January 2021,
https://www.nytimes.com/2021/01/06/us/politics/trump-congress.html (Accessed 7
January 2021); Nicholas Fandos and Emily Cochrane, "After Pro-Trump Mob
Storms Capitol, Congress Confirms Biden's Win" *New York Times,* 6 January 2021,
Updated 7 January 2021, https://www.nytimes.com/2021/01/06/us/politics/congress-
gop-subvert-election.html (Accessed 7 January 2021).

15 It is not clear, for example, that all those interdicted, were "black". I have to leave
determination of this issue to the self-appointed racial classification experts.

16 University of Cape Town v Davids and Others (2648/2016) [2016] ZAWCHC 56;
[2016] 3 All SA 333 (WCC) (11 May 2016), §62.

17 Hotz and Others v University of Cape Town [2017] ZACC 10, §32.

18 Adam Haupt, "Liquid racism, possessive investments in whiteness and academic
freedom at a post-apartheid university", p. 99.

19 University of Cape Town v Davids and Others (2648/2016) [2016] ZAWCHC 56;
[2016] 3 All SA 333 (WCC) (11 May 2016), §62; Hotz and Others v University of Cape
Town [2017] ZACC 10, §32.

20 Adam Haupt, "Shackville and the Securo-State", *The Con,* 26 February 2016,
http://www.theconmag.co.za/2016/02/26/shackville-the-securo-state/ (Accessed 28
February 2016). Some of what he describes in this piece, if accurate, would be illegal.
However, merely bringing security to campus in order to prevent criminal
behaviour, is not illegal.

21 Adam Haupt, "Liquid racism, possessive investments in whiteness and academic
freedom at a post-apartheid university", p. 94.

22 Adam Haupt, "Liquid racism, possessive investments in whiteness and academic
freedom at a post-apartheid university".

23 Rocco Zizzamia, Simone Schotte, and Murray Leibbrandt, "Snakes and Ladders
and Loaded Dice: Poverty dynamics and inequality in South Africa between 2008-
2017", Cape Town: SALDRU, UCT, 2019. (SALDRU Working Paper Number 235,
Version 1/ NIDS Discussion Paper 2019/2).

24 On 1 July 2020, the number of ministerial appointments to Council, UCT's
governing body, increased from three to five, thus giving the minister's proxies
proportionally more power.

25 Registrar Royston Pillay, responding to me in an email on 17 October 2017 said
"Unlike an entity like a formal union, where if the University is collecting
subscriptions from members, and where this would require the University to have a
list of members, as the BAC is not such an entity, we do not keep a list of its
members." Subsequent communication (5 June 2020) revealed that UCT does not
even know how many members the BAC has.

26 For example, Edward Said (in 1991), Gayatri Chakravorty Spivak (1992), Noam
Chomksy (1997), Kader Asmal (2002), Achille Mbembe (2007), Mahmood Mamdani
(2017), and Steven Salaita (2019),
https://www.news.uct.ac.za/news/lecturesandspeeches/tbdavie/lectures/all/
(Accessed 10 May 2020).

27 For some discussion about this, see this article and the debate with Nathan Geffen
that follows it: David Benatar, "Flemming Rose and academic freedom: a response

to Nathan Geffen", *GroundUp*, 1 August 2016, https://www.groundup.org.za/article/flemming-rose-and-academic-freedom-response-nathan-geffen/ (Accessed 10 May 2020).

[28] See Appendix 1.

[29] See Appendix 2. *Politicsweb* is one of the only media outlets I now have in South Africa.

[30] "Council", http://www.uct.ac.za/main/about/governance/council (Accessed 10 May 2020). That percentage seems to have increased with the Council that began its term on 1 July 2020.

[31] Adam Haupt, "Liquid racism, possessive investments in whiteness and academic freedom at a post-apartheid university", p. 99. It is revealing that, in support of this claim, he cites not Section 16 of the South African constitution, but rather his own work.

[32] Adam Haupt, "Liquid racism, possessive investments in whiteness and academic freedom at a post-apartheid university", p. 98.

[33] Mr Rose would not have been the first non-academic to deliver the TB Davie lecture. Former TB Davie speakers who were not academics, include Albert van der Sandt Centlivres, Harry Oppenheimer, Robert Tredgold, Alpheus Zulu, John Redcliff Maud, Geoff Budlender, Helen Joseph, Albert Nolan, Walter Sisulu, Wole Soyinka, Ferial Haffajee, and Max du Preez.

[34] Adam Haupt, "Liquid racism, possessive investments in whiteness and academic freedom at a post-apartheid university", p. 100.

[35] Ibid, p. 101.

[36] Ibid, p. 88.

[37] David Benatar and Anton Fagan, "On the genocidal fantasies of Masixole Mlandu", *Politicsweb*, 13 November 2018, https://www.politicsweb.co.za/opinion/on-the-genocidal-fantasies-of-masixole-mlandu (Accessed 11 May 2020). See Chapter 13 in this book.

[38] Adam Haupt, "Liquid racism, possessive investments in whiteness and academic freedom at a post-apartheid university", p. 88.

Chapter 16

[1] David Benatar, "Vindictive Victimhood at UCT", *Politicsweb*, 12 November 2019, https://www.politicsweb.co.za/opinion/vindictive-victimhood-at-uct .

[2] Jonathan Rauch, *Kindly Inquisitors*, Chicago: Chicago University Press, 1993.

[3] Tanya Farber and Claire Keeton, "#FeesMustFall to blame, say Mayosi family", *Sunday Times*, 5 August 2018, p. 9.

[4] Nkosikhona Duma, "Zuma: I'm being victimised because I'm Black", *Eyewitness News*, 16 October 2019, https://ewn.co.za/2019/10/16/jacob-zuma-i-m-being-victimised-because-i-m-black (Access date unknown).

[5] David Benatar, "Academic Climate Change at UCT: An Inconvenient Truth", *Politicsweb*, 30 March 2017, https://www.politicsweb.co.za/opinion/ucts-climate-

turns-toxic. Chapter 10 in this book.

[6] Greg Lukianoff and Jonathan Haidt, The Coddling of the American Mind: How good intentions and bad ideas are setting up a generation for failure, New York: Penguin, 2019.

[7] "A response to the "Vindictive victimhood at UCT" article", *Politicsweb*, 15 November 2019, https://www.politicsweb.co.za/opinion/we-reject-david-benatars-crybully-claims--uct-hssc (Accessed 15 November 2019).

[8] David Benatar, "Response to the University of Cape Town's Health Sciences Students Council", *Politicsweb*, 18 November 2019, https://www.politicsweb.co.za/opinion/a-response-to-ucts-hssc .

[9] Marc Hendricks and Zena Woodman, co-Chairs writing on behalf of the Faculty of Health Sciences Transformation and Equity Committee, 20 February 2020.

[10] Ibid.

[11] "Request to find an alternative lecturer for MBChB 3rd and 4th year Ethics teaching", 21 February 2020.

[12] Interim Dean's email to David Benatar, 4 March 2020.

[13] David Benatar email to Interim Dean, 5 March 2020.

[14] It took more than a further week before I heard from the Deputy Dean, and that was only after I notified DVC Lange that I had still not received a reply.

[15] Lis Lange email to David Benatar, 26 April 2021.

[16] David Benatar email to Lis Lange, 26 April 2021.

Chapter 17

[1] See, for example, "Justice, Diversity and Racial Preference: A Critique of Affirmative Action", *South African Law Journal*, Vol. 125, Part 2, 2008, pp. 274-306; "Just Admissions: South African universities and the question of racial preference", *South African Journal of Higher Education*, Vol. 24, No. 2, 2010, pp. 258-267; David Benatar, *The Second Sexism: Discrimination Against Men and Boys*, Malden MA: Wiley-Blackwell, 2012.

[2] For more on this, see David Benatar, *The Second Sexism: Discrimination Against Men and Boys*, Malden MA: Wiley-Blackwell, 2012.

[3] Max Price, "Proposed Admissions Policy Aimed at Diversity and Redress", *Admissions Focus: A Monday Monthly Supplement*, May 2014, p. 1.

[4] UCT Senate Agenda, 30 May 2014, p. 20.

[5] This is not always the case. There are many situations in which somebody is fluent in a language that is not his or her mother tongue.

[6] "Where are the males? Diversity, proportionality and Health Sciences admissions", *South African Medical Journal,* April 2016, Vol. 106, No. 4, pp. 323-4.

[7] I think that there *are* other reasons: David Benatar, *The Second Sexism: Discrimination Against Men and Boys*, Malden MA: Wiley-Blackwell, 2012.

[8] There is no pressure for affirmative action policies favouring males in these areas.

[9] "Identifying somebody one admires" is not necessarily the same as "identifying *with* somebody one admires". I have used the first formulation because I think it is broader, but the point could also be made about identifying with somebody, at least if one rejects the prejudicial view that one cannot identify with people who belong to a different demographic.

[10] For example, "by the mid-[nineteen-]twenties there were still probably less than one hundred Jews among the college and university professors in the liberal arts and sciences faculties in the United States ... As late as April 1930, the institution which had the largest Jewish student body in the world had not a single Jewish professor." That institution was the Washington Square College of New York University, where 93 per cent of the students were Jews. (Lewis S Feuer 'The stages of the social history of Jewish professors in American colleges and universities', *American Jewish History* Vol. 71, 1982, p. 455.)

[11] Robert Guest 'The world's most extreme affirmative action program' *The Wall Street Journal* 23 December 2004 at A10.

[12] I shall focus here on appointments but there are also some instances when admissions may fall foul of South African law. For example, at least one department employs racial *quotas* (as distinguished from racial preferences) in its postgraduate admissions decisions. This may be illegal.

[13] South African law is not clear on this. The Employment Equity Act, 15(4), says that "...nothing in this section requires a designated employer to take any decision concerning an employment policy or practice that would establish an absolute barrier to the prospective or continued employment or advancement of people who are not from designated groups." The Constitutional Court judgement in *Barnard* seems to have interpreted this, counter to the plain sense, as *prohibiting* "employment equity" practices that constitute an "absolute barrier" to the appointment or promotion of people from non-designated groups. This is also echoed in The Codes of Good Practice. The practice I have described may be regarded as an "absolute barrier" to appointment.

[14] Senate minutes, 22 November 2019, Appendix 2.

[15] Ibid.

[16] See, for example, Chapter 18.

[17] "Policy on Employment Equity", 14 January 2021, p. 4.

[18] Ibid.

[19] Ibid.

[20] Ibid, p. 6.

[21] Employment Equity Act, 1988, §20(3)d.

[22] "Policy on Employment Equity", 14 January 2021, p. 2; Employment Equity Act, 1988, §20(4-5).

[23] UCT Senate Additional Agenda, 18 September 2020.

[24] This provides an illustration of the level of conformity that has come to prevail at Senate meetings (and elsewhere at UCT).

[25] The Faculty of Humanities was notified of this on 13 May 2021.

[26] Email from Nomusa Makhubu to the Faculty of Humanities, 13 May 2021.

[27] The Faculty of Humanities was notified of this on 27 May 2021, but the document indicates that it took effect from 20 May 2021 – one week earlier than it was distributed.

[28] This was the creation of a clear absolute barrier against appointment of candidates from non-designated categories. As noted earlier, absolute barriers are prohibited under the Employment Equity Act §15(4).The revised Practice Note, as I shall show below, could also be interpreted as effecting such a barrier, but the new provision leaves more wiggle room.

[29] HR Practice Note entitled "Employment Equity Practice Note: Considerations for Recruitment and Selection Commitees" (sic), 20 May 2021, p. 4.

[30] Ibid.

[31] PASS = Professional, Administrative, and Support Staff.

[32] Ibid. p. 5.

[33] Ibid.

[34] Ibid, p. 6.

[35] Ibid.

[36] Ibid.

[37] Ibid.

[38] Ibid, p. 7.

[39] Some might argue that this claim is incompatible with my criticising these preferences. However, that is not the case. Those of us who openly criticise UCT's extreme preferences pay a heavy price for doing so. Even if it does not silence all of us all of the time, it silences some people some of the time and other people all of the time.

Chapter 18

[1] For more about this, see Chapter 1. Then Vice-Chancellor Dr Stuart Saunders subsequently wrote in his autobiography that disciplinary action taken against the disrupters of Dr O'Brien's visit "involved one of the students being substantially fined and others receiving strong reprimands". (Stuart Saunders, *Vice-Chancellor on a Tightrope: A personal account of climactic years in South Africa*, Cape Town: David Philip Publishers, 2000, p. 182.) Reprimands, no matter how strong, seem like an inadequate disciplinary response to actions that purportedly posed a threat to the safety of a visitor speaking on campus.

[2] Humanities Faculty Board Agenda, 22 November 2016.

[3] http://www.hr.uct.ac.za/hr/recruitment/exec_appointments/deans (Accessed 15 September 2018).

[4] Ibid.

[5] Humanities Faculty Board Minutes, 11 June 2019.

[6] Email from Lwazi Lushaba to Dean of Humanities, 1 November 2018.

[7] See Chapter 10.

[8] I agonized about whether to include that correspondence thread as an appendix in this book. While I think that the public interest in exposing the contortions and evasions defeats – perhaps only narrowly – the strong presumption that collegial correspondence not be published without permission from all relevant parties, I have erred on the side of charity to the Registrar, and desisted from including the correspondence thread.

[9] Email from Lwazi Lushaba to Dean of Humanities, 1 November 2018.

[10] Ibid.

[11] There were also some instances in which the South African Police used tear gas cannisters, albeit not at the request of UCT.

[12] George Hull, post on Vula, 22 November 2018.

[13] I am reminded of the following joke:

Man, praying: "God, just for once, could you please let me win the lottery?"

God, replying: "Could you at least buy a lottery ticket?"

[14] Lwazi Lushaba, Post on Vula, 22 November 2018.

[15] Lwazi Lushaba email to Humanities Transformation Committee and others, 4 December 2018.

[16] Humanities Faculty Board Minutes, 11 June 2019.

[17] Lwazi Lushaba email to all members of Humanities Faculty, 8 June 2019.

[18] BAC Statement (undated, but June 2019).

[19] Lwazi Lushaba email to all members of Humanities Faculty, 8 June 2019.

[20] Lwazi Lushaba email to various people, and copied to all members of the Humanities Faculty, 10 June 2019. It was released to the members of the Humanities Faculty by the listerve manager on 11 June 2019.

[21] Shose Kessi, writing on behalf of the Humanities Transformation Committee to David Wardle, 19 November 2018.

[22] Faculty Board Minutes, 11 June 2019.

[23] Ibid.

[24] Mamokgethi Phakeng email to Humanities Faculty, 14 June 2019.

[25] Mamokgethi Phakeng email to Humanities Faculty, 25 June 2019

[26] http://www.hr.uct.ac.za/hr/recruitment/exec_appointments/deans (Accessed 15 September 2018).

[27] Mamokgethi Phakeng email to Humanities Faculty, 25 June 2019.

[28] Letter reprinted in Faculty Board Agenda, 8 August 2019.

[29] For example, see the introduction to this book for a discussion of the case of the disbarred lawyer UCT hired to be its Deputy Registrar in charge of legal affairs!

[30] Msindisi Fengu, "'UCT Vice-Chancellor allowed use of resources to push dean appointment'", *City Press*, 27 October 2019, p. 6.

[31] Msindisi Fengu, "'I am the most qualified for this position' – Professor hits back at

UCT for prejudice", *City Press*, 5 November 2019, https://city-press.news24.com/News/i-am-most-qualified-for-this-position-professor-hits-back-at-uct-for-prejudice-20191105 (Accessed, 20 April 2020).

32 Tami Jackson, "Phakeng's UCT panders to radicals – Progress SA", *Politicsweb*, 18 February 2019, https://www.politicsweb.co.za/politics/phakengs-uct-panders-to-radicals--progress-sa (Accessed 3 June 2020).

33 One of these deans is an interim dean.

34 Lest it be thought that I hanker for the position of Dean, let me dismiss that thought. I have zero interest in such a position.

35 http://www.hr.uct.ac.za/hr/recruitment/exec_appointments/deans (Accessed 15 September 2018).

Chapter 19

1 It was also later noted that the "November Agreement was signed by 13 people out of the 30,000 at UCT". It was asked, perhaps rhetorically, whether they represented anyone other than themselves? (Jeremy Seekings and Nicola Illing, "Report back to Senate on 3rd IRTC Steering Committee Meeting, 18 April 2017", p. 2.)

2 IRTC - Background document (2016)

3 The full list of Steering Committee members was attached to "A Call for Nominations for Commissioners for the Institutional Reconciliation and Transformation Committee", 6 June 2017.

4 IRTC - Background document (2016)

5 In one of his reports, one of the Senate representatives noted that the "Executive took a back seat through most of the process, but in the end, and with the support of Ms Budlender (from Council), ... seems to have decided that the IRTC should be established along the lines demanded by the uncompromising ShackvilleTRC/BAC clique" and that the Executive's "view seems to be that the IRTC must be established at any cost". (Jeremy Seekings, "Another shortish note on the proposals for the Institutional Reconciliation and Transformation Commission (IRTC)", 9 June 2017.)

6 I draw on those reports in the account that follows.

7 Nicola Illing, "Report back on IRTC Steering Committee meeting, 24 August 2017.

8 Jeremy Seekings, "Report to Senate on the Meeting of the Steering Committee of the IRTC Held on Thursday 24th August", 3 September 2017.

9 Jeremy Seekings and Nicola Illing, "Report back to Senate on 3rd IRTC Steering Committee Meeting, 18 April 2017", p. 1.

10 Jeremy Seekings and Nicola Illing, "Report back to Senate on the Facilitated Workshop for the IRTC Steering Committee held on Saturday 20 May 2017, and the so-called 'Agreements' that have since been distributed to Steering Committee members", 29 July 2017.

11 Ibid.

12 Ibid, p. 4.

[13] Ibid

[14] Jeremy Seekings and Nicola Illing, "Report back to Senate on 3rd IRTC Steering Committee Meeting, 18 April 2017", p. 2.

[15] Ibid.

[16] Ibid, p. 1.

[17] "Agreement with SRC Candidates / ShackvilleTRC and other student formations", 7 November 2016, p. 2.

[18] More accurately, a meeting of the Steering Committee's subcommittee.

[19] Jeremy Seekings and Nicola Illing, "Report back to Senate on 3rd IRTC Steering Committee Meeting, 18 April 2017", p. 1.

[20] Report back to Senate on the Facilitated Workshop for the IRTC Steering Committee held on Saturday 20 May 2017, and the so-called 'Agreements' that have since been distributed to Steering Committee members", 29 July 2017.

[21] Nicola Illing, "31st October, 2017 IRTC Steering Committee Report back". This student evidently added that she had been "appealing for calm", but this should be viewed with a good dose of scepticism, especially in the context of breaking down the locked door.

[22] The commissioners were Mr Mosibudi Mangena, Judge Zak Yacoob, Dr Yvette Abrahams, Dr Malose Langa, and Ms Yasmin Sooka. (On 23 March 2017, one Yvette Abrahams responded to a tweet by noted Fallist Brian Kamanzi about Emeritus Professor Tim Crowe. Her comment was "Looks like a case of a 'sore loser' ☺ Funny how when democracy works against white supremacists they don't like it anymore". Was this the same Yvette Abrahams?)

[23] Jeremy Seekings, "Comments on IRTC Report", March 2019, p. 1.

[24] Ibid.

[25] Ibid.

[26] Initially, amnesty was granted to seven students who were named in this document: "Decision(s) of the Institutional Reconciliation and Transformation Commission of the University of Cape Town (IRTC)", 28 March 2018. The final report indicated that an eighth student had been granted amnesty. (*The Final Report by the Institutional Reconciliation and Transformation Commission of the University of Cape Town*, March 2018, p. 20). In the final report, all the students to whom amnesty was granted were left unnamed.

[27] The Final Report by the Institutional Reconciliation and Transformation Commission of the University of Cape Town, March 2018, p. 22.

[28] "Agreement with SRC Candidates / ShackvilleTRC and other student formations", 7 November 2016, p. 2.

[29] The Final Report by the Institutional Reconciliation and Transformation Commission of the University of Cape Town, March 2018, p. 73.

[30] Ibid, p. 33.

[31] See, for example: "Cape Town's universities shut down", *GroundUp*, 5 October 2016, https://www.groundup.org.za/article/uct-student-leader-vows-continue-

protests/ (Accessed 24 June 2020). This is exactly the same report in which Dr Lushaba's complaint about being called "black academics" is to be found.

[32] I am not suggesting that Dr Lushaba is a member of the BAC. He had a public spat with the BAC. See Chapter 18.

[33] Jeremy Seekings, "Notes on the IRTC Steering Committee meeting on 22 March 2019".

[34] "Summary of the PASS Forum feedback to the IRTC", Undated, but May 2019.

[35] Robert Morrell, "Submission: Response to IRTC Report, 21 March 2019".

[36] Although the panel said that it was *not* investigating why Professor Mayosi had taken his own life (*Enquiry into the Circumstances Surrounding Professor Bongani's Tenure: Crucible for Senior Black Staff?*, 16 June 2020, p. 16), it was in fact investigating the circumstances leading up to that suicide. The panel had been convened in response to the suicide.

[37] Enquiry into the Circumstances Surrounding Professor Bongani's Tenure: Crucible for Senior Black Staff?, 16 June 2020, p. 26.

[38] Ibid, pp. 34-35.

[39] David Benatar, "Academic Climate Change at UCT: An Inconvenient Truth", *Politicsweb*, 30 March 2017. Republished as Chapter 10 in this book.

[40] Enquiry into the Circumstances Surrounding Professor Bongani's Tenure: Crucible for Senior Black Staff?, 16 June 2020, p. 6.

[41] Ibid, p. 55.

[42] Ibid.

[43] "Fallists vandalised Bongani's soul – Ncumisa Mayosi", *Politicsweb*, 5 August 2018, https://www.politicsweb.co.za/news-and-analysis/the-fallists-completely-vandalised-bonganis-soul-- (Accessed 7 August 2018). For video footage see: https://www.youtube.com/watch?v=6Vz_xWoYpcM&feature=youtu.be&t=3778 .

[44] Tanya Farber and Claire Keeton, "#FeesMustFall to blame, say Mayosi family", *Sunday Times*, 5 August 2018, p. 9.

[45] Staff Writer, "Listen: UCT Vice Chancellor Blames Professor Mayosi's Death on Fees Must Fall", *Vernac News*, 30 July 2018, https://vernacnews.co.za/2018/07/30/listen-uct-vice-chancellor-blames-professor-mayosis-death-on-fees-must-fall/ (Accessed 30 July 2018).

[46] Mamokgethi Phakeng, "VC Desk: Building community after trauma", 31 July 2018.

[47] Phurah Jack, "Speakers ambushed students at Prof Mayosi's funeral", *The Sunday Independent*, 12 August 2018, p. 14.

[48] For details about his other outrageous behaviour at UCT see Chapter 21.

[49] "Fallists not to blame for Mayosi's death – Chumani Maxwele", *Politicsweb,* 31 July 2018, https://www.politicsweb.co.za/news-and-analysis/uct-must-take-responsibility-for-prof-mayosis-deat (Accessed 30 June 2020).

[50] Xolela Mangcu ordered a "soft omelette" at a restaurant in Cape Town. He got into an argument with the chef, Claudine Adams, whom he allegedly called a

"Coloured servant". The restaurant owner later asked him to leave. Professor Mangcu alleged that the owner had called him a criminal. The owner denied this, responding that he had said only that he would call the police. Professor Mangcu claimed that he was a victim of racism. See Lynette Johns, "Omelette meal ends in racism fracas", *Independent Online*, 22 May 2015, https://www.iol.co.za/news/south-africa/western-cape/omelette-meal-ends-in-racism-fracas-1861906 (Accessed 17 November 2015).

[51] Xolela Mangcu visited another restaurant in Cape Town. This time the spinach that should have accompanied his steak was not available. There are competing accounts of what happened next, but the upshot was that Professor Mangcu alleged more restaurant racism. See Xolela Mangcu, and Pierre van Tonder, "Restaurant Racism: what happened when a respected academic had enough", *City Press,* 16 September 2015, https://www.news24.com/citypress/voices/Spinach-chips-and-race-20150911 (Accessed 30 June 2020).

[52] Xolela Mangcu, "How many Mayosis must be martyred before UCT deals with its toxic racism", *Sunday Times*, 12 August 2018, p. 18.

[53] By contrast, the grievance complaints he laid against three of his colleagues were all found to be groundless. For the record, I am neither the person who laid the complaint nor one of the people against whom he brought a counter-complaint.

[54] Concerned Academics and the UCT Black Academic Caucus, "Statement on the Handling of Prof. Mayosi's Passing and a Call for an Inquiry", 31 July 2018.

[55] The #OccupyFHS singled her out for thanks as the occupation of the Dean's Suite came to an end. See https://twitter.com/noma_solwandle/status/783262149636423680 (Accessed 17 November 2020).

[56] Lydia Cairncross, "Thoughts on the death of Professor Bongani Mayosi", *Daily Maverick*, 31 July 2018, https://www.dailymaverick.co.za/article/2018-07-31-thoughts-on-the-death-of-professor-bongani-mayosi/#gsc.tab=0 (Accessed 31 July 2018).

[57] Ed Herbst, "Reflections on suicide of Professor Bongani Mayosi, persecuted to death", *BizNews*, 7 August 2018, https://www.biznews.com/thought-leaders/2018/08/07/suicide-professor-bongani-mayosi-death-ed-herbst (Accessed 7 August 2018).

[58] Enquiry into the Circumstances Surrounding Professor Bongani's Tenure: Crucible for Senior Black Staff?, 16 June 2020, p. 7.

[59] Ibid, pp. 93-101.

[60] Ibid.

[61] In keeping with the report's own findings, the subtitle should have focused on Fallist behaviour rather than on this issue.

[62] Enquiry into the Circumstances Surrounding Professor Bongani's Tenure: Crucible for Senior Black Staff?, 16 June 2020, p. 115.

[63] Reitumetse Obakeng Mabokela, "'We Cannot Find Qualified Blacks': Faculty Diversification Programmes at South African Universities", *Comparative Education* , Vol. 36, No. 1, February 2000, p. 100.

[64] Information provided by UCT's Institutional Planning Department. In 2018, the proportion of academic staff who were "black" South Africans was 26% (*University*

of Cape Town Transformation Report – 2018, p. 24), which provides some indication of the recent rate of "transformation".

[65] Based on information provided by UCT's Institutional Planning Department.

[66] There were many errors of fact in the report. Some are less consequential, but they do nonetheless suggest a certain sloppiness. For example, the report mistakenly claimed that Professor Stuart Saunders (not Sanders, as the report claimed), had been Dean of the Faculty of Health Sciences between being the Head of the Department of Medicine and being the Vice-Chancellor. It also erroneously claimed that Professor Mayosi had coined the term "the bottom billion" to refer to the world's poor[est]. (See Paul Collier, *The Bottom Billion: Why the Poorest Countries are Failing and What Can Be Done About It*, New York: Oxford University Press, 2007.)

[67] Enquiry into the Circumstances Surrounding Professor Bongani's Tenure: Crucible for Senior Black Staff?, 16 June 2020, p. 116.

[68] Ibid. p. 94.

[69] Ibid. p. 117. According to the report, there "are many prominent historical examples of eminent black scholars who are globally recognised for their outstanding work, who fell foul of the UCT system and subsequently suffered frustration and exclusion." (p. 117). The cases of Archie Mafeje and Mahmood Mamdani are cited. The Archie Mafeje case was in 1968, the midst of the Apartheid era, and thus hardly relevant to Professor Mayosi's situation. (For more on this case, see Howard Phillips, *UCT Under Apartheid: Part 1: From Onset to Sit-In, 1948-1968*, Sunnyside: Fanele, 2019.) It is much less clear that Mahmood Mamdani was a victim of UCT. He is often presented, including in this report, as having left UCT in frustration at not having been allowed to decolonize the teaching of African Studies, of which he was the head. The truth is more complicated. I know this because both Professor Mamdani and I were roped into participating in a new compulsory, multidisciplinary "Foundation Course" that was being introduced in the Faculty of Humanities. I was then a young, new lecturer in the Philosophy Department. I was asked to teach the critical thinking component of the course. I did not like the idea of the Foundation course, and I did not like the fact that other members of the design team wanted to design my component of the course with me. By the same token, I saw no role for myself in helping design *their* components. Despite my frustrations, I attended all the design meetings, holding the line on what I thought should be included in and excluded from the critical thinking component. I desisted from passing any opinions on the other components. My recollection is that Professor Mamdani attended almost none of these meetings – until a very late stage in the process, when he expressed his alternative conception of the African Studies components of the course. He met with resistance and he then made a public spectacle of his criticism. I do not have the expertise to comment on the merits of Professor Mamdani's critique. What I *can* say is that if he had been collegial, he would not have raised this critique only towards the end of the design process, expecting it to be reversed at that point. Put another way, I shared his frustration at being told how to teach one's own area of expertise, but he should either have put his foot down at the beginning of the process or he should have participated in it.

[70] It might be argued that *I* do not know "black" lives from the inside. I do not deny this. (The only life I know from the inside is mine, and I do not think that it is the same as the lives of others who may share my skin tone.) What I claim is that

subjective impressions are not sufficient. We need to present the evidence for such impressions, so that this evidence can be evaluated. If both "blacks" and "whites" feel more appreciated abroad than at home, then the fact that "blacks" feel more appreciated abroad than at home cannot constitute evidence of an environment hostile (only) to "blacks". If the claim is that "blacks" are actually appreciated less at home than "whites" are, then we need evidence for this, which can then be evaluated.

[71] Enquiry into the Circumstances Surrounding Professor Bongani's Tenure: Crucible for Senior Black Staff?, 16 June 2020, pp. 117-118.

[72] Ibid, p. 119.

[73] Ibid,, p. 120.

[74] Ibid, p. 133.

[75] Yolisa Tswanya, "Activists 'vindicated' by report after UCT Professor Bongani Mayosi's death", IOL, 24 June 2020, https://www.iol.co.za/capetimes/news/activists-vindicated-by-report-after-uct-professor-bongani-mayosis-death-49817572 (Accessed 2 July 2020).

[76] Unfortunately, the report attempted to shift some of the blame to the University by saying "that the protests would not have been as prolonged, nor as vicious at times, had the University's initial response been more measured and less reactionary" (p. 138). In other words, if the University had capitulated more quickly and more entirely, the students would not have behaved as badly as they did.

Chapter 20

[1] Until recently, the BAC's statements were typically not dated and often not titled. The statement was posted on Twitter on 4 June 2020.

[2] This was sent to its various recipients in an email on 6 June 2020.

[3] The BAC said that it is "not surprised when white academics design research framed in a fashion that disqualifies the aspirations of black people". It's convenient to dismiss Professor Nattrass's study as one designed by a "white academic". The truth, however, is that those designing it were from different purported races. Nor is it true, as will become apparent shortly, that the study disqualified the aspirations of black people. Instead, it sought to understand those aspirations.

[4] Data differ quite considerably. According to the 2016 South African household living standards survey, 47% of "white" households but only 5% of "black" households have companion animals (including herding and guarding dogs). According to data for the same year from the South African Audience Research Foundation, 71% of "white" respondents and 26% of "black respondents said that they had a cat or a dog. (Professor Nattrass's calculations).

[5] Robyn Dixon, "South Africa's Jacob Zuma: Pet dogs are part of 'white culture'", *Los Angeles Times*, 27 December 2012, https://www.latimes.com/world/la-xpm-2012-dec-27-la-fg-wn-southafrica-zuma-dogs-20121227-story.html (Accessed 14 June 2020).

[6] See Chapter 4.

[7] Adam Haupt, "Liquid racism, possessive investments in whiteness and academic freedom at a post-apartheid university", in Evangelia Kindinger and Mark Schmitt

(Eds.), *The Intersections of Whiteness*, Abingdon, Oxon: Routledge, 2019, pp. 87-104.

[8] Chapter 15 in this book.

[9] Jonathan Jansen, "What to write about black people? Make very sure of your facts?", *TimesLive*, 11 June 2020, https://select.timeslive.co.za/ideas/2020-06-11-want-to-write-about-black-people-make-very-sure-of-your-facts/# (Accessed 22 November 2020).

[10] "Statement by the UCT executive on research paper by academic", 5 June 2020.

[11] Personal testimony from Nicoli Nattrass.

[12] Jane Carruthers email to George Hull, 24 August 2020.

[13] UCT Senate, 5 March 2021.

[14] Jonathan Jansen, "What to write about black people? Make very sure of your facts?", *TimesLive*, 11 June 2020, https://select.timeslive.co.za/ideas/2020-06-11-want-to-write-about-black-people-make-very-sure-of-your-facts/# (Accessed 22 November 2020).

[15] Letter to the UCT Executive from Professor Nicoli Nattrass, 7th June 2020.

[16] See, for example: Nicoli Nattrass, "Tumult at UCT - Part 1: The Challenges of Transformation", *News24*, 9 June 2020, https://www.news24.com/news24/columnists/guestcolumn/opinion-professor-nicoli-nattrass-tumult-at-uct-part-1-the-challenges-of-transformation-20200609 (Accessed 9 June 2020); Nicoli Nattrass, "Tumult at UCT – Part 2: The Dangers of Allowing the Thought Police to Take Over", *News24,* 10 June 2020, https://www.news24.com/news24/southafrica/news/opinion-tumult-at-uct-part-2-the-dangers-of-allowing-the-thought-police-to-take-over-20200610 (Accessed 10 June 2020); Nicoli Nattrass, "The thought police at UCT should address transformation, not pass a judgment of racism" *Mail&Guardian*, 17 June 2020, https://mg.co.za/opinion/2020-06-17-the-thought-police-at-uct-should-address-transformation-not-pass-racist-judgment/ (Accessed 18 June 2020); Nicoli Nattrass, "Sloppy race science or sensationalist journalism?" *Daily Maverick*, 29 June 2020, https://www.dailymaverick.co.za/article/2020-06-29-sloppy-race-science-or-sensationalist-journalism/ (Accessed 30 June 2020).

[17] PsySSA Presidency, Psychological Society of South Africa, "Response from the Psychological Society of South Africa (PsySSA) on the commentary by Prof Nicoli Nattrass, published in the South African Journal of Science (*SAJS*; Vol 116; 5/6)", 16 June 2020.

[18] Hogarth, "Mampara of the Week: Prof Nicoli Nattrass", *Sunday Times*, 7 June 2020, p. 15. Non-South Africans may be unfamiliar with the term. A "mampara" is South African slang for a fool or buffoon.

[19] "Afriforum requests dismissal of UNISA-lecturer for gender and racial abuse of UCT professor", 20 July 2020, https://www.afriforum.co.za/en/afriforum-requests-dismissal-of-unisa-lecturer-for-gender-and-racial-abuse-of-uct-professor/ (Accessed 2 August 2020).

[20] He obviously does not understand what satire is.

[21] Belinda Bozzoli, "In defence of Nicoli Nattrass and academic freedom", *Politicsweb*, 8 June 2020, https://www.politicsweb.co.za/opinion/in-defence-of-nicoli-nattrass-

and-academic-freedom (Accessed 9 June 2020).

[22] "Statement by the veterans of the 1968 Mafeje protest on the treatment of Prof Nattrass by the University of Cape Town", 10 June 2020, https://martinplaut.com/2020/06/10/statement-by-the-veterans-of-the-1968-mafeje-protest-on-the-treatment-of-prof-nattrass-by-the-university-of-cape-town/ (Accessed 10 June 2020). They were promptly dismissed as "white liberals". See Koni Benson, et al, "The Nattrass Case and the Dangers of Ahistorical Analogy", *Daily Maverick*, 20 June 2020, https://www.dailymaverick.co.za/article/2020-06-20-the-nattrass-case-and-the-dangers-of-ahistorical-analogy/ (Accessed 20 June 2020).

[23] Paul Trewhela, "Der Fall Nattrass", *Politicsweb*, 11 June 2020, https://www.politicsweb.co.za/opinion/der-fall-nattrass (Accessed 12 June 2020).

[24] David Welsh et al, "Nicoli Nattrass: Executive's behaviour disturbing – former UCT academics", *Politicsweb*, 15 June 2020, https://www.politicsweb.co.za/documents/nicoli-nattrass-executives-behaviour-disturbing--f (Accessed 15 June 2020).

[25] The Council of the Academy of Science of South Africa, "Statement in response to the article published in the South African Journal of Science by Professor Nicoli Nattrass with the title *Why are black South African students less likely to consider studying biological sciences?*", 9 June 2020.

[26] *South African Journal of Science*, Vol 116 Special Issue, July 2020. If any of those to whom Professor Nattrass responded subsequently wrote a reply to her response, I am not aware of it.

[27] One of the charges brought against Professor Nattrass is that of "falsification". According to the relevant UCT policy, which is consistent with general usage, falsification means "deliberate misrepresentation of research including progress in research or inappropriate adjustment and/or selection of data, imagery, results and/or consents, or undisclosed duplication of publication, or inappropriate claims to authorship or attribution of work contrary to the UCT Authorship Practices Policy". ("UCT Policy and Procedures for Breach of Research Ethics Codes and Allegations of Misconduct in Research", 27 September 2014, http://www.uct.ac.za/sites/default/files/image_tool/images/328/about/policies/Policy_Research_Ethics_Breach_Misconduct_2014.pdf Accessed 16 October 2020). However, the reason why the charge was brought against Professor Nattrass was that she had not indicated in her original research proposal or in the consent forms that the research would be used to write a commentary. This does not constitute falsification. Moreover, it is common practice for research proposals and consent forms not to specific what papers will be produced as a result of the research. It is similarly common for data to be stored for future (unspecified) use.

[28] Draft statement, in Academic Freedom Committee Agenda, 31 August 2020, p. 21-22.

[29] Academic Freedom Committee Agenda 26 October 2020, p. 23. In the poll producing this result, eight of ten members voted, five denying that there had any infringement of academic freedom, and three saying that there had been such an infringement.

[30] Jane Carruthers email to George Hull, 24 August 2020.

[31] Email from Judith du Toit (Director, Office of the Vice-Chancellor) to George

Hull, 26 August 2020.

[32] At a subsequent meeting of Senate (on Friday 5 March 2021), the Vice-Chancellor, in a response to a question from Professor Nattrass, attempted to explain the discrepancy. She claimed that she had called Professor Carruthers in her "capacity as a member of the Academy of Science of South Africa and as a scholar concerned about the scholarly merit of the Commentary [and] not officially as Vice Chancellor of the University of Cape Town". She then suggested that this would explain why the Director of the Office of the Vice-Chancellor would have been unaware of the discussion" and that she was "correct in stating that the Executive never phoned the journal because the Executive never did". There are two arguments being made here. The second one sounds like Bill Clinton opining that whether he had perjured himself "depends on what the meaning of the word 'is' is". Given that Mamokgethi Phakeng *did* call Professor Carruthers, and given that Professor Phakeng is a member of the Executive, it is, at the very least, misleading to say that "The UCT Executive never phoned the Editor". The first argument also strains credulity. Before the Director of the Office of the Vice-Chancellor could answer the question about whether the Executive phoned the editor, she would have had to check with them whether they had done so. (She has not been accused of answering the question without first checking with the Executive.) In other words, the only way in which she would be aware of such a call is by asking the members of the Executive. Her awareness would not depend on whether the Vice-Chancellor was acting in her personal capacity or in her capacity as the Vice-Chancellor.

[33] Elelwani Ramugondo, Twitter, 9 June 2020, https://twitter.com/ERamugondo/status/1270453815880359938 . When another twitter user interpreted her comment as suggesting that "Prof Nattrass is not protected by principles of academic freedom", Professor Ramugondo replied: "Blatant lie ... yet again. Putting words in my mouth". In his response, her interlocutor asked: "So ... are you defending Prof Nattrass's right to publish her paper? YES OR NO?" Professor Ramugondo did not reply.

[34] Elelwani Ramugondo, Twitter, 7 June 2020, https://twitter.com/ERamugondo/status/1269616739781881856 .

[35] For some of her other tweets about academic freedom and the Nicoli Nattrass affair, see:

https://twitter.com/ewnreporter/status/1269251474053304320

https://twitter.com/ERamugondo/status/1278389548565872647

https://twitter.com/ERamugondo/status/1278600386019045377

https://twitter.com/ERamugondo/status/1278693840984080392

[36] Nithaya Chetty, "In a bid to placate politics on race UCT fails to protect academic freedom", *Mail&Guardian*, 30 June 2020, https://mg.co.za/opinion/2020-06-30-in-a-bid-to-placate-politics-on-race-uct-fails-to-protect-academic-freedom/ (Accessed 30 June 2020).

Chapter 21

[1] "Mthethwa's sorry 'middle-finger' story", *Mail&Guardian,* 8 May 2014, https://mg.co.za/article/2014-05-08-mthethwas-sorry-middle-finger-story/ (Accessed

27 August 2014); "Man who 'insulted' Zuma in limbo", *Mail&Guardian*, 7 June 2013, https://mg.co.za/article/2013-06-07-00-man-who-insulted-zuma-in-limbo/ (Accessed 27 August 2020).

2 "Minister dodges apology to blue-light victim again", *Mail&Guardian*, 6 January 2012, https://mg.co.za/article/2012-01-06-minister-dodges-apology-to-bluelight-victim-again/ (Accessed 3 September 2020).

3 Ibid.

4 Ibid.

5 The FW de Klerk foundation is not a "white" organization, but it does bear the name of the last Apartheid-era president of South Africa. That Mr de Klerk recognized the evils of Apartheid, was instrumental in paving the way to democracy, and established a foundation committed to the new South Africa, are all nuances that would be lost on Mr Maxwele.

6 "Blue-light 'victim' welcomes ruling against Mthethwa", *Mail&Guardian*, 21 June 2013, https://mg.co.za/article/2013-06-21-00-blue-light-victim-welcomes-ruling-against-mthethwa/ (Accessed 3 September 2020).

7 "Mthethwa's sorry 'middle-finger' story", *Mail&Guardian,* 8 May 2014, https://mg.co.za/article/2014-05-08-mthethwas-sorry-middle-finger-story/ (Accessed 27 August 2014).

8 Yazeed Kamaldien, "Rhodes statue: students occupy offices", *IOL*, 21 March 2015, https://www.iol.co.za/news/south-africa/western-cape/rhodes-statue-students-occupy-offices-1835276#.VSEO86g0WS0 (Accessed 10 November 2020). Video footage can be found here: https://www.iol.co.za/news/south-africa/western-cape/protesters-throw-poo-on-rhodes-statue-1829526 .

9 University of Cape Town v Chumani Maxwele, UCT Student Disciplinary Tribunal Judgement, 15/0017/HC, 10 July 2018, p. 2.

10 Ibid, p. 17.

11 Max Price, "Urgent update on the Rhodes statue and Bremner Occupation", 10 April 2015, https://www.news.uct.ac.za/article/-2015-04-10-urgent-update-on-the-rhodes-statue-and-bremner-occupation (Accessed 10 September 2020).

12 "Chumani Maxwele: These are the facts – UCT", *Politicsweb*, 5 June 2015,

https://www.politicsweb.co.za/news-and-analysis/chumani-maxwele-these-are-the-facts--uct?sn=Marketingweb%20detail (Accessed 11 August 2020).

13 Chapter 24.

14 Max Price, "UCT grants amnesty to protestors", 18 May 2015, https://www.news.uct.ac.za/article/-2015-05-18-uct-grants-amnesty-to-protesters (Accessed 9 September 2020). The astute will notice that the amnesty period included any protests that would still occur up to five days after the granting of the amnesty. This was to give time to those who were occupying Avenue House to vacate those premises.

15 "Chumani Maxwele: These are the facts – UCT", *Politicsweb*, 5 June 2015,

https://www.politicsweb.co.za/news-and-analysis/chumani-maxwele-these-are-the-facts--uct?sn=Marketingweb%20detail (Accessed 11 August 2020). It is not clear what became of this as there do not seem to be any rulings by the Equality Court on this matter. See: http://www.saflii.org/za/cases/ZAEQC/ (Accessed 28 February 2021).

16 "Chumani Maxwele: These are the facts – UCT", *Politicsweb*, 5 June 2015, https://www.politicsweb.co.za/news-and-analysis/chumani-maxwele-these-are-the-facts--uct?sn=Marketingweb%20detail (Accessed 11 August 2020).

17 Maxwele v University of Cape Town and Others (11766/2015) [2015] ZAWCHC 200 (15 September 2015), p. 5.

18 The hearing for the final suspension order had been held after the provisional suspension order had already lapsed. "Suspension of Mr Chumani Maxwele", 10 June 2015, https://www.news.uct.ac.za/article/-2015-06-10-suspension-of-mr-chumani-maxwele (Accessed 11 August 2020).

19 "UCT adapts Maxwele's suspension order", *News24*, 27 July 2015, https://www.news24.com/News24/uct-adapts-maxweles-suspension-order-20150727 (Accessed 15 September 2020).

20 Lisa Isaacs, "Maxwele beats UCT in court", *IOL*, 16 September 2015, https://www.iol.co.za/capetimes/news/maxwele-beats-uct-in-court-1916675 (Accessed 9 September 2020).

21 "UCT, Rhodes Must Fall, sign mediation agreement", 19 August 2015, https://www.news.uct.ac.za/article/-2015-08-19-uct-rhodes-must-fall-sign-mediation-agreement (Accessed 27 August 2020).

22 "Agreement between the University of Cape Town (UCT) and Rhodes Must Fall (RMF) movement", 18 August 2015, https://www.news.uct.ac.za/images/archive/dailynews/2015/RMFMediationStatement.pdf (Accessed 27 August 2020).

23 The Preliminary Investigating Committee (PIC) sat on 18 August 2015. A submission from Ms Mathematica implies that it was the 17th, but that is probably because the submission was written on the eve of the PIC meeting.

24 "Chumani Maxwele: These are the facts – UCT", *Politicsweb*, 5 June 2015, https://www.politicsweb.co.za/news-and-analysis/chumani-maxwele-these-are-the-facts--uct?sn=Marketingweb%20detail (Accessed 11 August 2020); "Suspension of Mr Chumani Maxwele", 10 June 2015, https://www.news.uct.ac.za/article/-2015-06-10-suspension-of-mr-chumani-maxwele (Accessed 11 August 2020).

25 "Disciplinary procedures for academic staff", Policy updated on 6 May 2005, http://www.hr.uct.ac.za/hr/employee_relations/disciplinary/academic_staff (Accessed 15 September 2020).

26 Ms Mathematica's email to Dr Price and others, 20 August 2015.

27 Anonymized, "Arguments in aggravation of sentence", p. 3.

28 Maxwele v University of Cape Town and Others (11766/2015) [2015] ZAWCHC 200 (15 September 2015), p. 17.

29 Anonymized, "Arguments in aggravation of sentence", p. 3.

30 This is a quotation from Judge Allie's judgement in "University of Cape Town v Davids and Others (2648/2016) [2016] ZAWCHC 56; [2016] 3 All SA 333 (WCC) (11 May 2016)", p. 16. The precise words are Judge Allie's and not necessarily Mr Maxwele's.

[31] University of Cape Town v Davids and Others (2648/2016) [2016] ZAWCHC 56; [2016] 3 All SA 333 (WCC) (11 May 2016)", p 16.

[32] *Hotz v UCT* (730/2016) 2016 ZASCA 159 (20 October 2016), p. 29.

[33] University of Cape Town v Davids and Others (2648/2016) [2016] ZAWCHC 56; [2016] 3 All SA 333 (WCC) (11 May 2016)", p. 16.

[34] Ibid, p. 17.

[35] *Hotz v UCT* (730/2016) 2016 ZASCA 159 (20 October 2016), pp. 29-30.

[36] Ibid, p. 30.

[37] Ibid, p. 30.

[38] Ibid.

[39] University of Cape Town v Davids and Others (2648/2016) [2016] ZAWCHC 56; [2016] 3 All SA 333 (WCC) (11 May 2016)", p. 17.

[40] Ibid.

[41] Ibid.

[42] Lisa Isaacs, "Maxwele under fire from #FeesMustFall feminists", IOL, 6 April 2016, https://www.iol.co.za/news/maxwele-under-fire-from-feesmustfall-feminists-2005721 (Accessed 11 August 2020).

[43] Ibid.

[44] Jenni Evans, "Chumani Maxwele arrested at pension protest outside Parliament", *News 24*, 5 May 2016, https://www.news24.com/news24/southafrica/news/rhodes-must-fall-activist-arrested-at-pension-protest-outside-parliament-20160505 (Accessed 24 September 2020).

[45] For those who cannot understand the significance of quotation marks, I note that they indicate that the word within them was used by Mr Maxwele. In quoting him I am not myself using this epithet or endorsing it. To the contrary, I am quoting his word in order both to make clear what he said and to convey my abhorrence. He did not say "n-word", and I condemn his use of the epithet he used.

[46] "Agreement with SRC Candidates / ShackvilleTRC and other student formations", 7 November 2016, p. 2.

[47] *Hotz v UCT* (730/2016) 2016 ZASCA 159 (20 October 2016), p. 43.

[48] See Chapter 19.

[49] It should have been lodged by 10 November, but the delay was condoned by the Constitutional Court. (Hotz and Others v University of Cape Town [2017] ZACC 10, p. 8.)

[50] Tammy Petersen, "Charges withdrawn against UCT students who burnt paintings", *News24*, 6 December 2016, https://www.news24.com/news24/southafrica/news/charges-withdrawn-against-uct-students-who-burnt-paintings-20161206 (Accessed 24 September 2020). My understanding is that this was at UCT's request and as a consequence of the "November agreement". However, I have been unable to have this confirmed.

[51] "The Convocation of the University of Cape Town is a statutory body administered by the Office of the Registrar. It comprises graduates and all holders

of diplomas and certificates of the university, the Vice-Chancellor, the Deputy Vice-Chancellors and the academic staff, as well as emeritus professors and emeritus associate professors." http://www.alumni.uct.ac.za/convocation (Accessed 24 September 2020).

[52] Nathan Geffen, "UCT Convocation descends into chaos", *GroundUp*, 16 December 2016, https://www.groundup.org.za/article/uct-convocation-descends-chaos/ (Accessed 9 September 2020).

[53] Ibid.

[54] Ibid.

[55] "Agreement with SRC Candidates / ShackvilleTRC and other student formations", 7 November 2016, p. 2.

[56] Hotz and Others v University of Cape Town [2017] ZACC 10

[57] Anonymized, "Arguments in aggravation of sentence", p. 3.

[58] It is viewable here: https://twitter.com/msakha/status/982173282442002434 .

[59] "The Final Report by the Institutional Reconciliation and Transformation Commission of the University of Cape Town (IRTC)", March 2018, p. 20.

[60] Ibid.

[61] Maxwele v University of Cape Town (18555/2019) [2020] ZAWCHC 188 (8 December 2020), p. 6.

[62] Noxolo Majavu, "Student activist Chumani Maxwele relieved as court slaps UCT", *Sowetan Live*, 18 December 2020, https://www.sowetanlive.co.za/news/south-africa/2020-12-18-student-activist-chumani-maxwele-relieved-as-court-slaps-uct/# (Accessed 18 December 2020).

[63] The relevant rule, DJP 5.6 states:

> When a proctor sits with assessors, a verdict may be reached by a majority. If, for any reason, an assessor is unable to assume or continue with their duties as an assessor, a proctor has an ordinary and a deciding vote on matters of verdict. If both assessors are unable to continue with their duties as assessors, the matter must be heard afresh.

The High Court understood this rule to apply only to the verdict stage of a hearing – that is, if one assessor was unable to continue at that stage, then a verdict could be delivered. According to Proctor's interpretation but not the High Court's, this provision did not apply to an earlier point in the process.

[64] Maxwele v University of Cape Town (18555/2019) [2020] ZAWCHC 188 (8 December 2020), p. 30.

[65] Ibid, pp. 30-31.

Chapter 22

[1] David Benatar, "Commandante Lushaba and the Führer", *Politicsweb*, 15 April 2021, https://www.politicsweb.co.za/opinion/commandante-lushaba-and-the-fhrer.

[2] https://youtu.be/TSv4A913050?t=1763

[3] Natasha Mazzone, "DA reports Lwazi Lushaba to Human Rights Commission over Hitler comments", Democratic Alliance, 9 April 2021, https://www.da.org.za/2021/04/da-reports-lwazi-lushaba-to-human-rights-commission-over-hitler-comments (Accessed 9 April 2021).

[4] Sisonke Mlamla, "UCT's SRC defends lecturer's 'Hitler committed no crime' comments", *IOL*, 12 April 2021, https://www.iol.co.za/capeargus/news/ucts-src-defends-lecturers-hitler-committed-no-crime-comments-f0b28a87-4220-48f0-82d8-6aa2bd19a9c4 (Accessed, 12 April 2021).

[5] "UCT academic reprimanded after vote for new dean ends in chaos", *TimesLive*, 25 July 2019, https://www.timeslive.co.za/news/south-africa/2019-07-25-uct-academic-reprimanded-after-vote-for-new-dean-ends-in-chaos/ (Accessed 25 July 2019).

[6] Staff Reporter", *Mail&Guardian*, 24 August 2015, https://mg.co.za/article/2015-08-24-habib-defends-suspension-of-wits-eff/ (Accessed 16 November 2017).

[7] This self-endowed promotion is to be found in an email he sent to the Humanities Faculty (9 September 2019). This particular email began "Dear Staff, Student and fellow black people" (sic).

[8] Simnikiwe Hlatshaneni, "My 'combi-court' rant wasn't racist, Mazibuko tells SAHRC", *The Citizen*, 16 April 2019, https://citizen.co.za/news/south-africa/general/2119286/my-combi-court-rant-wasnt-racist-mazibuko-tells-sahrc/ (Accessed 13 April 2021).

[9] "Bulhoek Massacre", *Wikipedia*, https://en.wikipedia.org/wiki/Bulhoek_massacre (Accessed 13 April 2021).

[10] "Herero and Namaqua genocide", *Wikipedia*, https://en.wikipedia.org/wiki/Herero_and_Namaqua_genocide (Accessed 13 April 2021).

[11] Matthew White, *The Great Big Book of Horrible Things*, New York: W.W. Norton, 2012, pp. 280-281.

[12] "Mfecane", *Wikipedia*, https://en.wikipedia.org/wiki/Mfecane (Accessed 13 April 2021).

Chapter 23

[1] This was borne out by the Inclusivity Survey conducted in 2019: Aephoria Partners, UCT Staff Inclusivity Survey: Findings of the Staff Inclusivity Survey", 20 December 2019, p. 79.

[2] I say "some" because, technically, the "IRTC dealt only with the cases arising directly from the 'Shackville protest', in particular the events that happened around 16 February 2016". *The Final Report by The Institutional Reconciliation and Transformation Commission of the University of Cape Town*, March 2019, *p. 23*.

[3] One can only imagine the scruples such doctors will have in completing medical certificates for UCT students a few years from now.

[4] Rule G17.3, *General Rules and Policies*, University of Cape Town, 2015, p. 9.

[5] Chair's action on behalf of the Faculty (of Humanities) Examinations Committee, 5 June 2018.

[6] There were further technical problems with Mr Pillay's arguments. For example, the rules he cited for justifying a "review" did not apply to the case at hand. Email from David Benatar to Royston Pillay, 8 October 2018.

[7] Rorisang Moseli, 28 May 2020, https://twitter.com/RoriMoseli/status/1265924578313977859 .

[8] Nicholas Woode-Smith, "Academic Bias in UCT Political Theory", *Rational Standard*, 29 July 2016; C. Tsampiras, *Power, Privilege, and Intersecting Identities*, Critical Health Humanities Handbook, MBChB 2, 2018.

[9] Another problem is that when in-person interviews were conducted, those interviewed were obliged, I was told, to provide a racial classification of themselves. This would exclude anybody refusing to make such a self-classification.

[10] See Chapter 20.

[11] Aephoria Partners, UCT Staff Inclusivity Survey: Findings of the Staff Inclusivity Survey", 20 December 2019, p. 79.

[12] Zetu Makamandela-Mguqulwa, UCT Ombud Report 2019, p. 3. The number of complaints about the Vice-Chancellor was later reported as being 37 (Murray Williams, "Fear and Loathing at UCT as University Ombud calls VC Mamokgethi Phakeng a 'bully'", *News24*, 9 July 2020, https://www.news24.com/news24/southafrica/news/fear-and-loathing-at-uct-as-university-ombud-calls-vc-mamokgethi-phakeng-a-bully-20200709 (Accessed 9 July 2020).)

[13] Zetu Makamandela-Mguqulwa, UCT Ombud Report 2019, p. 3.

[14] Ibid.

[15] Ibid.

[16] Ibid, p. 2.

[17] Zetu Makamandela-Mguqulwa, "The Ombud's Response to the Vice-Chancellor's Email sent to the Chair of Council on 2 March 2020", 13 March 2020.

[18] Zetu Makamandela-Mguqulwa, UCT Ombud Report 2019, p. 2.

[19] Murray Williams, "Fear and Loathing at UCT as University Ombud calls VC Mamokgethi Phakeng a 'bully'", *News24*, 9 July 2020, https://www.news24.com/news24/southafrica/news/fear-and-loathing-at-uct-as-university-ombud-calls-vc-mamokgethi-phakeng-a-bully-20200709 (Accessed 9 July 2020).

[20] Ibid.

[21] A legal opinion obtained by the Chair of Council, suggested that she had not. Advocate Michelle O'Sullivan, Memorandum of Advice, 8 April 2020.

[22] Michelle O'Sullivan mentions this number, quoting from a response of the Ombud to a request from the Council Executive Committee. (Advocate Michelle O'Sullivan, Memorandum of Advice, 8 April 2020, p. 43.)

[23] Sipho Pityana and Shirley Zinn, "Fanal (sic) Report to UCT Council",10 June 2020.

[24] Ibid.

[25] At the time of Professor Phakeng's appointment, the Vice-Chancellor was the chief executive officer. However, a new post of Chief Operating Officer has since been created. This position is subordinate to that of Vice-Chancellor.

[26] Zetu Makamandela-Mguqulwa, UCT Ombud Report 2019, pp. 15-16.

[27] See, for example, Chapter 21.

[28] @popazana_, 28 December 2018.

[29] Black Land First member, Lindsay Maasdorp, 28 December 2018.

[30] #LettersToQueers @Adv_Nchodu, 2 January 2019. "Poes" is Afrikaans for "pussy".

[31] In the Neville Alexander Building, September 2019.

[32] Associate Professor Xolela Mangcu, 14 September 2015.

[33] 8 to 11 October 2019.

[34] Adam Haupt, 6 March 2018. This seminar seems to be a prelude to his subsequent paper by the same title. See Chapter 15.

[35] For example, 11 April 2018.

[36] Department of English Seminar by Professor Michelle Wright (Emory University), 14 October 2019.

[37] Public seminar by Professor Rozena Maart, 3 February 2020.

[38] Speakers were Dr Robin di Angelo, Dr Mandisa Haarhoff, and Dr Wilhelm Verwoerd", 30 July 2020.

[39] 22 September 2020.

[40] Email from Lwazi Lushaba to Faculty of Humanities, 9 September 2019.

[41] "UCT invites 'conspiracy theorist' to talk about decolonization of science", *GroundUp*, 28 September 2017, https://www.groundup.org.za/article/uct-invites-conspiracy-theorist-talk-about-decolonisation-science/ (Accessed 30 September 2020).

[42] Ibid.

[43] Ibid.

[44] Ibid.

[45] See Chapter 19.

[46] Faculty of Health Sciences, *Transformation Framework*, Undated, but distributed on 16 June 2020.

[47] Contrary to what many people think, "woman" is not derived from "man". For more, see David Benatar, "Sexist Language: Alternatives to the Alternatives", in *Public Affairs Quarterly*, Vol. 19, No. 1, January 2005, pp. 1-9.

[48] And to the male and "white" student minorities of students in the Faculty of Health Sciences, and to the pro-life Christians who are hounded in some quarters of the Faculty and University. (Re males see, David Benatar, "Where are the males? Diversity, proportionality and Health Sciences admissions", *South African Medical Journal,* April 2016, Vol. 106, No. 4, pp. 323-4; re "whites" see Chapter 16 of this book. Re pro-life Christians, see Chapter 10 and below.)

⁴⁹ George Orwell, *Animal Farm*, Harmondsworth: Penguin, 1982.

⁵⁰ Edited by RD Hoekstra.

⁵¹ See Chapter 19.

⁵² Temwa-Dango Mwambene, "Anti-Choice culture is allowed to flourish at UCT. Why?", *Daily Vox*, 22 August 2018, https://www.thedailyvox.co.za/anti-choice-culture-is-allowed-to-flourish-at-uct-why-temwa-dango-mwambene/ (Accessed 17 June 2020).

⁵³ Natalie Pertsovksy, "Here is the list of art destroyed on UCT", *GroundUp*, 9 June 2017. http://www.groundup.org.za/article/here-list-art-destroyed-uct/ (Accessed 9 June 2017).

⁵⁴ Gerda Kruger, "UCT condemns RMF vandalism and violence", 16 February 2016. https://www.news.uct.ac.za/article/-2016-02-16-uct-condemns-rmf-vandalism-and-violencereleased-20h20-16-february-2016 (Accessed 8 July 2020).

⁵⁵ Gabriel Clark-Brown, "Art Under Threat at the University of Cape Town", Undated.

⁵⁶ Natalie Pertsovksy, "Here is the list of art destroyed on UCT", *GroundUp*, 9 June 2017.

⁵⁷ Azwi Mufamadi, "UCT statement on the David Goldblatt Collection", 24 February 2017.

⁵⁸ Natalie Pertsovksy, "Here is the list of art destroyed on UCT", *GroundUp*, 9 June 2017.

⁵⁹ "UCT Works of Art Collection – return to lender", undated UCT document.

⁶⁰ "UCT Works of Art Collection – in storage", undated UCT document.

⁶¹ Paul Weinberg letter to Renate Meyer, Appendix to Saam Niami Jalinous, "Photographer demands his photo of Mandela back from UCT", *GroundUp*, 7 November 2018, https://www.groundup.org.za/article/photographer-demands-his-photo-mandela-back-uct/ (Accessed 31 December 2018.)

⁶² William Daniels, email to Elijah Moholola and Renate Meyer, 31 December 2018.

⁶³ Paul Weinberg letter to Renate Meyer, in the appendix to Saam Niami Jalinous, "Photographer demands his photo of Mandela back from UCT", *GroundUp*, 7 November 2018, https://www.groundup.org.za/article/photographer-demands-his-photo-mandela-back-uct/ (Accessed 31 December 2018).

⁶⁴ Max Price, "A subtle kind of racism", *News24*, 16 July 2017, https://www.news24.com/news24/columnists/guestcolumn/a-subtle-kind-of-racism-20170716-2 (Accessed 5 August 2020).

⁶⁵ Paul Weinberg letter to Renate Meyer, Appendix to Saam Niami Jalinous, "Photographer demands his photo of Mandela back from UCT", *GroundUp*, 7 November 2018, https://www.groundup.org.za/article/photographer-demands-his-photo-mandela-back-uct/ (Accessed 31 December 2018).

⁶⁶ Max Price, "Right of Reply: We should think more carefully about what artworks are displayed in everyday public spaces", *Daily Maverick*, 14 August 2017, https://www.dailymaverick.co.za/article/2017-08-14-right-of-reply-we-should-think-more-carefully-about-what-artworks-are-displayed-in-everyday-public-spaces/

(Accessed 31 July 2020).

[67] Elisa Galgut and William Daniels argued that when "works of art are covered, boarded up, or removed for ideological purposes, and we are told 'this is not censorship', we are in the realm of bullshit. See Elisa Galgut and William Daniels, "Coverings and Cover-Ups: The Art of Bullshit", *Politicsweb*, 1 November 2018, https://www.politicsweb.co.za/opinion/the-art-of-bullshit-at-uct (Accessed 8 July 2020).

[68] Max Price and Belinda Bozzoli, "UCT and art: an exchange between Max Price and Belinda Bozzoli", 9 May 2017, http://www.groundup.org.za/article/uct-and-art-exchange-between-max-price-and-belinda-bozzoli/ (Accessed 9 May 2017). Similarly, the Artworks Task Team said: "In response to the destroyed artworks and what at the time were continuing protests, a decision was made by the Works of Art Committee to remove artworks in selected places for safe keeping." "Report by the Artworks Task Team" (a Task Team of the Council of the University of Cape Town) February 2017.

[69] Max Price and Belinda Bozzoli, "UCT and art: an exchange between Max Price and Belinda Bozzoli", 9 May 2017, http://www.groundup.org.za/article/uct-and-art-exchange-between-max-price-and-belinda-bozzoli/ (Accessed 9 May 2017).

[70] Jay Pather, "Right of Reply: UCT is not a closed and controlled gallery", 11 August 2017, https://www.dailymaverick.co.za/article/2017-08-11-right-of-reply-uct-is-not-a-closed-and-controlled-gallery/ (Accessed 14 January 2019). Elijah Moholola, a spokesperson from UCT's Communication and Marketing Department, offered a similar argument the following year: "'Censorship' of artworks: UCT's response", *Politicsweb*, 4 October 2018, https://www.politicsweb.co.za/opinion/censorship-of-artworks-ucts-response (Accessed 8 July 2020).

[71] The Artworks Task Team also claimed that male artists were disproportionately represented. This is true, but by a relatively narrow margin – 53% versus 41% female and 6% of unknown sex.

[72] Ramabina Mahapa, "Little at UCT saying 'Black child be proud'", *Independent Online*, 15 July 2014, https://www.iol.co.za/capeargus/little-at-uct-saying-black-child-be-proud-1720099 (Accessed 8 July 2020).

[73] William Daniels, "UCT: Censorship in plain sight", *Politicsweb*, 3 January 2019, https://www.politicsweb.co.za/opinion/uct-censorship-in-plane-sight (Accessed 3 January 2019).

[74] Natalie Pertsovsky, "Sarah Baartman sculptor speaks out against art censorship", *GroundUp*, 5 June 2017, http://www.groundup.org.za/article/sara-baartman-sculptor-speaks-out-against-art-censorship/ (Accessed 5 June 2017).

[75] "Sarah Baartman (sculpture), *Censorpedia*, National Coalition Against Censorship, http://www.wiki.ncac.org/Sarah_Baartman_(sculpture) (Accessed 9 July 2020).

[76] Natalie Pertsovsky, "Sarah Baartman sculptor speaks out against art censorship", *GroundUp*, 5 June 2017.

[77] Ibid.

[78] Gwenda Thomas, "Sarah Baartman Sculpture: Position of the University Librarian", 23 January 2018.

[79] Natalie Pertsovsky, "Quarrel over Sarah Baartman sculpture at UCT", 2 March

2018, https://www.groundup.org.za/article/quarrel-over-sarah-baartman-sculpture-uct/ (Accessed 2 March 2018).

80 Ibid.

81 Elijah Moholola, "UCT artworks committee to host an exhibition", 22 August 2018.

82 William Daniels, "UCT: Censorship in plain sight", *Politicsweb*, 3 January 2019, https://www.politicsweb.co.za/opinion/uct-censorship-in-plane-sight (Accessed 3 January 2019).

83 Elijah Moholola, "UCT artworks committee to host an exhibition", 22 August 2018.

84 Natalie Pertsovksy, "Here is the list of art destroyed on UCT", *GroundUp*, 9 June 2017.

85 William Daniels, "UCT: Censorship in plain sight", *Politicsweb*, 3 January 2019, https://www.politicsweb.co.za/opinion/uct-censorship-in-plane-sight (Accessed 3 January 2019).

86 See Chapter 6.

87 See Chapter 20.

88 Email from the Director of the School of Economics to all staff in the Department, 2 September 2020.

89 "Proposal for UCT School of Economics: Transformation, Equity & Belonging Intervention", L&N Advisors, 5 August 2020, p. 8.

90 William Daniels, "When banning things was bad", *Politicsweb*, 19 September 2018, https://www.politicsweb.co.za/opinion/when-banning-things-was-bad (Accessed 19 August 2020).

91 Ibid.

92 Helen Swingler, "Vision 2030: virtual staff engagements roll out", 31 July 2020, https://www.news.uct.ac.za/article/-2020-07-31-vision-2030-virtual-staff-engagements-roll-out (Accessed 31 July 2020).

93 *Vision 2030: Unleash Human Potential to Create a Fair and Just Society*, p. 5, http://vision2030.uct.ac.za .

94 Niémah Davids, "Vision 2030: Initiating Change", https://www.news.uct.ac.za/article/-2020-09-16-vision-2030-initiating-change (Accessed 29 September 2020).

95 Ibid.

96 Nicoli Nattrass and Jeremy Seekings, "UCT says no to non-racialism: A Freudian slip, or an embracing of the cult of 'anti-racism'?", *Daily Maverick*, 25 September 2020, https://www.dailymaverick.co.za/opinionista/2020-09-25-uct-says-no-to-non-racialism-a-freudian-slip-or-an-embracing-of-the-cult-of-anti-racism/ (Accessed 26 September 2020).

97 "All-women executive academic leadership for UCT", *UCT News*, 16 May 2019, https://www.news.uct.ac.za/article/-2019-05-16-all-women-executive-academic-leadership-for-uct (Accessed 1 June 2021).

98 Sisonke Mlamla, "Women head UCT's top leadership staff", *Cape Argus*, 20 May 2019, p. 1.

99 Both accounts were created at the same time, shortly before these tweets. Both accounts have only a few tweets, most of which are devoted to this issue.

100 Nkosikhona Duma, "Zuma: I'm being victimised because I'm black", *Eyewitness News*, 16 October 2019, https://ewn.co.za/2019/10/16/jacob-zuma-i-m-being-victimised-because-i-m-black (Accessed, 12 July 2020)

101 "Women and black academics still under-represented at SA's institutions of higher learning", 8 July 2020. https://www.youtube.com/watch?v=IaAvG7XIdtg . In this interview, she was being asked about a more general issue, but her prolix response was a very thinly veiled reference to, in part, her own experience with the Ombud, which hit the news the following day.

102 Kabelo Khumalo, "UCT Vice-Chancellor Phakeng subject of withering Ombud report", *Sunday World*, 12 July 2020, p. 6.

103 Biénne Huisman, "Clouds continue to gather over UCT vice-chancellor", *Daily Maverick*, 15 July 2020. https://www.dailymaverick.co.za/article/2020-07-15-clouds-continue-to-gather-over-uct-vice-chancellor/ (Accessed 15 July 2020).

104 Ibid.

105 Ibid.

106 See, for example, Ismail Lagardien, "Mamokgethi Phakeng has shaken the edifice(s) of white social certification", *Daily Maverick*, 22 July 2020, https://www.dailymaverick.co.za/opinionista/2020-07-22-mamokgethi-phakeng-has-shaken-the-edifices-of-white-social-certification/#gsc.tab=0 (Accessed 22 July 2020). This piece is devoid of any actual evidence, but is laden with personal anecdote and explicit hypotheticals.

107 Tim Crowe, "Who is Chumani Maxwele? (Part 2), *Rational Standard*, 25 February 2018, https://rationalstandard.com/chumani-maxwele-pt-2/ (Accessed 30 March 2018). Professor Crowe claims that my name was *intentionally* mispronounced. I have no reason for thinking that. It is more likely, in my view, that Mr Maxwele mispronounced my name in ignorance.

108 "UCT's People Of Colour Dinner Now Open To All After Backlash" *SAfrica24*. 25 June 2018, http://www.safrica24.com/south-africa/ucts-people-of-colour-dinner-now-open-to-all-after-backlash/90406-news (Accessed 25 June 2018).

109 Mohammed Jameel Abdulla, "Decolonial School 'POC' Supper had no white people despite backlash", *Daily Vox*, 26 June 2018, http://www.thedailyvox.co.za/decolonial-school-poc-supper-had-no-white-people-despite-backlash-mohammed-jameel-abdulla/ (Accessed 26 June 2018).

110 Twitter, 21 June 2018.

111 Shaazia Ebrahim, "A POC Supper at UCT's Decolonial School is Causing White Tears", *The Daily Vox*, 23 June 2018, https://www.thedailyvox.co.za/a-poc-supper-at-ucts-decolonial-school-is-causing-white-tears-shaazia-ebrahim/ (Accessed 24 June 2018).

112 Ciaran Heywood, as quoted by Mohammed Jameel Abdulla, "Decolonial School

'POC' Supper had no white people despite backlash", *Daily Vox*, 26 June 2018, http://www.thedailyvox.co.za/decolonial-school-poc-supper-had-no-white-people-despite-backlash-mohammed-jameel-abdulla/ (Accessed 26 June 2018).

[113] Shaazia Ebrahim, "A POC Supper at UCT's Decolonial School is Causing White Tears", *The Daily Vox*, 23 June 2018.

[114] Mohammed Jameel Abdulla, "Decolonial School 'POC' Supper had no white people despite backlash", *Daily Vox*, 26 June 2018.

[115] Ed Herbst, "Assessing the need to exclude others", *The Messenger*, 25 June 2018.

[116] Catherine Heron, "Anti-semitism, anti-choice and anarchy at Plaza week", *Varsity*, Vol. 76, Edition 1, 28 March 2017, p. 3.

[117] 15 February 2019. Photographed and posted on Twitter by Ed Rybicki, https://twitter.com/edrybicki/status/1096411916115808256 .

[118] Louen Kleinsmidt, Twitter, 19 February 2019.

[119] Karin Morrow, Twitter, 20 May 2019.

[120] Chris Barron, "So Many Questions", *Sunday Times,* 15 January 2017, https://www.timeslive.co.za/sunday-times/opinion-and-analysis/2017-01-15-so-many-questions-on-feesmustfall-in-2017/ (Accessed 16 June 2020). Curiously, he elsewhere denied that he could be racist "because some of my best friends are white"! "'I'm not racist – some of my best friends are white': Ntokozo Qwabe", *Business Tech*, 1 June 2016, https://businesstech.co.za/news/lifestyle/125357/im-not-racist-some-of-my-best-friends-are-white-ntokozo-qwabe/ (Accessed 16 June 2020).

[121] I use this term in its technical sense: https://en.wikipedia.org/wiki/Useful_idiot (Accessed 26 February 2020).

[122] J Geldenhuys and M Kelly-Louw, "Hate Speech and Racist Slurs in the South African Context: Where to Start?, *PER / PELJ*, 2020(23), DOI http://dx.doi.org/10.17159/1727- 3781/2020/v23i0a7043.

[123] Simnikiwe Hlatshaneni, "My 'combi-court' rant wasn't racist, Mazibuko tells SAHRC", *The Citizen*, 16 April 2019, https://citizen.co.za/news/south-africa/general/2119286/my-combi-court-rant-wasnt-racist-mazibuko-tells-sahrc/ (Accessed 19 April 2021). The relevant commissioner, Priscilla Jana, provided two explanations for this bias – "historical context" and on the grounds that "racism from whites towards other races was more pervasive". It is hard to know whether that second claim is true or whether, instead, victims of racism from "whites" are much more likely to report such racism than are victims of anti-"white" racism, perhaps because victims of racism from "whites" can expect to receive a more sympathetic hearing.

[124] I argued this primarily with reference to sexism, but the point applies, *mutatis mutandis*, to racism. See David Benatar, *The Second Sexism: Discrimination Against Men and Boys*, Malden: MA, Wiley-Blackwell, 2012, pp. 5ff.

Chapter 24

[1] David Benatar, "Must UCT now fall?", *Politicsweb*, 30 June 2015, https://www.politicsweb.co.za/news-and-analysis/must-uct-also-now-fall . Chapter 3

in this book.

[2] For the latter see, for example, Chapters 12, 16, 18, 20, and 21.

[3] University of Cape Town General Rules and Policies: 2019.

[4] Ibid.

[5] "UCT Black academic caucus statement", 21 October 2016, https://thoughtleader.co.za/blackacademiccaucus/2016/10/23/uct-black-academic-caucus-statement/ (Accessed 4 August 2020).

[6] "Memorandum of Understanding Between the University of Cape Town and The Black Academic Caucus –University of Cape Town", 26 January 2017.

[7] https://en.wikipedia.org/wiki/Postmodernism_Generator

[8] Constitution of the Black Academic Caucus of the University of Cape Town, Adopted 3 November 2015.

[9] "Memorandum of Understanding Between the University of Cape Town and The Black Academic Caucus –University of Cape Town", 26 January 2017.

[10] Emails from Registrar Royston Pillay, 9 October 2017 and 17 October 2017.

[11] Email from Registrar Royston Pillay, 5 June 2020.

[12] "UCT Black academic caucus statement", 21 October 2016, https://thoughtleader.co.za/blackacademiccaucus/2016/10/23/uct-black-academic-caucus-statement/ (Accessed 4 August 2020).

[13] Chapter 10.

[14] Chapter 4.

[15] Chapter 7.

[16] Chapter 4.

[17] Chapter 10.

[18] Chapter 12.

[19] Chapter 10, and Elijah Moholola, "Fallist dropped rock on security guard's head – UCT", *Politicsweb*, 20 October 2016, https://www.politicsweb.co.za/news-and-analysis/fallist-dropped-rock-on-security-guards-head--uct (Accessed 1 October 2020); "Security guard attacked at UCT during #FeesMustFall protests", Multimedia Live, Youtube, 19 October 2016, https://www.youtube.com/watch?v=qMmolu8f--s (Accessed 1 October 2020).

[20] Chapter 20.

[21] Chapter 10.

[22] Chapter 10.

[23] Chapter 10.

[24] Chapters 10, 12, 21.

[25] Chapter 10. In the article reproduced in that chapter, I did not identify the parties involved. They have since been publicly identified. Xolela Mangcu defamed Nicoli Nattrass. See Tim Crowe, "Who is Chumani Maxwele? Part 2", *Rational Standard*, 25

February 2018, https://rationalstandard.com/chumani-maxwele-pt-2/ (Accessed 20 March 2018).

[26] Chapter 10.

[27] Chapters 10, 23.

[28] "Campus Announcement: UCT Condemns Hate Speech in any form", 11 February 2016.

[29] Chapter 10.

[30] Chapter 10.

[31] Chapter 18.

[32] Chapter 10

[33] Chapter 10.

[34] Chapters 13, 23.

[35] Alexis Haden, "UCT student says that there is an 'extreme hatred of whites'", *The South African*, 18 February 2016, https://www.thesouthafrican.com/news/uct-student-says-there-is-an-extreme-hatred-of-whites/ (Accessed 19 August 2020).

[36] Chapter 10.

[37] Chapters 10, 23.

[38] Chapter 5.

[39] When "blacks" who share the BAC's political agenda are in conflict with other "blacks" who are not serving that agenda, the BAC takes the side of the former, irrespective of what these allies do.

[40] "UCT Black academic caucus statement", 21 October 2016, https://thoughtleader.co.za/blackacademiccaucus/2016/10/23/uct-black-academic-caucus-statement/ (Accessed 4 August 2020).

[41] There is actually a technical gap in UCT's policies on grievances. There is no explicit provision for grievances to be brought against post-doctoral students, who are neither staff members nor students. I noted this gap and indicated that it needed to be filled. It should come as no surprise, that nothing has been done to rectify this problem.

[42] "Memorandum of Understanding Between the University of Cape Town and The Black Academic Caucus –University of Cape Town", 26 January 2017.

[43] Republished as Chapter 2 in this book.

[44] See Chapter 12.

[45] See Chapter 4.

[46] See, for example, Benjamin Ginsberg, The Fall of the Faculty: The rise of the all-administrative university and why it matters, New York: Oxford University Press, 2011.

[47] Justice Malala, We have now begun our descent: How to stop South Africa losing its way, Johannesburg: Jonathan Ball Publishers, 2015.

[48] *Report of the Ministerial Task Team on the Recruitment, Retention and Progression of Black South African Academics,* November 2019, p. 33,

https://www.dst.gov.za/images/2020/02/Report_MTT_RRP_of_Black_Academics_we
b_final1.pdf (Access date unknown).

[49] See Chapter 1.

[50] L.D. Mazibuko, Questions in the National Assembly (Question 1658). *Politicsweb*,
24 November 2009, https://www.politicsweb.co.za/documents/paul-ngobeni-
receiving-r601761-per-annum-from-dod (Accessed 23 March 2010).

[51] Lindiwe Sisulu, "Paul Ngobeni is not a fugitive from justice", *Politicsweb*, 19 March
2010, https://www.politicsweb.co.za/documents/paul-ngobeni-is-not-a-fugitive-
from-justice--lindi (Accessed 23 March 2016).

[52] Thuli Madonsela, "Report on an investigation into the alleged irregular
appointment of the special advisor to the Minister of Defence and Military
Veterans", *Politicsweb*, 26 April 2012, https://www.politicsweb.co.za/documents/paul-
ngobeni-what-the-public-protector-found (Accessed 26 April 2012).

[53] Emma Powell MP, "DA gives Sisulu 24 hours to refute or clarify allegations before
laying criminal charges", 10 May 2020, https://www.da.org.za/2020/05/da-gives-
sisulu-24-hours-to-refute-or-clarify-allegations-before-laying-criminal-charges
(Accessed 10 August 2020).

[54] See Chapter 21.

[55] See Chapter 23.

[56] The Ratcatcher, "How to ruin a newspaper group", *Politicsweb*, 24 April 2012,
https://www.politicsweb.co.za/news-and-analysis/how-to-ruin-a-newspaper-group
(Accessed 13 August 2020).

[57] Ibid.

[58] Sam Sole and Craig Mckune, "What's black and white and in the red all over?",
Mail&Guardian, 28 August 2014, https://mg.co.za/article/2014-08-28-whats-black-
and-white-and-in-the-red-all-over/ (Accessed 12 August 2020).

[59] John Yeld, "Remember the Sekunjalo Scandal?", *Politicsweb*, 13 September 2016,
https://www.politicsweb.co.za/opinion/remember-the-sekunjalo-scandal (Accessed
12 August 2020).

[60] Stephen Grootes, "The Firing of Cape Times Editor: A sign of things to come?",
Daily Maverick, 10 December 2013, https://www.dailymaverick.co.za/article/2013-12-
10-the-firing-of-cape-times-editor-a-sign-of-things-to-come/#.WcYuT7Kg-po
(Accessed 12 August 2020).

[61] Ibid; Ricky Stoch, Framing Transformation: An Exploration into the Cape Times'
Coverage of the University of Cape Town During the Formation of Rhodes Must
Fall, Thesis for Honours Degree in Transitional Justice, University of Cape Town,
2016; Alide Dasnois and Chris Whitfield, *Paper Tiger: Iqbal Survé and the downfall of
Independent Newspapers*, Cape Town: Tafelberg, 2019.

[62] Ricky Stoch, "Did Iqbal Survé's personal agenda influence newspaper's coverage
of UCT?", *Daily Maverick*, 15 September 2017,
https://www.dailymaverick.co.za/article/2017-09-15-op-ed-did-iqbal-survs-personal-
agenda-influence-newspapers-coverage-of-uct/#.Wbu4urKg-po (Accessed 12
August 2020); Ed Herbst, "Did the Survé-controlled Cape Times defame Max
Price?", *BizNews*, 28 September 2017, https://www.biznews.com/thought-

leaders/2017/09/28/ed-herbst-iqbal-surve-cape-times-max-price (Accessed 11 August 2020).

63 Ricky Stoch, *Framing Transformation*, p. 46.

64 Ricky Stoch, "Did Iqbal Survé's personal agenda influence newspaper's coverage of UCT?", *Daily Maverick*, 15 September 2017.

65 Ibid.

66 7 April 2015. A series of video clips of him speaking are available here: https://www.youtube.com/watch?v=M9O-hoawFzk

67 Ricky Stoch, *Framing Transformation*; Ed Herbst, "Did the Survé-controlled Cape Times defame Max Price?", *BizNews*, 28 September 2017.

68 Ricky Stoch, *Framing Transformation*, p. 35.

69 Ibid, p. 36

70 Ibid, p. 35.

71 Ibid, p. 50.

72 Ibid, pp. 50-51.

73 Ibid, p. 50

74 Carlo Petersen, "Disciplinary action over 'racist, defamatory' remarks between student and lecturer", *Cape Times,* 15 March 2016, p. 3. The article also appeared online under the heading "UCT student in hot water over social media slurs", 14 March 2016, https://www.iol.co.za/capetimes/news/uct-student-in-hot-water-over-social-media-slurs-1997740 (Accessed 15 March 2016).

75 Chapter 12.

76 Carlo Petersen, "Disciplinary action over 'racist, defamatory' remarks between student and lecturer", *Cape Times,* 15 March 2016, p. 3.

77 David Benatar, "Independent Online out of line: What readers of Independent Online (IOL) should know", *Politicsweb,* 12 August 2015, http://www.politicsweb.co.za/opinion/what-iol-readers-need-to-know . This article can be found as Appendix 1 in this book.

78 Alide Dasnois and Chris Whitfield, *Paper Tiger: Iqbal Survé and the downfall of Independent Newspapers*, Cape Town: Tafelberg, 2019.

79 See Appendix 2.

80 See, for example, Rekgotsofetse Chikane, *Breaking a Rainbow, Building a Nation: The Politics behind #MustFall Movement*, Johannesburg: Picador Africa, 2018.

81 Chapter 12.

82 Monday 4 May 2020.

83 James Myburgh, "The Fallist and the Professor", *Politicsweb*, 30 April 2020, https://www.politicsweb.co.za/opinion/the-fallist-and-the-professor (Accessed 30 April 2020).

84 "Busisiwe Mkhumbuzi: Timeline of Disciplinary Matters", *Politicsweb*, https://www.politicsweb.co.za/politicsweb/action/media/downloadFile?media_fileid=4456 (Accessed 30 April 2020).

[85] John Lamola, Friday 8 May 2020.

[86] Bernhard Weiss and Elisa Galgut, 11 May 2020.

[87] This includes the UCT Humanities Students Council of 2016 (Nickita Maesela, Precious Bikitsha, Reon van der Merwe, Priyanka Naidoo, Nonkululeko Moyo, Nandi Ntshiliza, Aphelele Mjana, Tandie Nkosi, Ally Dlamini and Sakhile Tembe) as well as the BAC.

[88] Katherine Eyal of UCT's Department of Economics.

[89] She did take down the original post, which is something, but given that people were unlikely to go back to it, the best way to counter the earlier damage was to make a new public statement and ask for that to be widely distributed (even though it's very unlikely that it would have been distributed as widely as the original defamatory statement.)

[90] PEN South Africa, https://pensouthafrica.co.za/about-us/who-we-are/ (Accessed 18 August 2020).

[91] For example, Elisa Galgut wrote to them on 29 August 2017, 8 December 2017, 7 February 2018, and 2 March 2018, and William Daniels wrote to them on 23 April 2018, 26 April 2018, 7 May 2018, 16 November 2018, 4 January 2019, 22 March 2019, 27 March 2019, 19 April 2019, 29 April 2019, 7 May 2019, 22 May 2019, 30 May 2019, and 25 October 2019.

[92] PEN Charter, http://pensouthafrica.co.za/about-us/who-we-are/pen-charter/ (Accessed 19 August 2020).

[93] Email to Elisa Galgut, 11 December 2017.

[94] "PEN SA Notes the Re-Classification of Inxeba to X18", 15 February 2018, https://pensouthafrica.co.za/pen-sa-notes-the-re-classification-of-inxeba-to-x18/ (Accessed 19 August 2020).

[95] PEN SA Statement on the UCT Artworks Case: Members Encouraged to Submit Views", 23 March 2018, http://pensouthafrica.co.za/pen-sa-statement-on-the-uct-artworks-case-members-encouraged-to-submit-views/ (Accessed 18 August 2020). See also, Nick Mulgrew and Nokukhanya Mncwabe, "Curation or Censorship? A timeline of events and articles relating to art at UCT", 11 April 2018, http://pensouthafrica.co.za/curation-or-censorship-a-timeline-of-events-and-articles-relating-to-art-at-uct/ (Accessed 19 August 2020).

[96] PEN SA, "Clarifying Statement Regarding Previous Statements on UCT Artworks Case", 10 May 2018.

[97] Library and Information Association of South Africa, "Statement by LIASA on University of Cape Town censorship", 17 August 2018.

[98] The sculpture was first covered in April 2015 until approximately the end of that year. It was covered again on 9 March 2016. LIASA's statement was on 17 August 2018.

[99] https://www.liasa.org.za/page/statements (Accessed 20 August 2020).

[100] See Chapter 20.

[101] The play can, at the time of writing, be viewed here: https://www.standard.co.uk/go/london/theatre/watch-the-fall-play-online-cecil-

rhodes-statue-oxford-south-africa-a4473106.html

[102] See, for example, David Smith, "The Fall: what the hit South African play can teach us about the US", *The Guardian*, 1 November 2018, https://www.theguardian.com/stage/2018/nov/01/the-fall-review-south-africa-play-washington (Accessed 19 August 2020); Ben Brantley, "Review: 'The Fall' Delivers Stirring Protest in South Africa", *New York Times,* 12 March 2018, https://www.nytimes.com/2018/03/12/theater/the-fall-review.html (Accessed 10 August 2020).

[103] Olivia Goldhill, "Philosophy is the new battleground in South Africa's fight against colonialism", *Quartz*, 30 September 2018.

[104] See Appendix 3.

[105] Linda Nordling, "South African university probe finds 'rife' racism", *Nature*, Vol. 568, 11 April 2019, pp. 151-152.

[106] See Chapter 19.

[107] Linda Nordling, "After Rhodes Fell: the Battle to Tackle a Racist Legacy", *Nature*, Vol. 593, 20 May 2021, pp. 465-467.

[108] I use this term in its technical sense: https://en.wikipedia.org/wiki/Useful_idiot (Accessed 26 February 2020).

[109] Students' Health and Welfare Centres Organization.

[110] Is the very act of contributing to this charity part of the purported "chronic liberal saviour elitism"? Who will make that determination? The author of those words?

[111] Facebook, 30 September 2016.

[112] Facebook, 10 March 2016.

[113] For more details see Appendix 3.

[114] Indeed, there was initially some opposition to Professor Chirwa's appointment to the deanship, given that he is not a South African. Fortunately, the xenophobia did not prevail in that particular case.

[115] Nithaya Chetty and Christopher Merrett, The Struggle for the Soul of a South African University: The University of KwaZulu-Natal: Academic freedom, corporatisation and transformation, 2014, p. 82.

[116] See Chapter 20.

[117] Mamokgethi Phakeng, "Vice-Chancellor's submission to the Chair of Council in response to the 2019 Annual Report of the Ombud", 8 March 2020, p. 13.

[118] Murray Williams, "Fear and Loathing at UCT as university Ombud calls VC Mamokgethi Phakeng a 'bully'", 9 July 2020, https://www.news24.com/news24/SouthAfrica/News/fear-and-loathing-at-uct-as-university-ombud-calls-vc-mamokgethi-phakeng-a-bully-20200709 (Accessed 9 July 2020).

[119] Ibid.

[120] Sipho Pityana and Shirley Zinn, "Fanal (sic) Report to UCT Council",10 June 2020, p. 2.

[121] Ibid, p. 4.

[122] Edwin Naidu, "Ombud faces axe after report labels UCT vice-chancellor 'a bully'", *IOL*, 27 September 2020, https://www.iol.co.za/sundayindependent/news/ombud-faces-axe-after-report-labels-uct-vice-chancellor-a-bully-c663b93d-c545-4769-9e9f-68396cf800dc (Accessed 28 September 2020).

Appendix 1

[1] "Independent Online, out of line: What readers of Independent Online (IOL) should know", *Politicsweb*, 12 August 2015, http://www.politicsweb.co.za/opinion/what-iol-readers-need-to-know (Accessed 12 August 2015).

[2] Republished as Chapter 2 in this book.

[3] Republished as a postscript to Chapter 2 in this book.

Appendix 2

[1] David Benatar, "What Mail&Guardian readers need to know", *Politicsweb*, 13 November 2017, http://www.politicsweb.co.za/opinion/what-mg-readers-need-to-know (Accessed 13 November 2017).

[2] Appendix 1 in this book.

[3] https://thoughtleader.co.za/author/blackacademiccaucus/

[4] BAC, "Parading White Privilege", 1 October 2017, https://www.facebook.com/785908911530731/photos/a.834547000000255.1073741830.785908911530731/1407602572694692/?type=3&theater (Accessed date unknown).

[5] Jenna Etheridge, "UCT test concession for Rocking the Daisies festival is 'parade of white privilege", *Mail&Guardian*, 3 October 2017, https://mg.co.za/article/2017-10-03-uct-test-concession-for-rocking-the-daisies-festival-is-parade-of-white-privilege/ (Accessed 7 October 2017).

[6] Staff Reporter, "Transforming UCT: Reflections on the road ahead", *Mail&Guardian*, 13 October 2017, https://mg.co.za/article/2017-10-13-transforming-uct-reflections-on-the-road-ahead/ (Accessed 14 October 2017).

[7] "UCT Philosophy Department statement on the Rocking the Daisies concession", 20 October 2017, https://www.news.uct.ac.za/article/-2017-10-20-uct-philosophy-department-statement-on-the-rocking-the-daisies-concession (Accessed date unknown).

Appendix 3

[1] David Benatar, "Philosophy and SA's 'battle against colonialism'", *Politicsweb*, 8 October 2018, http://www.politicsweb.co.za/opinion/philosophy-and-sas-battle-against-colonialism

[2] Olivia Goldhill, "Philosophy is the new battleground in South Africa's fight against colonialism" *Quartz,* 30 September 2018, https://qz.com/1332351/philosophy-is-the-new-battleground-in-south-africas-fight-against-colonialism/ (Accessed 30

September 2018).

[3] David Benatar, "Academic Climate Change at UCT: An Inconvenient Truth", *Politicsweb*, 30 March 2017, https://www.politicsweb.co.za/opinion/ucts-climate-turns-toxic . Chapter 10 in this book.

[4] David Benatar, "The University of Capitulation", *Politicsweb*, 21 September 2016, https://www.politicsweb.co.za/opinion/uct-capitulation-isnt-working . Chapter 7 in this book.

[5] "Fallists vandalised Bongani's soul – Ncumisa Mayosi", *Politicsweb*, 5 August 2018, https://www.politicsweb.co.za/news-and-analysis/the-fallists-completely-vandalised-bonganis-soul-- (Accessed 7 August 2018). For video footage see: https://www.youtube.com/watch?v=6Vz_xWoYpcM&feature=youtu.be&t=3778

[6] Zodidi Dano, "Did protestors contribute to UCT professor's suicide?", IOL, 30 July 2018, https://www.iol.co.za/capeargus/news/did-student-protests-contribute-to-uct-professors-suicide-16314839 (Accessed 19 August 2020).

[7] David Benatar, "Those who seek changes must show they are desirable", *Cape Times*, 29 June 2015, p. 11. Chapter 2 in this book.

[8] David Benatar, "Not enough space to address all Mangcu's mistakes, but here's a summary", *Cape Times*, Friday 3 July 2015, p. 9. Postscript to Chapter 2 in this book.

[9] Xolela Mangcu, "Racially offensive diatribe has no place", *Cape Times*, 2 July 2015.

[10] David Benatar, "Philosophy and SA's 'battle against colonialism'", *Politicsweb*, 8 October 2018, http://www.politicsweb.co.za/opinion/philosophy-and-sas-battle-against-colonialism .

[11] https://qz.com/about/#values (Accessed 19 August 2020).

INDEX

Printed in Great Britain
by Amazon